QUALITATIVE DATA ANALYSIS

For information address:

SAGE Publications, Inc.
275 South Beverly Drive
Beverly Hills, California 90212

SAGE Publications India Pvt. Ltd.   SAGE Publications Ltd
C-236 Defence Colony   28 Banner Street
New Delhi 110 024, India   London EC1Y 8QE, England

Printed in the United States of America

Library of Congress Cataloging in Publication Data

Miles, Matthew B.
    Qualitative data analysis.

    Bibliography: p.
    Includes index.
      1. Social sciences—Research.   2. Education—Research.
I. Huberman, A. M.   II. Title.
H62.M437   1984   300′.72   84-2140
ISBN 0-8039-2274-4

FIRST PRINTING

QUALITATIVE DATA ANALYSIS

A Sourcebook of New Methods

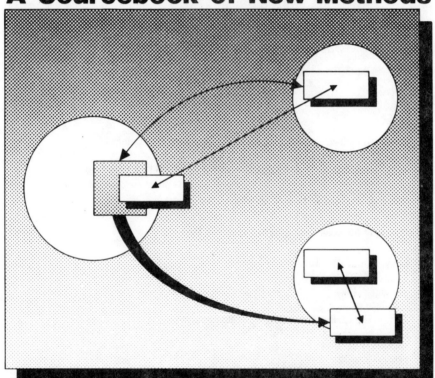

Matthew B. Miles
A. Michael Huberman

 SAGE PUBLICATIONS Beverly Hills London New Delhi

Contents

List of Charts and Figures

Charts

Figures

Acknowledgments

This book grew out of our experience in two linked research projects. The first, beginning in 1978, was the field study component of the Study of Dissemination Efforts Supporting School Improvement (Department of Education Contract 300-78-0527), led by David P. Crandall of The Network, Inc. We are indebted to him for his steady encouragement and support. Ann Bezdek Weinheimer, as project officer from the Office of Planning, Budgeting and Evaluation, gave active support to the idea of the field study and thoughtful commentary along the way. DESSI project staff who gave feedback and suggestions included Joyce Bauchner, Pat Cox, Gene Hall, Ronald Havelock, Susan Heck, Susan Loucks, Glenn Shive, and Charles Thompson.

In the field study itself, we had as strong colleagues Beverly Loy Taylor and Jo Ann Goldberg; their competent fieldwork and case study analysis along with ours led to Vol. IV of the DESSI final report, *People, Policies and Practices: Examining the Chain of School Improvement*, now published as *Innovation Up Close* (Plenum, 1984).

The Center for Policy Research and the Knowledge Transfer Institute of American University supplied basic administrative services; our special appreciation to Sophie Sa, Marcia Kroll, Ann MacDonald, and Nanette Levinson.

The second project, "The Realities of School Improvement Programs: Analysis of Qualitative Data," NIE grant G-81-0018, gave us the opportunity to develop our methodological ideas further, and to write this book. Rolf Lehming of the Program on Dissemination and Improvement of Practice was our project officer; we value his sustained interest and stimulating suggestions.

The ideas presented here, of course, do not necessarily reflect the views or policies of the Department of Education, or of the National Institute of Education. But we are grateful for their sponsorship of these studies.

Earlier versions of this book were capably reviewed and critiqued by Beverly Loy Taylor and by Rein van der Vegt. Their suggestions helped to improve both the book's format and its substance.

A book of this sort could not have been easily produced and revised through multiple drafts without capable word-processing people. We express our strong thanks to Tim Barnum and Mindy Wexler-Marks, and to the noble Xerox 850.

We are grateful to David Crandall, William Firestone, Klaus Krippendorff, Michael Patton, Allen Smith, and Suzanne Stiegelbauer for permission to use previously published material as exhibits.

The final version of the manuscript was reviewed by several interested colleagues; our thanks for the thoughtful suggestions of Jean Cardinet, Pat Cox, Judith Dawson, Mats Ekholm, William Firestone, Robert Herriott, Patricia Holborn, David Kelleher, Harold Levine, Allen Smith, Beverly Loy Taylor, Uri Trier, and Marvin Wideen.

Finally, we thank each other for four years of energetic, stimulating collaboration. The process was always rich and satisfying; it brought on pleasure and excitement with the product. What more can one ask of shared work?

—M.B.M.
A.M.H.

I

Introduction

We wrote this book to address a critical need faced by researchers in all fields of the human sciences. Put simply, that need is this: How can we draw valid meaning from qualitative data? What methods of analysis can we employ that are practical, communicable, and non-self-deluding—in short, *scientific* in the best sense of that word?

In this introduction we first outline the need and why we consider it critical just now. Next, we explain the nature of this book and its intended public. We then describe our experience base—what led us to produce this book—and describe our general stance toward matters of qualitative analysis, including what we consider "qualitative analysis" to consist of. Finally, we give a short overview of the book, along with suggestions for using it fruitfully.

I.A THE GENERAL PROBLEM

Qualitative data, in the form of words rather than numbers, have always been the staple of certain social sciences, notably anthropology, history, and political science. In the past decade, however, more and more researchers in fields with a traditional quantitative emphasis (psychology, sociology, linguistics, public administration, organizational studies, urban planning, educational research, program evaluation, and policy analysis) have shifted to a more qualitative paradigm.

Qualitative data are attractive. They are a source of well-grounded, rich descriptions and explanations of processes occurring in local contexts. With qualitative data one can preserve chronological flow, assess local causality, and derive fruitful explanations. Then, too, qualitative data are more likely to lead to serendipitous findings and to new theoretical integrations; they help researchers go beyond initial preconceptions and frameworks. Finally, the findings from qualitative studies have a quality of "undeniability," as Smith (1978) has put it. Words, especially when they are organized into incidents or stories, have a concrete, vivid, meaningful flavor that often proves far more convincing to a reader—another researcher, a policymaker, a practitioner—than pages of numbers.

So it is not surprising to see more and more researchers committed to qualitative data collection—enough so in educational research, for example, that one experienced researcher (Rist, 1980) has denounced what he calls "blitzkrieg ethnography." Anthropologists wonder out loud whether researchers in other fields are reinventing the wheel (Wolcott, 1980), and seem wary of claim jumping. Superficial "case studies" are not rare. But the expansion of qualitative inquiry continues, advanced in no small way by the reformulations of methodologists (for example, see Snow, 1974; Cronbach, 1975; Campbell, 1975; Cook & Campbell, 1979) who originally took "hard-nosed," quantitatively oriented approaches to problems of generating valid knowledge; they have now shifted substantially toward the endorsement of context-embedded qualitative inquiry.

The demands of conducting good qualitative research are not small. Collecting data is a labor-intensive operation, traditionally lasting for months if not years. Field notes mount up astronomically, so that data overload is a given. It may take from many months to several years to complete a thoughtful analysis. To these ordinary demands have been added others. Qualitative research is typically no longer the province of the lone fieldworker immersed in a local setting, but is now often part of a "multisite, multimethod" effort (Smith & Louis, 1982), combined qualitative and quantitative inquiry carried out by a team of researchers whose data collection and analysis methods must be executed in a formalized, comparable way (Herriott & Firestone, 1983).

There are also real problems with the output of qualitative studies. Even if a study goes beyond the classic single case to a multiple-site study, the bulk of data makes it unlikely that a sample of more than a few dozen cases can be managed. So there is a serious question of *sampling* involved. Are the cases examined a reasonable sample of a larger universe? Put another way, what is the *generalizability* of qualitatively derived findings? And given the fact that words are slippery, ambiguous symbols, the possibility of researcher *bias* looms quite large; we must be concerned with the *replicability* of qualitative analyses.

But the deepest, darkest question about qualitative studies lies beyond these issues. As one of us has written:

> The most serious and central difficulty in the use of qualitative data is that methods of analysis are not well formulated. For quantitative data, there are clear conventions the researcher can use. But the analyst faced with a bank of qualitative data has very few guidelines for protection against self-delusion, let alone the presentation of unreliable or invalid conclusions to scientific or policy-making audiences. How can we be sure that an "earthy," "undeniable," "serendipitous" finding is not, in fact, *wrong*? (Miles, 1979)

In short, we have few agreed-on canons for qualitative data analysis, in the sense of shared ground rules for drawing conclusions and verifying their sturdiness. A few years ago, an examination of seven well-respected textbooks on field methods found that less than 5%-10% of their pages were devoted to analysis (Sieber, 1976). Most attention went to issues such as gaining access and avoiding bias during data collection. Recent textbooks have redressed the balance somewhat (for example, see Patton, 1980; Bogdan & Biklen, 1982; Dobbert, 1982; Guba & Lincoln, 1981; Spradley, 1979). But many qualitative researchers still consider analysis as "art" and stress intuitive approaches to it. There has been a somewhat magical belief in "bracketing," or in the "intuitive insights" generated by the experienced ethnographer, who progressively discerns clear classifications and an overarching pattern from the welter of field data, and does this in ways that are presumably irreducible or even incommunicable.

Some researchers have hesitated to focus on analysis issues on the grounds that unequivocal determination of the validity of findings is not really possible (Becker, 1958; Bruyn, 1966; Lofland, 1971). More profoundly, for some phenomenologically oriented researchers there is no social reality "out there" to be accounted for, so there is no need to evolve a robust set of methodological canons to help explicate its laws (see Dreitzel, 1970). Social processes in this view are ephemeral, fluid phenomena with no existence independent of social actors' ways of construing and describing them.

This degree of uncertainty about qualitative analysis has another consequence: Analysis methods are rarely reported in detail in published case studies or in cross-site synthesis reports. One cannot ordinarily follow how a researcher got from 3600 pages of field notes to the final conclusions, sprinkled with vivid quotes though they may be. And even when researchers try to be explicit about their methods, the lack of a common language and the labor-intensiveness of the analysis process make for much ambiguity: Using the same basic field notes, could another researcher write a case study that was plausibly similar to the original? Under these circumstances, as Dawson (1979, 1982), LeCompte and Goetz (1982) and others have pointed out, the validity of qualitatively derived findings is seriously in doubt.

In brief, the field of qualitative research badly needs explicit, systematic methods for drawing conclusions, and for testing them carefully—methods that can be used for replication by other researchers, just as correlations and significance tests can be by quantitative researchers. This is the need our book addresses.

I.B THE NATURE OF THIS BOOK

This is a practical sourcebook for all researchers who make use of qualitative data. It draws on our experience over the past eight years in the design, testing, and use of innovative qualitative data analysis methods. Strong emphasis is placed on new types of data displays, including graphs, charts, matrices, and networks, that go beyond the limitations of ordinary narrative text. Each of 49 specific methods of data display and analysis is described and illustrated in detail, with practical suggestions for the user. We also refer to helpful, relevant work of other researchers.

Audiences

The book is aimed at *professional researchers* in all fields whose work, whether basic or applied, calls for qualitative data analysis—or whose interests are shifting in that direction.

Naturally, the book will also be useful in undergraduate and graduate courses for *students* who are learning fieldwork and qualitative analysis methods. We have encountered large numbers of students in graduate departments being carried along in the Zeitgeistlike drift toward more and more qualitative research who feel that their training is inadequate for resolving data analysis issues. We hope this book will be useful to them, and possibly to their mentors as well.

A third audience is that of *staff specialists and managers*, who rely on qualitative information as a routine part of their work, and need practical methods for making the best use of it.

The examples used in the book are largely drawn from our own educational research (in implementation of innovations, dissemination studies, the development of new schools), although we also include some other public-sector illustrations. Since everyone has experienced life in schools, we believe the illustrative material will be clear and comprehensible to readers in other fields (anthropology, linguistics, health care, political science, program evaluation, public administration, social services, sociology).

Furthermore, we believe the methods can easily be used in any size of qualitative study, down to the level of the single individual. The fact that many of the methods grew out of multiple-site, large-scale, demanding studies served to test them under extreme circumstances. They can be useful in more modest case studies—of individuals, small groups, or single organizations.

Approach

We should say a few things about the book's approach. First, our subtitle ("A Sourcebook of New Methods") is deliberate. We do not consider the volume a "handbook," which usually implies a sort of encyclopedic finishedness, a compilation and synthesis that attempts to bring all readers in touch with the "state of the art." Rather, we have tried to bring together a useful set of resources in a coherent way, to encourage their use—and, above all, their further development, testing, and elaboration.

Second, as we have already explained, most of the illustrations come directly from our own work (see section I.C for more detail). Though we thereby run the risks of parochialism and blithely taken-for-granted shorthand, we wanted to anchor our descriptions and advice in our own direct experience as much as possible. Where we knew of others' work that seemed directly relevant to a particular method, we of course have added such examples as well. We have thus opted for the gritty, happy reality of "research-in-use," to use Kaplan's (1964) term, rather than the sanitized structures of "research-in-theory."

We do not attempt to review prior work in detail in such fields as ethnography, anthropology more generally, or content analysis, though we acknowledge its pertinence, point to specific areas of relevance, and suggest a wide range of readings.

This book is about *analysis*. Though, as we explain shortly, that term is broad, encompassing data reduction and data display as well as what is ordinarily construed as "analysis," our emphasis is still a limited one. We focus only partially on questions of research design and data collection, and hardly at all on matters such as access to field sites and trust-building with informants, since others have dealt with them repeatedly and well.

We have taken as concrete and direct an approach as possible, staying close to the reader's elbow. We feel that much of what is written elsewhere about qualitative data analysis tends to be general, abstract, and unanchored to hands-on work with actual data (Spradley, 1979, is a notable exception). One gets the principles, but hardly ever their concrete workings-out during the course of analysis. So for each of the methods we outline, we give specific illustrations, with enough detail so the reader can see how things work, can try the method—and, most important, can revise and develop the method in future work.

We also tend to be pragmatic. Though we outline our epistemological positions in section I.D below, the book tends not to get into discussions about whether X or Y approach is "pure," "emic/etic," "correct," "fatally flawed," "problematic," or "methodologically unacceptable." We just want to do good analysis, and we believe, perhaps less naively than the reader might think at first, that any method that works—that will produce clear, verifiable, replicable meanings from a set of qualitative data—is grist for our mill, regardless of its antecedents.

Most of the methods we describe from our own projects were invented—or, sometimes, *reinvented*—by us as we struggled with qualitative data. In doing this we found two things. First, the methods are manageable and straightforward. They do not require prolonged training or an arcane vocabulary. Second, we found the invention process so enjoyable and productive that we believe others will also thrive on a similarly inventive, method-creating stance. So the strongest message of this book is *not* that these particular methods should be applied scrupulously, but that the creation, testing, and revision of simple, practical, and effective analysis methods is the highest priority for qualitative researchers.

The spirit of that quest is well summed up by a thoughtful remark on our work by a European sociologist (W. Hutmacher, personal communication, 1983):

> I think you've worked out a comprehensive solution to many of the methodological problems we *have* to resolve, that we resolve poorly and, as a result, that we often cover up when reporting out to our peers. But

yours isn't the only solution nor the last one we'll come upon. We have to admit that we're *all* casting about, you included.

This book was written to share our "casting about," and to encourage much wider experimentation and sharing by concerned colleagues.

I.C   OUR EXPERIENCE BASE

Prior Work

We have come to qualitative analysis from different yet converging routes. Miles has had a career-long interest in the assessment of social environments (groups and organizations) and, more particularly, in the effects of attempts to change their behavior, climate, and structures. While he had always been interested in nonqualitative inquiry, his first full-scale venture into qualitative research was a four-year study of the processes involved in the creation of new, innovative organizations (Miles et al., 1978; Miles, 1980). This involved following six public schools through the course of their design, creation, and stabilization. In the study, direct observation and informal interviewing were supplemented by document collection, structured interviewing, and two-wave surveys. It was here that Miles came to grips with the problems of qualitative analysis we have alluded to earlier; the "attractive nuisance" paper (Miles, 1979) was at the same time a rueful reflection on his experience and a sort of manifesto for work to follow.

Huberman's long-term interests have been in scientific epistemology—how scientific theories are developed and validated—and in adult cognition, in the perspective of the Swiss psychologist Piaget and the French epistemologist Bachelard. Like Miles, Huberman had worked empirically with "softer," more clinical methodologies in combination with harder-nosed psychometric techniques. But his first extensive project with a qualitative emphasis was a four-year study of an experimental elementary school seeking to implement Piagetian theories in a classroom setting (Huberman, 1978, 1980). Aside from the conventional mix of data-gathering devices (formal and informal interviewing, nonparticipant and participant observation documents, questionnaires, and tests), Huberman tried two data-analytic approaches often advocated by field study methodologists but seldom executed. The first involved testing the emerging pattern of findings from the experimental school against a second school with similar characteristics, in a staggered replication design (see Cronbach, 1975;

Yin, 1981). The second experiment was to quantify the nonnumeric data and conduct parallel and comparative analyses using standard psychometric procedures alongside more descriptive, thematic, and configural techniques. It was here that he too confronted some of the problems of conducting and verifying qualitative research, and of meshing qualitative and quantitative data sets. *His* reflection/manifesto paper (Huberman, 1981a) spoke of the "splendors and miseries" of qualitative research.

These experiences set the stage for the work we have done together in the past four years. When the opportunity to collaborate on a major field study arose, we leaped at it. The dead ends and dilemmas each of us had confronted in earlier work had generated lessons learned and techniques *not* to try again. And with the relative lack of canons, decision rules, agreed-upon procedures, and even any shared *heuristics* for analyzing qualitative data, each of us had begun to evolve a small arsenal of what looked like promising analysis devices. Perhaps they could help us cope with some of the more intractable problems we had run into earlier: imprecise measurement, weak generalizability of findings, vulnerability to several sources of bias, an overload of data—some of it dross—and extreme labor-intensiveness. Many of these lessons and devices were brought into the new collaborative effort, a four-year study of the dissemination of educational innovations. Since many of the examples and exhibits we shall be using in this text come from that study, let us describe it briefly.

The Field Study

The field study was nested in an overall study of school improvement (Crandall et al., 1983), covering some 145 school buildings throughout the United States involved in the implementation of educational innovations.[1] In all, the larger study collected survey and interview data from nearly 4000 respondents, including teachers, principals, central office administrators, people assisting the projects, and developers of the innovations.

The field study component was designed to look intensively at a stratified sample of the survey population. Twelve field sites across the country were selected and visited repeatedly throughout the school year 1979-1980, with follow-up contacts the next year to verify the main findings. The study had a four-person research staff: each of us worked 60% time, and we were joined by two colleagues, Beverly Loy Taylor and Jo Anne Goldberg, at 80% time. We were not doing "ethnographies," but a repeated-visits field study of much smaller scope. Still, the data collection was highly intensive; the volume of data collected included over 400 interviews, 85 observations, some 250 documents, and over 2500 pages of transcribed field notes.

In the course of the school year, we typically visited a site three or four times, for two to three days, with interim contact by telephone. The number of visits and total days on site varied with the proximity of the site, the number of informants, the complexity of the program, and the difficulty of getting credible accounts from site informants. We collected data chiefly through *interviews*—usually multiple interviews with key informants and single interviews with more peripheral actors—using a common, semistructured schedule across sites, covering the principal research questions. There were also informal talks (in empty classrooms, cars, cafes, and so on) that yielded valuable "backstage" information. Our *observations* were typically unstructured, though we usually had specific things we were looking for. Similarly, whenever a piece of paper looked or sounded significant, we asked to look at it and/or copy it, and abstracted each *document* on a document analysis form. We dictated interview and observation notes in narrative form along with any pertinent analytical or methodological notes, and had them transcribed. Finally, about midway in the school year, site-specific *raw questionnaire and interview data* became available from the larger study; we used them as a verification device, as a source of new leads to follow, and as puzzles to solve.

For each of the 12 field sites, we wrote a report. These reports ranged from 70 to 140 pages[2] and followed a common data-reporting and display format. The subsequent cross-site analysis (Huberman & Miles, 1983b) was then built from the appropriate sections of the 12 site reports.

The NIE Study

In the course of the cross-site analysis, we began another study, sponsored by the National Institute of Education, on the procedures involved in the analysis of qualitative data (Miles & Huberman, 1982). The task was to document in detail the successive procedures we used for within-site and cross-site analyses, all the way from the initial coding of site-level notes to the more explanatory cross-site analyses. Each of the analyses fed into a detailed self-documentation form (see Section VII.C) on which we recorded the analytic steps taken, the decision rules used, the bases for drawing conclusions, the confidence held in the conclusions, and the strengths and weaknesses of the analysis. This exercise provided many of the illus-

trations and rules of thumb contained in the present book.[3]

Further Work

The basic corpus of analytic methods has since been debugged, refined, and extended as we have worked with it and incorporated the procedures used by colleagues. In a second multiple-site field study (Huberman, 1981b; Havelock, Cox, Huberman, & Levinson, 1983), we replicated many of the techniques for collecting, reducing, and analyzing qualitative data that had been used in the school improvement study, finding that they "traveled" very well. We have also conducted, in the United States, Canada, and Switzerland, a series of training sessions for qualitative researchers, where we debugged some sections of the book and added new material based on participant reactions. In addition, the tools shown in this text have been used in whole or in part in about a dozen M.A.-level dissertations. Finally, thirteen researchers carefully reviewed an initial version of this manuscript; their critiques and amendments have been incorporated.

I.D OUR STANCE

It is good for researchers to make their preferences clear. All too often, the reader has to intuit whether the author is, for example, operating from the standpoint of a logical positivist, a symbolic interactionist, or a social phenomenologist. These people all look differently at the world of social affairs and social science. We think of ourselves as logical positivists who recognize and try to atone for the limitations of that approach. Soft-nosed logical positivism, maybe.

In other words, we believe that social phenomena exist not only in the mind but also in the objective world—and that there are some lawful and reasonably stable relationships to be found among them. In part, of course, these phenomena exist objectively in the world *because* people construe them in common or agreed-upon ways, so those perceptions are crucial in understanding why social behavior takes the form it does. Still, even if people do not themselves apprehend the same analytical constructs as those derived by researchers, this does not make such constructs invalid or contrived. (We are all, for example, surrounded by lawful physical processes and mechanisms of which most of us are, at best, remotely aware.) Given our belief in social regularities, there is a corollary: Our task is to express them as precisely as possible, attending to their range and generality and to the local and historical contingencies under which they occur.

[handwritten notes in margin:]
analytic steps
decision rules used
bases for drawing conclusions
confidence held in conclusions
strengths + weaknesses of analysis

So, unlike some schools within social phenomenology, we consider it important to evolve a set of valid and verifiable *methods* for capturing these social relationships and their causes. We want to interpret and explain these phenomena *and* have confidence that others, using the same tools, would arrive at analogous conclusions. This stance does not exclude "verstehen" or intersubjective resonance, and we refuse to draw an arbitary conceptual line between "idiographic" and "nomothetic" approaches to research. No social phenomenon is wholly idiosyncratic; no overarching social pattern is unconditional.

We do, however, tilt toward a more inductive methodology for illuminating social processes. In our view, traditional positivists have been too concerned with *internal* validity and conceptual certainty, coming to grief when their data lacked authenticity and meaning—*external* validity. The traditional experimental and correlational studies are not enough. Note that we are joined in this view by some premier positivists (such as Campbell, Bronfenbrenner, Cronbach, and Snow) who have been searching for more fruitful methodologies.

In fact, it is getting harder to find *any* methodologists solidly encamped in one epistemology or the other. More and more "quantitative" methodologists, operating from a logical positivist stance, are using naturalistic and phenomenological approaches to complement tests, surveys, and structured interviews. On the other side, an increasing number of ethnographers and qualitative researchers are using predesigned conceptual frameworks and prestructured instrumentation, especially when dealing with more than one institution or community. Few logical positivists will now dispute the validity and explanatory importance of subjective data, and few phenomenologists still practice pure hermeneutics—and even those believe that there are generic properties in the ways we idiosyncratically "make" rules and common sense (see Mishler, 1979).

So, without our realizing it very clearly, the paradigms for conducting social research have shifted beneath our feet, and most people now see the world with more ecumenical eyes. However, we have sometimes found that standing in the middle between mainstream deductivists and dyed-in-the-wool inductivists is like Saint Sebastian standing in between the archers. For the former, the approach taken in this book is that of "fuzzy" or "flabby" social science, or of "misplaced precision." For the latter, we come on as reductionist wolves in qualitative sheep's clothing, closet psychometricians who write of "collecting data" rather than of "compiling information," of "measuring" and even of "predicting" rather than of simply "describing" and "interpreting."

We address ourselves explicitly in this book to the latter critics. We have read their corpus of methodological literature carefully, and have found it wanting. Although there are frequent references to, and general descriptions of, such procedures as "bracketing," "illuminating," "structural corroboration," "referential adequacy," and "compelling credibility," it is never precisely clear how the analyses to which they give rise are achieved. We do not know about their replicability or validity. For example, the anthropological literature has more than a few instances of two bracketed, illuminating, coherent accounts of the same culture or subculture that are at fundamental odds with each other.[4]

Methodologically, our beef is with the somewhat magical approach to the analysis of qualitative data advocated on the grounds that such an approach is idiosyncratic, incommunicable, and artistic—and that only those who have been fully socialized and apprenticed in its practice can claim to comment upon it. That, it seems to us, is mostly mystification. We suspect that, protests to the contrary, many of the procedures actually *used* by ethnographers and social phenomenologists are akin to those used by epistemologists using canons of inductive inference—and even akin to some used by qualitative researchers when they count instances of a phenomenon or try to assess its intensity relative to other phenomena.[5]

If this is so, it is worth the risk of dissecting and reassembling the actual procedures and underlying heuristics that a qualitative researcher actually uses. We may then get far clearer about what we mean when we say that a qualitative analysis is "coherent" or "plausible" or "credible" or "compelling." Doing that might also be a step in the direction of enabling others to achieve similar results, without necessarily ending up with the sort of sterile, fetishist canons that have tied up methodologists for so many years and produced so much fruitless research.

One more thing is worth saying. Our stance necessarily involves *orderliness*, a certain degree of formalization of the analysis process. There are many qualitative researchers who prefer intuitive, relaxed, nonobsessive voyages through their data, and we wish them well. But for us, as the reader will find, thoroughness and explicitness are quite paramount. We are committed to clarity in qualitative analysis procedures, a commitment that requires a good deal of explicit structure in our approach to inquiry. That is *not* the same thing as "positivism" or "deductiveness." One can be an inductively oriented phenomenologist *and* rather structured in one's approach to empirical work.

Our methods are described methodically, in a structured way. That is because vague descriptions are of no practical use to others. But if your research preferences tend toward less structure and formalization, do not be put off. You can still easily borrow from this book. Look behind the structure to see what will be useful in your own work.

I.E OUR VIEW OF QUALITATIVE ANALYSIS

We owe the reader a brief discussion of the territory we are covering in the book. What, in short, do we consider qualitative analysis to consist of?

First, the data concerned appear in *words* rather than in numbers. They may have been collected in a variety of ways (observation, interviews, extracts from documents, tape recordings), and are usually "processed" somewhat before they are ready for use (via dictation, typing up, editing, or transcription), but they remain words, usually organized into extended text.[6]

What, then, do we consider to be "analysis"? Our general view is outlined in Figure 1a. We consider that analysis consists of three concurrent flows of activity: data reduction, data display, and conclusion drawing/ verification. We shall explore each of these themes in more depth as we proceed through the book. For now, we make only some overarching comments.

Data Reduction

Data reduction refers to the process of selecting, focusing, simplifying, abstracting, and transforming the "raw" data that appear in written-up field notes. As we see it, data reduction occurs continuously throughout the life of any qualitatively oriented project. In fact, *even before* the data are actually collected (see Figure 1a), anticipatory data reduction is occurring as the researcher decides (often without full awareness) which conceptual framework, which sites, which research questions, which data collection approaches to choose. As data collection proceeds, there are further episodes of data reduction (doing summaries, coding, teasing out themes, making clusters, making partitions, writing memos). And the data-reduction/ transforming process continues after fieldwork, until a final report is complete.

Data reduction is not something separate from analysis. It is *part* of analysis. The researcher's choices of which data chunks to code, which to pull out, which patterns summarize a number of chunks, what the evolving story is, *are all analytic choices.* Data reduction

is a form of analysis that sharpens, sorts, focuses, discards, and organizes data in such a way that "final" conclusions can be drawn and verified.

We should make one thing plain: By "data reduction" we do not necessarily mean quantification. Qualitative data can be reduced and transformed in many ways: through sheer selection, through summary or paraphrase, through being subsumed in a larger pattern, and so on. Sometimes it may be well to convert the data into numbers or ranks (for example, the analyst decides that the site being looked at has a "high" or "moderate" degree of administrative centralization), but this is not always wise. Even when it does look like a good analytical strategy, our counsel is this: Keep the numbers, and the words you used to derive the numbers, *together* in your ensuing analysis. That way one never strips the data at hand from the contexts in which they occur.

Data Display

The second major flow of analysis activity is data display. We define a "display" as an organized assembly of information that permits conclusion drawing and action taking. Displays in daily life vary from gasoline gauges to newspapers to computer screens. Looking at displays helps us to understand what is happening and to do something—further analysis or action— based on that understanding.

The most frequent form of display for qualitative data in the past has been *narrative text.* As we shall note later, text (in the form, say, of 3600 pages of field notes) is terribly cumbersome. It is dispersed, sequential rather than simultaneous, poorly structured, and extremely bulky. Under those circumstances, it is easy for a qualitative researcher to jump to hasty, partial, unfounded conclusions. Humans are not very powerful as processors of large amounts of information; the cognitive tendency is to reduce complex information into selective and simplified Gestalts or easily understood configurations. Similarly, vivid information, such as an exciting episode, "jumps out" of page 124 of the field notes after a long "boring" passage and gets drastically overweighted. Pages 109 through 123 have suddenly been collapsed, and the criteria for weighting and selecting may never be questioned. Narrative text, in this sense, overloads humans' information-processing capabilities (Faust, 1982) and preys on their tendencies to find simplifying patterns.

In the course of our work, we have become convinced that better displays are a major avenue to valid qualitative analysis. The displays discussed in this book include many types of matrices, graphs, networks, and charts. All are designed to assemble

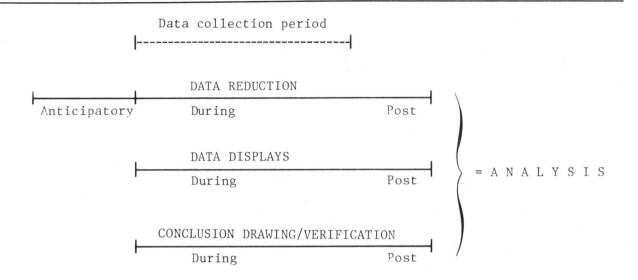

Figure 1a   Components of Data Analysis: Flow Model

organized information in an immediately accessible, compact form, so that the analyst can see what is happening and either draw justified conclusions or move on to the next-step analysis the display suggests may be useful.

Once again, take careful note: As with data reduction, the creation and use of displays is not something separate from analysis, it is a *part* of analysis. Designing the rows and columns of a matrix for qualitative data and deciding which data, in which form, should be entered in the cells are *analytic* activities. (They are also, note, *data-reductive* activities.)

In short, as we have remarked elsewhere, the dictum "You are what you eat" might be transposed to "You know what you display." In this book we advocate much more systematic, powerful displays, and urge a more inventive, self-conscious, iterative stance toward their generation and use.

Conclusion Drawing/Verification

The third stream of analysis activity is conclusion drawing and verification. From the beginning of data collection, the qualitative analyst is beginning to decide what things *mean*, is noting regularities, patterns, explanations, possible configurations, causal flows, and propositions. The competent researcher holds these conclusions lightly, maintaining openness and skepticism, but the conclusions are still there, inchoate and vague at first, then increasingly explicit and grounded, to use the classic term of Glaser and Strauss (1967). "Final" conclusions may not appear until data collection is over, depending on the size of

the corpus of field notes, the coding, storage, and retrieval methods used, the sophistication of the researcher, and the demands of the funding agency—but they have often been prefigured from the beginning, even when a researcher claims to have been proceeding "inductively."

Conclusion drawing, in our view, is only half of a Gemini configuration. Conclusions are also *verified* as the analyst proceeds. That verification may be as brief as a fleeting "second thought" crossing the analyst's mind during writing, with a short excursion back to the field notes—or it may be thoroughgoing and elaborate, with lengthy argumentation and review among colleagues to develop "intersubjective consensus," or with extensive efforts to replicate a finding in another data set. In short, the meanings emerging from the data have to be *tested* for their plausibility, their sturdiness, their "confirmability"—that is, their *validity*. Otherwise we are left with interesting stories about what happened, of unknown truth and utility.

We have presented these three streams—data reduction, data display, and conclusion drawing/verification—as interwoven before, during, and after data collection in parallel form, to make up the general domain called "analysis." The three streams can also be represented as shown in Figure 1b. In this view, the three types of analysis activity and the activity of data collection itself form an interactive, cyclical process. The researcher steadily moves among these four "nodes" during data collection, then shuttles among reduction, display, and conclusion drawing/verification for the remainder of the study. The coding of data, for

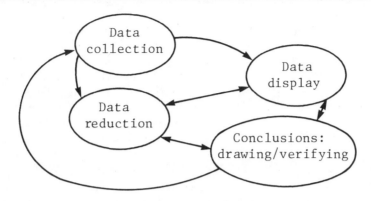

Figure 1b Components of Data Analysis: Interactive Model

example (*data reduction*), leads to new ideas on what should go into a matrix (*data display*). Entering the data requires further data reduction. As the matrix fills up, preliminary *conclusions* are drawn, but they lead to the decision (for example) to add another column to the matrix to *test* the conclusion.

In this sense, qualitative data analysis is a continuous, iterative enterprise. Issues of data reduction, of display, and of conclusion drawing/verification come into figure successively as analysis episodes follow each other. But the other two issues are always part of the ground.

Such a process is actually no more complex, conceptually speaking, than the analysis modes used by quantitative researchers. They, too, must be preoccupied with data reduction (computing means, standard deviations, indexes), with display (correlation tables, regression printouts), and with conclusion drawing/ verification (significance levels, experimental/control differences). The point is that these activities are carried out through well-defined, familiar methods, have canons guiding them, and are usually more sequential than iterative or cyclical. Qualitative researchers, on the other hand, are in a more fluid— and a more pioneering—position.

There is a consequence of that position: As we elaborate later (in section VII.C), qualitative analysis needs to be *documented* as a *process* far more fully than it has been to date. This is needed not only for purposes of "auditing" any specific analysis enterprise, but also for purposes of *learning*. As qualitative researchers, we need to understand more clearly just what is going on when we analyze data, so we can develop methods that are more generally reproducible.

I.F USING THIS BOOK

Overview

Anticipatory explanations of what is in a book are usually somewhat hollow until the reader is further in, but we'll give a brief outline. We proceed roughly according to the chronology of qualitative research efforts. Chapter II, just ahead, discusses the bounding and focusing of data collection, the sort of anticipatory analysis that occurs *prior* to fieldwork, when a study is designed.

Chapter III reviews methods especially useful *during the first stages of data collection*, including coding, memoing, and various techniques of data summary.

Chapter IV emphasizes *within*-site analysis (a "site" means a single case, at the level of an individual, a family, a work group, an organization, a community, etc.). The methods are best used *later during data collection*, or *after* it is complete.

Chapter V explores methods of *cross*-site analysis, also usable *during or after data collection*. How does one make sense of findings across a series of cases or sites without distorting, throwing away, or forcing the patterns found within sites?

Chapter VI reviews "rules of thumb" useful in building and using matrices, which we see as a fundamental type of data display.

Chapter VII deals with the tactics of analysis that a researcher employs when working with the methods discussed in Chapters IV and V. It discusses twelve specific tactics for *conclusion drawing*, such as noting patterns, themes, and clustering. Then it reviews twelve specific tactics for *verifying* conclusions, such as triangulation and looking for negative evidence.

The chapter also explains methods for documentation and auditing of qualitative analysis.

In time-honored fashion, Chapter VIII includes some general reflections, along with concluding advice for qualitative researchers.

Format

When specific methods are discussed, the format is as follows:

Name of method.

Analysis problem. The problem, need or difficulty faced by a qualitative data analyst, for which the method proposed is a useful solution.

Brief description. What the method is and how it works.

Illustration. In more detail, a "minicase," showing how the method is developed and used. Usually, this section has a variety of subheadings, such as "building the display," "entering the data," and "analyzing the data."

Variations. Alternative approaches using the same general principle. Relevant work of other researchers is cited.

Advice. Summarizing comments about use of the method, and tips for using it well.

Time required. Approximate estimates (naturally contingent on subject matter, researcher's skill, research questions being asked, number of sites, and so on).

The text also includes *supplementary* methods, described in a briefer format, that can be used in conjunction with the principal method being discussed.

Suggestions for the User

Ideas as to what a reader should "do" with any particular book are usually presumptuous, mistaken, or both. As someone has pointed out, a book is essentially a random-access display that users activate merely by turning their eyes toward it. Authors have no control over what readers end up doing. However, we can think of several modes of use that we and preliminary readers of the manuscript have found fruitful; we list them here.

Browsing. There is a wide range of material in the book, so simply exploring it in an unstructured way may be fruitful.

Problem solving. Anyone opening the book comes to it with more or less specifically defined problems in conducting qualitative data analysis. The index has been designed to be "problem sensitive," in order to permit easy access to appropriate sections of the book. The table of contents can also be used in this way.

A to Z. Some readers (such as conscientious book reviewers, docile students, and obsessive professionals) prefer to go through a book sequentially, from start to finish. We have organized the book so it makes sense that way. Some A-to-Z readers have told us that they found it useful to jump forward from the first part of Chapter IV (within-site analysis) to VI (matrix displays) and VII (tactics), then return to IV and V.

Operational use. For readers who are members of an ongoing qualitative research project, we have found it useful to have staff members read particular sections focusing on *upcoming* analysis tasks (for example, on the formation of research questions, coding, or time-ordered matrices), then discuss them, and engage in direct planning of next steps in the project, revising the methods outlined here, or developing new ones.

Training/teaching. The book can be used profitably in short-term, intensive training workshops or in longer courses. In both cases, it is soundest to proceed through the book's topics in approximately the present sequence. A typical teaching sequence has been as follows:

Chapter II (pre-data collection work)
    A. conceptual framework
    B. research questions
    C. sampling
    D. instrumentation
Chapter III (analysis during data collection)
Chapter IV (within-site analysis)
Chapter VII (conclusion drawing and verification tactics)
Chapter V (cross-site analysis)
Chapter VI (matrix building and use)

For a short (three-day) training workshop (maximum size: thirty participants), the most profitable experience has been that of directing careful attention to the four sections of Chapter II, then reviewing introductory sections of following chapters, and then focusing in more depth on two or three display modes (for example, conceptually clustered matrices, progressive matrices, causal networks in Chapter IV, and unordered meta-matrices and site-ordered predictor-outcome matrices in Chapter V).

For each specific method, we have used a learning approach like this, carried out by individuals or working pairs:

(1) Introductory lecture and/or reading to clarify the main conceptual points of the section.
(2) A brief learning task (for example, drawing a conceptual framework, designing a section of a coding

scheme, designing a matrix, drawing an event-state network, interpreting a filled-out matrix). Time here is usually 30 minutes or less.

(3) Comparing the products of individuals or pairs, using an overhead projector or newsprint; drawing generalizations, giving advice.

(4) If step 2 has not involved actual data from the participants' current or projected research, there should be a period for application to one's own work. Consultative help should be available from the workshop leader.

Our experience with Chapter VII on tactics for conclusion drawing/verification is that a rapid overview of the tactics is useful *after* people have had direct experience with several analysis episodes. They can then give deeper attention to the specific tactics that are most immediately relevant.

The same general principles apply when the book is being used in a semester-long course, although the coverage will be much deeper and more leisurely. Interim exercises, critiqued in class, are particularly productive. Self-documentation can also be done profitably (section VII.C).

Consulting. The book can also be used by people with an advisory or consulting role in ongoing research projects. Assuming good problem identification, a consultant can work with the client in either the problem-solving or direct training/teaching modes mentioned above.

So, enough curtain-raising. On with the book.

NOTES

1. For a display showing the school settings, and the kinds of innovation involved, see Charts 2 and 3, section II.C.

2. The twelve case reports are available at cost from the principal investigator (D. P. Crandall, The Network, Inc., 290 S. Main St., Andover, MA 01810). We recommend the Carson and Masepa cases for readers interested in comprehensive treatment, and the Lido case for a condensed treatment.

3. Beverly Loy Taylor contributed much to the development of the documentation form and helped design the format of the book.

4. The most recent is Freeman's (1983) reading of Samoan society, 180 degrees away from Margaret Mead's (1928). Similar differences appear in Redfield's (1930) and Lewis's (1963) studies of Tepoztlan, and Spiro's (1982) reanalysis of Malinowski's 1923 data on Trobriand islanders.

5. We concur with Cook and Reichardt (1979) that qualitative and quantitative approaches are not operationally (or paradigmatically) incompatible. We also agree with their careful debunking of the stereotypes that qualitative researchers must necessarily be phenomenological, naturalistic, subjective, inductive, and holistic, while quantitative researchers must necessarily be positivistic, obtrusive, objective, deductive and particularistic.

6. We do not deal with qualitative data in image form, but suggest useful references.

II

Focusing and Bounding the Collection of Data

Prior to fieldwork, how much shape should be a qualitative research design have? Should there be a preexistent conceptual framework? A set of research questions? Some predesigned devices for collecting data? Does such prior bounding of the study blind the researcher to important features in the site, or cause misreading of local informants' perceptions? Does *lack* of bounding and focusing lead to indiscriminate data collection and data overload? These are recurrent questions in qualitative analysis, and they have stirred up lively debate. Let us try briefly to order the terms of the debate and explain our own position within it.

To begin with, any researcher, no matter how unstructured or inductive, comes to fieldwork with *some* orienting ideas, foci, and tools. A highly inductive sociologist, for example, will focus on families or organizations (rather than, say, on rock formations or anthills) and, *within* those families or organizations, will be after data marked by preexisting conceptual tags (such as roles, relationships, routines, norms). If that researcher looks at closets or lunchrooms, it is not with the *eyes* of an architect, but with an interest in what the room and its contents have to say about the people using it. Similarly, a psychologist would orient differently toward the same phenomena, by seeing, for example, motivation, anxiety, communication, cognitive dissonance, and learning.

The conventional image of field research is one that keeps prestructuring and tight designs to a minimum. Suggesting that the qualitative researcher use a standardized instrument or lay out a conceptual framework to orient the data collection effort is likely to raise the hackles of some people who, up to now, have done the most qualitative research: social anthropologists and social phenomenologists. From their perspective, social realities are usually too complex, too relative, or too exotic to be approached with conventional conceptual maps or standardized instruments. They advocate a more loosely structured, emergent, inductively "grounded" approach to gathering data. The conceptual framework should emerge empirically from the field in the course of the study; the most important research questions will become clear only later on; the most meaningful settings and actors cannot be predicted prior to fieldwork; instruments, if any, should derive from the properties of the setting, and from the ways its actors construe them.

We go along with this vision—up to a point. Highly inductive and loosely designed studies make good sense when researchers have plenty of time and are exploring exotic cultures, understudied phenomena, or very complex social realities. But when one is interested in some better-understood social phenomena within a familiar culture or subculture, a loose, highly inductive design is a waste of time. Months of fieldwork and voluminous case studies will yield a few banalities.

We should also remember that qualitative research can be outright "confirmatory." For example, one may have been studying a key relationship—let's say, the father-daughter relationship—through a series of laboratory experiments. This preliminary work suggests that a good deal of what goes on between fathers and daughters can be subsumed under flirtation and withdrawal, a sort of approach-avoidance conflict. The researcher might then want to know how this works in natural settings, and would go into the field with a nearly complete theory and set of hypotheses, *and* a validated instrument to look only at flirtation/withdrawal and its consequences.

So one can make a case for tight, prestructured qualitative designs *and* for loose, emergent ones. Predictably enough, most of the qualitative research now being done lies between these two extremes. *Something* is known conceptually about the phenomenon, but not enough to house a theory. The researcher has a fairly good idea of the parts of the phenomenon that are *not* well understood, and knows where to look for these things—in which settings, among which actors, within which processes or during what class of event. Finally, the researcher usually has some initial ideas about how to gather the information—through interviews, observations, document collection, perhaps even with a well-validated instrument that will allow for some comparison between the proposed study and earlier ones. At the outset, then, we usually have at least a rudimentary conceptual framework, a set of general research questions, some notions about sampling, and some initial data-gathering devices.

How prestructured should a qualitative research design be? Enough to reach the ground, as Lincoln said when asked about the proper length of a man's legs. It depends on the time available, how much is already known about the phenomena under study, the instruments already available, and the analysis that will be made. Our stance lies off center, toward the structured end. To our earlier epistemological reasons, we should add a couple that are more mundane.

First, the looser the initial design, the less selective the collection of data; *everything* looks important at the outset to someone waiting for the key constructs or regularities to emerge from the site, and that wait can be a long one. The researcher, awash in data, will need months to sort it out. Much "contract" research must produce results under time pressure, with a limited budget, and looseness is unwise.

Second, much current fieldwork involves *multiple-site* (multiple-case) research rather than single-site studies. If different fieldworkers are operating inductively, with no common framework or instrumentation, they are bound to end up with the double dilemma of data overload *and* lack of comparability across cases.[1]

A word on notation. We use the word "site" to mean the same thing as "case." Both refer to the same phenomenon: a bounded context in which one is studying events, processes, and outcomes. Note that a "case" could include a wide range of settings; a school, a program, a specific project, a network, a family, a community, and even the behavior of an individual over time in a specified environment. We prefer the word "site" because it reminds us that a "case" always occurs in a specified *setting*; we cannot study individual "cases" devoid of their context in the way that a quantitative researcher often does.

There are trade-offs here: The looser the initial framework, the more each researcher can be receptive to local idiosyncrasies, but cross-site comparability will be hard to get and the costs and the information load will be colossal. Tightly coordinated designs face the opposite dilemma: They yield more economical, comparable, and potentially generalizable findings, but they are less site-sensitive and may entail bending data

out of contextual shape to answer a cross-site analytic question.

One final note. Focusing and bounding data collection can be seen usefully as anticipatory *data reduction*; it is a form of preanalysis, ruling out certain variables and relationships, and attending to others.

With this backdrop, let us look more closely at the aspects of a study design involving decisions about bounding and focusing the collection of qualitative data in the field. These aspects include developing a conceptual framework, formulating research questions, sampling, and instrumentation.

II.A BUILDING A CONCEPTUAL FRAMEWORK

Rationale

Theory-building relies on a few general constructs that subsume a mountain of particulars. Terms such as "social climate," "stress," or "role conflict" are typically labels we put on bins containing a lot of discrete events and behaviors. When we assign a label to a bin, we may or may not know how all the contents of the bin fit together, or how this bin relates to another one. But any researcher, no matter how inductive in approach, knows which bins to start with and what their general contents are likely to be. Bins come from theory and experience, and (often) from the general objectives of the study envisioned. Laying out those bins, giving each a descriptive or inferential name, and getting some clarity about their interrelationships is what a conceptual framework is all about.

Doing that exercise also forces the researcher to be selective—to decide which dimensions are more important, which relationships are likely to be most meaningful, and, as a consequence, what information should be collected and analyzed. And as we have noted, the conceptual framework allows multiple researchers to be sure they are studying the same phenomenon in ways that will permit an eventual cross-site analysis.

Brief Description

A conceptual framework explains, either graphically or in narrative form, the main dimensions to be studied—the key factors, or variables—and the presumed relationships among them. Frameworks come in several shapes and sizes. They can be rudimentary or elaborate, theory-driven or commonsensical, descriptive or causal.

Illustrations

Let us look at a few examples. First, Figure 2a presents a rudimentary, mostly descriptive framework from a large-scale contract research study (The Network, Inc., 1979). The study's general objectives were to examine several programs aimed at school improvement through dissemination of exemplary innovations, to understand reasons for implementation success, and to make policy recommendations. But within this context, there needed to be more conceptual specificity.

Here we see a good example of the "bins" approach. The framework is mostly a visual catalogue of *roles* to be studied (policymakers, linkers, adopters), and, within each role, where these people work and what they do (context, characteristics, behavior). A second main aspect of the study is the *innovations*, notably their characteristics, and a third aspect is the *outcomes* of the innovations (improvement effort success indicators) as a result of their interactions with the three types of people.

What does this framework do for the researcher? First, it specifies who and what will and will not be studied. For example, it looks as if the people who developed the innovations will not be studied. It also appears that the study is focusing on *successful* outcomes, and is going to collect data specifically on four kinds. Second, the framework assumes some *relationships*, as indicated by the arrows. Some of these relationships are purely logical—for instance, the idea that adopters and the innovations will influence one another—but the arrows also mirror empirical findings: Such relationships have actually operated this way in the real world. The success indicators also derive in part from previous empirical work.

We see here the focusing and bounding function of a conceptual framework. Some, not all, actors are going to be studied, along with some, not all, aspects of their activity. Only some relationships will be explored and certain kinds of outcomes measured. By scanning the chart, the researcher can see where to get information and, equally important, what should be done with the information once it has been collected—that is, which analyses will be made.

Now for a slightly more complex and more inferential conceptual frame, using some of the same variables (Figure 2b). It comes from the same study (The Network, Inc., 1979). This is essentially an unbundling and refinement of the first illustration, but there are heavier bets being made on the interrelationships. For example, "policymakers" are hypothesized to influence "linkers" through the provision of technical assistance and through interventions in the linkers' network. There are few two-way arrows in this cut, and specific within-role relationships are not hypothesized. In other words, the researcher is deciding to collect information *selectively*, to test some hypotheses. Similarly, it looks as if the study will focus more heavily on "linker behavior," "adopter behavior," and "implementation effectiveness," that is, on variables coming *later* in the causal chain indicated by the arrows. "Linker perspective," for example, will be studied only as a presumed consequence of "network embeddedness" and as a predictor of "linker behavior."

On our continuum from exploratory to confirmatory designs, the first illustration is closer to the exploratory end and the second to the confirmatory. Let's have a look at one about midway along the continuum (Figure 3). This framework is of particular interest in that it lays out the study from which we will draw most of our subsequent exhibits (Huberman & Miles, 1983b).

Once again, we have the "bins," in the form of general labels for *events* (e.g., "prior history"); *settings* (e.g., "community," "district office"); *processes* (e.g., "assistance," "changes in user perceptions and practices"); and *theoretical constructs* (e.g., "organizational rules"). Some of the outcomes are hypothesized (e.g., "degree of institutionalization"), but most are open-ended. The directional arrows follow time flow, but there are still some bets being made (e.g., that most assistance comes early, and that there will be reciprocal changes among the innovation, its users, and the organization). But overall, the level of specificity of each bin and the direction of influence between and within bins are far less predetermined than in the preceding framework. Each researcher in the study will have to find out what the "assumptions" and "characteristics" of the innovations are at the field site, and how these factors will affect "user purposes," but this is still a very general brief.

It is, moreover, a brief that can change en route, as in fact this conceptual framework did. Frameworks are focusing and bounding devices that need not work as blinders and straitjackets. As qualitative researchers collect data, they revise their frameworks—make them more precise, replace empirically feeble bins with

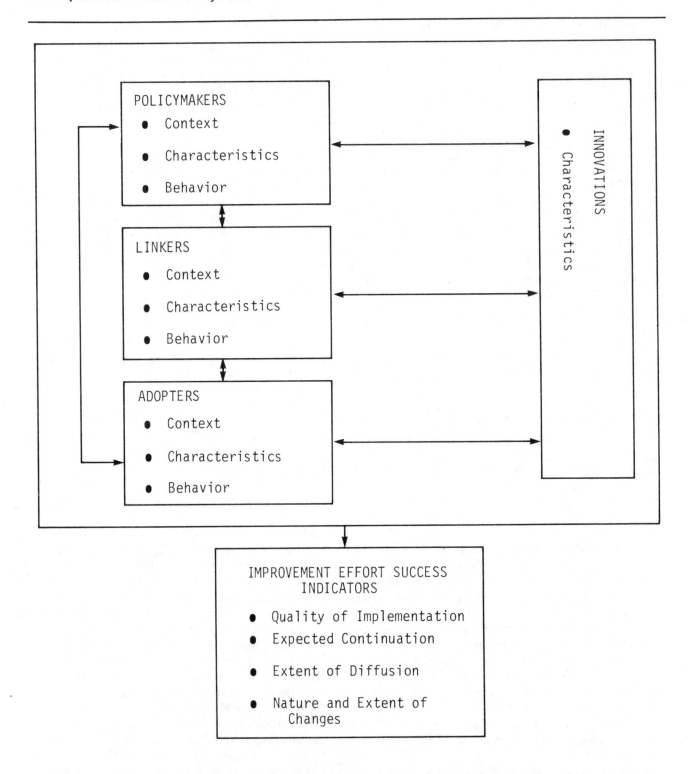

Figure 2a   Conceptual Framework for a Study of the Dissemination of Educational Innovations

SOURCE: The Network, Inc. (1979). Reprinted by permission.

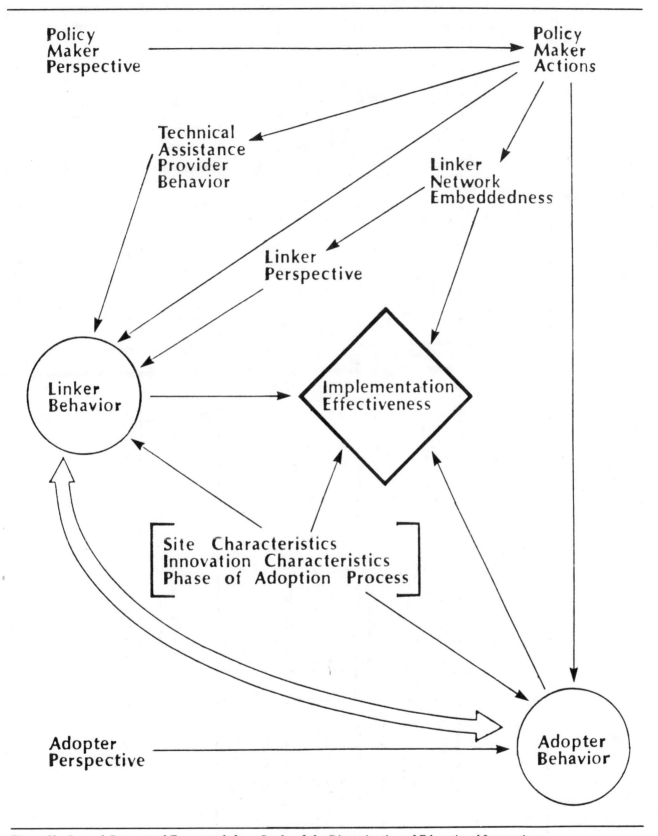

Figure 2b Second Conceptual Framework for a Study of the Dissemination of Educational Innovations
SOURCE: The Network, Inc. (1979). Reprinted by permission.

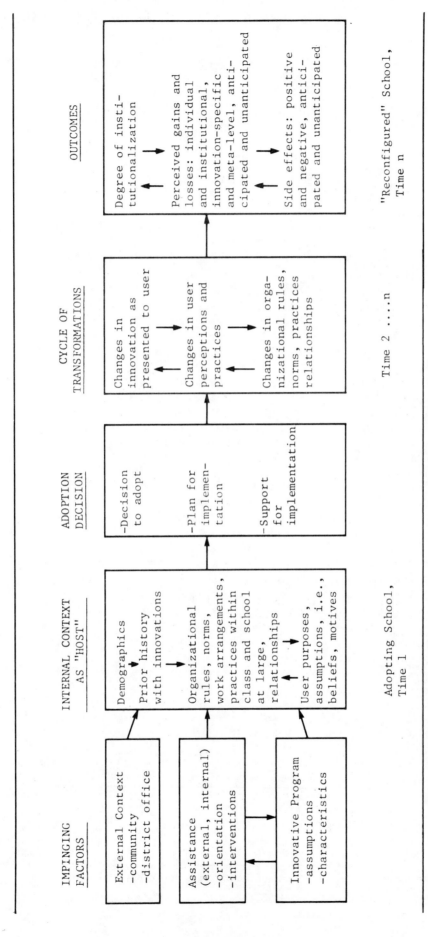

Figure 3   Conceptual Framework for a Multiple-Site "School Improvement" Field Study (initial version)

more meaningful ones, reconstrue relationships. The great advantage of qualitative research is that it *can* change direction easily and refocus data collection for the next field trip. Conceptual frameworks are simply the current version of the researcher's map of the territory being investigated. Without such a map, the search is slipshod; and if several researchers are involved, fruitless empirical anarchy can result. As the explorer's knowledge of the terrain improves, the map becomes correspondingly more differentiated and integrated, and researchers in a multiple-site study can coordinate their data collection even more closely.

Advice

Here are some suggestions that summarize and extend what's been said in this section.

(1) Conceptual frameworks are best done graphically, rather than in text. Having to get the entire framework on a single page is salutary; it obliges the researcher to *find* the bins that hold the discrete phenomena, to map relationships, to divide variables that are conceptually or functionally distinct, and to work with all the information at once.

(2) One should expect to do several iterations, right from the outset. There are probably as many ways of representing the main variables as there are variables to represent, but some—typically later cuts—are more elegant and parsimonious than others.

(3) Early in a multiple-site study, have each field researcher do a cut at an overarching framework, then compare the several versions. This will show, literally, where everyone's head is at and usually leads to an explication of contentious or foggy areas that otherwise would have surfaced later on with far more loss of time and data. Note: Good conflict management skills are needed.

(4) Avoid the no-risk framework, that is, one that keys variables at a very global level and has two-directional arrows everywhere. This amounts essentially to making *no* focusing and bounding decisions, and is little better than the strategy of going indiscriminately into the field to see what the site has to "tell." One can legitimately *begin* with such an omnibus framework—Figure 2a is close to the no-risk framework—as a way of getting to a more selective and specific one.

(5) Prior theorizing and empirical research are, of course, important inputs. It helps to lay out your own orienting frame, then map onto it the variables and relationships from the principal studies available to see where there are overlaps, contradictions, refinements, and qualifications.

Time Required

Taken singly, each iteration of a conceptual framework is not a time-consuming exercise. If the researcher has already done a lot of thinking about the study and is on top of the research literature, an initial cut might take 45 minutes to an hour. For the reader who doubts this, we should mention that in training workshops using these materials, participants have routinely been able to develop preliminary conceptual frameworks for their qualitative studies in under half an hour. The issue is usually *not* developing a giant scheme *de novo*, but making explicit what is already in one's mind. Furthermore, working briskly helps to cut away the superfluous and encourages synthesis and creativity.

Successive cuts of a framework are more differentiated and have to resolve the problems of the prior one, so they take longer—more like an hour or two. If the researcher is new to the field, the first try may take two hours or so.

II.B FORMULATING RESEARCH QUESTIONS

Rationale

It is a direct step from the elaboration of a conceptual framework to the formulation of research questions. The former sets up the latter. If I have a bin labeled "policymaker," as in Figure 1, and within it a subhead called "behavior," I am asking myself some questions about policymakers' behaviors. If I have a two-way arrow from the policymaker bin to an "innovation" bin, as again in Figure 1, my question has to do with how policymakers behave in relation to the introduction of innovations and, reciprocally, how different kinds of innovations affect policymakers' behaviors. If my bins are as general as those in Figure 2a, I can ask a variety of general and specific questions. If, by contrast, my conceptual framework is more constrained, so are my questions. In Figure 2b my interest in "policymaker actions" is more focused; I want to know whether and how they affect adopter behavior, linker network embeddedness, linker behavior, and technical assistance provider behavior. Here, I am down to specific variables in a bin and specific relationships between bins. Naturally, the nature and quality of the relationships may well take some careful pondering before research questions are clear.

What do these questions do for me? First, they are a way of making my theoretical assumptions even more explicit than they may have been in the conceptual framework. Second, they tell me what I want to know *most* or *first*; I will start by channeling energy in this direction rather than in the direction of other variables and relationships. My collection of data will be more focused and limited than if I simply tracked an innovation as it passed through the hands of policymakers and linkers.

I am also beginning to make some sampling decisions; I will look only at *some* actors in *some* contexts dealing with *some* issues. The questions also tell me I will need data-gathering devices that could include specific types of observation, interviewing, document collection, or questionnaires.

Finally, the rough boundaries of my analysis have been set, at least provisionally. If I ask, "How do policymaker actions affect adopter behavior?" I will be looking at data on adopter behaviors, policymaker actions, and their influences on each other, not at *what else* affects adopter behaviors. The research questions make it easier for me to move from the conceptual framework to considerations about sampling, instrumentation, and eventual analysis; they *operationalize* the conceptual framework.

This is, of course, a deductive model. We begin with some orienting constructs, extract the questions, then line the questions up with an appropriate sampling frame and methodology. Inductivists argue that we could have the wrong concepts, the wrong questions, and the wrong methodology for studying the phenomena we are interested in, and would only find how wrongheaded we were when our ultimate analysis turned up equivocal or shallow findings. We will chip away at that argument throughout this text. For now, however, we want to make the point that inductivists are *also* operating with research questions, conceptual frameworks, and sampling matrices, but their choices are simply more implicit and the links between framework and procedures are less linear. Nevertheless, these choices, of necessity, serve to bound and focus the study.

Take, for example, the problem of understanding police work—a domain that remains somewhat arcane and obscure despite (or perhaps because of) TV shows. It deserves an inductive approach. But *which facets* of police work will be studied? One can't look at them all. And *where* will one study them? One can't look everywhere. If one "delays" that decision for a few months until one has spent some time, let us say, at the precinct station, that simply reflects two tacit sampling decisions (start at the precinct house, then recheck after a while). The "recheck'" is inevitably constrained by the first decision.

Suppose the choices were to focus on arrests and bookings. That immediately excludes many other issues and leads to *sampling* and *instrumentation* choices (for example, observation as a useful contrast to official documents; selection of different kinds of suspects, crimes, styles of apprehending suspects, types of officers). These sampling and instrumentation decisions, often inexplicit, are actually delimiting the settings, actors, processes, and events to be studied. In turn, the types of analysis possible are constrained by these choices.

In such a study, the conceptual framework can come at the beginning, at the end, or both, but it is always present. Let us illustrate. Manning (1977) conducted just such a field study of police work. He found, for instance, that police officers often made "discretionary" arrests, bending laws and regulations to fit their own, often private, purposes. Arrests were also often justified after the fact ("situationally justified actions"), and whether or not something was a "crime" turned out to be extremely fluid. In each case, there appeared to be a series of implicit "negotiations" that brought informal and formal rules into play.

Readers of Schutz and Goffman will immediately recognize the language of social phenomenology: situational actions, negotiated rule meanings, front-stage and backstage agendas, and the like. This is a powerful but *particular* way of conceptualizing social activity. Alternatively, a Marxist analyst doing an analysis of the same research questions, operationalized in the same settings around the same classes of events and behaviors, would probably show us how the police serve class-bound interests by stabilizing existing social arrangements. A mainstream social psychologist might focus on autonomy and social influence as the core issues.

Conceptualization can occur up front—the researcher says something like, "I am a social phenomenologist and I am interested in socially negotiated rule meanings in police work"—or at the end, when the implicit conceptual framework is trained on the analysis. But it is invariably *there*, even when one is unaware of belonging to a school of thought. In other words, people, including research people, share common "bins" and causal "arrows" in the ways they construe and carve up social phenomena, and they will use them explicitly or implicitly to decide which questions they think are the most important and how one should go about getting the answers. We believe better science happens when one makes one's framework—and associated choices of research questions, sample, and instrumentation—*explicit*, rather than pretending a sort of inductive purity.

Brief Description

The formulation of research questions can precede or follow the development of a conceptual framework, but in either case represents the facets of an empirical domain that the researcher most wants to explore. Research questions can be general or particular, descriptive or explanatory. They can be formulated at the outset or later on, and can be refined or reformulated in the course of fieldwork.

Illustration

The school improvement study shows how a conceptual framework hooks up with the formulation of research questions. Look back at Figure 3, where the main variable sets of the school improvement study were laid out. Look at the third column, entitled "adoption decision." Its component parts are listed inside the bin: the decision to adopt, the plan for implementation, requisite support for implementation. The task then is to decide what one wants to find out about these topics—which aspects are essential to an overall understanding of the school improvement process. The procedure used here was to cluster specific research questions under more general ones, as shown in Chart 1.

Notice that there are choices being made *within* each topical area. For example, in the first two areas, the main things we want to know about the "decision to adopt" are who was involved, how the decision was actually made, and how important this project was relative to others. All the questions seem to be *functional*, rather than theoretical or descriptive—they have to do with getting something done. And there is the implicit idea that more is better, for example, more priority and centrality is a plus, anticipating eventual problems is desirable, and implementation will be better if the "requisite conditions" are met. This is simply another type of bounding given to a study, one that looks instrumentally at a social phenomenon.

We can also see that, conceptually, more is afoot than we saw in the conceptual framework. The "requisite conditions" in the last clump of questions indicate that the researchers have some a priori notions about which factors make for the greatest preparedness. When such a research question gets operationalized, there will be an attempt to determine whether these conditions were present or absent at the various field sites, and whether that made any difference in the execution of the project. This is a good example of how research questions feed directly into data collection. It does *not* mean, however, that field researchers will be

Chart 1
General and Specific Research Questions Relating
to the Adoption Decision
(school improvement field study)

How was the adoption decision made?

Who was involved (for example, principal, users, central office people, school board, outside agencies)? How was the decision made (top-down, persuasive, consultative, collegial-participative, or delegated styles)?

How much priority and centrality did the new program have, at the time of the adoption decision?

How much support and commitment was there from administrators? How important was it for teachers, seen in relation to their routine, "ordinary" activities, and any other innovations that were being contemplated or attempted? Realistically, how large did it loom in the scheme of things? Was it a one-time event or one of a series?

What were the components of the original plan for implementation?

These might have included front-end training, monitoring and debugging/troubleshooting unexpected problems, ongoing support. How precise and elaborate was this plan? Were people satisfied with it at the time? Did it deal with all the problems anticipated?

Were the requisite conditions for implementation assured before it began?

These might have included commitment, understanding, materials and equipment, skills, time allocation, organizational backup. Were any important conditions seen as missing? Which were *most* missing?

---

inattentive to other, as yet undreamed-of, "requisite conditions," nor even that the entire construct of "requisite conditions" will be retained throughout the study.

Advice

(1) Even if you are in a highly inductive mode, it is a good idea to start with some general research questions. They need not overly constrain the study; rather, they allow you to get clear about what, in the general domain, is of most interest. They make the implicit explicit, without necessarily freezing or limiting your vision.

(2) If you are foggy about your priorities or about the ways they can be framed, begin with a foggy research question and then try to defog it. Most research questions do not come out right on the first cut, no matter how clear the researcher is about the domain of study.

(3) Formulating more than a couple of dozen general questions is looking for trouble. One can easily lose the forest for the trees and overly fragment one's collection of data. The research endeavor becomes more actuarial than generative. Furthermore, having a large number of research questions makes it harder to see emergent links across different parts of the data base and to achieve successful integration of findings. As we saw in the illustration, a solution to research question proliferation is the use of major questions, each with a series of subquestions, for clarity and specificity. It also helps to consider whether there is a *key* question, the "thing you really want to know."

(4) In a multiple-site study, be certain that *all* fieldworkers understand *each* question and see its importance. Multiple-site studies have to be more explicit so that site researchers can be aligned as they collect information in the field. Poor alignment—unclear questions, different understandings—makes for noncomparable data across cases.

(5) It is sometimes easier to generate a conceptual framework *after* one has made a list of research questions. You look at the list for common themes, common constructs, implicit or explicit relationships, and so on, and *then* begin to map out the underlying framework joining these pieces. Some researchers operate better in this mode.

(6) Once the list of research questions is generated and honed, look it over to be sure that each question is, in fact, researchable. You can always think of trenchant questions that you or your informants have no real means of answering.

(7) Keep the research questions in hand and review them during fieldwork. This will focus data collection; you'll think twice before observing or noting down what informants have for lunch or where they park their cars. Unless something has an *obvious*, fairly direct, or potentially important link to a research question, it should not indiscriminantly fatten the corpus of field notes. If a datum initially ignored does turn out to be important, you will know it. The beauty of qualitative field research is that there is (nearly) always a second chance.

Time Required

Formulating the questions is an iterative process; the second version is sharper and leaner than the first, and the third cut gets the final few bugs out. Most of the time should be spent on the *general* questions, since the range and quality of specific ones will depend on how good the overarching question is.

Iterating a set of six or seven general research questions, if done scrupulously, should not take *less* than two to three hours and should not be done in one sit-

ting. A question that looks spellbinding usually loses some of its appeal when one has another look a few hours later. Specific research questions should come easier. If a general question breaks down into, let us say, three or four subquestions, the first cut at the subquestions should take under an hour and the next cut slightly less. So a set of research questions comprising five general questions and twenty specific ones might add up to four to five hours in all, spread over two or three sittings. Naturally, the times will vary with the nature of the study, the researcher's experience, the complexity and explicitness of the conceptual framework, and so on, but these estimates are, in our experience, reasonable.

II.C SAMPLING: BOUNDING THE COLLECTION OF DATA

Rationale

Empirical research is often a matter of progressively lowering your aspirations. You begin by wanting to study *all* the facets of an important problem or a fascinating social phenomenon. But it soon becomes clear that choices must be made. Unless you are willing to devote most of your professional life to a single study, you have to settle for less.

Qualitative researchers may have an initial sense of having licked this problem. Most of their work, after all, has to do with a single "case," usually a social setting. There are only so many parameters to a setting: a finite number of people, processes, and events. But a closer look reveals that settings have subsettings (schools have classrooms, groups have cliques, cultures have subcultures, families have coalitions), so that fixing the boundaries of the setting in a nonarbitrary way is tricky. Life proliferates endlessly.

Knowing, then, that one cannot study everyone everywhere doing everything, even within a single case, how does one limit the parameters of a study? More specifically, how are such decisions made *prior* to fieldwork? The issue brings out some of the differences between qualitative and quantitative studies. For example, qualitative researchers usually work with smaller samples of *people* in fewer global *settings* than do survey researchers. Also, qualitative samples tend to be more purposive than random, partly because the initial definition of the universe is more limited (for example, arrest-making in an urban precinct) and partly because social processes have a logic and coherence that random sampling of events or treatments usually reduces to uninterpretable sawdust.

Finally, and most crucially, samples in qualitative studies can *change*. Initial choices of informants lead to the recommendation of new informants; observing one class of events calls for a comparison with a different class; understanding one relationship reveals several facets that have to be teased out and studied individually.

In other words, qualitative research is essentially an *investigative* process, not unlike detective work, as Douglas (1976) has argued convincingly. One makes gradual sense of a social phenomenon, and does it in large part by contrasting, comparing, replicating, cataloguing, and classifying the object of one's study. Basically, these are all *sampling* activities—finding the variabilities and commonalities of a social universe—and they are conducted progressively and iteratively by the qualitative field researcher. Some of these procedures can be replicated in quantitative research—snowball sampling is an example—but they are far more cumbersome. In terms of sampling maneuverability, surveys are jumbo jets and qualitative case studies are superlights.

However, when we move from single-site studies to multiple-site studies (remember that "site" is equivalent to "case" throughout the book), qualitative research comes up against some of the same constraints as survey research. Fieldworkers looking at different places, phenomena, and people are likely to find little in common. Or their commonalities will be at such a general level that they might have spared themselves and their readers the trouble. In multiple-case research, the question of *which* sites to look at becomes focal. Beyond this, each investigator must *begin* with a common class of within-site settings or events and a consensual catalogue of types of informant.

How are these initial choices made? They are driven in large part by the conceptual framework and research questions. If, for instance, I am interested in the deterrent effects of capital punishment on hard-core criminals, and I want to do a field study, I will probably have to talk with criminals in states where the death penalty is present or absent. I may also want to talk to *other* people (judges, sociologists, relatives of criminals, psychologists). Or I may decide to do a life history of a small number of criminals, but *this* option is also a sampling decision that bounds and focuses my universe of inquiry. I will have to choose my cases from a larger candidate pool and identify my initial sources of information from a still larger pool. If I am one of several researchers doing life histories of hard-core criminals, there has to be initial consensus and coordination around actions, events, and settings.

Sampling issues are also, of course, tied up with issues of generalizability. Multiple-site studies are especially appealing because they can purposively sample, and thereby make claims about, a larger universe of people, settings, events, or processes than can single-site studies.

Finally, being explicit about what you want to study and why is the best way of attending primarily to *that* topic in the field. You thereby avoid the pitfalls faced by researchers who are unsure of what they are studying: indiscriminate, vacuum-cleanerlike collection of every datum; accumulation of far more information than there will be time to analyze; and detours into alluring but ultimately blind alleys that use up time, goodwill, and analytic possibilities.

Brief Description

Sampling involves not only decisions about which *people* to observe or interview, but also about *settings*, *events*, and social *processes*. Multiple-site studies also demand clear choices about which *sites* to include. Qualitative studies call for continuous refocusing and redrawing of the parameters of the study during fieldwork, but some initial selection is still required. The conceptual framework and research questions determine the foci and boundaries within which samples are selected.

Illustrations

Let us look briefly at two ends of the qualitative continuum: the relatively unfettered, exploratory single-case study and the more constrained and focused multiple-case study.

To provide continuity, let us stay with the "police work" and "school improvement" studies discussed earlier. In the first case, we have no mapped-out conceptual framework, but rather a general perspective on social processes emphasizing how people literally "make sense" of their habitual surround. Part of this sense-making activity involves developing and interpreting rules about legitimate and illegitimate behavior.

The decision to illustrate this general perspective by studying the arrest and booking of suspects is a good example of a sampling choice. It can, in fact, even *precede* the research question. You can either ask, "How are laws interpreted by people enforcing them in face-to-face situations?" and *then* select police officers as a sample of such "people" (rather than judges or fire inspectors), or you can move *right away* from the general domain to the sample and then ask, "How do police officers interpret laws when arresting and booking suspects?"

However you proceed, the sampling parameters are set by the framework and the research question: police work, rule interpreting, arrests, and booking. There is still much room for choices within each dimension of the study, but the universe is now far more bounded and focused than that of the conceptual framework or the general research question. To get a sense of a minimal set of *initial* sampling choices within this universe, let us array some options:

Sampling Parameters	Possible Choices
settings:	precinct station, squad car, scene of the crime, suspect's residence or hangout
actors:	police officers with different characteristics (e.g., rank, seniority, experience, race, beliefs, education) and suspects (age, race, beliefs, education, type of offense)
events:	arrests, bookings, possibly pursuits of suspects, and post hoc justifications of booking to other actors
processes:	making the arrest, doing the booking, relating to suspects, interpreting laws, justifying laws, generally "negotiating" law enforcement within the precinct.

Eventually, the researcher will have to touch most or all of these bases to get the research question well answered. The first base will usually be the *setting* (staying home or going up in a hot air balloon are unlikely to produce good answers to the research questions). From there, *several options emerge:*

(1) Start with the precinct station, one kind of police officer, all bookings during the working day, and all instances of the social processes that occur.
(2) Start with the precinct station and all types of officers, bookings, and justifications for the booking.
(3) Start with the precinct station and one officer, and follow the officer through several episodes of arrests, pursuits, bookings, and justification.
(4) Start with the precinct station with a booking, then reconstitute the prior events.

All permutations are possible, as are many different nestings (officers within events, events within processes, and so on) in this general universe, but there *is* a selection process at work. An ethnographer setting out to "hang around" a precinct is continuously making sampling decisions about what to observe, who to talk to, what to ask, what to write down, whether to stay in one room or another. And these choices, in turn, are determined by the questions being asked and the framework—implicit or explicit—that determines

why *these* questions, and not others, are being asked.

There is also the question of practicality. There is a finite amount of time, with variable access to different actors and events, and an abundance of logistical problems. Very seldom does a start-up sampling frame survive the lovely imperfection and intractability of the field. It must be bent and reframed.

Finally, sampling means just that: taking a smaller chunk of a larger universe. If I focus on one precinct station and one kind of police officer making one kind of booking, I can make few legitimate claims about other precincts, or about other officers and bookings within the precinct I have studied. If, on the other hand, I hang around one precinct long enough and track a variety of arrests and bookings, I will probably have a large enough sample of settings, actors, and events to make confident claims not only about these variables but also about how laws are enforced and interpreted within the precinct, which is the conceptual focus of my study. That process, however, may well be precinct-specific; to make sure it is not, we would have to study several precinct stations.

To illustrate a multiple-site study, let us look at the final sample of sites for the school improvement study (Chart 2). Notice that there are twelve sites and eight sampling dimensions, which means that the probability is very high that each of the twelve sites will form a uniquely different configuration; the choice here was for representative diversity across sites. To see this graphically, look at Chart 3. It shows the final sampling frame. Site uniqueness means our findings may *illustrate* school improvement activity in the programs studied across the country, but they cannot support *generalizations* about it with much confidence. Rather, we are betting that, within any given site, a large enough variety of actors, events, subsettings, and processes will be captured that the findings will *characterize* a far larger population of sites than might be legitimate on purely statistical grounds.[2] Whether the outcomes found for the three rural NDN projects in this sample obtain for the full population of rural NDN projects is not an answer that this sample can provide. It *can*, however, help define the parameters for a follow-up survey or a follow-up series of case studies focused on this subpopulation.

The sample was also nested in a larger sample of sites from which survey data were collected; findings from our field study were expected to speak to what might be going on in that larger population. Note that some sampling dimensions reflect this (for example, focusing only on NDN and IV-C programs, each an important part of the larger study; or the break by region and setting); other dimensions (year of start, project status) follow from the conceptual framework,

Chart 2

Characteristics of Field Study Sample

| | SITE CONTEXT | | | ASPECTS OF THE INNOVATION | | | | |
SITE	PROGRAM SPONSORSHIP #	U.S. REGION	SETTING	YEAR BEGAN PROJECT	STATUS (as initially assessed)	PROGRAM TYPE	PROGRAM NAME OR INITIALS x	PROGRAM CONTENT
ASTORIA	NDN	Southeast	Small city	1978	Expanding	Add-on	EPSF	Early Childhood
BANESTOWN	NDN	Southeast	Rural	1979	Expanding	Pull-out	SCORE-ON	Reading/Math
BURTON	NDN	Midwest	Suburban	1979	Expanding	Add-on	IPLE	Law and government
CALSTON	NDN	Midwest	Center city	1978	Ongoing	Drop-in	Matteson 4D	Reading
CARSON	IV-C	Plains	Rural	1977	Expanding	Add-on	IPA	Individualized educational planning*
DUN HOLLOW	IV-C	Northeast	Urban sprawl	1977	Dwindling	Add-on	Eskimo Studies	Social studies*
LIDO	NDN	Northeast	Rural	1976	Dwindling	Add-on	KARE	Environment
MASEPA	NDN	Plains	Rural	1978	Ongoing	Drop-in	ECRI	Language Arts*
PERRY-PARKDALE	NDN	Midwest	Suburban	1977	Ongoing	Sub-system	EBCE	Career education
PLUMMET	IV-C	Southwest	Center city	1976	Ongoing	Sub-system	Bentley Center	Alternative school
PROVILLE	IV-C	Southwest	Urban sprawl	1977	Dwindling	Pull-out	CEP	Vocational education
TINDALE	IV-C	Midwest	Urban sprawl	1976	Ongoing	Drop-in	Tindale Reading Model	Reading

\# NDN = National Diffusion Network
   IV-C = Title IV-C

x IV-C program names are pseudonyms, to avoid identifying specific sites.

* Program is used in this site with a comprehensive sample of learners, rather than with low-achieving or marginal populations.

39

Chart 3
Final Sampling Frame for Field Study

	National Diffusion Network Projects (NDN)			Title IV-C Projects (IV-C)		
	1979	1978	Earlier	1978	1977	Earlier
EXPANDING	SCORE-ON Banestown Rural Pull-out, in-school	EPSF Astoria Town/suburb Add-on, in-school			IPA Carson Rural Add-on, in-school	
ONGOING	IPLE Burton Suburb Drop-in, in-school & field	ECRI Masepa Rural Drop-in, in-school Matteson 4-D Calston Metro urban Drop-in, in-school	EBCE Perry-Parkdale Suburb Subsystem, in-school/field			Tindale Reading Tindale Urban sprawl Subsystem, in-school Bentley Center Plummet Urban Subsystem, in-school
INACTIVE, DWINDLING			KARE Lido Rural Add-on, field	Eskimo Curr. Dun Hollow Urban sprawl Add-on, in-school	CEP Proville Urban sprawl Pull-out, in-school	

which stressed changes over time; and still other dimensions (program type, name, content) are generated from what was known about properties of the innovation being tried.

Note the focusing and bounding decisions that have already been made. For example, this study of the school improvement process is going to look only at *sponsored* programs of two types and, within these, at twelve projects. Each aspect acts like a decision tree that takes us into increasingly particularistic domains of study. What we may eventually have to say about the school improvement process can only encompass these facets; we have taken a small bite out of a far larger pie and have no way of being certain that other bites would have the same ingredients.

On the other hand, multiple-case samples enable us to speak with some confidence about projects like the ones being sampled. These projects are located in different *regions* and *settings*, are at different points in their *life cycles* (just under way at the start of the study, or up to three years old), exemplify the possible range of *growth* ("status") and *program type*, and cover all the main *content* areas.

Some of these dimensions, in fact, allow us to address some important conceptual issues economically. For example, by sampling for variability on the year the project began, we can follow the innovation process over time but only spend a year doing it. By stratifying levels of growth, we have a proxy measure of success (presumably, "dwindling" is a poor harbinger and "expanding" a good one) that could help tell us *how* success is achieved (we can contrast various levels of success and need not study serially a successful project, then a less successful one, and so on).

In sum, multiple-site sampling prior to fieldwork, while limiting the universe of study and constraining the individual field researcher, also pays some handsome rewards. It allows one to look simultaneously at several settings and to get enough variability to increase the explanatory power of the study as a whole.

Note that this sampling matrix does not yet resolve some of the within-site focusing and bounding decisions the police work study had to make. If one site researcher interviews only administrators and another only teachers, the comparability of the two sites is minimal. For these decisions, we need the conceptual framework or the research questions. Using them, we can set up a chart of sampling parameters and possible choices for initial fieldwork, as follows:

Sampling Parameters	Possible Choices
settings	schools, classrooms, offices, meeting rooms
actors	teachers, administrators, pupils, assistants
events	meetings, daily use of the innovation training sessions, visits
processes	making decisions about use, assisting users, mastering the innovation, changing routines, supervising use, changing the innovation

Once again, the sequence and mix of these choices can be researcher-specific, but making cross-site generalizations is going to be hard if individual site researchers are talking with different actors and looking at different events. It will be downright impossible if researchers are operating in radically different settings or, most of all, focusing on different processes. The processes in sites flow out of the interplay of actors, events, and settings. They are usually at the core of the conceptual framework, and serve as the glue holding the research questions together. Being explicit about processes is the best way to ensure careful data collection, and avoid costly distractions. It also improves your chances of getting to a new and better set of underlying constructs as you get deeper into data collection.

Advice

(1) Just *thinking* in sampling-frame terms is healthy methodological medicine. If you are talking with one kind of informant, you need to consider *why* this kind of informant is important and, from there, which *other* people should be interviewed. This is a good, bias-controlling exercise.

(2) Remember that you are not only sampling *people*, but also *settings, events, and processes*. It is important to line up these parameters with the research questions as well, and to consider whether your choices are doing a representative, time-efficient job of answering them. The settings, events, or processes that come rapidly to mind at the start of the study may not be the most pertinent or data-rich ones. A systematic review can sharpen early and later choices.

(3) There is never "enough" time to do any study. So taking the tack, "I'll start somewhere, and take it from there," is asking for trouble. It's probably a good idea to start with a *fallback sample* of informants and subsettings: the things one *has* to cover in light of what one knows at that point. That sample may—probably will—change later on, but not massively.

(4) In qualitative research, as well as in survey research, there is a danger of sampling too narrowly. In fact, points 1 and 2 above tug in that direction: Go to the meatiest, most study-relevant sources. It is also important to work a bit at the peripheries—to talk with people who are not central to the phenomenon but are neighbors to it, to people no longer actively involved, to dissidents and renegades and eccentrics. Spending a day in the adjoining village or school is also worth the time.

In all such cases, there are two possible payoffs. First, you may learn a lot. Second, you get contrasting and comparative information that helps you understand the phenomenon at hand. As we all know, traveling abroad gives us insights into our own cultures.

Time Required

It is very difficult to provide workable guidelines here. Within-site sampling decisions, as we have noted, tend to get made gradually, over time. Even so, a first cut at within-site choices should not take more than two or three hours—assuming that the conceptual framework and the research questions are reasonably clear. At least one iteration before the first site visit is a good idea.

Sampling sites in a multisite study is nearly always a demanding experience. There are usually so many contending dimensions, and so many alternate realizations of those dimensions, that it is easy for researchers to lose intellectual control, get overwhelmed with the multiple possibilities and finally say, "There's no rational way to do this." Setting up the possibilities in matrix form helps.

In our experience, you can usually expect to spend three or four hours for a first cut when a dozen or so sites are involved; two or three additional sessions, involving the entire research team, are typically required. The work isn't simple, and can't be hurried. After all, you are making some long-term commitments to where your basic data will be collected.

II.D INSTRUMENTATION

Rationale

We have been emphasizing that conceptual frameworks, research questions, and sampling matrices have a legitimate focusing and bounding role within a study. They give some direction to the researcher, prior to fieldwork, by clarifying *what* he or she wants to find out from *whom* and *why*. Some direction is needed—but not too much; it is important not to foreclose on other ways of construing and addressing the main research issues that the field site can disclose.

Knowing what you want to find out leads inexorably to the question of *how* you will get that information. If, for example, I want to find out how suspects are arrested and booked, I will presumably do such things as *interview* people associated with this activity (police officers, suspects, attorneys), *observe* bookings, and *collect documents* having to do with arrests (such as regulations or transcripts). I may also take *pictures* of bookings or *record* them on tape. In sort, the qualitative researcher usually has a kit of data-collecting devices that are keyed, directly or indirectly, to the conceptual framework and reseach questions. But how much of this instrumentation has to be designed *prior* to going out to the field? And how much structure should such instrumentation have?

There are several possible answers, ranging from "none" (no prior instrumentation to all) to "a lot" (of prior instrumentation, well-structured) to "it depends" (on the nature of the study). Each view has supporting arguments; let us review them in capsule form.

Arguments for no prior instrumentation:
(1) Predesigned and structured instruments blind the researcher to the site. If the most important phenomena or underlying constructs at work in the field are not in the instruments, they will be overlooked or misrepresented.

(2) Prior instrumentation is usually context-stripped; it lusts for universality, uniformity, and comparability. Qualitative research is the one place where contexts can and should be studied; it is the particularities that produce the generalities, not the reverse.

(3) Most qualitative studies involve single cases, with few people involved. Who needs questionnaires, observation schedules, or tests—whose prime function is to yield economical, comparable, and parametric distributions for large samples?

(4) The lion's share of fieldwork consists of taking notes, recording things (conversations, meetings), and picking up samples (documents, products, artifacts). "Instrumentation" is a misnomer. Some orienting questions, some headings for observations, a rough and ready document analysis form are all one needs at the start—perhaps all one will *ever* need in the course of the study.

Arguments for a lot of prior instrumentation:
(1) If you know what you are after, there is no reason not to plan out in advance how to collect the information.

(2) If interview schedules or observation schedules are not focused, too much superfluous information will be collected. Data overload will then compromise the efficiency and power of the analysis.

(3) Using the same instruments as in prior studies in the only way we can converse across studies. Otherwise, the work will be noncomparable, except in an overly global, meta-analytic form. So we need common instruments to build theory, to improve predictions, and to make recommendations about practice.

(4) A biased or uninformed researcher is going to ask partial questions, take selective notes, make unreliable observations, and skew the information recorded. The data will be invalid and unreliable. Using validated instruments, and using them as they are designed, is the best guarantee of dependable and meaningful findings.

Arguments for "it depends":

(1) If you are running an *exploratory*, largely descriptive study, you don't know the parameters or dynamics of a social setting with any certainty. So heavy front-end instrumentation or closed-ended devices are inappropriate. If, on the other hand, you are doing a *confirmatory* study, with relatively focused research questions and a well-bounded sample of persons, events or processes, well-structured instrument designs are the logical choice. Even *within* a given study, there can be exploratory and confirmatory aspects that call for differential front-end structure, or there can be exploratory and confirmatory *times*, with exploration often called for at the outset and confirmation near the end.

(2) A *single-site study* calls for less front-end preparation than does a *multiple-site study*. The latter is looking forward to cross-site comparison, which requires some standardization of instruments so that findings can be laid side by side during analysis. Similarly, a *freestanding study* has fewer constraints than a *field study tied to a survey* as a follow-up or parallel exercise. A *"basic"* study often needs less advance organizing than an *applied, evaluation* or *policy* study. In the latter cases, the focus will be far tighter and the instrumentation more closely keyed to the variables, items, and scales of the survey.

(3) A lot depends on the *units of analysis*. A researcher studying the "social climate" in an elementary school might choose to look intensively in 3 of the building's 35 classrooms, and would probably be right to start with a looser, orienting set of instruments. If, however, there will be an attempt to say something about the building as a whole, a more standardized, validated instrument—a questionnaire, a group interview schedule—will also be required.

It seems to us—and, we hope, to the reader as well—that there is wisdom in all three stances toward front-end instrumentation and its degree of structure. The first stance (minimal prior instrumentation) puts the emphasis on *construct* and *contextual validity*, where qualitative studies can be especially strong. The second (heavy preinstrumentation) emphasizes *internal validity, generalizability,* and *manageability,* all worthy causes. The third stance is both contingent and ecumenical, the idea being that it is unhelpful to reach for absolute answers in relative instances. Figure out first what kind of study you are doing and what kind of instruments you are likely to need at different moments within that study, then go to work on the ones needed at the outset. But in all cases, as we have argued, the amount and type of instrumentation should be a function of one's conceptual focus, research questions, and sampling criteria. If not, the tail is likely to be wagging the dog, and the ultimate analysis will suffer.

Illustrations

Let is illustrate how front-end instrument design can be driven in different ways by a study's scope and focus. First we will look at a study design calling for some loose and some tight front-end instrumentation. Next, we will illustrate a semistructured interview schedule for studies involving multiple cases.

One of us was recently involved in a study of how schools and universities link up to move research knowledge into the community of school practitioners and get practice knowledge into the university (Huberman, 1981b). Essentially, we focused on *units* (within the school system and within the university) and the *links* between these units. The units (shown by letters) and links (shown by numbers) are shown in Figure 4.

We won't detail the conceptual framework we used to understand the units and links; it was derived from theories of knowledge transfer and interorganizational relationships. As we have said, the framework informs the choice of research questions. Here are four examples from the list:

(1) How are such interorganizational arrangements *managed*?
(2) Which *kinds of knowledge* are transferred from one unit to another, notably from university to school and vice versa?
(3) What is the *relative influence* of school and university personnel in the arrangement?
(4) Which kinds of *bargains* or exchanges, if any, are made between school and university personnel?

The research questions, in turn, inform the *sampling frame*: where one goes to get answers, with whom one talks, what one observes. It turned out that an ideal

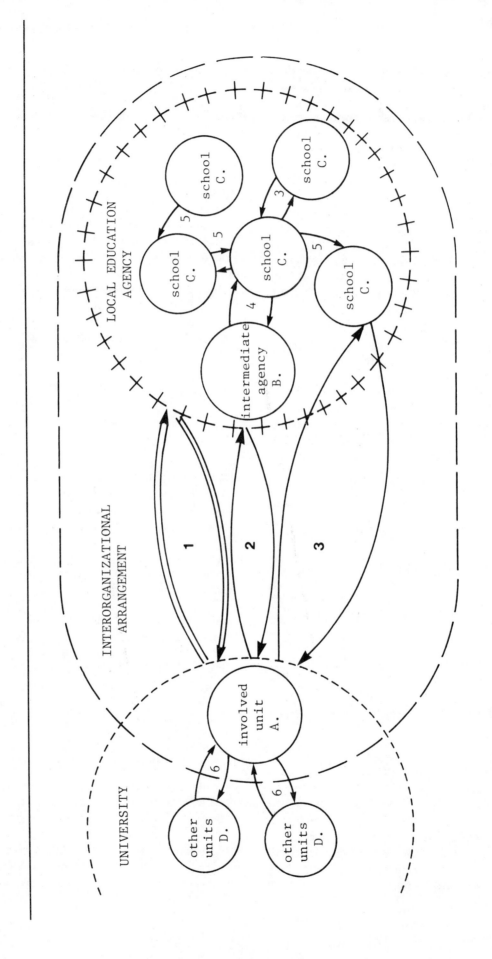

Figure 4 Interorganizational Linkages Involving Universities and Schools

place to get answers to all four questions was the monthly governance meeting held in the intermediate agency (B on Figure 4), including representatives from both school and university units. These meetings were presumably the hub of the interorganizational arrangement (question 1). They regularly reviewed and assessed the activities linking schools and universities (question 2). The key formal decisions and arrangements were likely to be made here (questions 3 and 4).

The *sampling* decision for these questions, then, is clear. Within the arrangement, we would sample *meetings*; within meetings, ones having to do with *governance*, ones held in the *intermediate agency*, and ones including *delegates* of the various units. Within such governance meetings, we would sample *knowledge types*, *influence patterns*, and *bargains or exchanges*. Notice the progressive funneling as we move from conceptual framework to research questions to sampling.

So, essentially, we are observing meetings, with an eye to gathering information that can answer these four research questions. What kind of instrumentation is needed for observing such meetings, and how much should we prepare beforehand? We will probably need *both* loose and tight front-end instrumentation, depending on the research question. Let's look at this question by question.

(1) How are such interorganizational arrangements managed? This question is the most general. From it we developed data collection activities such as (a) taking general notes on discussion of agenda points; (b) listening for the gist and flow of the conversation; and (c) jotting down points that appear salient, mysterious, worth following up, or frequently mentioned. In terms of front-end instrumentation, only point a calls for some predesigned cueing system for the observer (for example, a list of possible facets of an interorganizational governance system, such as policy, finance, activity format, decision-making process, role of school and university delegates). The list helps the observer attend to these features when they crop up.

(2) Which kinds of knowledge are transferred from one unit to another? Here, there has to be some prior consensus about kinds of knowledge, and some quick way to register transfers. We can handle this by generating in advance a taxonomy of knowledge types, with a list of examples, a code for each, and an arrow to indicate who provided the knowledge and who received it. The field researcher then records the example when it comes up, draws the arrow, and, if appropriate, adds the code. This is simply a form of shorthand, with a prespecified glossary in back of it. Items in the glossary are changed iteratively when recorded examples show that better definitions are needed.

(3) What is the relative influence of school and university personnel? Here again, some front-end instrumentation can be helpful. When the agenda calls for a decision to be made, the field researcher can take out a separate, predesigned sheet. There is space on it for recording the initial (and possibly revised) stance of each delegate on the issue being decided, and the final decision itself. In addition, for ten minutes of each quarter hour, the observer notes who had intervened and for how long, the idea being that frequency and length of intervention can be indicators of influence.

(4) Which kinds of bargains or exchanges are made? This question is downright exploratory. We have no way of knowing at the outset what kind of bargains or exchanges could be made in this kind of arrangement, except that they are likely to be implicit, and will probably turn around money, influence, knowledge or expertise, solutions to problems, and the like. While prior conceptual *orientation* is important (for instance, what does an interorganizational bargain mean, and what might be examples of one?), prior *instrumentation* in the form of checklists, catalogues, or frequency counts seems counterproductive. The main task here is to watch and listen carefully and get an initial sense of how the construct operates, if at all, in this arena.

In sum, we have a good mix of predesigned and open-ended instrumentation corresponding to the demands of the different research questions, and to the extent of our prior knowledge about the phenomenon being studied. And in some cases, when we say "instrumentation," we mean little more than some shorthand devices for observing and recording events—devices that come from initial conceptualizations loose enough to be reconfigured readily as the data suggest revisions.

For a second illustration, let us take another look at the school improvement study. It's worth looking back for a moment to the *conceptual framework* (Figure 3) to recall the main variables and their flow over time. Remember also that (a) this is a multiple-site (N = 12) study and (b) the phenomenon under study is moderately well, but not fully, understood from prior empirical research. As we have noted, both these points suggest that some front-end instruments are likely to be called for.

One important *research question* in the study was as follows:

> In which ways did people redefine, reorganize, or reinvent the new program in order to use it successfully?

Looking back at Figure 3, we can see that the question derives from the fourth bin, "cycle of transformations," and, within that bin, from the first variable cluster, "changes in innovation as presented to the user." The assumption here, relying on previous empirical research and on basic cognitive theory, is that people will adapt or reinvent practices while using them locally.

The *sampling* decision is straightforward. The question addresses teachers in particular and, to get the answer, we will have to observe or interview them or, ideally, do both. Let's look at the interview component of the *instrumentation*.

For many of the study's questions, there was an interview guide, which all field researchers used. Two features of the guide are noteworthy. First, it is a guide, not a schedule. Each field researcher was closely familiar with the guide, but had latitude to use a personally congenial way of asking and sequencing the questions and to segment them appropriately for different respondents. Second, the guide was designed before the questions were addressed systematically, but *not* before fieldwork had begun. There had been an initial wave of site visits to get a sense of the context, the actors, and the ways the school improvement process appeared to be configured locally. The guide was designed after this initial fieldwork, but *prior* to deeper and broader data collection.

Now to dip into the guide near the point where the research question will be explored (Chart 4). Note that there are several research questions addressed here, all set chronologically. The idea is to take the informant back to the original point in time, then go progressively forward. The probes can be handled in various ways: as aids to help the interviewer flesh out the question, as prompts for items the informant may have overlooked, or as systematic subquestions derived from previous conceptual and empirical research. Four questions later (question 40), we find the interview item directly focused on answering our research question.

Later in the interview, the same question recurs, as the interviewer evokes the teacher's retrospective views of early and later use, then into the present (what

changes are you making now?) and the future (what changes are you considering?). So all field researchers are addressing the same general question, and addressing it in similar ways (chronologically, as a process of progressive revision), although the question formulation and sequencing may vary slightly from one researcher to the next. If the response opens up other doors, the interviewer will probably go through them, coming back later to the "transformation" question. If the response is uncertain or looks equivocal when the researcher reviews the field notes, the question will have to be asked again—perhaps differently—during the next site visit.

Advice

(1) People and sites in field studies can be observed more than once. Not everything is riding on the single interview or observation. So front-end instrumentation can be revised—in fact, *should* be revised. You learn how to ask a question in the site's terms, and to look with new eyes at something that began to jump out during the first visit. Instrumentation can be modified steadily to explore new leads, address a revised research question, or interview a new class of informant.

(2) Continuously revising instruments puts qualitative research at odds with survey research, where instrument stability (for example, test-retest reliability) is required to assure reliable measurement. This means that in qualitative research issues of instrument validity and reliability ride largely on the skills of the researcher. Essentially, a *person*—more or less fallibly—is observing, interviewing, and recording, while modifying the observation, interviewing, and recording devices from one field trip to the next.

We shall return to this issue later on. For now, we only note that it is not too extreme to ask of yourself and your colleagues, "How valid and reliable is this person likely to be as an information-gathering instrument?" The topic is a hotly debated one.

Very briefly, our own stance is that the best investment is in people with the following characteristics:

- some familiarity with the phenomenon and the setting under study
- strong conceptual interests
- a multidisciplinary approach, as opposed to a narrow grounding or focus in a single discipline
- good "investigative" skills, including doggedness, the ability to draw people out, and the ability to ward off premature closure

This is not, to put it midly, the kind of list one finds in many sociological or anthropological textbooks. There, *lack* of familiarity with the phenomenon and setting, and the importance of a strong single-disciplinary

Chart 4
Excerpts from Interview Guide, School
Improvement Study

CYCLES OF TRANSFORMATION: Pre-implementation

What I'd like to do now is to go through your experience with _____--what you were doing and thinking and feeling while you were working with it BEFORE you started using it with students.

I really want to find out what your experience with _____ has been without trying to put it into any framework. I do have some questions I'll need answers to, and I'll be interjecting them now and then. But, feel free to float a little with your answers.

32. Let's go back first to the time just before you started using _____. Say, a week or so before you were going to use it with students.

   A. When was that? (Year, month)

      Do you remember what that was like? What was going on at school--or maybe at home or, elsewhere--that week? Where were you located? Were you working alone or with other people? I'm just trying to bring your memory back to that point in time.

   B. How were you feeling about starting in? What concerns did you have?

      Probes

      --Looking forward/feeling neutral/feeling apprehensive

      --General anxiety about starting something new

      --Thinking about evaluation by others

      --Wondering about children's reactions

      --Considering dynamics in the school or central office

      --Feeling unsure that you'd be good at this

      --Feeling not ready

33. Probably you have a certain idea of how _____ looks to you now, but keep thinking back to how it first looked to you then, just before students came. How did it seem to you then?

   Probes

   --Clearly connected, differentiated vs. unconnected, confusing

   --Clear how to start vs. awesome, difficult

   --Complex (many parts) vs. simple and straightforward

   --Prescriptive and rigid vs. flexible and manipulatable

34. What parts or aspects seemed ready to use, things you thought would work out OK?

35. What parts or aspects seemed not worked out, not ready for use?

36. Could you describe what you actually did during that week or so before you started using _____ with students?

   Probes

   --Reading

   --Preparing materials

   --Planning

   --Talking (with whom, about what)

   --Training

. . . .

40. Did you make any changes in the standard format for the program before you started using it with students?   What kind of changes with things you thought might not work, things you didn't like, things you couldn't do in this school?

   Probes

   --Things dropped

   --Things added, created

   --Things revised

grounding, are considered assets. For us, the danger of that view is twofold. First, while unfamiliarity with the phenomenon or setting allows for a fertile "decentering," it also engenders relatively naive, easily misled, easily distracted, and data-overloaded field research.

The problem is that of getting beyond the superficial or the merely salient, of becoming "empirically literate." Quite simply, you can understand little more than your own evolving mental map allows for; a naive, undifferentiated map will translate into global, surface-oriented data and conclusions—and usually into self-induced or informant-induced bias as well. You have to be knowledgeable to collect good information (Markus, 1977).

Inexperience and single-discipline grounding also lead to a second danger: plastering a ready-made explanation on phenomena that might well be construed in far more compelling ways. Thus, on closer inspection, presumably "grounded" theorizing can turn out to be conceptual heavy-handedness, *without* the researcher's being aware of it. We feel, by contrast, that a savvy practitioner, with strong conceptual interests and more than one disciplinary perspective, is usually a better research "instrument" in a qualitative study: more refined, more bias-resistant, more economical, quicker to home in on the core processes that hold the site together, and more ecumenical in the search for conceptual meaning.[3]

(3) Simply *thinking* in instrument-design terms from the outset strengthens data collection as you go. If you regularly ask, "Given that research question, how can I get an answer?" it sharpens *sampling* decisions (I'll have to observe/interview this class of people, these events, those processes), usually clarifies *concepts* further, and sets *priorities* for actual data collection. You also learn the skills of redesigning instrumentation as new questions, new subsamples, or new lines of inquiry develop.

Not thinking in instrument-design terms can lead to self-delusion: You feel "sensitive" to the site, but may in fact be stuck in reactive, seat-of-the-pants interviewing that yields only flaccid data.

Time Required

It is not really possible to specify time requirements for instrumentation, because so very much depends on the modes of data collection involved, how prestructured you choose to be, the nature of the research questions, the complexity of the sample, and so on. Clearly, more structured instrumentation, done with diverse samples, with a confirmatory emphasis, will take substantially more time to develop.

NOTES

1. There is a paradox here (R. E. Herriott, personal communication, 1983): We may have more confidence in a finding across multiple sites when it was *not* anticipated or commonly measured, but simply "jumps out" of all the sites. Of course, researchers should stay open to such findings—but we cannot guarantee that they will appear.

2. This is a variation of the famous "degrees of freedom" argument made by Campbell (1975) when he displaced the unit of analysis from the case to each of the *particulars* making up the case, with each particular becoming a test of the hypothesis or theory being tested. The greater the number of such particulars and the greater their overlap, the more confidence in the findings and their potential generalizability.

3. For some extra ammunition on this point, we can note Freeman's (1983) revisionist attack on Margaret Mead's (1928) pioneering study of Samoan culture. He considers Mead's findings invalid as a result of her unfamiliarity with the language, lack of systematic prior study of Samoan society, and residence in an expatriate rather than in a Samoan household during her stay. For instance, well-meant teasing by adolescent informants may have led to her mistaken thesis of adolescent free love in Samoa. In addition, says Freeman, just *because* Mead was so untutored in the setting, she had heavy recourse to a preferred conceptual framework (that is, cultural determinism), further weakening her main findings. Some epistemologists (for example, see Campbell, 1975) have also made a strong case for fieldwork done by "an alert social scientist who has thorough local acquaintance."

III

Analysis During Data Collection

In this chapter we describe methods for qualitative data analysis that are especially useful during the ongoing process of data collection. Most analysis methods can be used during data collection, of course—these methods are especially helpful ones.

Why analyze during data collection at all? Some qualitative researchers put primary energy into data collection for weeks, months, or even years, then retire from the field to "work over their notes." We believe this is a serious mistake. It rules out the possibility of collecting new data to fill in gaps, or to test new hypotheses that emerge during analysis; it tends to reduce the production of what might be termed "rival hypotheses" that question the fieldworker's routine assumptions and biases; and it makes analysis into a giant, overwhelming task that both demotivates the researcher and reduces the quality of the work produced.

To take the approximate obverse of these points: Analysis during data collection lets the fieldworker cycle back and forth between thinking about the existing data and generating strategies for collecting new—often better quality—data; it can be a healthy corrective for built-in blind spots; and it makes analysis an ongoing, lively enterprise that is linked to the energizing effects of fieldwork. Furthermore, ongoing analysis permits the production of the interim reports that are a part of most evaluation and policy studies. So the ideal model for data collection and analysis is one that interweaves them from the beginning. Periodic field visits are interspersed with time for data reduction and display, for drawing conclusions, and for testing those conclusions—either through other analyses in the existing data base, or through a new round of data collection. We are only reiterating here the interactive, cyclical nature of qualitative data analysis already outlined in Chapter I.

This chapter describes seven major methods useful for analysis during data collection, along with seven supplementary ones. As we have indicated, each of the *major methods* is presented in this format:

- *Name of method.*
- *Analysis problem.* The problem, need, or difficulty faced by a qualitative data analyst, for which the method is a useful solution.
- *Brief description.* What the method is and how it works.
- *Illustration.* In more detail, a "minicase," showing how the method is developed and used. Usually, this section will have a variety of subheadings, such as "developing the format," "entering the data," and "analyzing the data."
- *Variations.* Alternative approaches that use the same general principle. Work of other researchers is cited.
- *Advice.* Summarizing comments about the use of the method, and tips for using it well.
- *Time required.* Approximate estimates to guide the researcher (these will naturally vary according to subject matter, the researcher's skill, the research questions being asked, the number of sites, and so on).

The *supplementary methods* are described in boxes, usually on one or two pages. The aim is to suggest simple methods that can be used profitably in conjunction with the major method being discussed. The format varies, but usually includes a brief statement of the problem for which the method is a solution, plus a brief exhibit or illustration, and concluding advice.

Our assumptions about "data." The methods being described in this and following chapters assume that the fieldworker has collected information in the form of handwritten field notes, or notes dictated in the field, or (more rarely) tape recordings of events in the field setting. In all cases we are focusing on *words* as the basic form in which the data are found.[1]

We further assume that the basic, raw data (the scribbled field notes, the dictated tapes, the direct tape recordings) are subjected to more *processing* before they are available for analysis. Field notes must be converted into "write-ups," either through typing or dictation. A write-up is a product intelligible to anyone, not just the fieldworker. It can be read, coded, and analyzed using any of the methods we are about to describe. Raw field notes themselves are usually partially illegible, and contain many private abbreviations. They are also sketchy. One estimate is that field notes of an interview usually contain one-half or less of the actual content. But a write-up will usually add back some of the missing content, since the raw field notes, when reviewed, stimulate the fieldworker to remember things said at that time that are not in the notes. Such additions should, of course, be marked specially, to guard against bias.

Similarly, dictated notes are not ready for analysis, but must ordinarily be transcribed onto paper and usually edited for accuracy by the fieldworker before they are ready for use.

Finally, direct tape recordings of field events must be either transcribed fully (if the aim is to have a full record of speech and other audible events), or processed in some way (for example, the fieldworker listens to the recording, makes notes, selects excerpts, makes judgments or ratings, and so on).

Thus, for the methods we review below, we are focusing on *words* as the basic medium, and we assume that the words involved have been *refined* one step beyond their form at the point of data collection (raw notes, tape recordings), so that they are clear to any reader or analyst.

Now, on to the methods. They are roughly arranged from early to late in data collection, and from simple to complex. Beginning with the *contact summary sheet*, a simple way to summarize time-limited data, we proceed through first-level *coding*, second-level or *pattern codes*, and the process of deriving even more general themes called *"memoing."* As more and more data pile up, the *site analysis meeting* and the *interim site summary* prove more and more crucial for understanding.

III.A CONTACT SUMMARY SHEET

Analysis Problem

After an intensive field contact (from one to several days) has been completed, and field notes are written up in systematic form, there is often a need to pause and consider: What were the main themes, issues, problems, and questions that I saw during this contact? Without such reflection, it is easy to get lost in a welter of detail. And communicating important things about a contact to one's colleagues is essential for any project with more than one fieldworker.

Brief Description

A contact summary is a single sheet containing a series of focusing or summarizing questions about a particular field contact. The fieldworker reviews the written-up field notes, and answers each question briefly to develop an overall summary of the main points in the contact.

Illustration

Deciding on the questions. The main thing here is being clear about what you (or your colleagues) need to know *quickly* about a particular field contact (which may itself have run to anywhere from a half dozen to a hundred or more pages of written-up field notes), and which questions will locate the *essence* of the data in the contact. Some possibilities follow:

- What people, events, or situations were involved?
- What were the main themes or issues in the contact?
- Which research questions did the contact bear most centrally on?
- What new hypotheses, speculations, or guesses about the field situations were suggested by the contact?
- Where should the fieldworker place most energy during the next contact, and what sorts of information should be sought?

Making the form. The questions should be arranged on a single sheet of paper (using more than both sides of one sheet defeats the purpose), with space for the fieldworker's answers. Identifying information on the site, the contact, the fieldworker, and the date should be indicated as well.

Entering the data. A contact summary sheet is usually best filled out as soon as fully written-up field notes have been reviewed and corrected by the fieldworker. At that point, one has a perspective that combines reasonable immediacy with a reflective overview of what went on in the contact. One can include one's own reflective remarks (see Box III.B.a), as well as unanswered questions for the next contact.

On the other hand, waiting until a contact has been thoroughly and fully coded is probably too late. In addition, the process of coding usually adds so many additional hunches and thoughts about the contact that summarizing what was originally there in the notes may get distorted or lost.

The data on a contact summary sheet are essentially phrases or sentences that the fieldworker considers an adequate answer to the form's questions, after the complete write-up of the contact has been reviewed. Note-taking while the write-up is being reviewed helps. Excerpts from a filled-out example of an illustrative form follow (Chart 5a). Note that the second and fourth questions of this form are built around the fact that the fieldworker was entering the site with a focused set of target questions, a useful approach when one's time is limited. Information gained on each question is summarized, and new target questions are posed for the next visit. Some of these come from the background research questions ("How do users really perceive the innovation?") and some are provoked by data collected during the visit (for example, English teacher Reilly's "fall from the chairmanship").

Using the data. The filled-out sheet can be used in several ways: (1) to guide planning for the next contact; (2) to suggest new or revised codes (see sections following); (3) to help with communication and coordination when more than one fieldworker is involved in the study; (4) to reorient oneself to the contact when returning to the write-up for any reason; (5) to serve as the basis for data analysis itself (the summary sheets for a number of contacts can themselves be coded and analyzed).

It usually helps to attach a copy of the summary form to the top page of the write-up, so it is close to the data it summarizes. In addition, depending on one's purposes, it is often useful to circulate photocopies of the filled-out form to other fieldworkers or colleagues, as well as to build a site file, with all contact summary forms for that site.

Variations

Contact summary sheets, as just noted, can be used in a more systematic and less open-ended way, through applying codes to them. An excerpted illustration appears in Chart 5b. Here the analyst had a list of codes (called "themes" or "aspects"), which were applied to "salient points" in the write-up.

Still another possibility involves supplying *ratings* of the same set of dimensions, across a number of contacts. Chart 5c presents an excerpted illustration from our new schools study. This type of contact summary sheet involves considerable abstraction, and moves quite far from the original raw data. However, if terms are well defined (a "thesaurus" is needed) and if notes are appended at the right, it can be illuminating in providing an overview of a particular contact. It is best used in conjunction with summary sheets like the ones we have already seen.

Advice

The contact summary form sounds rather simple-minded. It is. It is a rapid, practical way to do first-run data reduction—without losing any of the basic information (the write-up) to which it refers. It captures thoughtful impressions and reflections; it pulls together the data in the "soft computer"—the fieldworker's mind—and makes them available for further reflection and analysis, not only by the fieldworker but by others.

Keep contact summary forms simple. Focus on the primary issues. A form that proves difficult, over-demanding, or confusing after one or two uses should be simplified. The basic need is to have an instrument that makes it *easy* for the fieldworker to make a rapid retrieval/synthesis of what the contact was all about.

During the first few uses of the form, it is a very good idea to have someone *else* read the basic write-up, and independently fill out a summary form. That way, one can surface systematic bias or selectivity that is serious enough to need correction. One needs to be able to *rely* on summaries, to be reasonably sure that they are a good capsule of what is in the write-up.

Time Required

Filling out a good contact summary form takes as much time as necessary to read/review the write-up, plus less than an hour's time to do the filling in. If more time is needed, it is a signal that the form is too complex or demanding.

III.A.a Document Summary Form

Fieldworkers often pick up documents from their sites, ranging widely (meeting agendas, evaluation reports, newspaper articles, budgets, brochures, lunch menus, minutes of meetings, rosters—the list is not quite endless, but very large). Documents are often lengthy and typically need explaining or clarifying, as well as summarizing. One needs a clear awareness of the document's *significance:* what it tells us about the site that's important.

It helps to create and fill out a document summary form, which can be attached to the document it refers to. Box III.A.a provides an illustration. This form puts the document in context, explains significance, and gives a brief content summary. Note the fieldworker's

Chart 5a
Contact Summary Form: Illustration

Contact type: Site __Tindale__
    Visit __X__   Contact date __11/28-29/79__
    Phone_____   Today's date __12/28/79__
    (with whom?)   Written by ___BLT___

1. What were the main issues or themes that struck you in this contact?

    Interplay between highly prescriptive, "teacher-proof" curriculum
    that is top-down imposed and the actual writing of the curriculum
    by the teachers themselves.

    Split between the "watchdogs" (administrators) and the "house masters"
    (dept. chairs & teachers) vis-a-vis job foci.

    District curric. coord'r as decision maker re school's acceptance of
    research relationship.

2. Summarize the information you got (or failed to get) on each of
    the target questions you had for this contact.

Question	Information
Nature of the innov'n	Prescriptive reading prog'm (4 yrs in English, 1 yr each in math & science)
History of dev. of innov'n	Conceptualized by Curric. Coord'r, English Chairman & Assoc. Chairman; written by teachers in summer; revised by teachers following summer with field testing data
School's org'l structure	Principal & admin'rs responsible for discipline; dept. chairs are educ'l leaders
Demographics	Racial conflicts in late 60's; 60% black stud. pop.; heavy emphasis on discipline & on keeping out non-district students slipping in from Chicago
Teacher response to innov'n	Rigid, structured, etc. at first; now, they say they like it//NEEDS EXPLOR'N
Research access	Very good; only restriction: teachers not required to cooperate

3. Anything else that struck you as salient, interesting, illuminating
    or important in this contact?

    Thoroughness of the innov'n's development and training.

    Its embeddedness in the district's curriculum, as planned and
    executed by the district curriculum coordinator.

    The initial resistance to its high presc ptiveness (as reported by
    users) as contrasted with their current acceptance and approval of
    it (again, as reported by users).

4. What new (or remaining) target questions do you have in considering
    the next contact with this site?

    How do users really perceive the innov'n? If they do indeed
    embrace it, what accounts for the change from early resistance?

    Nature and amount of networking among users of innov'n.

    How much attention to give to the other high school using the
    innov'n (Tindale West).

    Effects upon non-users of receiving students from the innov'n who
    are "mainstreamed" into regular English classes.

    Info on "stubborn" math teachers whose ideas weren't heard initially
    -- who are they? Situation particulars? Resolution?

    Particulars of content teachers' work with reading specialist to
    develop curriculum of innov'n.

    Follow-up on English teacher Reilly's "fall from the chairmanship."

    Talk of security needs from old-timers like Reilly and Kennedy raise
    issue of possible threat from above (the district) if they don't
    use the innov'n well. How much of a squeeze play did Crowden make,
    if any?

    Follow a team through a day of rotation, planning, etc.

    Talk with Mr. Macduff in English.

    CONCERN: The consequences of eating school cafeteria food two days
             per week for the next four or five months...

                                        Stop.

Chart 5b
Contact Summary Form: Illustration with Coded Themes

CONTACT SUMMARY FORM   SITE _Westgate_

Type of contact: Mtg. _Principals_ ___Ken's office___ _4/2/76_   Coder _Matt_
                       Who, what group   place   date

                                                                Date coded _10/6/76_

                  Phone_____ _____ _____
                       With whom, by whom   place   date

                  Inf. Int. _____ _____ _____
                           with whom,by whom place   date

1. Pick out the most salient points in the contact. Number in order on this sheet and
   note page number on which point appears. Number point in text of write-up. Attach theme
   or aspect to each point in CAPITALS. Invent themes where no existing ones apply and asterisk
   those. Comments may also be included in double parentheses.

PAGE   ZONING   SOCIO-POLIT SUPPORT
 1   *1. Ken reports Board decision: approval of rezoning plan (was
         put off deliberately until after the election).
             STAFF
 1   2. Staff decisions have to be made by April 30.
             STAFF / RESOURCE MGMT   their present
 1   3. Teachers will have to go out of∧grade-level assignment
         when they transfer.
             STAFF / RESOURCE MGMT
 1   4. Supplemental teachers to be distributed across schools
         --3 for #1, 3 for #2, 2 for #3, 1 for #4 (covering 9 classes).
             *RESISTANCE
 2   5. Teachers vary in their willingness to inetgrate special ed
         kids into their classrooms---some are "a pain in the elbow".
             INTERNAL COMMUNIC   teachers
 2   6. Ken points out that tentative teacher assignment lists got
         leaked from the previous meeting ((implicitly deplores this)).
             POWER DISTRIB
 2   7. Ken says "teachers act xx as if they had the right to decide
         who should be transferred" (make would make outcry, etc.)
             POWER DISTRIB / CONFLICT MGMT
 2   8. Tacit/explicit decision: "It's our decision to make"(voiced by
         Ken, agreed to by Ed)
             * STEREOTYPING   & Brown
 2   9. Principals and Ken,John, agree that Ms. Epstein is a "bitch"
             STAFF / RESOURCE MGMT
 2   10. The equivalent of 10 teachers will have to be moved (#1 has
         surplus of 7½, #4 has surplus of 2½, #2 needs 8, #3 needs 2).
             PLAN for PLANNING / TIME MGMT
 2   11. Ken decides not to tell teachers ahead of time (now) about
         transfers ("because then we'd have a fait accompli")

       . . . .

Chart 5c
Contact Summary Form: Illustration with Ratings

Considering this contact as a whole, circle the statement(s) that fit(s) for each theme. Don't
force it. Use the "uncertain" box if relevant. Add comments at right if you wish.

Planning/implementation styles   UNCERTAIN   NOTES

1. Plan for planning   Explicit,   Mid   (Implicit,   ☐
                            thought-thru   vague)

2. Adaptiveness   High _____ (Mid) _____ Low   ☐

3. Reflexivity   Sought,   (Resisted,   ☐   Said the dots would
                            open to _____ Mid _____ closed to   be like "poison ivy".
                            data   data)

4. Time management   Long run _____ Mid _____ (Short run)   ☐   Detailed dates.

                            (Clear) _____ Mid _____ Unclear   ☐   Argued, but smoothed over

5. Goals for school   Agreement, _____ Mid _____ Disagreement, ☒
                            consensus   dissensus

                            Real, linked (Mid) _____ Rhetorical, not ☐
                            to action   action-linked

                            Explicit _____ (Mid) _____ Implicit   ☐

                            Reaffirmed _____ (Mid) _____ Abandoned ☐

6. Planning/Implementation Linkages
   Planners-implementers as a sub-system

1. Commitment   High _____ (Mid) _____ Low   ☐

2. Educational   Innovative _____ Mid _____ (Traditional) ☐
   orientation

3. Task orientation   (High) _____ Mid _____ Low   ☐   Very strong, almost
                                                                              amazing

4. Socio-emotional   (High) _____ Mid _____ Low   ☐   Old-boyism again
   orientation

5. Division of labor   High _____ Mid _____ Low   ☒   very hard to see who's
                            differen-   differen-   doing what
                            tiation   tiation

                            High _____ (Mid) _____ Low   ☐
                            integration   integration

---

reflective commentary, set off in double parentheses.

Document summary forms can also be coded, not only for later analysis, but to help in rapid retrieval when the document is needed. For a good review of methods of document analysis (including content analysis), see Bailey (1982), as well as Holsti (1968, 1969) and Krippendorff (1980b).

III.B CODES AND CODING

Analysis Problem

Working with words. A chronic problem of qualitative research is that it is done chiefly with words, not with numbers. Words are fatter than numbers, and usually have multiple meanings. This makes them harder to move around and work with. Worse still, most words are meaningless unless you look backward or forward to *other* words. Take, for example, the pronoun "it" in the first sentence above. Or take the noun "board" in such an ambiguous phrase as "The board is on the fence." Are we talking about a piece of wood or a decision-making body?

Numbers, by contrast, are usually less ambiguous and may be processed with more economy. Small wonder, then, that most researchers prefer working with numbers alone, or getting the words they collect translated into numbers as quickly as possible.

Despite all this, we argue several times in this book that although words may be more unwieldy than numbers, they also enable "thick description," as Geertz (1973) suggests. That is, they render more meaning than numbers alone, and should be hung onto throughout data analysis. Converting words into numbers, then tossing away the words, gets a researcher

---

Box III.A.a
Document Summary Form: Illustration

DOCUMENT FORM

Site ___Carson___
Document # ___2___
Date received or picked up: ___Feb.13___

Name or description of document:

    The Buffalo (weekly sheet)

Event or contact, if any, with which document is associated:

    Paul's explanation of the
       admin. team's functioning   Date ___Feb. 13___

Significance or importance of document:

    Gives schedule for all events in the district for the week.
    Enables coordination, knots 2 schools together.

Brief summary of contents:

    Schedule of everything from freshman girls'basketball to "Secret Pals Week"
    in the elemntary school.

    Also includes "Did you know" items on the IPA program (apparently integrating
    the IPA News).

    And a description of how admin team works (who is on team, what regular
    meetings deal with, gives working philosophy ("ex: " we establish personal
    goals and monitor progress"..We coordinate effort, K-12, and all programs"..
    "We agree on staff selection".) Concluding comment: "It is our system of
    personnel management".

    Also alludes to the 26 OPERATIONAL GUIDELINES (Document 16)

    ((I'll guess that the admin explanation does not appear every week----need
    to check this.))

IF DOCUMENT IS CENTRAL OR CRUCIAL TO A PARTICULAR CONTACT (ex: a meeting
agenda, newspaper clipping discussed in an interview, etc.), make a
copy and include with write-up. Otherwise, put in document file.

---

into all kinds of mischief. One is thus assuming that the chief property of the words is that there are *more* of some than of others. This, of course, is only *one* of the things that the words are, and certainly not the most important one. Focusing solely on numbers shifts our attention from substance to arithmetic, and thereby throws out the whole notion of qualitativeness; one would have done better to have started with numbers in the first place and saved a lot of time.

Also, when word-derived numbers don't make sense, there is usually no very satisfactory way of making them more intelligible with more numbers, which is all one has at hand. The solution to this problem, as we will see in later sections, is to keep words and any associated numbers *together* throughout the analysis. Essentially, words and numbers keep one another analytically honest.

Word overload. The words that the qualitative analyst works with are usually in the form of written-up field notes and various kinds of documents that have words on them. They tend to pile up quickly during data collection. Two weeks at a field site can result in something like 300-400 pages of typed-up field notes and ancillary materials, even with some restraint. *Everything* looks important, especially at the outset, and the analyst wants to get it *all*. What at first seemed simple gets rapidly more complex and has to be fleshed out. New leads surface and need checking out. All this adds bulk. The real danger is that, at the end of data collection, the analyst will be overloaded with more data than can be processed. Furthermore, the narrative text of field notes is very difficult to use during analysis. It is spread over many pages, laid out in sequence rather than by topic, and usually has little inherent structure. It becomes difficult to *retrieve* the words that are most meaningful, to *assemble* chunks of words that go together, and to *reduce* the bulk into readily analyzable units. How then to contend with this?

Brief Description

A common solution is that of *coding* field notes, observations, and archival materials. A code is an abbreviation or symbol applied to a segment of words—most often a sentence or paragraph of transcribed field notes—in order to *classify* the words. Codes are *categories*. They usually derive from research questions, hypotheses, key concepts, or important themes. They are *retrieval and organizing devices* that allow the analyst to spot quickly, pull out, then cluster all the segments relating to the particular question, hypothesis, concept, or theme. Clustering sets the stage for analysis.

Illustration

Types of codes. Let us assume that an analyst is interested, as we were in our school improvement study, in the reasons for which a new educational practice is adopted. This may be the sole or one of several research questions to be addressed in a study. The researcher will typically begin by asking informants at the field site why they or others decided to try out the practice. A piece of the field notes might look like this:

> I asked him what the need for the new program was, and he responded that the students coming into the 9th grade were two years below grade lvel, and that the old curriculum was ineffective. Through testing (the Nelson Reading Test) it was determined that students were growing academically only five to six months during the ten-month school year.

Assuming that the analyst found it possible to apply a single summarizing notation to this chunk, it might be "MOT" to indicate "motivation." That code would appear in the left-hand margin beside the segment (the right-hand margin might be used for a comment; see Box III.B.b). If the analyst wanted a little more differentiation, the code might separate teachers' motivations from administrators'; we then get "ADM-MOT." Or perhaps one might want to specify the *time period* or phase in which that motivation appeared, (for instance, the "adoption" phase, by lengthening the code to read "AD/MOT." Or, to include all these things, "AD/ADM-MOT."

These are *descriptive* codes; they entail no interpretation, but simply the attribution of a class of phenomena to a segment of text. The same segment could, of course, be handled more *interpretively*. Let us assume that, as the field researcher gets more savvy about local dynamics, a more complex, more back-stage web of motives turns up. Some people may have adopted the new practice chiefly to attract attention to themselves and thereby to set up a desirable promotion. We then have the official motive, such as the one in the segment shown above, and the more private or backstage motive. The segment we just saw could then be coded "OFF-MOT" (for official motivation) and the other segments "PRIV-MOT."

A third class of codes is even more inferential and *explanatory*. The idea here is to indicate that a segment of field notes illustrates an emergent leitmotiv or pattern that the analyst has deciphered while unraveling the meaning of local events and relationships. These codes can be called what they are—LM (leitmotiv), PATT (pattern), TH (theme), CL (causal link)—and should include a word indicating the theme or pattern. They typically get used *later* in the course of data collection, as the patterns come clear.

Here is an example. In the field study of educational innovations, this segment appeared:

> But he (Mr. Walt) says that he does not know that much about what is exactly involved in the SCORE-ON program. He thinks that "it is a combination of a lot of things." The resource lab appears to be used in the morning for the FACILE program, which Mr. Walt knows a great deal more about. . . . In the afternoon, Mrs. Hampshire uses the lab for SCORE-ON purposes. Mr. Walt says that this is a different program, and therefore it is a different use.

That clump looks innocent enough to be taken descriptively, which is the way the field researcher saw it during initial interviewing. Several interviews and some causal observations later, however, it looked different. There was apparently an intense power struggle between different factions or "teams" in the district central office—which the researcher later likened to a "lot of rattlesnakes in a jug"—and people were lining up in one or the other camp. Mr. Walt was in the FACILE camp, not in the SCORE-ON camp; both projects were competing for funds and supervisory posts. The segment thus got coded PATT-TEAM.

These illustrations tell us three important things about codes. First, they can be at *different levels* of analysis, ranging from the descriptive to the higher inferential. Second, they can happen at *different times* during analysis; some get created and used at the start and others come later—typically the descriptive ones first and the inferential ones later.

Finally, and most important, *codes are astringent; they pull a lot of material together*, permitting analysis. The PATT-TEAMS code, for example, signals a theme that accounts for a lot of other data—makes them intelligible, suggests causal links, and functions like a statistical factor in grouping disparate pieces into a more inclusive and meaningful whole.

Creating codes. One method—the one we prefer—is that of creating a "start list" of codes *prior* to fieldwork. That list comes from the conceptual framework, list of research questions, hypotheses, problem areas, and key variables that the researcher brings into the study. In our school improvement study, for example, we conceptualized the innovation process in part as one of "reciprocal transformation" among the innovation itself, its users, and the host classroom or school. Teachers changed the characteristics of new practices. Those practices, in turn, changed the teachers and modified the working arrangement in the classroom, which in turn influenced how much of the innovation could be used, and so on.

We began, then, with a master code—TR—to indicate the transformational process we had hypothesized, and some subcodes—TR-USER, TR-CLASS (classroom changes), TR-ORG (organizational changes), TR-INN (changes in the innovation)—to mark off segments of data in each class of variables.

A start list can have from 80 to 90 codes; this number can be kept surprisingly well in the analyst's short-term memory, without constant reference to the full list—if the list has a clear structure and rationale. It is a good idea to get that list on a *single sheet* for easy reference. Chart 6a is an example. Note the three columns. The first one gives a short descriptive label for the general categories and the individual codes. The second column shows the codes, and the third keys the code to the research question or subquestion from which it derives.

There are at least two other, equally honorable, methods of generating codes. First, a more inductive researcher may not want to precode *any* datum until he or she has collected it, seen how it functions or nests in its context, and determined how many varieties of it there are. This is essentially the more empirically "grounded" approach advocated by Glaser (1978), and it has a lot going for it. Data get well molded to the codes that represent them, and we get more of a code-in-use flavor than the generic-code-for-many-uses generated by a prefabricated start list.[2] The analyst is more open-minded and more context-sensitive.

The trade-off here is that earlier segments may have different codes than later ones. Or, to avoid this, *everything* may have to be recoded once a more empirically sculpted scheme emerges. This means more overall coding time, and longer uncertainty about the coherence of the coding frame. And there is another risk: the danger of finding *too* much coherence in the data during recoding of earlier segments— retrospective hindsight is at work.

A second alternative, part way between the two approaches, is that of creating a general accounting scheme for codes that is not content-specific but that points to the general domains in which codes will have to be inductively developed. Lofland (1971), for example, says that codes in any study can deal with the following sorts of phenomena, from microscopic to macroscopic levels:

(1) *acts:* action in a situation that is temporarlly brief, consuming only a few seconds, minutes, or hours
(2) *activities:* action in a setting of more major duration—days, weeks, months—constituting significant elements of people's involvements
(3) *meanings:* the verbal productions of participants that define and direct action
(4) *participation:* people's holistic involvement in, or adaptation to, a situation or setting under study
(5) *relationships:* interrrelationships among several persons considered simultaneously
(6) *settings:* the entire setting under study conceived as the unit of analysis

He further notes that codes at each level can be static or dynamic, focusing on changes over time.

Another accounting scheme is suggested by Bogdan and Biklen (1982), who divide codes the following way:

(1) *setting/context:* general information on surroundings
(2) *definition of the situation:* how people define the setting of topics
(3) *perspectives:* ways of thinking, orientation
(4) *ways of thinking about people and objects:* more detailed than above)
(5) *process:* sequences, flow, changes over time
(6) *activities:* regularly occurring kinds of behavior
(7) *events:* specific activities
(8) *strategies:* ways of accomplishing things

Chart 6a
Illustration of a Start List of Codes

INNOVATION PROPERTIES	IP-OBJ	3.1
IP: OBJECTIVES	IP-OC	3.1.1
IP: ORGANIZATION	IP-ORG/DD, LS	3.1.1
IP: IMPLIED CHANGES–CLASSROOM	IP-CH/CL	3.1.4
IP: IMPLIED CHANGES–ORGANIZATION	IP-CH/ORG	3.1.5
IP: USER SALIENCE	IP-SALIENCE	3.1.2
IP: (INITIAL) USER ASSESSMENT	IP-SIZUP/PRE, DUR	3.1.3, 3.4, 3.5
IP: PROGRAM DEVELOPMENT (IV-C)	IP-DEV	3.1.1, 3.3.3, 3.3.4
EXTERNAL CONTEXT	EC (PRE) (DUR)	3.2, 3.3, 3.4
EC: DEMOGRAPHICS	EC-DEM	
In county, school personnel	ECCO-DEM	3.2.3, 3.3, 3.4
Out county, nonschool personnel	ECEXT-DEM	3.2.3, 3.3, 3.4
EC: ENDORSEMENT	EC-END	3.2.3, 3.3, 3.4
In county, school personnel	ECCO-END	3.2.3, 3.3, 3.4
Out county, nonschool personnel	ECEXT-END	3.2.3, 3.3, 3.4
EC: CLIMATE	EC-CLIM	3.2.3, 3.3, 3.4
In county, school personnel	ECCO-CLIM	3.2.3, 3.3, 3.4
Out county, nonschool personnel	ECEXT-CLIM	3.2.3, 3.3, 3.4
INTERNAL CONTEXT	IC (PRE) (DUR)	3.2, 3.3, 3.4
IC: CHARACTERISTICS	IC-CHAR	3.2.2, 3.4, 3.5
IC: NORMS AND AUTHORITY	IC-NORM	3.2.2, 3.4.3, 3.5
IC: INNOVATION HISTORY	IC-HIST	3.2.1
IC: ORGANIZATION PROCEDURES	IC-PROC	3.1.1, 3.24, 3.3, 3.4
IC: INNOVATION-ORGANIZATION CONGRUENCE	IC-FIT	3.2.2
ADOPTION PROCESS	AP	3.2, 3.3
AP: EVENT CHRONOLOGY–OFFICIAL VERSION	AP-CHRON/PUB	3.2.4, 3.3.1
AP: EVENT CHRONOLOGY–SUBTERRANEAN	AP-CHRON/PRIV	3.2.4, 3.3.1
AP: INSIDE/OUTSIDE	AP-IN/OUT	3.2.5
AP: CENTRALITY	AP-CENT	3.2.2
AP: MOTIVES	AP-MOT	3.2.6
AP: USER FIT	AP-FIT	3.2.7
AP: PLAN	AP-PLAN	3.3.3
AP: READINESS	AP-REDI	3.3.4, 3.2.1
AP: CRITICAL EVENTS	AP-CRIT	3.3.1
SITE DYNAMICS AND TRANSFORMATIONS	TR	3.4
TR: EVENT CHRONOLOGY–OFFICIAL VERSION	TR-CHRON/PUB	3.4.1, 3.4.2, 3.4.3
TR: EVENT CHRONOLOGY–SUBTERRANEAN	TR-CHRON/PRIV	3.4.1, 3.4.2, 3.4.3
TR: INITIAL USER EXPERIENCE	TR-START	3.4.1, 3.4.2, 3.4.3
TR: CHANGES IN INNOVATION	TR-INMOD	3.4.1
TR: EFFECTS ON ORGANIZATIONAL PRACTICES	TR-ORG/PRAC	3.4.3
TR: EFFECTS ON ORGANIZATIONAL CLIMATE	TR-ORG/CLIM	3.4.3
TR: EFFECTS ON CLASSROOM PRACTICE	TR-CLASS	3.4.2
TR: EFFECTS ON USER CONSTRUCTS	TR-HEAD	3.4.2, 3.4.3
TR: IMPLEMENTATION PROBLEMS	TR-PROBS	3.4.1
TR: CRITICAL EVENTS	TR-CRIT	3.4.1, 3.4.2, 3.4.3
TR: EXTERNAL INTERVENTIONS	TR-EXT	3.4.3
TR: EXPLANATIONS FOR TRANSFORMATIONS	TR-SIZUP	3.4.1, 3.4.2, 3.4.3
TR: PROGRAM PROBLEM SOLVING	TR-PLAN	3.4.1, 4.4.2, 3.4.3

Chart 6a (Continued)

NEW CONFIGURATION AND ULTIMATE OUTCOMES	NCO	3.5
NCO: STABILIZATION OF INNOVATION–CLASSROOM	NCO-INNOSTAB/CLASS	3.5.1
NCO: STABILIZATION OF USER BEHAVIOR	NCO-STAB/USER	3.5.2
NCO: USER FIRST-LEVEL OUTCOMES	NCO-USER 1OC	3.5.4
Positive and negative	NCO-USER 1OC/+, –	
Anticipated and unanticipated	NCO-USER 1OC/A, U	
Combinations (when appropriate)	NCO-USER 1OC/A+, A–	
	U+, U–	
NCO: USER META OUTCOMES	NCO-USER META	
Positive and negative	NCO-USER META OC/+, –	
Anticipated and unanticipated	NCO-USER META OC/A, U	
Combinations (when appropriate)	NCO-USER META OC/A+, A–	
	U+, U–	
NCO: USER SPINOFFS AND SIDE EFFECTS	NCO-USER SIDE	3.5.5 (3.5.2)
Positive and negative	NCO-USER SIDE OC/+, –	
Anticipated and unanticipated	NCO-USER SIDE OC/A, U	
Combinations (when appropriate)	NCO-USER SIDE OC/A+, A–	
	U+, U–	
NCO: CLASSROOM INSTITUTIONALIZATION	NCO-INST/CLASS	3.5.5
NCO: STABILIZATION OF INNOVATION–ORGANIZATION	NCO-INNOSTAB/ORG	3.5.6
NCO: STABILIZATION OF ORGANIZATIONAL BEHAVIOR	NCO-STAB/ORG	3.5.7
NCO: ORGANIZATIONAL INSTITUTIONALIZATION	NCO-INST/ORG	3.5.8
NCO: ORGANIZATIONAL FIRST-LEVEL OUTCOMES	NCO-ORG 1OC	3.5.9
Positive and negative	NCO-ORG 1OC/+, –	
Anticipated and unanticipated	NCO-ORG 1OC/A, U	
Combinations (when appropriate)	NCO-ORG 1OC/A+ A–	
	U+, U–	
NCO: ORGANIZATIONAL META OUTCOMES	NCO-ORG META	3.5.9
Positive and negative	NCO-ORG META OC/+, –	
Anticipated and unanticipated	NCO-ORG META OC/A, U	
Combinations (when appropriate)	NCO-ORG META OC/A+, A–	
	U+, U–	
NCO: ORGANIZATIONAL SPINOFFS AND SIDE EFFECTS	NCO-ORG SIDE	3.5.9 (3.5.7)
Positive and negative	NCO-ORG SIDE OC/+, –	
Anticipated and unanticipated	NCO-ORG SIDE OC/A, U	
Combinations (when appropriate)	NCO-ORG SIDE OC/A+, A–	
	U+, U–	
NCO: INSTITUTIONAL EXPANSION	NCO-INNOGRO/ORG	3.5.8
NCO: ORGANIZATIONAL REDUCTION	NCO-INNODWIN/ORG	3.5.8

EXTERNAL AND INTERNAL ASSISTANCE (SEPARATE CODES FOR EXTERNAL, PEER, ADMINISTRATIVE)

ASS: LOCATION	ASS-LOC	3.6.1
ASS: RULES, NORMS	ASS-RULE	3.6.1
ASS: ORIENTATION	ASS-ORI	3.6.2
ASS: TYPE	ASS-TYPE	3.6.3
ASS: EFFECTS	ASS-EFF	3.6.4
ASS: ASSESSMENT BY RECIPIENTS	ASS-ASS	3.6.5
ASS: LINKAGE	ASS-LINK	3.6.6

EMERGING CAUSAL LINKS   CL

CL: NETWORKS	CL-NET	N.A.
CL: RULES	CL-RULE	N.A.
CL: RECURRENT PATTERNS	CL-PATT	N.A.
Within site	CL-PATT/LS	N.A.
Intersite	CL-PATT/OS	N.A.
CL: EXPLANATORY CLUSTER (researcher)	CL-EXPL	N.A.
(respondent)	SITECL-EXPL	N.A.

QUERIES   QU

QU: SURPRISES	QU-!	N.A.
QU: PUZZLES	QU-Q	N.A.

(9) *relationships and social structure:* unofficially defined patterns

(10) *methods:* research-related issues

Such schemes help the researcher think about categories in which codes will have to be developed; any particular study, of course, may focus on only a few of the categories.

Revising codes. For *all* approaches to coding—predefined, accounting-scheme guided, or postdefined—codes will change and develop as field experience continues. Researchers with start lists know that codes will change; there is more going on out there than our initial expectations have dreamed of, and few field researchers are foolish enough to avoid looking for these things.

Furthermore, some codes don't work; others decay. No field material fits them, or the way they slice up the phenomenon isn't the way the phenomenon appears empirically. This calls for doing away with the code or changing its level.

Other codes flourish, sometimes too much so. Too many segments get the same code—the familiar problem of bulk. This calls for breaking codes down into subcodes, something that can be saved for later on if necessary.

Still other codes emerge progressively during data collection. These are better grounded empirically and are especially satisfying to the researcher who has uncovered an important local factor. They also satisfy other readers, who can see that the researcher is open to what the site has to say, rather than force-fitting the data into preexisting codes.

The importance of structure. Whether codes get created and revised early or late, however, is basically less important than whether they have some conceptual and structural *order.* Codes should relate to one another in coherent, study-important ways; they should be part of a governing structure. Incrementally adding, removing, or reconfiguring codes produces a ragbag that usually induces in turn a shapeless, purely opportunistic analysis. It also makes the codes harder to memorize and use; the retrieval and organization of the material becomes burdensome and difficult.

Chart 7 is an illustration of a poorly structured set of codes. It comes from a study of the creation of new schools (Miles et al., 1978). The study developed inductively, and over two years the number of codes mushroomed. The only structure is a sorting of 175 different codes into four general bins (formal and informal actors, processes, and aspects of the new school); the codes are alphabetically arranged only

within each bin. The scheme proved more and more difficult to remember and use; eventually it was collapsed in sheer desperation to a series of 28 more general categories including "adaptiveness," "time management," "sociopolitical support," "internal communication," and the like. This exhibit can be compared profitably to the conceptual structure underlying the coding scheme shown in Chart 6; that one was focused around families of variables, was easily remembered and usable, and led directly to our analysis.[3]

Definitions of codes. Whether codes are prespecified or developed along the way, clear operational definitions are indispensable, so that they can be consistently applied by a single researcher over time, and so that multiple researchers will be thinking about the same phenomena as they code. A code is usually a single term—"incentives," "institutionalization," "linkage"—that suggests different meanings to different analysts. Since codes will drive the retrieval and organization of the data for analysis, they have to be precise and their meaning shared among analysts. Defining them helps to get both these things done.

The actual mechanics of retrieval are not a minor issue (see section III.B.c for some ideas). Later sections of this and following chapters will also deal with the use of retrieved data "chunks" in analysis.

Chart 6b presents an excerpt from the list of definitions for the codes shown in Chart 6a. Such definitions will naturally get improved/focused further as the study proceeds. We wish to emphasize, however, that *conceptual structure,* whether prespecified or evolving, must underlie the definitions. In the new schools study, we developed rather clear, operational, and reliably usable definitions. But the codes *as a whole* had little intellectual shape, and thus proved unfruitful.

Naming codes. A short word of advice: Give a name to a code that is closest to the concept it is describing. If you have the term "motivation," the code should be MOT and not, for example, AIM or INC (for incentive). And *don't use numbers*—162, 29, or 29A. The rationale is that the analyst must be able to get back to the original concept as quickly as possible, without having to translate the code into the concept. It is also important that a second reader—a teammate or secondary analyst—be able to do the same.

Double-coding. Definitions get sharper when two researchers code the same data set and discuss their initial difficulties. Disagreements show that the definition has to be expanded or otherwise amended. Time

Chart 7
Illustration of a Poorly Structured List of Codes (excerpt)

Actors		Planning/Implementation Processes		Aspects of New School	
Formal		201	commitment	301	boundary maintenance
101	administrator	202	complexity management	359	budget (district)
127	advisory group	203	conflict management	302	budget (school)
128	architect	204	constituency development	303	collective sentiments
102	Board (central)	205	cooptation	360	community control
129	Board (district)	253	decision-making	304	communication (formal)
130	builder	207	designing	305	communication (informal)
131	chairperson	208	energy depletion	306	conflict management
103	citizen	209	energy mobilization	307	curriculum
132	community liaison	210	energy overinvestment	308	data collection/feedback
	. . .	211	future-envisioning	309	discipline
118	principal (focal)	212	goal clarification (stud. outcome)	310	departmentalization
119	principal (other)	213	goal clarification (sys. prop.)	311	equipment
130	researcher (other)	214	goal clarification (benefits)	312	evaluation (of school)
120	researcher (SA)	215	goal succession	313	extracurricular activities
131	salesman	254	group-building	314	food service
121	specialist (central off.)		. . .	315	friendship grouping
122	specialist (school)	227	planning	316	goals (student outcomes)
123	supt. (central)	231	planning horizon	317	goals (system properties)
135	supt. (district)	228	planning/implementation linkage	318	goals (benefits)
124	student	229	planning model	319	governance
125	teacher	232	policy-making	320	group definitions
136	teaching team	233	power base-building	321	influence (informal)
126	union representative	234	power struggle	361	inter-organizational linkage
112	voluntary organization	237	recruitment		. . .
		238	redesign	341	role definition
Informal*		239	reflexivity	342	rules
151	buffer	240	rehearsal	343	salaries
106	core group	257	research relationship	365	school-community linkage
107	core member	242	resource acquisition	366	security
152	evaluator	241	resource allocation	344	space use
113	implementer	243	resource identification	345	staff assignments
153	leader (socio-emotional)	258	role accumulation	346	staff characteristics
154	leader (task)	235	role confusion	347	staff selection
155	linker	236	role strain	367	staff utilization
156	mass media	246	start-up	353	status/prestige
157	opinion leader	260	task behavior	368	student characteristics
117	planner	247	thoroughness	369	student grade levels
		248	time investment	349	student grading/evaluation
		249	timetabling	350	student grouping basis
		250	training	351	student population
		251	uncertainty management	352	student personnel services
		252	variety pool expansion	370	student recruitment
				371	student selection
				372	supplies
				354	teaching methods
				355	technology (non-stud. oriented)
				356	time use
AFTER CODING, LOOK AT PROCESSES AND ASPECTS LISTS, AND				357	transportation
PUT (*) BY THE MOST IMPORTANT KEY WORDS (MAXIMUM = 6).				372	zoning

*For actors actually present at the contact, circle the number. If an actor was not present, but is *discussed* in the contact, put parentheses around the key word.

Chart 6b
Definitions of Selected Codes from Chart 6a

Site Dynamics and Transformations—TR

Event chronology— official version: TR-CHRON/PUB	Event chronology during initial and ongoing implementation, as recounted by users, administrators or other respondents.
Event chronology— subterranean version: TR-CHRON/PRIV	Event chronology during initial or ongoing implementation, as recounted by users, administrators or other respondents, and suggesting (a) a consensual but different scenario than the public version or (b) varying accounts of the same events.
Initial user experience: TR-START	Emotions, events, problems or concerns, assessments, made by teachers and administrators during first six months of implementation.
Changes in innovation: TR-INMOD	Reported modifications in components of the new practice or program, on the part of teachers and administrators, during initial and ongoing implementation.
Effects on organizational practices: TR-ORG/PRAC	Indices of impact of new practice or program on: (a) intraorganizational planning, monitoring, and daily working arrangements (e.g., staffing, scheduling, use of resources, communication among staff) and (b) interorganizational practices (e.g., relationships with district office, school board, community, and parent groups).
Effects on organizational climate: TR-ORG/CLIM	Indices of impact of new practice or program on institutional norms and interpersonal relationships, including effects on power and influence, social networks, institutional priorities for investing time and energy.
Effects on classroom practice: TR-CLASS	Indices of impact of new practice or program on regular or routine classroom practices (instructional planning and management).
Effects on user constructs: TR-HEAD	Indices of effects of new practice or program on teacher and administrator perceptions, attitudes, motives, assumptions or theories of instruction, learning, or management (e.g., professional self-image, revised notions of what determines achievement or efficiency, other attitudes toward pupils, colleagues, other staff members, stance toward other innovative practices).
Implementation problems: TR-PROBS	Difficulties or concerns relating to implementation at the personal, classroom, organizational, or extraorganizational levels, including reasons given for presence of difficulty or concern.

spent on this task by members of a research team is not hair-splitting casuistry, but reaps real rewards by bringing researchers to an unequivocal and common vision of what the codes signify and which blocks of data best fit which code.

Double-coding not only aids definitional clarity, but is a good reliability check. Do two coders, working separately, agree on how big a codable block of data is? And do they use the same codes for the same blocks of data? If not, they are headed for different analyses. Or the lone cross-site analyst working from field notes coded idiosyncratically by different researchers will soon be going crazy.

The best advice here is for all members of a field research team to code, separately, 5-10 pages of the first set of transcribed field notes, then to review each rendition collectively. When doing this, one shouldn't initially expect better than 70 percent intercoder reliability, using this formula:

$$\text{reliability} = \frac{\text{number of agreements}}{\text{total number of agreements plus disagreements}}$$

Each coder will have preferences—sociologists see organization-level codes for the same blocks of data that are intrapersonal for psychologists and interpersonal for social psychologists—and each vision is usually legitimate, especially for *inferential* codes. Clarifying these differences is also useful; each analyst tends to be more ecumenical during later coding for having assimilated a colleague's rival vision of data that looked, initially, codable in only one way.

Similarly, each coder is well advised to double-code the first dozen pages of field notes, once right away and again (on an uncoded copy) a few days later. How good is the internal consistency? We should look here for higher initial code-recode reliability—something closer to 80 percent—than was the case for between-coder agreements. Eventually, both intra- and intercoder agreement should be up in the 90 percent range.

Levels of detail. How fine should coding be? That depends on the study. Some linguistic analyses require line-by-line or even word-by-word coding. More typically, codes get applied to larger units—sentences, naturally occurring "chunks" of sentences, or paragraphs in the written-up field notes.

The important thing is that the researcher be reasonably clear about what constitutes a unit of analysis. In our work to date, we have usually defined the unit of analysis as a sentence or multisentence chunk, and have used the following heuristic: Assign the single most appropriate code among those derived from a given research question. For example, each segment, like the ones that are shown on page 56, drew a single code—the better one when two looked good, and the more encompassing rather than the narrower one. Any block of data—a clause, sentence, or paragraph—is usually a candidate for more than one code. But if the margin gets piled up with dual codes for each block, the researcher is in for heavy sledding when the notes are reviewed for site-level analysis. This problem is less critical when computer retrieval is used (Becker, Gordon, & LeBailly, 1984); multiple coding is actually useful in exploratory studies, they note.

A good case can be made for dual-coding segments with both a descriptive and inferential code; these are legitimately two necessary levels of analysis. But keep in mind that inferential codes don't have to be exhaustive. The analyst is looking for good explanatory *exemplars*, not for all instances.

Similarly, the codes themselves should not be overbuilt. In another study, we experimented with multiple-facet coding. For example, if a segment showed administrators providing problem-solving assistance to teachers who found that help useful, the code was AD/PS-T/+. This made the codes difficult to scan, and absolutely maddening to cluster during final write-ups. Two or three facets in a single code seem to be as much as the brain can process efficiently.

Finally, *not every piece of the notes must be coded.* Field notes usually contain much dross—material that is unrelated to the research questions, either prespecified or emerging. There are such things as trivial, useless data. The aim is to keep the dross rate down, but it will never be zero.

When to code. This is an important issue. Some analysts reserve coding for the end of data collection. We think this is a serious mistake, even for inductively oriented researchers. Why?

Basically, late coding *enfeebles the analysis.* Coding is not just something one does to "get the data ready" for analysis, but something that drives ongoing data collection. It is, in short, a form of continuing analysis. Qualitative fieldwork should be iterative; one pass at a site leads to a reshaping of one's perspective and of one's instrumentation for the next pass.

Futhermore, coding is hard, obsessive work. It is not nearly as much fun as getting the good stuff in the field. Trying to do the coding all at one time tempts the researcher to get sloppy, resentful, tired, and partial, thus damaging data quality.

One simple rule of thumb is this: Always code the previous set of field notes before the next trip to the site. If the researcher is several weeks at the site, dictated notes should be sent home regularly for transcription and coding. This plan can be foiled by coding backlogs and slow turnaround in typing up transcripts, but ongoing coding is the right plan.

Coding field notes while you are still in the data collection process uncovers real or potential sources of bias and, overall, sets the agenda for the next wave of data collection. Incomplete or equivocal data can get resolution next time out.

The more important point is that, since the ultimate power of field research lies in the researcher's emerging map of what is happening and what the strongest determinants appear to be, *any* device that will force more differentiation and integration of that map is a good investment.

Advice

Codes are efficient data-labeling and data-retrieval devices. They empower and speed up analysis. To generate and use them to their best advantage, we have offered a number of tips.

Creating codes prior to fieldwork is helpful; it forces the analyst to tie research questions or conceptual interests directly to the data. But the analyst should be ready to bend the codes when they look inapplicable, overbuilt, empirically ill-fitting, or overly abstract. One can also work more inductively, waiting for the field notes to suggest more empirically driven labels. One should not, however, wait too long or change the codes too often.

Make certain that all the codes fit into a structure, that they *relate to* or are *distinct from* others in meaningful, study-important ways. Don't casually add, remove, or reconfigure codes.

Keep the codes semantically close to the terms they represent. Don't use numbers as codes.

Have the codes on a single sheet for easy reference.

Define the codes operationally and be sure all analysts understand the definitions and are able to identify rapidly a segment fitting the definition.

Ordinarily, use a single code for a segment. Dual or even multiple coding is warranted if a segment is both descriptively and inferentially meaningful.

Double-coding the same transcripts is essential for studies with more than one researcher and very useful for the lone researcher (get code-recode consistencies over 90 percent before going on).

Coding should not be put off to the end of data gathering. Qualitative research depends heavily on ongoing analysis, and coding is a good device for forcing that analysis.

Time Required

The time required for generating initial codes and definitions depends, of course, on how many you start with, and on the clarity of the conceptual framework and research questions. For the start list and definitions shown earlier, the first cut took two full days—one for the codes and one for the definitions. Revisions and completions added another two days.

Coding itself takes varying amounts of time, depending on the code's conceptual structure and complexity, the quality of the field notes, and the coder's skill. Here is some typical arithmetic from our experience.

A single-spaced page of transcribed field notes has about 45 lines. As a rough rule of thumb, it might contain 8-10 codes. A 2-3-day field trip usually generates 40-80 such pages, even when the researcher is disciplined. Coding each page runs about 5-10 minutes once the codes are committed to memory; in the beginning, one should count 10-15 minutes. So "inexperienced" coding of such a data set would take perhaps 2 days; later, it could be done in a day or so. Taking longer than this is a signal that there are too fine units of analysis, too much dual coding, too many codes, or a weak conceptual structure.

Coding is tiring. If often feels "longer than it really is." It helps very much to use written-in marginal remarks (see Box II.B.b) of an active, musing sort—rather than just dully plowing through the application of codes. Breaking from time to time to do other related work—such as arguing with other coders, writing memos (see section III.D), or jotting down notes about what to look for in the next site visit—also helps.

III.B.a Reflective Remarks

Raw field notes (the scribbles and jottings that enter your notebook as you are watching a situation or talking with someone) must, as we have pointed out, be converted into a write-up, a transcription that is legible to any reader.

When doing a write-up, whether by typing or dictation, the temptation is to plod along, converting raw notes into a coherent account. But that misses an important resource: the fieldworker's reflections and commentary on issues that emerge during the process.

As a write-up is being produced, reflections of several sorts typically swim into awareness. For example:

- what the relationship with the respondents was like

Box III.B.a
Reflective Remarks: Illustrations

```
    Mike joked, "maybe I could go and act like a senior."
He made a dumb monkey face as he was speaking. ((This
staff does not seem to put down students, really, but they
can not resist occasional jokes of this sort - more of this
later.))
....
    Jim indicated that they had unofficially done their own
analysis of attendance data and said, "I'm sure it's been
effective", (that is, CARED in increasing attendance rates).
((This sounded pretty soft and vague to me.))

....
    John went on to explain that during the second semester
he would be doing pretty much the same, that is, "nothing
much at all." ((This denial of his activity was later
picked up informally by Jim, I think, in a conversation
with me. It was, in fact, a sort of minimization, and
perhaps a deflection from the fact that he was away a great
deal of the time, when presumably, he might be able to be
helpful with issues in the program itself.))
```

- second thoughts on the meaning of what a respondent was saying
- doubts about the quality of data being recorded
- a new hypothesis explaining what was happening
- a mental note to pursue an issue further in the next contact
- cross-allusions to something in another part of the data
- own feelings about what was being said or done
- elaboration or clarification of something said or done

When something like this arises in your mind, it is useful to enter it directly into the write-up. A good convention is to mark off the remark with double parentheses, to signal that it is of a different order than the data it comments on. The material in Box III.B.a gives some examples. Remarks such as these add substantial meaning to the write-up for other readers. And they usually are an aid during coding, because they often point to deeper or underlying issues that deserve analytic attention.

Note: The ((reflective remark)) technique can also be used while you are jotting down raw field notes as well. Doing so, in fact, improves the usefulness of field notes considerably; one is simultaneously aware of events in the site, and of one's own feelings, reactions, insights, and interpretations, as Patton (1980) suggests. See Bogdan and Biklen (1982), who divided reflective remarks into those on analysis, method, ethical dilemmas, own frame of mind, and points of calibration.

III.B.b Marginal Remarks

Coding, as we have noted, can get boring and tedious, if one treats oneself as a sort of machine picking out chunks of data and assigning category labels to them. The sensation of being bored is usually a signal that you have ceased to think. One way of retaining a thoughtful stance to coding is the marginal remark. It is analogous to the reflective remark (see Box III.B.a).

As coding proceeds, if you are being alert and nonroutine about what you are doing, ideas and reactions to the meaning of what you are seeing will well up steadily. These ideas are important: They suggest new interpretations, leads, connections with other parts of the data—and they usually point toward analytic work, like the pattern codes discussed in the next section, and the memoing (Section III.D) that leads further and further into analysis.

Assuming that your convention is that codes appear in the left margin, it is useful to put preanalytic remarks of all sorts in the right margin. Box III.B.b presents a couple of examples. Marginal remarks, like reflective remarks, add meaning and clarity to field notes. They

Box III.B.b

Marginal Remarks: Illustrations

IC-NoRM/DAR
CL-PATT

Jim looked past me for a minute and asked Dawn, the aide, to go out and check the kids in the hall. I asked what that was about and he explained that "we don't release them until the bell", and that some students had already stepped outside in the hall even though the bell for the next period had not yet rung.

Control concerns.

. . .

CL-PATT

Largely the group free-associated from topic to topic. Certain themes recurred from time to time, including Mary's tendency to reassure the other two that the community relations work would be easy for them to carry out, and her steady advice not to give "professional" tasks to the aides. There was a good deal of advice-seeking from Mary. Finally, there did not seem to be any very specific planning or decision making about particular procedures or how things would occur in detail.

Reassurance.
Conflict over aide role
"Organic coping"

. . .

CL-PATT

. ((I think it was along through here that Mary said for the first of several times that "I'll still be available," implying that she wasn't really going to go away, this wasn't irrevocable, she would still be accessible.))

Reassurance theme

. . .

CL-PATT

John mentioned that there would be more girls than boys and suggested "should we go through the first day?" as if to launch discussion of how the program would start up. But this did not get a very direct response.

Organic coping theme

---

also point to important issues that a given code may be missing or blurring. As such, they may suggest needs for revision in codes.

III.B.c Storing and Retrieving Text

Codes are *category labels*, but they are not a filing system. Every research study needs a systematic way to *store* coded field data, and a way to *retrieve* those data when they are needed during analysis.

As in other aspects of life, the simplest way is not necessarily the best. The simplest way is to put coded field notes into a folder or notebook. Then, when you want to retrieve, say, all the coded chunks that deal with "motivation," you scan through the field notes for all the MOT codes to see what you have, making notes as you read and jotting down page numbers so you can get back if necessary. This works all right if field notes are not massive; otherwise it is often inefficient and time-consuming.

Generally speaking, it pays to consider the basic structure of your storage and retrieval system. Levine (1982) has provided a comprehensive guide, with examples, to the information-science principles involved in physical formatting, indexing (coding) of data,

cross-referencing, abstracting, and (a nonminor issue) pagination. Let's discuss the first two of these briefly.

Physical formatting. There are many possibilities in addition to the single "notebook/folder" method. One is *coded chunks on cards*. Coded field notes can be photocopied, cut into chunks and each chunk attached to a 5×8 card. Cards can be filed by code. If this is done, the card should also indicate the site, date, page number, and so on so you can get back to the chunk's content easily. Meaninglessness of isolated chunks is the potential problem here.

If McBee cards are use for chunks, they can be edge-punched, and subsets of cards pulled out easily. This permits, for example, locating all chunks coded MOT and some other, perhaps higher-level code, such as PATT in our example. Or edge punches can be given for specific respondents (administrators, teachers, and so on) as well.

One can also use differentiated *file folders*. Lofland (1971) suggests two types of files. "Mundane files" organize the field notes by people, settings, events, projects, groups, or other sensible categories, so that you don't have to search all the way through a complete site visit's field notes to find what, say, the school principal was doing (see also Levine, 1982).

"Analytic files" contain cut-up chunks of field notes. Each analytic file contains material on some major issue, theme, code, or family of codes. New analytic files get generated as the fieldwork proceeds, often through "memos" (see Section III.D). Material in one file may be cross-referenced to another. A loose-leaf notebook can also be used.

Bogdan and Biklen (1982) also suggest folders organized by single codes, and note that analysis usefully involves clumping/rearranging/connecting data chunks, perhaps on a thumbtack board. For a fascinating survey of procedures for field note storage and retrieval, see also Bolton (1982).

Cards and file folders are reasonably workable if the number of sites is small and the data collection not extended. But they are increasingly difficult and very time-consuming as the data base gets larger. The obvious way to store and retrieve text quickly and easily is to use a *computer*. As Werner (1982) has noted, it's fully practical to use a microcomputer in the field to write up and code field notes directly. For various approaches using computers for storage and retrieval, see the thoughtful collection of articles edited by Conrad and Reinharz (1984), Patton (1980, pp. 301-302), Dow (1982), and Sproull and Sproull (1982), whose TEXTAN program also permits easy analysis of text line by line. For a good discussion of one large-scale application of computerized storage and retrieval, see Stern (1977) and Yates (1977).

The main things to avoid in developing a computerized approach are (a) elaborateness—for example, assigning each chunk complex and multiple codes, just because retrieval is so easy, forgetting that this chews up large amounts of coding time, and (b) atomism and context-stripping. We have seen, for example, a program that produced something like this when asked to retrieve lines with the word "principal" in them, ordering them by position of the word:

622 PRINCIPAL OF THE SCHOOL IS JOHN NEUMANN. HE IS NOT

673 PRINCIPAL REMAINED QUIET, BUT I WAS UNSURE AS TO HIS

501 THE PRINCIPAL IS WIDELY SEEN AS SUPPORTIVE OF THE EFFORT BUT

998 THE PRINCIPAL STAYS IN THE OFFICE, NEVER SEEMING TO

443 TASK GROUP AGREED THAT PRINCIPAL WOULD FOLLOW

999 AND IN ANY CASE THOMPSON AS PRINCIPAL WOULD BE

The net result was that one could never understand the semantic, let alone the event *context* in which the retrieved word appeared.

The rapid diffusion of microcomputers and associated word-processing software is making for decided advances in text storage and retrieval (not to mention analysis) capabilities; anyone planning a field study should take a serious look at what's available before settling for cards and file folders.

Indexing. As Levine (1982) explains, "indexing" is a generic term including three processes: (a) defining clear categories (codes); (b) organization of these into a structure using an "index language"; and (c) pairing of the codes with appropriate places in the data base. As such, "indexing" is the heart of storage and retrieval; a strong, well-organized indexing sytem takes a good deal of energy to set up, but is crucial for data reduction, display, and conclusion drawing.

To avoid semantic confusion, let's focus for a minute on *tables of contents*, also called "indexes." Here we mean only a list of places where specific data chunks can be found. Such a list is often a useful part of the overall "indexing" system. For example, file cards can be prepared, one for each code. Each card has a notation on it for each instance of a coded chunk in the field notes, giving the page number and line number (this requires use of prenumbered paper for typed-up notes). Retrieval is slow this way; its best use is for small data bases. Some researchers add an index to the front of each meaningful block of field notes (Dobbert, 1982).

Tables of contents can of course easily be produced through available microcomputer programs (for example, GETSTUD.BAS; W. A. Firestone, personal communication, 1983), helping enormously in rapid access to a large body of field notes.

III.C PATTERN CODING

Analysis Problem

Given a working set of reasonably clear codes that describe the phenomena and events that are depicted in transcribed field notes, how can the researcher move to a second, more general, perhaps more explanatory level? Just naming or classifying what is out there is usually not enough. We need to understand the patterns, the recurrences, the *whys*. As Kaplan (1964) remarks, the bedrock of inquiry is the researcher's quest for "repeatable regularities."

Brief Description

Pattern codes are explanatory or inferential codes, ones that identify an emergent theme, pattern, or explanation that the site suggests to the analyst. They act to pull a lot of material together into more meaningful and parsimonious units of analysis. They are a sort of *meta*-code.

First-level coding is a device for summarizing segments of data. Pattern coding is a way of grouping those summaries into a smaller number of overarching themes or constructs. It is, for qualitative researchers, an analogue to the cluster-analytic and factor-analytic devices used in statistical analysis. The quantitative researcher works with sets of variables that either put *people* into distinct families built around what they do or say (Q analysis) or, alternatively, cluster such *actions and perceptions* across informants (R analysis).[4]

For the qualitative analyst, pattern coding has four important functions:

(1) It *reduces* large amounts of data into a smaller number of analytic units.
(3) It gets the researcher into *analysis during data collection*, so that later data collection can be more focused.
(3) It helps the researcher build a *cognitive map,* an evolving schema for understanding what is happening locally.
(4) When several researchers are engaged in individual case study work, it *lays the groundwork for cross-site analysis* by surfacing common themes and causal processes.

Illustrations

These four functions can be clarified as we discuss how pattern codes are generated, what they look like, and what the field researcher does with them in the course of data collection.

Generating pattern codes. This is easy—sometimes too easy. As in everyday life, the researcher needs to reduce and channel the stimuli with which he or she is being bombarded into a smaller number of chunks that can be mentally encoded, stored, and readily retrieved. Already during the initial fieldwork, the researcher is looking for threads that tie bits of data together. For example, if two or three informants say independently that they resent a decision made by their boss, we may be on to several different phenomena—a conflict, an organizational climate factor, or a disgruntled subgroup of employees. Any of these interpretations involves sorting and chunking data (function 1, above). These first bits of data are also leads; they suggest to the researcher what may be important variables to check out, factors that may account for other local perceptions and behaviors (function 2, above). Seeing the "resentment" data in any of these alternative ways also helps the researcher make sense of observations that had up now been puzzling or surprising. These several bits come together into an initial plot of the terrain to be gone over in progressively greater detail (function 3). Finally, if another field researcher in a multisite study comes across a similar batch of resentment or, alternatively, finds no resentment of decisions at all in a place otherwise similar to the more "resentful" site, we have the first threads of cross-site comparisons (function 4).

The danger is that of getting locked too quickly into naming a pattern and assuming you understand it, then thrusting the name onto data that fit it only poorly. Premature analytic closure is hard to shake, in part because the analyst often isn't aware of what is happening (a second analyst, reading over the field notes, usually *is*, however). Patterning happens fast because it is the way we habitually process information.[5] The trick here is to work with loosely held chunks of meaning, to be ready to unfreeze and reconfigure them as the data shape up otherwise, to subject the best patterns to merciless cross-checking, and to lay the most tenuous ones aside until other informants and observations give them more persuasive empirical grounding.

What pattern codes look like. Pattern codes usually turn around four, often interrelated, summarizers: themes, causes/explanations, relationships among people, and more-theoretical constructs. Here are some examples from a recent study, with codes we assigned in capital letters.

Themes:
 PATT (pattern): All supervisors seem to be using benevolent, fatherly terms when talking about employees ("my" staff, "my" people, "my" junior guys), but employees use mostly bureaucratic, regulation-type terms ("the office," "upstairs," "the management").
 RULE: You don't talk earnestly about your problems or your successes in the staff lounge.
 PATT/OS (theme appearing in other sites as well as this one): It seems easier to get new projects adopted among lower-class students or in vocational tracks.

Causes/Explanations:
 EXPL multiple role of the "helping teacher" seems to be an important ingredient of success.
 SITE-EXPL (informants' explanations): The best projects are ones that put together the best practitioner's recipes.
 MET (metaphor): The idea of career "trajectories"—people are using these projects to get away from some jobs and places to other ones.

Relationships Among People:
 NET (social network): The money-and-support club: A. Becker, P. Harrison, V. Wales.

Theoretical Constructs:
 BSP (basic social processes, as in Glaser, 1978): Negotiating or bargaining seems to be the way decisions get made; a conflict model is more plausible than a rational-technological model.

Using pattern codes in analysis. There are at least three ways to use pattern codes. First, they are added in tentative form to the list of codes, and tried out on the next set of transcribed field notes or documents to see whether they fit.

Next, the most promising ones are written up in the form of a *memo* (see next section) that expands on the significance of the code. This helps the writer get less fuzzy about the theme or construct, helps other researchers to think summatively about their own data set, and gets cross-site analytic energy flowing.

Finally, pattern codes get checked out in the next wave of data collection. This is largely an inferential process. The analyst tries out the theme on a new informant, engages in if-then procedures (if the pattern holds, other things will happen or won't happen), or checks out a rival explanation. What typically happens is not that a pattern code get discounted, but rather that it gets *qualified*; the conditions under which it holds are specified. For example, the role "No earnest talk in the lounge" can be bent in cases of conflict, crisis, or socializing of new members. This sort of clarification sets more precise parameters for verifying the pattern and strengthens its external validity.

Variations

If a general pattern code (such as RULE) is being used a good deal, it helps to create subcodes that explain the content and enable easy retrieval:

RULE: INF—Rules about informant behavior.

RULE: PUB—Rules about behavior in public settings.

RULE: WORK—Rules that specify how formal work tasks are to be carried out.

Stay open to the idea of inventing new *types* of pattern codes. For example, we developed the pattern code QU!, meaning a query about something surprising that happened in the site. Being surprised is an important event in fieldwork, and we wanted to track it in our notes.

Advice

Pattern coding is crucial for getting the next step above (or below) the immediate ebb and flow of events in the site. It should be done habitually and regularly as the initial set of first-level codes is being applied.

Don't try to force the use of pattern codes, pretending that because they are a meta-level code they can in principle be applied to *every* bit of data that already has a first-level code.

How many pattern codes, and when? This is largely a matter of analytic style. Some analysts are unregenerate pattern coders, others are more cautious. Some prefer to generate pattern codes very early, then check them out and qualify them; others are more resolutely inductive and wait until enough data accumulate to support a pattern or construct unequivocally. The important point is that pattern codes are *hunches*: Some pan out, but most don't.

Judging from our recent experience, the analyst for a site typically starts out with 3-4 pattern codes during initial analysis, then expands these to as many as a dozen, and finally comes back down to a half dozen (possibly different or reconstrued) themes. Pattern coding is an intellectually pleasurable process, and we sense correctly that those codes that survive the onslaught of several passes at the site, and several attempts to disqualify them, will turn out to be the conceptual hooks on which the analyst hangs the meatiest part of the analysis.

Time Required

Developing and applying pattern codes is an integral part of first-level coding; the activities are concurrent. Early on, doing pattern coding might occupy only 5-10 percent of total coding time; later somewhat more, as the analyst gets more and more preoccupied with making sense of the data.

III.D MEMOING

Analysis Problem

Fieldwork is so fascinating, and coding usually so energy-absorbing, that you can get preoccupied and overwhelmed with the flood of particulars—the poignant quote, the appealing personality of a key informant, the telling picture on the hallway bulletin board, the gossip after a key meeting. You forget to *think*, to make deeper and more general sense of what is happening, to begin to explain it in a conceptually coherent way. Reflective remarks, marginal remarks, and pattern coding are all a step away from the immediate toward the more general. But how is this done, more particularly?

Brief Description

We can hardly do better than Glaser's (1978) definition: "[A memo is] the theorizing write-up of ideas about codes and their relationships as they strike the analyst while coding. . . . it can be a sentence, a paragraph or a few pages . . . it exhausts the analyst's momentary ideation based on data with perhaps a little conceptual elaboration."

Memos are always *conceptual* in intent. They do not just report data, but they tie different pieces of data together in a cluster, or they show that a particular piece of data is an instance of a general concept.

Illustrations

Here are some memos written during the school improvement study, showing different facets of memoing. We'll comment on them as we go.

The first memo, A, responded to a colleague's earlier memo suggesting the "welcoming structures" concept and adapting it from the field of cognitive psychology. Note that the memo writer (a) aims at clarifying the idea; (b) ties it to information from a site; and (c) differentiates the idea from already-existing codes.

A. On "welcoming structures"   March 6, 1980

Your idea of a durable structure (typically combined with learned skills, procedures, etc.) at the organizational level which would facilitate adoption of innovations is a useful one, I think. We should be looking for it. In Perry-Parkdale there are so many Gov't programs that the concept clearly exists at the district level, at least for attracting money. At the building level there is prior experience with work experience programs, demonstration programs, etc.

The sheer ORG-FIT concept is not it; that only implies some sort of congruence. What we are talking about here is more of an active capability. I suggest a label that would recognize that what is at issue here is not merely a structure or mechanism, but working procedures, flows, and the associated skills and techniques. The cue you get is when you notice that people are in effect telling you that "we know how to handle these things."

Memo B, below, is an example of a "place-holding" memo—always a useful idea when an idea strikes.

B. Memo: Comparison processes   3/19/80

Introducing a new program inevitably induces a comparison process, notably comparison-for-alternatives (see FACILE and SCORE-ON). Just wanted to hold a place for this idea—more to come.

Memo C, below, is a rather thorough, integrative discussion, pulling together data from many sites and reformulating them around the issue of career patterns. It came part way through data collection, paved the way for a major addition to the study's outcome measures, and (in the last paragraph) encouraged specific means of data collection on the topic.

C. Memo: Career patterns   2/22/80

In a general sense, people are riding the innovations in a state of transition; they are on their way *from* somewhere *to* somewhere *via* the project . . .

Where could people be going? They could be going

—*up:* from a classroom to a supervisory or administrative role or to a higher administration slot. Innovations are a lot faster than waiting for someone else to move on or going back for a degree. They get you visibility and good positioning. If it gets institutionalized, you get institutionalized with it in the new role. Also, they're less brutal than getting promotions by doing in the person above you and more convenient than having to move away to move up.

—*away:* from teaching by easing into a part-time or more flexible job. These projects tend to be marginal, loosely administered (although Tindale is the contrary), transition-easing. They also can allow for permutations, as in the up-and-away pattern Cary may be following at Plummet.

—*in:* the remedial programs are less choosy about formal credentials. They provide access to civil services like education to people with weird backgrounds. Aides can get positioned to become certified teachers; people from business or the arts can come into a marginal or experimental universe and ease gradually into a more formal role incumbency.

At "my" sites, the innovation services the purposes of two teachers moving into supervisory roles ("helping teachers"). One has now become Title I coordinator. The administrator at this site (Masepa) is now well positioned for promotion, since he has won (ECRI has been mandated). At Banestown, the aide moves "in"; the head lab teacher does what the teacher at Masepa did with Title I: She gets the other half of her job in the same sector, thereby becoming "specialized" and ready to move "up" as *her* patron, the reading supervisor, moves "up" herself into a higher administrative post. The other lab teacher moves (back) "in" from non-teaching with a part-time post.

All this is very tentative, but it might focus us on this dimension, which is being independently flagged by 2-3 of us.

It is especially worth keeping track, as we dictate and code, of where these people have come from and where they are, or think they are, on their way to. I suggest we ask each informant:
   —a little more directly, *why* he/she is doing this, in terms of roles and role changes.
   —what he/she expects to be doing in 2-3 years.
   —if he/she has a sense of being in a transitional period.

The next memo, D, is an example of an idea that struck the researcher early during data collection. As it turned out, this particular idea went nowhere; the "miracle case" concept didn't seem to explain much when it was followed up further.

D. On "miracle cases"   19 March, 1980

We've now seen several times the story of the kid (impossible, low-achieving, *etc.*) who the program changed for the better in a miraculous way (ex: Masepa visit 1).

Maybe there's a sort of pious hope: Miracles of the program will lead to its canonization. Success stories about program outputs are a form of primitive legitimizing/justification. A high frequency of success-story telling possibly indicates basic unsecurity about low or unstable status of the program within the school and its curriculum.

Memos E and F, on "barometric events," illustrate how preexisting concepts can be useful in clarifying an idea. The memos tie the basic idea to site events, and to the coding system. They also show the importance of using memos as a dialogue among staff.

E. "Barometric events"   19 March, 1980

We can sometimes see a noticeable/identifiable change in the (weather) conditions of the system. It reminds me of Lewin's term "region of instability/uncertainty," or Redl's concept "dynamics of focal event." The event has a future-shaping quality: Thereafter things won't be the same; the state of the system will be different. Or they lead to a new developmental stage. Events are "preludes in prologues," and fulfill a linking (transitional) function in time.

Key actors in the event provide a clue: What is the domain or subsystem affected by the event? For example, Ms. Spiess's seminar attendance (Banestown) was a sort of boundary activity, a crucial event linking the school system with external professional information sources, not to mention "inspiration."

F. Return memo on barometric events   4/4/80

I think the idea is felicitous. It's very true that there is a sea change thereafter in several sectors of the subsystem. The codes AP-CRIT and TR-CRIT help to flag this. We can stay with a diachronic approach, even while doing some cross-sectional comparisons.

Memos should always be *dated*, entitled with key *concept* being discussed, and *anchored* to particular places in the field notes, to previous site analysis discussions, or to site summaries.

Memos should be filed under the *concept* they are about, and kept separate from data files. As a study proceeds—especially a strongly inductive one—memos will accumulate, and can themselves be sorted into more comprehensive categories (see Glaser, 1978, p. 87).

Memoing helps the analyst move easily from data to a conceptual level, refining and expanding codes further, developing key categories and showing their relationships, and building toward a more integrated theory of events, processes, and outcomes in the site.

Memoing is crucial when you are taking a strongly inductive, "grounded theory" approach, as Glaser does, but it is equally important, for other reasons, when you begin with a preliminary framework. Without memoing, there is little opportunity to understand how adequate the original framework is, and where it needs to be revised.

Variations

Memos can also be written (1) on what is intensely puzzling or surprising about a site; (2) as alternate hypotheses in response to someone else's memo; (3) to propose a specific new pattern code; (4) to integrate a set of marginal or reflective remarks already made on written-up field notes; (5) when the analyst does *not* have a clear concept in mind, but is struggling to clarify one; (6) around a general metaphor that organizes discrete observations (see section VII.A.5).

There can also be different types of memos for different phases of the study. For example, Lee et al. (1981, p. B43) have described the use of "insight journals"—memos of a page or less, perhaps stored in a card-file format—for the later stages of a study, when one is specifically after cross-case comparability and synthesis. They can include cross-site patterns, "bright ideas," policy implications, and ideas for next-step syntheses. Insight journals can themselves be coded for later retrieval.

Advice

Once again, we draw on Glaser (1978, pp. 83-92). Our advice is an amalgam of his experience and ours.

(1) Always give priority to memoing. When an idea strikes, STOP whatever else you are doing and write the memo. Get it down; don't worry about prose elegance or even grammar. Include your musings of all sorts, even the fuzzy and foggy ones. Give yourself the freedom to think. Don't self-censor.

(2) Memoing should begin as soon as the first field data start coming in, and will usually continue right up to the production of final report text. Just as codes should stabilize reasonably well by half or two-thirds of the way through data collection, the basic concepts pointed to by memos will usually start settling down then or shortly afterward, as the analyst approaches what Glaser calls "saturation" (no significantly new explanations for data). Memoing contributes strongly to the development/revision of the coding system.

(3) Keep memos "sortable." Caption them by basic concept, and mark or underline other concepts discussed during the text of the memo. Like coded data, they can be stored and retrieved using a wide variety of methods (see section II.B.c).

(4) Once again, memos are about *ideas*. Simply recounting data examples is not enough. Data should be referenced, but the issue is placing those data in a broader/deeper/higher conceptual frame.

(5) Memo writing is *fun*. Protect time to have fun in projects.

Time Required

Any given memo ordinarily occupies only a few minutes of time. Even one synthesizing a lot of data, such as memo C in our examples, should not occupy more than a half hour. Memos are simply a rapid way of capturing thought processes that occur all the way through data collection, data reduction, data display, conclusion drawing, conclusion testing, and final write-up.

III.D.a Developing Propositions

Memoing captures the thoughts of the analyst on the fly, so to speak, and is precious for that reason. As a study proceeds, the usual need is to formalize and systematize the researcher's thinking into a coherent set of explanations. One way to do that involves generating propositions, or connected sets of statements, reflecting the findings and conclusions of the study.

A good illustration appears in Stearns et al. (1980). They were studying 22 school sites implementing a new special education law (PL 94-142). Five fieldworkers prepared case study reports for each site. But how to describe commonalities, note differences, and develop powerful explanations across all 22 sites?

Stearns et al. rightly assumed that much useful material of this sort resided in fieldworkers' heads, and took an ingenious and thorough approach to eliciting the material, clarifying it, synthesizing it, and verifying it. The process had seven major steps, managed by three analysts who had themselves visited all the sites.

(1) Each fieldworker made an unstructured list of statements he or she "would like to see in the final report." Example:

> Although teachers spend a lot of time doing individualized education plans for special education students they don't find them all that useful on a daily basis.

Other statements were retrieved from documents and staff meeting notes; the total was 1500. One statement to a card.

(2) The 1500 were reduced through sorting and reduction of duplication to 1000.

(3) The more general, abstract statements were retained (N = 250), and specific instances set aside for later use.

(4) The 250 cards were sorted into "assumptions," "findings," and "conclusions," and divided into 30 general categories. The analysts displayed the 30 sets of cards on the wall to see their interrelationships; considering the information needs of their report audience as well, they developed a working outline for the findings sections of the report.

(5) Now for verification. The analyst developed from the 250 a draft list of propositions for fieldworker review. Example:

> The greatest impact of the law at the school level has been to add new duties to old ones.

The propositions were listed in organized sequence, under each of 21 headings.

(6) Fieldworkers examined the proposition list (33 pages), commenting on how true each was, what qualifications or conditions needed to be added, and said "don't know" or "doesn't apply" when relevant. This was done on a site-by-site basis, yielding 22 reports for each of the 21 categories.

(7) The analysis staff wrote a findings report for each of the 21 topics, using only the sites where relevant and valid data were available, and discarding confusing or mystifying findings. They checked back against a prior list of state and site characteristics for further explanations, and also noted explanations that emerged during the final step.

The Stearns et al. illustration is a fine example of an inductive approach to proposition generation, with safeguards against premature and invalid closure. Though they were faced with a very large data base, the approach can of course be used at any level, down to the individual case.

We should also note that propositions can also be prespecified more closely as to their form (not their content). For example, propositions can be cast in any of the following ways:

X exists (across a specified set of actors, sites, etc.)

X exists because . . .

Given X, then Y will follow, ("If . . . then . . . ").

X is necessary but not sufficient for Y to occur.

X causes Y.

Finally, although this illustration describes proposition generation in the later stages of a study, it can be very productively used much earlier—after the first round or two of site visits. Writing one proposition to a card, posting cards on the wall, then clustering them, helps a study staff see rather clearly what their preliminary understandings look like, as a guide for next-step analysis and further data collection.

III.E SITE ANALYSIS MEETING

Analysis Problem

In any study that has multiple sites (cases) and more than one staff member, the meaning of what is happening at each site tends increasingly to get lost in the welter of fieldwork, write-ups, coding, and other preliminary analysis. Even the fieldworker (or workers) who know most about a particular site can get overloaded and lose perspective. In studies with intensive field contact, coding tends to lag, so that there is usually a backlog of uncoded write-ups. How can a research staff understand quickly and economically what is happening in a site, and keep themselves current, and develop shared constructs to guide later analysis?

Brief Description

At a site analysis meeting, the fieldworker(s) most conversant with a site and other staff members meet to summarize the current status of events at the site. The meeting is guided by a series of questions, and notes are taken on answers to the questions as the meeting progresses.

Illustration

In a study of the creation of new schools (Miles et al. 1978) that included six sites, we wanted to keep as current as we could on events in the planning and implementation of each new school. We were also seeking explanations and hypotheses—and we were in addition feeling strongly that a too complex and overloaded coding scheme needed to be revised.

Structuring the meeting. We settled on the idea of a site analysis meeting that would be held for each of the six sites in rotation. To help focus and manage the meeting, there needed to be a note-taking form, which appears in compressed form below.

Site Analysis Meeting Form   Date_____

     Site_____

Recorder_____
Meeting Attendance_____

1. MAIN THEMES, IMPRESSIONS, SUMMARY STATEMENTS about what is going on in the site. Comments about the general state of the planning/ implementation system.
2. EXPLANATIONS, SPECULATIONS, HYPOTH-ESES about what is going on in the site.
3. ALTERNATIVE EXPLANATIONS, MINORITY REPORTS, DISAGREEMENTS about what is going on in the site.
4. NEXT STEPS FOR DATA COLLECTION: follow-up questions, specific actions, general directions fieldwork should take.
5. Implications for REVISION, UPDATING OF CODING SCHEME.

The actual form, of course, should have such questions spread out over three or four pages, to allow space for note-taking.

Assembling the data. In using the form, the meeting can profitably begin with the most involved field-worker(s) launching a discussion of item 1, main themes. Others ask questions for clarification. The recorder follows the discussion, taking notes under that heading, and asking for further clarification if needed.

Often the discussion will jump forward to later questions (for example, a theme suggests an explanation), and the recorder enters those data under appropriate headings. Points or items under each heading should be numbered to mark them off and aid reference to them during discussion.

If the group does not move to later questions, the recorder should ask them to do so.

The recorder should summarize the notes from time to time to be sure that the discussion is being accurately followed.

Using the data. Usually photocopies should be made for all staff members; they can be reviewed at the end of the meeting and specific plans made (to revise codes, how to collect new data of a certain sort), or such review and planning can be done afterward.

Chart 8 shows some excerpts from a filled-out site analysis form for the new schools study. The field-worker had been observing the start-up of a new open-space elementary school. In this exhibit, we can see that a main theme was the researchers' effort to describe (item 1) and then understand (item 2) why early implementation of the open-space teaching was going relatively smoothly, even though there had been poor advance preparation. The hypotheses and hunches in item 2 (such as the "retreatability" concept, the principal-teacher relationship or teacher pro-fessionalization) lead to additional data collection plans in item 4 (for instance, teacher interviews), as do the alternate, rival hypotheses suggested in item 3. One can also see that the meeting allows people to entertain opposing views (for example, the idea of retrieval interviews on summer planning in item 4 opens up the possibility that perhaps there was more advance planning and preparation than the field-worker had thought).

Variations

Many other questions can be generated to guide site analysis meetings:

- What is puzzling, strange, or unexpected about recent site events?
- What is the state of our rapport with various people in key roles?
- What additional analyses do we need of existing data to understand the site better?
- What is definitely *not* true of the site at this point?
- What will probably happen over the next few days/ weeks at the site?

These are content-free examples; the research questions for any particular study can also generate additional substantive issues that can go on the site analysis meeting form (for example, "What are the current outcomes of the innovation?" "How politically stabilized is the program?" "What is the level of parent involvement?" "What are the main channels of information transfer?").

The notes from site analysis meetings, as well as guiding specific next steps in data collection, can be returned to after the next round or two of data collection for confirmation/disconfirmation. In our illustration, it turned out that Ed's preoccupation with

Chart 8
Site Analysis Form: Exhibit with Data

1. MAIN THEMES, IMPRESSIONS, SUMMARY STATEMENTS about what is
   going on in the site.

1. Ed (principal) is efficient "technical" manager, not dealing with
social system; doesn't think about it. When Ken (asst supt) pointed out
need for Ed to work with Janet, a complaining teacher ("treat her with
kid gloves....good luck.") Ed said, "She'll be the one needing good luck."
   Not supportive especially: one teacher asked the field worker for help,
seemed reluctant when FW referred her back to Ed.
2. Implementation of the open space approach is incredibly smooth in
light of the minimal advance preparation and training. There is still
a "walking on cracked eggs" feeling, though.
3. Teachers seem cautiously willing to see how it will work out, not
directly optimistic. Uncertainty, feeling unprepared. "If it doesn't work
out I hope we can undo it" suggests weak commitment, is called "retreatability."
4. Children relaxed.
5. Teachers feel principal had no idea of what would be involved, really,
in start-up.
.....

2. EXPLANATIONS, SPECULATIONS, HYPOTHESES about what is going
   on in the site

1. Ed's "efficiency" emphasis helps smoothness.
2. People know who to go to for support.
3. Many teachers were students of asst supt and   trust him,
4. Things aren't being imposed by outsiders.
5. Teacher attitudes may be related to the "retreatability" concept
6. Principal knew teachers well enough to compose workable teams to implement
the open space concept. Also sent complaining teachers to another school.
7. Principal respects the teachers--even though during the administrative
planning they were treated like cattle.
....

3. ALTERNATIVE EXPLANATIONS, MINORITY REPORTS, DISAGREEMENTS
   about what is going on in the site.

1. Perhaps the teachers' considerable past experience and training, their
professionalization makes for the smooth implementation.
2. The size of Ed's faculty has doubled; there are many strangers. That
may be increasing the uncertainty as much as the lack of preparation.

.....

4. NEXT STEPS FOR DATA COLLECTION: follow-up questions, specific
   actions, general directions field work should take.

1. Ask Ed about Janet, how she's adjusting. Get to know her.
2. Need time to talk with teachers, not just observe the start-up.
Teachers are probably bothered more than their "professional" surface
behavior shows.
3. Will or can Ken give the teachers technical help?
4. What happened in yesterday's faculty meeting?
5. We should do a careful retrieval interview with Ken and Ed about
the summer work, planning decisions, etc. that preceded the start-up.
6. Ask key people: what are your hopes for the way the school will
be by Christmas? by June? What indicators would they use for good
teacher collaboration? humanization of teaching?
....

5. Implications for REVISION, UPDATING OF CODING SCHEME.

1. Consider adding a code for support.
2. Something on teacher commitment or ownership of the innovation.
3. Use a pattern code for the "retreatability" idea, which seems
   quite key.
4. Our codes on "planning-implementation linkage" are too complicated;
   need to simplify them considerably.
....

"technical" issues and apparent nonsupportiveness was seen by teachers as helpful; they believed that he was granting them much autonomy as professionals, and they appreciated that.

Site analysis meetings can also be focused on a *single theme* in one site, such as "stabilization of the innovation," or treat such a theme across *several sites.* See Stiegelbauer, Goldstein, and Huling (1982) for further suggestions.

Advice

Site analysis meetings are good devices for rapid retrieval of impressions, and the formation of preliminary descriptive and explanatory generalizations. The back and forth of colleague interaction helps to keep the fieldworkers honest. Even so, care should be taken not to get locked into premature generalizations. The themes and suggestions from site analysis meetings should always be checked against events in the site, as noted in carefully coded write-ups of field notes.

Don't let a fieldworker's generalization or impression go unquestioned or unillustrated. The tone should not be one of arguing, but of friendly skepticism and efforts at concreteness and shared clarity. There must be a balance between getting reasonable consensus and testing alternative, rival hypotheses. Summarize frequently to check understandings.

If the staff group is bigger than three or four, it will help to have someone chairing as well as recording.

Time Required

A site analysis meeting longer than an hour and a half or so begins to lose focus and bite. The frequency of such meetings depends, of course, on such factors as staff size, number of sites, and the frequency of site visits. In our illustration, each of six sites was visited once a week, and site analysis meetings for a given site were held every three weeks (thus two meetings a week). The rule of thumb is this: Don't let a large amount of site data pile up before an analysis meeting is held. In our school improvement project, we found it useful to hold short site analysis meetings after each site visit (which usually occupied two to three days).

III.F INTERIM SITE SUMMARY

Analysis Problem

Researchers have four recurring nightmares about data analysis. In the first nightmare, the data are no good. They haven't measured what they were supposed to measure. In the second nightmare, there has been systematic measurement error (commonly in the form of biased responses) on the most important measures. In the third nightmare, conclusions come out of the wringer of successively more sophisticated analyses looking either trival or trite ("You spent $75,000 to tell us *that*?"). And in the last nightmare, the data resist analysis, are opaque, even inscrutable.

In conventional survey research, these nightmares may materialize *too late* (that is, after the close of data collection). As a result, much preventive care is given earlier to proper sampling, validated and reliable instrumentation, and methodical data collection. In qualitative research, the nightmares typically appear *early* in the game, and the analyst works on correcting them during further data collection. But these problems do not always appear spontaneously; they become clear only as the analyst examines the data as they are collected.

These are methodological worries. Usually one also has substantive concerns as well. What is really going on in the site so far? What's the big picture? Are there patterns and themes emerging?

Typically, interim data examining is done on the run or is done for some subsets or data but not for others, as, for example, in generating *pattern codes* (III.C) or writing *memos* (III.D). One needs an integrative exercise that obliges the analyst to audit *what* is known and *how well* it's known—to collate the main findings to date, to estimate the confidence held in those findings, and to list gaps, puzzles, and data that still need to be collected. The *interim site summary* serves these purposes.

Brief Description

The interim site summary is a provisional product of varying length (between 10 and 25 pages) which provides a synthesis of what the researcher knows about the site, and indicates what is still left to find out. It reviews findings, looks carefully at the quality of the data supporting them, and states the agenda for the next waves of data collection. The summary is the first attempt to derive a coherent account of the site.

Illustration

We have used interim summaries in several field studies. Taking the most recent one, Chart 9 presents the table of contents given to each researcher in the school improvement study as an outline for the interim site summary. Note that common formatting like this will enable cross-site comparability. This, in turn, might suggest promising avenues for other analysts for their next site visits, and it will certainly dredge up themes and concepts that exist at more than one site. In other words, the interim summary is the first formalized shot at cross-site analysis and has the big advantage of yielding emergent explanatory variables that can be checked out, rather than generated post hoc, as is often the case in cross-site analysis work.

Organizing the summary. Assuming that the codes have been derived from the research questions, it

Chart 9
Interim Site Summary Outline: Illustration

Table of Contents

A. The Site

1. Geography, setting
2. Demographics of community and district
3. Organization chart (showing key actors and their
    relationships)

B. Brief Chronology

1. Adoption (includes brief description of the innovation)
2. Planning (anything postadoption and pre-actual use with
    pupils)
3. Implementation up to present

C. Current Status of Research Questions

1. The innovation (deal with all subquestions; summarize
    what is currently known / if unknown, say so / if puzzles,
    describe them.)
2. The school as a social organization, preimplementation
3. The adoption decision
4. Site dynamics during implementation/transformation
5. New configurations/outcomes
6. Role of external and internal assistance

(CONCLUDE THIS SECTION WITH A LIST OF
UNCERTAINTIES/PUZZLES)

D. Causal Network

1. Graphic network of variables, at this site, seen as affecting
    outcomes (draws on pattern codes)
2. Discussion of network, including ties to other previous
    conceptual/empirical work on dissemination that seems
    especially salient or relevant

E. Brief Methodological Notes (how analysis was done, problems
    encountered, etc.; confidence in results, suggestions for next
    summary, etc.)

---

makes sense to scan the write-ups, looking for the primary codes for each research question, jotting down notes as one goes, then writing the summary. The problem with this procedure is that it chews up a lot of time. It is, however, the best way of synthesizing the findings to date and of becoming aware of the questions still unanswered or equivocally answered. Short of that, some analysts prefer to reread the write-ups carefully, then tackle the research questions *en bloc*. They then use the *pattern codes* to pull the material together for the summary. Doing the summary can also be the occasion for setting up a *data accounting sheet* (see Box III.F.a).

Using the summary. The interim summary exercise, as we have noted, forces the researcher to digest the materials in hand, to formulate a clearer sense of the site, *and* to self-critique the adequacy of the data that have been collected. This leads to next-step data collection, planning, and usually reformulation of codes and further analysis plans.

When the researcher is not working alone, but has colleagues working in other sites, the interim site summary is collectively helpful. Exchanging interim summaries among site researchers is a good means of bringing one another up to date. It also surfaces blind spots that are usually obvious to a second reader. And it provides good occasion for individual analysts to subject their emerging constructs or recurrent themes to a more thoroughgoing, critical review, both in their own and in their colleagues' minds. Finally, exchanging and discussing interim summaries is good cross-site medicine: People can get their visions better aligned,

Box III.F.a
Data Accounting Sheet: Illustration

Research Questions \ Data Sources	Background Materials			Informant Group 1					Informant Group 2, etc.			
	1	2	3	1	2	3	4	5	1	2	3	4
Q 1.1	✓	✓⁄	✓	N.A.		N.A.	N.A.	N.A.	N.A.	✓⁄		
Q 1.2	✓⁄		✓	✓	✓	✓⁄				✓⁄		✓
Q 1.3		N.A.	✓	✓⁄		✓⁄	✓	✓		✓⁄	✓⁄	
Q 2.1, etc.	N.A.	N.A.	N.A.	✓⁄	✓⁄							✓

Legend   blank = missing data   ✓ = data complete
          ✓⁄ = incomplete data   N.A. = not applicable

argue on the basis of shared and documented instances, and get resolution on fuzzy or shadowy issues that need clarification for the study as a whole to move forward.

Variations

Interim summaries can come in all shapes and sizes. The best ones are shapely and small—something on the order of 15-20 pages. (The outline shown earlier produced summaries of 25-35 pages.) Summaries can also be more specialized. For example, rather than collating material both for individual research questions and overarching themes, one might do two consecutive summaries, one reviewing the research questions and, a month or so later, another tackling the larger issues, which, by that time, should have become clearer.

Very brief summaries can be produced rapidly by the method outlined in Stiegelbauer et al. (1982): the case study interview. One fieldworker interviews another for an hour, using a standard set of questions. The interviewee prepares by reviewing all available data, but leaves them aside during the interview. The transcribed interview is then edited by the interviewee, referring back to available data as needed. This method is good at helping the fieldworker to be integrative, pulling together impressions of the site and core themes that are beginning to appear.

Advice

There is never a "good time" to draft interim summaries, because they usually get done on time stolen from data collection. Strategically, the best moment is about one-third of the way into fieldwork, when there are initial data to report and enough months left to

atone for the gaps or weaknesses the summary has revealed to the analyst.

In a multisite study, be sure to allow time for individual researchers to study and discuss one another's summaries. These are usually focused and informed interactions, springing from a common exercise, and they are typically more intellectual—and therefore more mind-expanding—than logistically oriented staff meetings. Discussion of interim summaries is also a fertile and risk-free arena for individual researchers to try out their sense of how the data—theirs and others'—are coming together, and to get the analytic juices flowing.

Time Required

Unless the researcher has a leisurely schedule, the exercise should be brief. Two days should do the basic job, one for review and note taking, the second for drafting. Reading and discussion takes another two or three hours. The most difficult part seems to be accepting the fact that interim summaries are *interim*, and likely to be incomplete, rapidly written, and fragmented. To do them "well" would require upwards of a week, which is too much time proportionate to the yield. Do them rapidly and dirtily, then *think* about them with your colleagues.

III.F.a Data Accounting Sheet

Doing an interim site summary can also be the opportunity for setting up a data accounting sheet. The sheet simply arrays each research question by informant or class of informants, as shown in Box III.F.a. As the legend shows, the analyst checks the cell when a set of data is in hand, with the ultimate objective of filling all the cells. This may look laborious, even overzealous, but it pays handsome rewards. In field research, one loses sight all too quickly of how much—and which sort of—data have been collected from different informants. Since these data are often corroborative—verifying an explanation given by others, testing an emerging thesis—their absence is more serious than just having "missing data," as in a quantitative survey. They are the evidential bricks upon which the analysis must be built.

The accounting sheet accompanies subsequent coding; the analyst checks off each cell while coding each interview, observation, or document. At the end of coding a particular site contact, a photocopy of the data accounting sheet can be attached to the contact summary form (III.A) and used in planning next-step data collection.

NOTES

1. There is a long and well-worked-out tradition of *photographs* as a form of data, which we will not explore in this book. For good treatments of problems of photographic data collection and analysis, see Bogdan and Biklen (1982), Becker (1978), Wagner (1979), and Templin (1982). On film and videotape, see the very thorough compendium of methods, with extensive annotated bibliography, by Erickson and Wilson (1982).

Similarly, data may sometimes appear in the form of *drawings* made by the fieldworker (for example, the set-up of a room) or by field informants (such as an organization chart). See section IV.A for further discussion.

Finally, data may also appear in the form of *documents* that have been collected from a field site. See Box III.A.a.

2. For a systematic approach to doing this, with illustrations, see also Turner (1981).

3. The classic reference on approaches to building a systematic set of codes (categories) is Lazarsfeld and Barton (1972).

4. The Q versus R distinction was first made by Stephenson (1953). For the reader new to the idea, an example may help. If one measured several different *attitudes* in a population of, say, college students, and correlated the attitude measures, one might find that conservative political attitudes were somewhat positively related to attitudes to beer drinking. That would be an R analysis.

Using the same data set, one could also see if there were clusters or families of students. It might turn out that the students fell into four main clusters: (a) conservative beer drinkers (the largest group); (b) progressive beer drinkers; (c) total abstainers; (d) middle-of-the-roaders. That would be a Q analysis.

Pattern codes for qualitative data can be used for either Q or R analysis.

5. For a good review of how people tend to cling to their beliefs, even when faced with countering evidence, see Ross and Lepper (1980); the best full-scale treatment is by Nisbett and Ross (1980).

IV

Within-Site Analysis

This chapter explores methods for drawing and verifying conclusions about a *single site*—the phenomena in a bounded context that make up a single "case study," whether that case is an individual in a setting, a small group, or a larger unit such as a department, organization, or community. They can be used either during or after data collection, but they tend to be most useful when the data base is substantially complete, and the work is in the stage of final analysis and write-up.

Displays

The idea of a *display* is very central to this book. By "display," we mean a spatial format that presents information systematically to the user. Newspapers, gasoline gauges, computer screens, and organization charts are all displays. They present information in a compressed, ordered form, so that the user can draw valid conclusions and take needed action.

For qualitative researchers, the typical mode of display has been *narrative text*. The text appears in the form of written-up field notes, which the analyst scans through, extracting coded segments and drawing conclusions. The analysis then usually goes to a second form of narrative text: a case study report.

Our experience tells us that narrative text alone is an extremely weak and cumbersome form of display. It is hard on analysts, because it is *dispersed,* spread out over many pages and is hard to look at; it is *sequential* rather than simultaneous, making it difficult to look at two or three variables at once; it is usually only *vaguely ordered;* and it can get monotonous and overloading. The same objections apply with even stronger force for final readers. Indeed, some observers (for example Mulhauser, 1975) have claimed that narrative text case studies are almost useless for policymakers, who cannot afford the time and energy required to comprehend a long account and draw conclusions for their work.[1]

The argument of this book, as an analogue to "You are what you eat," is *"You know what you display."* Valid analysis requires, and is driven by, displays that are as simultaneous as possible, are focused, and are as systematically arranged as the questions at hand demand. While such displays may sometimes be overloading, they will never be monotonous. Most important, the chances of drawing and verifying valid conclusions are very much greater than for narrative text.

Looking at typical work styles of quantitative researchers helps reinforce this claim. Quantitative researchers like to use statistical packages, such as SPSS and BMD, because they can compute a very large amount of data in a matter of seconds. But one often overlooks an equally important function of canned packages: They also *display* the data they compute in ways that (a) show the data and analysis in one place; (b) allow the analyst to see where further analyses are called for; (c) make it easier to compare different data sets; and (d) permit direct use of the results in a report. These virtues are commonplace to survey researchers, who simply *expect* to see computed data appear in histograms, correlation matrices, scatterplots, factor plots, and vector and box-and-whisker displays. The qualitative analyst has to hand-craft all such data displays. As yet there are no agreed-upon data set-ups among qualitative researchers, so each analyst has to invent his or her own. A major purpose of this book is to encourage the creation and dissemination of innovative and reliable data displays for qualitative data.

Building displays. Generating formats for displaying qualitative data turns out to be fairly easy and enjoyable. Formats can be as various as the imagination of the analyst, but they usually turn out as a summarizing *table* (matrix, chart, checklist) or *figure*. The data entries are also multiform: short blocks of text, quotes, phrases, ratings, abbreviations, symbolic figures, and so on.

Obviously, the type of format and shape of the entries depend on what the analyst wants to do with the display: eyeball data; carry out detailed analyses; set data up for another, more differentiated display; combine parallel data for a single site, or combine data from several sites; report findings. A good format will allow all these uses to some degree, but emphases will naturally vary.

This chapter emphasizes formats for displays of *single-site* data—but displays that can be easily folded into multiple-case analysis, which is discussed in the next chapter. The basic idea is that if the formats of displays for all sites in a multisite study are comparable, the work of the cross-site analyst will be immeasurably aided.

We can make several general points about the process of building appropriate displays. They will be illstrated more fully as we proceed. First, as we have suggested, it is an interesting and not overly demanding task. Second, creating a good display format usually requires a number of iterations (sometimes with new data collection intervening). Third, form follows function: Formats must always be driven by the research question(s) involved, and their associated codes.

Some typical display formats: Matrices. Let us take a look at some formats, explaining and labeling them as we go. Chart 10a is a matrix that blocks descriptive data segments around a particular event or experience, partitioning the data between early and later participants. Chart 10b shows what an excerpt from a filled-in table looks like.

The matrix excerpted in Chart 10b has words only—short quotes and summarizing remarks. Entries for each informant are simply *listed:* almost no attempt has been made to standardize the entries by categorizing the entries or scaling them along a continuum. Still, one should bear in mind that this table has boiled down about 8-10 page of coded transcriptions. To do that, a lot of data reduction and data weighting have gone on. The analyst has summarized the data for each informant, has *selected* illustrative excerpts from interviews, and has set up the rudiments of a *dichotomous scale* (the + and − entries in column 4).

Which functions are performed in this table? The five we mentioned earlier. The analyst can *eyeball* the table to see where the common threads and contrasts are. The table also allows for a more *refined analysis* and can lead to *new displays and analyses.* The table can be *compared with other, similarly formatted tables*—those for the same site, but during other time periods, and those from other sites. Finally, the table can figure in a case *report,* with a short interpretive analysis and commentary attached.

Chart 11a presents a checklist format calling for heavier data transformation by the case analyst. For the filled-in matrix, see Chart 11b. We have another 8-10 pages of interview notes reduced to a single summary table (of which the illustration is an excerpt). There are, as before, quotes and other summarizing remarks. But much reduction and standardization

has gone on to get the data ready for entry into this format. In particular, informants' responses have been pooled and *scaled* (absent to ideal). The table lets the analyst sum up the components of "preparedness" vertically, and also compare different roles' preparedness by looking at columns. During later cross-site analysis, one can assemble a full set of such tables, one for each site, and compare sites on each supporting condition, and/or on a total "preparedness" index. We discuss such examples later on in this and the following chapter.

Tables and charts can be more heavy-duty. Chart 12a shows a format calling for the researcher to address five related variables, to distinguish two of them according to time, to pool responses, to align some responses along an evaluative scale, and to explain the response pattern for each respondent type. The filled-in table (Chart 12b) shows how much can be packed into a single page. Nearly twenty pages of field notes have been assembled in this table. The data are more abstract: There are no quotes, and one finds *inferential* remarks, in the last two columns. The "consequences" and "explanations" are not direct transpositions of informants' remarks nor of researchers' observations. Rather, for any given "consequence," such as the one in the top row, "Users are helped administratively and substantively, feel obligated to do ECRI with minor adaptations," the researcher has looked at the data segments in the three preceding columns, checked to see if they covary in some patterned way, and drawn a second-order generalization. In this case (see first row) the themes of "relieving pressure," "easing schedules," "feeling backed up," "controlling fidelity," and users' positive assessment all suggested the reception of help and a sense of user obligation for reasonably faithful implementation. A similar process of inductive inference occurs for the "researcher explanations." Here, too, we see that the table collects data for easy viewing in one place, permits detailed analysis, and set the stage for later cross-site analysis.

In this preliminary overview, we have not discussed just how one goes about selecting/reducing data from field notes for entry into matrices. We shall return to this issue recurrently as we discuss specific display methods. Here we can say generally that the choice of data for entry must be driven by the particular row and column headings involved, *and* that keeping a precise record of the actual criteria and decision rules used (which will vary from display to display) is essential. See also the suggestions in Chapter VI on entering data.

Display formats: Figures. Now for some graphics. Figures are easily formatted and can hold a large amount of readily analyzable information.

(Text continues on page 89)

Chart 10a
User Behavior and Attitudes During Implementation (format)

Users	Feelings/Concerns	Understanding/ How it Looked	Parts ready/ Parts not ready	What doing/ Spending time on
Early Users				
E.U. 1				
E.U. 2				
E.U. 3, etc...				
Later Users				
L.U. 1				
L.U. 2				
L.U. 3, etc...				

Chart 10b

User Behavior and Attitudes at Masepa: Mid-November to May (second six months)

Users	FEELINGS/CONCERNS	UNDERSTANDING/ HOW IT LOOKED	PARTS READY/ PARTS NOT READY	WHAT DOING/ SPENDING TIME ON
R. Quint	Same as earlier—"not settling down"	Basic format clear Only 1-2 parts very clear, but appear arbitrarily put together	+"Survival cycle" in place -Errors in materials	Getting minimally through cycle; creating, borrowing materials
F. Morelly	"More comfortable — can do the minimum" Can't do it as pre-scribed, will have to make changes Low retention? going through skills too quickly	"Saw major features" "Looked disconnected"	+"Basic things in place.. not even looking at anything else"	Consolidating skills, practice time (not trying to add com-prehension skills) Beginning to add grammer, work sheets
L. Brent	"Some kids wasting time" Exhaustion Insecure and afraid Boredom: "every day the same thing" Doing too little of the program	Focusing on 2-3 com-ponents, even these not clear Aware that "more in it than I thought"	+Pieces of each component ready -Aware of not doing many key parts	Perfecting the basic cycle Trying to control actual mastery levels Trying to put together a group of core materials – misplacing, forgetting, not finding

Chart 11a
Conditions Supporting Preparedness: Checklist Format

Conditions	Users	Principals	Central Office Administration
Commitment			
Understanding			
Resources/Materials			
Skills			
Training			
Provisions for Follow-up			
School Adm. Support			
Central Office Support			

NOTE: Cell entries are as follows: absent, inadequate, adequate, ideal, and a quote or remark.

Chart 11b

Excerpt from a Checklist Matrix (Masepa site)

Conditions	Early Users (n=2) 1977-78	Later Users (n=6) 1978-80	Administrators 1977-78	Administrators 1978-80
Commitment	Adequate-Ideal Bayes: "I was committed." Quint: "I don't know why I stayed with it."	Inadequate-Adequate: "I had no choice." (3) "I was excited about it" (1) Why not? (2)	Bldg. Level Inadequate "I wasn't that sold on it" Central office Adequate	Bldg. Level: Adequate "pushing it hard" Central office: Adequate
Understanding	Absent:Didn't know what was going on" "All very confusing"	Absent--Inadequate: "Didn't know what it was all about" "Understandable" "Not bad, but not how it all fit together"	Bldg.Level: Absent "little jumbled" Central office: Absent-Inadequate "I don't know anything about reading"	Bldg.Level: Adequate Trained and experienced Central office: Absent Delegated to trainers
Materials	Absent: "Nothing was ready" "Had to do it all myself"	Ideal: Emily Boud just marveled at that" "Everything was ready"	N.A.	N.A.
Front-end Training	Inadequate;"I should have had more training" "They really only knew what they had done themselves"	Inadequate "Short and strenuous" "I was overwhelmed-- too much thrown at me" "Better than I had thought before starting in. It worked"	Absent	Adequate; short, intensive training at D/D site
Skills	Inadequate "Can't think of anything I was prepared in" "Just had the very basics"	Minimally Adequate "enough to get started with"	N.A.	N.A.

N.A. = not applicable

Chart 12a
Effects Matrix: Assistance Location and Types (format)

Location of Assistance	User's Assessment	Types Provided	Short-run Effects (user's "state")	Longer-run Consequences	Researcher's Explanations
Building Admin.					
Central Office Admin.					
Helping Teacher					
User-helping Teacher					
Teacher Users in Other Schools					
Trainers					

Chart 12b

Effects Matrix: Assistance Location and Types (Masepa site)

Location	User's Assessment	Types Provided	Short-Run Effects (User's 'State')	Longer-Run Consequences	Researcher Explanations
Building Admin.	++ ++ -| +	1. authorizes changes 2. eases schedules, assigns aides 3. controls fidelity 4. consults, offers solutions	1. relieves pressure, encourages 2. helps early implementation 3. feeling policed 4. feeling backed-up, substantially helped	Users are helped administratively and substantively, feel obliged to do ECRI with minor adaptations	admin. authority, servicing, availability and flexibility lead to sustained, faithful implementation model
Central Office Admin.	+ ++	1. promotes ECRI 2. answers building admin., trainers' requests	1. pressures non-users 2. bldg.admins. have material, administrative support	program is perceived as supported, assisted, 'protected' by central office	central office able to push program and answer requests, yet not perceived as main actor by users
Helping Teacher	++ + ++ ++ +|	1. provides materials 2. demonstrates, models 3. answers requests 4. encourages 5. circulates, controls	1. reduces effort, increases repertoire 2. trains, facilitates use 3. problems solved rapidly 4. maintains level of effort 5. ambivalent: helped yet coerced	new, experienced users receive systematic instruction, follow-up, materials; stay with program and are careful about making changes in it	personalized in-service mechanism, with both training and assistance allows for mastery and spread of ECRI in 'faithful' format
User-Helping Teacher Meetings	++ + + +	1. comparing practices with others 2. debugging, complaining 3. learning about new parts 4. encouragement	1. encourages, regulates 2. cathartic, solves short-run problems 3. expands repertoire 4. gets through rough moments	creates reference group, gives users a voice, solves ongoing problems and lowers anxiety	multi-purpose forum which consolidates use and users, defuses opposition
Teacher-Users in Other Schools; Target School	+ + +	1. sharing materials 2. exchanging tips, solutions 3. comparing, encouraging	1. increases stock 2. new ideas, practices; problems solved 3. motivates, stimulates	increases commitment, regulates use (decreases deviance)	additional source of assistance, which increases as numbers of users grows
Trainers in Target School, Other School	++ ++ + +	1. tips for presentation 2. solution to short-term problems 3. encourages 4. serves as successful model	1. facilitates practice 2. helps expand beyond core format 3. maintains effort 4. stimulates	reliable, unthreatening backup provided in school	elaborate and effective lateral network; trainers seen as peers

Legend: ++ = very effective
+ = effective
+\| = mixed response
\|\| = ineffective

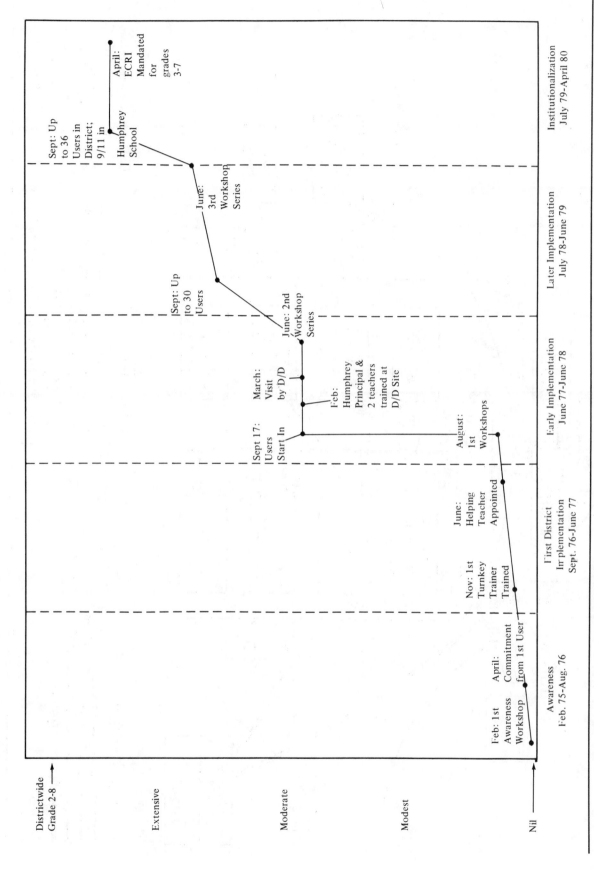

Districtwide
Grade 2-8 ⟶

Extensive

Moderate

Modest

Nil

April:
ECRI
Mandated
for
grades
3-7

Sept: Up
to 36
Users in
District;
9/11 in
Humphrey
School

June:
3rd
Workshop
Series

Sept: Up
to 30
Users

June: 2nd
Workshop
Series

March:
Visit
by D/D

Feb:
Humphrey
Principal &
2 teachers
trained at
D/D Site

Sept 17:
Users
Start In

August:
1st
Workshops

June:
Helping
Teacher
Appointed

Nov: 1st
Turnkey
Trainer
Trained

April:
Commitment
from 1st User

Feb: 1st
Awareness
Workshop

Awareness
Feb. 75-Aug. 76

First District
Implementation
Sept. 76-June 77

Early Implementation
June 77-June 78

Later Implementation
July 78-June 79

Institutionalization
July 79-April 80

Figure 5   Growth Gradient for ECRI Innovation at Masepa Site

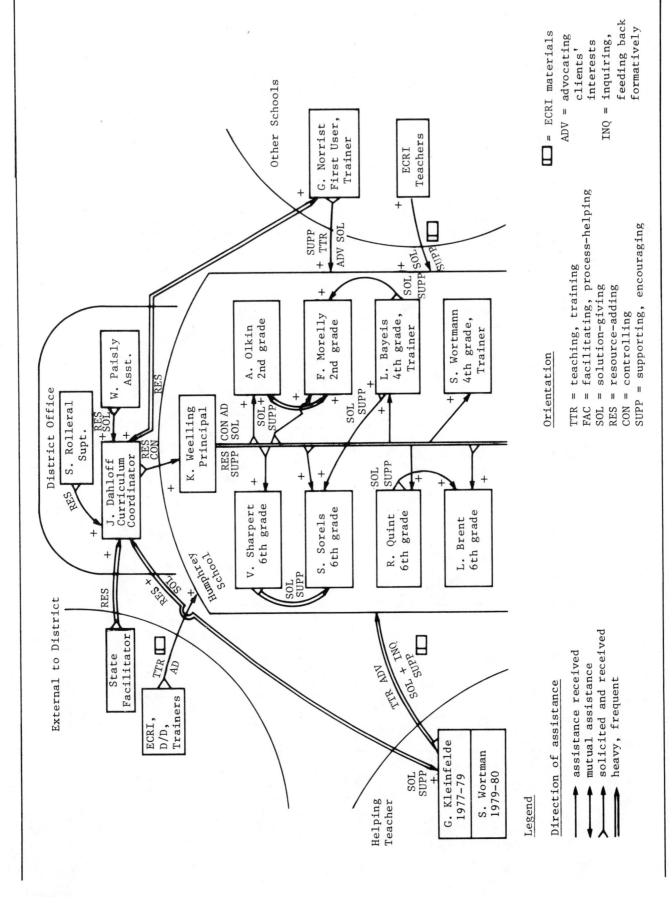

Figure 6   Illustration of Context Chart with Assistance Flows (Masepa site)

In Figure 5 we see a relatively simple display, designed to show the "growth gradient" of usage of an innovation at one site in our school improvement study. The line showing expansion of numbers of users is amplified/explained by brief descriptions of events related to that expansion.

In another part of our school study, we were interested in how to display the sources of "assistance" that users of an innovation received (and requested). Since assistance occurs in an organizational context, we decided on showing a quasi-organizational chart, with arrows showing where assistance came from and who received it. An illustration of how this worked out appears in Figure 6.

Figure 6 incorporates a very large amount of information. A look at the legend shows that the figure displays the organizational position of givers and receivers of help; depicts whether the assistance was solicited or not, mutual or not; labels the type of assistance received; and indicates how the receiver felt about it.

We can see immediately that a fair amount[2] of rather diverse assistance was received; that much of it was solicited; that the helping teachers and the principal were prime sources; and that virtually all assistance was positively received. Note too that there was much within-building help among teachers in the form of support and solution-giving. The figure was produced from about twenty pages of "longhand" data in the form of transcribed field notes. Note that the analyst had to reduce it into categories, ratings, and directional influences.

When the conceptual focus of the study changes, so do the graphics. Figure 7, for example, from another study (Huberman, 1981b), depicts linkage patterns and knowledge flows resulting from the creation of a teacher center. Note that several analytic avenues can be pursued in a simple figure like this one without overwhelming the reader. This figure handles strength of linkage, multiplicity of linkage, directional influence, and knowledge types.

Advice. When should formats be generated? If the format is at hand during data collection it helps save energy, cutting by 60 percent at least the total time from field note transcription to filled-out table or figure. But there are at least two cautions here. First, qualitative *data* evolve; later accounts round out, qualify, put in perspective, and disqualify earlier ones. Analysts don't march through data collection as in survey methodology; they scout around, sleuth, and take second and third looks. So entering the data to a set format as they are collected can get rapidly self-defeating. The displays will probably have to be redone at least once, and the total time involved begins to mount up.

Second, display *formats* nearly always evolve too. The later ones are more data sensitive than the earlier ones, as technologies and relationships come clearer. For instance, the headings in the display format of Chart 10a came from relationships observed in the course of data collection; the display allows the within-case (and later, the cross-case) analyst to test those relationships more rigorously. One might have built such a format directly from a conceptual framework, but real clarity on the workability of any framework typically comes later, when the empirical data begin to take shape.

Bear in mind that formatting is a decisive operation; it determines which variables are to be analyzed in which ways. If a variable isn't on the format sheet, it doesn't get compared to another variable. Displays can be excellent ways of summarizing and comparing findings within and across cases, but they are also straitjackets; they can bully the data into shapes that are superficially comparable across cases but that, on closer inspection, may be comparing intrinsically different things on dimensions that turn out to be trivial. All the more reason, then, to generate the formats near the end of data collection when they can be more contextually and empirically grounded.

Note: For any given research question or issue, using the same set of variables, *many* different displays can be developed. Each makes somewhat different assumptions; each has advantages and costs. We give an example of the typical pluralism among possible display types in section IV.B (p. 96-99).

Expect to make several passes or iterations before the format of the display is working right. The only way to test a proposed format is to start entering data. Unworkable or confusing formats, or those that don't incorporate all the relevant data, will show themselves rapidly.

As you enter data, be aware of, and *jot down* your criteria or decision rules: how ratings or judgments are arrived at; the basis for selecting particular quotes; how you balance reports from different people.

Stay open on the question of whether the format you use for analysis should be the same one used for reporting. The usual answer is yes, but sometimes a display will be used for intermediate purposes, and will not necessarily be shown to readers of the final report. For further advice on matrix building and use, see Chapter VI.

Time required. Creating formats is usually a matter of a few minutes. Revising them as the early items of data are entered is also quick work. What takes time is *data entry* itself. Coded data segments have to be located in the transcribed field notes; they have to be clustered, or notes taken summarizing key content.

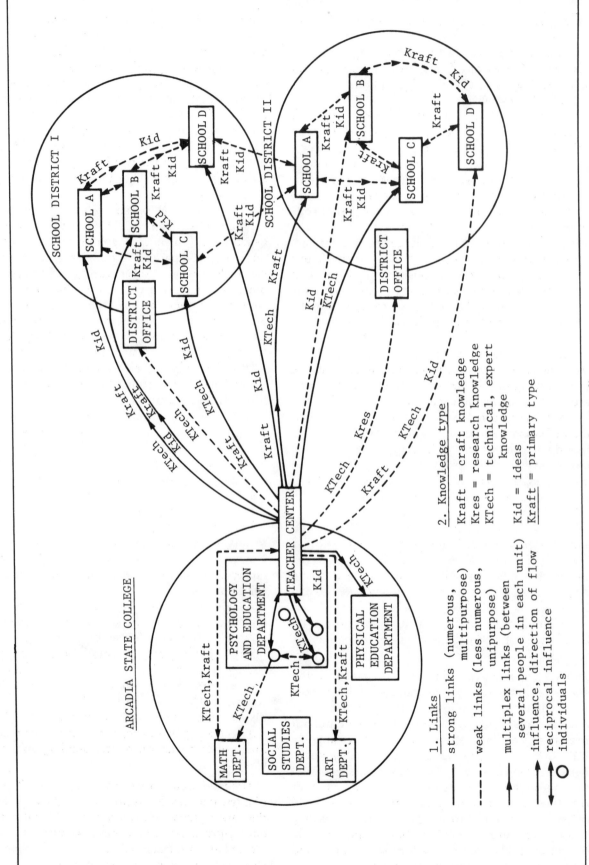

Figure 7 Linkage Patterns and Knowledge Flows Related to Teacher Center Activity: Arcadia

(The speed at which this is done will depend on the technology of storage and retrieval being used—see our earlier comments in Box III.B.c.) Usually, in addition, some data transformation and selection may be involved: doing ratings, making judgments, picking quotes.

Generally, of course, the time taken to enter data will depend on (a) the number of variables or dimensions in the display; (b) the number of respondents; and (c) the kind and number of transformations. As a general indication for reasonably experienced researchers, a display like that shown in Chart 10a can be expected to take 3-5 hours; one like Chart 12b will occupy perhaps 810 hours. Analysts vary, but we suspect that for most people, a traditional narrative-text display for the same data set would not be accomplished more quickly. And the formats illustrated here, in our view, very substantially increase both the readability and the analytic power of the results.

There may be shortcuts, which we have begun to try out. For example, one can collect raw data, in transcribed or freehand form, and enter them *immediately* into a previously formatted matrix or figure. The ratings and data transformations get made on the spot, corresponding to the "value labels" on the format. Doing this by hand, however, is very time-consuming; we believe it will require adaptation of existing word-processing programs using either mainframe or microcomputer facilities, a task we are now pursuing. Just as interactive data analysis programs for quantitative data permit the "sculpting" of analysis and display frames to fit the shape of the data as they undergo progressive transformations, so adapted word-processing (and data-base) programs can enable reformatting as data are entered and considered.

The time required for analyzing data displays and writing associated text (activities that, as we have noted, are intimately intertwined) usually runs to 20 percent or less of the time required for data entry. Well-formatted displays, with data entries in which one has confidence, almost "write the text" for the analyst, in our experience.

This discussion of displays and formatting has served as a general introduction to the substance of this chapter, which is concerned with methods for within-site analysis. We now move on to specific methods.

Since ten major methods (and nine supplementary ones in boxed format) are involved, some advance organizers may help. The methods are roughly arranged from simple to complex, and from sheerly descriptive to more broadly explanatory. We begin with the *context chart* and the *checklist matrix,* both used for straightforward description. Then we consider matrices that are ordered or arranged in some systematic way: *time-ordered matrix, role-ordered matrix,* and *conceptually clustered matrix.*

How can one arrive at good explanations? We discuss the *effects matrix,* which looks at outcomes or results of a process, then turn to the *site dynamics matrix,* a way of seeing "what leads to what." The next method is the *event listing,* a systematic method of arranging data to see underlying chronological flows. Then we turn to *causal networks,* which pull independent and dependent variables and their relationships together into a coherent picture. Finally, we consider the ultimate test of explanatory power: *making and testing predictions.*

A note: We'd like to make two general points about analysis of matrices and other displays. It's possible to make suggestions about how to analyze data in a display (looking down columns, across rows, comparing certain cells, and so on), and our sections VII.A and VII.B on tactics of analysis are designed to help with this. We should also emphasize that the act of *writing* text as one ruminates over the meaning of a display is itself a focusing and forcing device that guides further analysis. Perhaps we can profitably quote Lofland (1971, p. 127) here:

> It seems, in fact, that one does not truly begin to think until one concretely attempts to render thought and analysis into successive sentences. . . . For better or for worse, when one actually writes he begins to get *new* ideas, to see new connections, to remember material that he had not remembered before. . . . One is never truly inside a topic—or on top of it—until he faces the hard task of explaining it to someone else.

Or, as Mills (1959) has pointed out in his fine essay "On Intellectual Craftsmanship," writing begins in the context of discovery, then must needs turn to the context of *presentation.* That effort turns us, often, back to the context of discovery once more. Writing, in short, does not come after analysis; it *is* analysis, happening as the writer thinks through the meaning of data in the display. Writing is thinking, not the report of thought.

IV.A CONTEXT CHART

Analysis Problem

Qualitative research is usually focused on the words and actions of people that occur in a specific *context.* Though it is possible to collect purely "individual" data (for example, through interviews, observations, or analysis of tape-recorded speech), most qualitative researchers believe that a person's behavior has to be understood in context, and that context cannot be ignored or "held constant."

The context can be seen as immediately relevant aspects of the situation (where the person is physically, who else is involved, what the recent history of their contact is, and so on), as well as the relevant aspects of the social system in which the person is functioning (a classroom, a school, a department, a company, a family, an agency, a local community). To focus solely on individual behavior without attending to contexts amounts to "context-stripping" with attendant risks of misunderstanding the meaning of events. Take the individual behavior noted below:

> Bill picks up telephone, listens for a while, says, "No, Charlie, I don't think we should do that. See you tomorrow. Bye."

Your interpretation of this event, without context, can be limited only to matters such as individual decisiveness, economy of speech, and the like. So, as you read this, you probably constructed a context to help you interpret it. Reflect on that context for a minute, and decide what the event means.

Now consider some alternative contexts:

> Charlie is Bill's attorney, and they are going to court tomorrow. (The issue is something about a strategy to be followed, but Bill is certainly not a passive client.)

> Charlie is Bill's boss. (What inferences do you make about the relationship? Is Bill giving requested advice, or in effect vetoing something?)

> Charlie is Bill's subordinate, who is proposing that someone new should be invited to a meeting. (It feels like an abrupt dismissal.)

> Charlie is Bill's wife, calling from out of town to suggest meeting for a gallery visit before dinner tomorrow. (What kind of a marriage is implied? Distant? Routine? Independence-respecting?)

Understanding contexts is usually critical. Even that adjective is too mild. We should quote here the title of Mishler's (1979) thoughtful article on this topic: "Meaning in Context: Is There Any Other Kind?" Contexts drive the way we understand the meaning of events, or, as Mishler notes, "Meaning is always within context and contexts incorporate meaning."

The problem a qualitative researcher faces is how to map the social context of individual actions economically and reasonably accurately, without getting overwhelmed with detail. A context chart is one way to accomplish these goals.

Brief Description

A context chart maps in graphic form the interrelationships among the roles, groups (and, if appropriate, organizations) that go to make up the context of individual behavior.

Illustration

Most people do their daily work in organizations: They have superiors, peers, subordinates; they do work that differs in important respects from that of other people; they have different relationships with a range of people occupying other roles in their social vicinity. Context charts can be drawn for people in families, or informal groups, or communities, but more often than not, researchers are interested in the organizational context.[3]

Suppose that you were interested, as we were, in organizations called schools and school districts—and with the general problem of how innovations enter and are implemented in those organizations. What are some simple ways of displaying our understanding of those contexts?

Building the display. Such a context chart ought to reflect the ubiquitous characteristics of organizations: authority/hierarchy and division of labor. So it ought to show who has formal authority over whom, and what the role names are. But that doesn't tell us very much: We should also know about the quality of the working *relationships* between people in different roles.

And since we are talking about the introduction of an innovation, the display should show us who advocated it, who is actually using the innovation, and people's attitudes toward it (regardless of whether they are using it or not). The display should also show us how the specific school we are studying is embedded in the larger district organization. Above all, we need a display that will not overload us with information, but will give us a clear, relevantly simplified version of the immediate social environment.

Figure 8 shows how these requirements were met after a fieldworker made a first visit to Tindale East, a high school involved in implementing a new reading program through the departments of English, science, and math. The analyst has selected out from the larger organization the roles and groups that are most critical for understanding the context. District office roles are above, school roles below. For each individual, we have a name, age (a feature the analyst thought was important in understanding working relationships and career aspirations), a job title, whether the individual was a user of the innovation or not, and his or her attitude to the innovation (positive, ambivalent, neutral). Special codes were also applied when the individual was an innovation advocate or influenced implementation strongly. The relationships between individuals are also characterized (positive, ambivalent, neutral). Note that once past the upper echelons the display simply counts individuals, without giving detail (a secondary context chart at the level of individual teachers was also developed, but is not shown here).

Entering the data. The analyst consults field notes and available organization charts and documents.

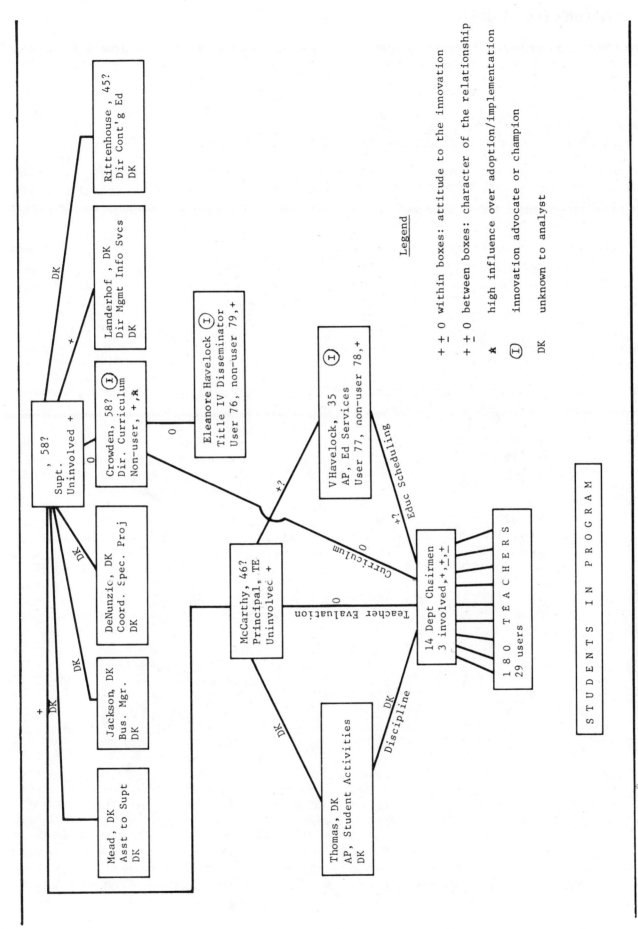

Figure 8   Context Chart for Tindale East High School and District

This is a preliminary mapping, subject to later correction. The decision rules look like this:

(1) If there is ambiguous or unknown information, enter "DK."
(2) A relationship rating (how X gets along with Y) should not be *disconfirmed* by the other party to the relationship, though it need not be directly confirmed.
(3) Similarly, the "innovation advocate" and "high influence" ratings should only be given if there is at least one confirmation and no disconfirmations.
(4) For information such as job title, number of persons, etc., assume accuracy for the moment and enter it.

Analyzing the data. Looking at lines of authority, we can see that only one central office person (Crowden) has direct authority over department chairmen as they work on the innovation; we see also that Crowden is not only an advocate but has high influence over implementation, and seems to have a license from the superintendent to do this. The department chairs, it appears, have three other masters, depending on the immediate issue involved (discipline, teacher evaluation, scheduling). Since, in this case, the innovation does involve scheduling problems, it's of interest that V. Havelock is not only an advocate, but has actually used the innovation and is positive toward it. We might draw the inference that Crowden serves as a general pusher, using central office authority, and V. Havelock aids directly with implementation issues; the field notes support this. We can also see that principal McCarthy is (a) not accountable to the superintendent for curriculum issues, and (b) has a good relationship with V. Havelock. Perhaps McCarthy gets his main information about the innovation from Havelock, and thus judges it positively.

We can also see that the 3 chairs involved are ambivalent to positive about the innovation, a finding that will require more data than displayed here to elucidate. A next-level context chart will have to display the 3 chairs, plus the 29 users and *their* attitudes.

So, in general, the chart shown in Figure 8 helps us to place the behavior of individuals (such as Crowden or V. Havelock) in a clear context, and understand its meaning. For example, when Crowden, discussing the innovation, says, "It is not to be violated; its implementation is not based on the whim of a teacher at any moment in class, and its success is not dependent upon charismatic teachers," the chart helps us understand that this very prescriptive stance is backed up with direct authority over department chairs for curriculum issues—an authority that is accepted neutrally. So it is not surprising when a department chair from Tindale says, "If you want to depart from the guide, ask me and also tell me why you want to do it and how it will fulfill the guide's objectives. The Tindale West department chair and I mostly decide no before teachers even ask to make changes."

Variations

Still staying with organizational context charts, there are naturally many possible variations. For example, working groups can be enclosed with circles (in this example, all the district office managers plus principal served as the "superintendent's cabinet").

Circles can also be drawn enclosing *informal* groups. In one study of a rural high school, we asked people to draw pictures of the faculty as they saw it, and interviewed them about the meaning of their drawings. This helped us find six major informal subgroups among the faculty. They included the "old new guard" (progressive teachers who had been around a good while); "boy coaches" ("the last great disciplinarians in the world"); "girl coaches"; "newcomers"; "structuralists" ("a 1950-1960 kind of teacher"); and "goners" ("people who might just as well be in a labor union . . . at 3:30 they're gone"). We also found one person, James Colley, who was a group unto himself, according to several respondents.

Dotted lines can be used to show informal influence. Linkages to other organizations in the environment can be shown. In an organizational context that has shown considerable change over a short period of time, successive context charts can be drawn (for example, in our study, the structure and relationships in an alternative school changed rather substantially for each of the three years of its existence, and we needed three charts). The specific functions or types of behavior involved in the relationships between roles can be identified on the chart as well (see Section IV.A.a).

Our illustration emphasized certain *social-system* aspects of the context. It is sometimes important to map the *physical* aspect of an immediate context (for example, a classroom, with indications of the teacher's desk, resource files, student tables and chairs, entrances, and so on) if we are to understand the ebb and flow of events in the setting.

Advice

Keep in mind the study's main research questions, and design the context chart to display the information most relevant to them.

Remember that you are *not* simply drawing a standard organizational chart, but mapping salient properties of the context. Remember, too, that your chart will not be exhaustive or complete: it is a collection of organizational *fragments* or excerpts, so to speak. (Figure 6 does not include custodians, secretaries, or the immediate subordinates of most of the district office personnel.)

Use context charts *early* during fieldwork to summarize your first understandings and to locate questions for next-step data collection. Colleagues' reactions are often useful in this respect.

Time Required

If the fieldwork has involved focused attention to the issues mapped in a context chart, one of the size shown in our illustration can ususlly be put together quite rapidly—in an hour or less. You usually find that an implicit chart has been materializing in your head as you talk to different people in the site, and drawing it, filling in the associated details, quickly makes it explicit.

IV.A.a Variable-Specific Context Chart

Sometimes an analyst may be preoccupied with understanding a particular variable in a context, especially one that involves inter-role transactions of some kind. Context charts can be easily elaborated to accommodate this need.

Figure 6 shows a context chart that focuses in detail on the question of "assistance"—the help given and received between different roles as people struggle with the implementation of an innovation. Note that the chart uses a defined list of assistance "orientations" (teaching/training, facilitation, and so on), and shows who gave help to whom, with what sort of orientation. The arrows also show whether the assistance was received, solicited and received, or done mutually. Double lines show heavy or frequent assistance. Another code shows how the assistance was perceived by the receiver. The chart also notes other relevant social units beyond the school (district office, state facilitator, other schools, and so on) that gave assistance.

With such a display, the analyst can see patterns rapidly. For example, the helping teachers and the curriculum coordinator form a mutually helping team; the helping teachers provide strong assistance to teachers of many different sorts; there is a good deal of peer assistance among teachers; the principal too gives assistance, but of a different sort (more control, advocacy, resource giving, along with support and solution giving).

In writing up this chart, the analyst referred to field notes for *when* assistance was provided (early, later, stabilized implementation periods) and could see

trends in types given. The chart itself could be modified to include time periods.

IV.B CHECKLIST MATRIX

Analysis Problem

Let's look at some contrasting stereotypes of survey and field researchers. The survey researcher is a purposeful, industrious and efficient worker who designs instrumentation in advance, marches into a site to administer it to all the people in the sample, marches out, gets the data into readily retrievable files, and analyzes the output. By contrast, the field researcher comes off as a near-aimless loiterer who throws together some orienting instrumentation, hangs around a field site for days, collects all manner of data that may not look remotely connected to the key independent variables, fiddles with the instrumentation, talks to some people more than to others, does observations without an observation schedule, gradually accumulates pages upon pages of words, then spends days coding and entering them onto a complicated homemade chart for analysis—and does all this for only one or two sites, to boot.

Of course we could turn these stereotypes upside down, speaking of the methodological rigidity and blindness of the survey researcher, and the "groundedness" of the fieldworker alert to local reality. There are grains of truth in stereotypes, whichever way they're slanted. We note here, though, that there are some instances when field researchers behave like surveyors by collecting predetermined data from all key respondents and entering them in a prespecified form for analysis. This usually happens under conditions such as these:

- The analyst believes in the conceptual importance of the variable, regardless of its empirical payoff.
- The variable can be easily unbundled into distinct indicators or components that are codable, and can be built into an interview schedule.
- The analyst needs the variable badly (for example, as an outcome measure with enough variance to permit sorting out main predictors).
- Analysis occurs in the context of a multiple-case study that requires comparability of formatting and measurement.
- The analyst is interested in relating field data to survey measures of the same variable.

When the first two, or more, of these conditions are at hand, the field researcher is likely to collect checklist-type data and to analyze them in the form of a *checklist matrix*.

Brief Description

A checklist matrix is a format for analyzing field data that can be combined into a summative index or scale.

Often, but not always, the scale has a normative function; cases with more of the items on the scale tend to be "better" in some way the researcher considers important. The basic principle behind the checklist matrix is that it organizes several components of a single, coherent variable.

An Illustration

Let's look first at a checklist for assessing "preparedness" prior to executing a new practice. In our school improvement study, we met most of the conditions described on the previous page. User and administrator preparedness were conceptually tied to implementation success in our conceptual framework, and had strong construct validity in the literature. It also made good common sense that people do better those things for which they are prepared. Empirical studies had broken preparedness down to distinct components that correlate well with good project execution. In short, the variable had a lot going for it. In addition, we were studying twelve cases and needed parallel measures of the variable; we were also trying to commune with a large survey that had a "preparedness" checklist in its questionnaire.

We did have some doubts about the variable, and about the appropriateness of measuring it in checklist form. We saw fieldwork as the ideal way of resolving those doubts. It seemed to us that the preparedness-good execution logic was mechanistic. We also suspected that other variables were getting mixed up with the measure. For example, a highly experienced user could look well prepared, although the technical training itself may have been dismal. In addition, we thought that some aspects of preparedness mattered more than others, so perhaps checklist items needed to be differentially weighted. Finally, we believed that many unpredictable and institution-level factors were at play during project execution. So a largely *individual* and *technical* factor such as preparedness could hardly account by itself for varying degrees of successful use of the new practice. These were all things that on-site observation and interviews with new and older users could capture far better than reliability and validity coefficients. In this way, field study measures could inform and qualify survey measures.

The display. Chart 13a shows a checklist matrix with data from one of the field sites (this is the completely filled-out version of the format shown in Chart 11a). The rows give ratings and quotes for each component of preparedness—each "supporting condition" on the table—and the columns show responses for each respondent group. The quotes are useful devices; notice how they both help *justify* and *illustrate* the rating. In this way, qualitative data can put flesh on the more bony survey measures—provided the two measures are parallel.

In the course of data collection, the analyst found that later users and administrators were far better prepared than earlier ones. That contrast then drove subsequent data collection on this issue and got built into the format. In a conventional survey, data from earlier and later actors might have been pooled, with the result that a misleading average checklist score could have emerged, *unless* the survey team thought *in advance* that late levels of preparedness would be different from earlier ones, or unless the survey analyst picked up on a bimodal distribution across sites and began to sniff around for its cause.

Entering the data. The analyst reviews relevant sections of the write-ups, aided by assigned codes, forms a general judgment or rating as to the level of adequacy of the component at hand, and locates relevant quotes. Notice that the quotes and the ratings are *kept together* in the cell. The idea here—an important one, we think—is that ratings only tell you *how much* there is of something, not what that something *means.* Two or three brief quotes per cell are enough to communicate—and to help another analyst judge, by going back to the write-ups, whether the rating is justified.

Analyzing the data. It is possible now to look down the columns of the matrix and form a general idea of the level of preparedness for, say, early users. The analysis tactic here is one of *noting patterns, themes* (see section VII.A.2 for more on this). Here it looks sketchy in terms of understanding, materials, training, and skills, but stronger on such items as commitment, support, and debugging. The picture is one of administrative enthusiasm and user bewilderment—not exactly superb "preparedness." (Note that simply adding up the ratings for a column is not necessarily the best way to proceed.)

Similarly, one can compare one column with another—early and later users, for example. One can also go across a row (for example, "understanding") and note how different users stacked up on that particular component of the checklist.

Variations. For any given research question and set of variables, there can be many different displays generated. Each has advantages and limitations. Let's illustrate: The research question here asked whether conditions supporting "preparedness" were assured before implementation began. The variables included a set of "conditions," with data for users and administrators, for "early" and "late" time periods. Chart 13a is only one possible display. Charts 13b, 13c, and 13d show three others.

The cell entries in Chart 13b are a rating of "strong," "moderate," "weak," or "absent," accompanied by

Chart 13a
Checklist Matrix: Presence of Conditions Supporting
Preparedness (Masepa site)

Conditions	Early Users (n=2) 1977-78	Later Users (n=6) 1978-80	Administrators 1977-78	Administrators 1978-80
Commitment	Adequate-Ideal Bayeis: "I was committed." Quint: "I don't know why I stayed with it."	Inadequate-Adequate: "I had no choice (3) "I was excited about it" (1) Why not? (2)	Bldg. Level Inadequate (3) "I wasn't that sold on it" Central office Adequate	Bldg. Level: Adequate "pushing it hard" Central office: Adequate
Understanding	Absent:Didn't know what was going on" "All very confusing"	Absent--Inadequate: "Didn't know what it was all about" "Understandable" "Not bad, but not how it all fit together"	Bldg.Level: Absent "little jumbled" Central office: Absent-Inadequate "I don't know anything about reading"	Bldg.Level: Adequate Trained and experienced Central office:Absent Delegated to trainers
Materials	Absent: "Nothing was ready" "Had to do it all myself"	Ideal: "Emily Boud just marveled at that" "Everything was ready"	N.A.	N.A.
Front-end Training	Inadequate:"I should have had more training" "They really only knew what they had done themselves"	Inadequate "Short and strenuous" "I was overwhelmed-too much thrown at me" "Better than I had thought before starting in. It worked"	Absent	Adequate: short, intensive training at D/D site
Skills	Inadequate "Can't think of anything I was prepared in" "Just had the very basics"	Minimally Adequate "enough to get started with"	N.A.	N.A.
Time allocation	Minimally Adequate	Minimally Adequate	N.A.	N.A.
Ongoing Inservice	Adequate:Meetings, consultant aid, demonstrations	Adequate: same provisions. Also, helping teacher has her office at ,Humphrey school.	N.A.	N.A.
Debugging	Adequate:helping teacher weekly meetings	Adequate;helping teacher monthly meetings	Adequate :periodic meetings with trainers	Adequate;periodic meetings with trainers
School administrator support	Perceived as Adequate (in fact lukewarm): "very important" "never would have made it without... the principal behind it"	Adequate-Ideal: "I'm sold on it...I try to help out" "It's very important that Mr. Welling is sold on the program"	N.A.	N.A.
Central office support	Adequate-Ideal "I didn't push it that hard [but]...I wanted to see it in." "Never would have made it without Jeanne behind us"	Adequate-Ideal "Jeanne and I agree on everything" "She sold me on it... nothing but good vibes about it"	N.A.	N.A.

N.A. = not applicable

a brief explanatory phrase showing what the condition consisted of, as the respondent saw it. (Under "materials," for example, a user might have said, "The basic notebook, plus the file cards and prep sheets.") If a respondent gave no illustrative example, the cell entry is NE (no example).

In Chart 13b the analyst has chosen to stay concrete. We can follow the responses of a specific *individual* easily across all conditions rather than pooling and deidentifying them as in Chart 13a. Chart 13b also bunches early and late responses, so that an easy user-administrator comparison can be made per condition at each time period. But note, we will have much more detailed, diverse data, rather than a general judgment such as "adequate" for any given condition, as we had in Chart 13a.

Chart 13c takes a still different cut. The cell entries here are the names of *conditions*, together with the N

Chart 13b
Checklist Matrix on Preparedness (alternate format 1)

Conditions

		Commitment	Understanding	Materials	Training	Etc.
EARLY	Users 1 2					
	Admin- 1 istrators 2					
LATER	Users 1 2 3 4 5 6					
	Admin- 1 istrators 2					

98

Chart 13c
Checklist Matrix on Preparedness (alternate format 2)

Conditions	Users		Administrators	
	Early	Late	Early	Late
Missing				
Weak				
Adequate				
Strong				

of users or administrators reporting. An asterisk appears near condition names seen as "most" missing, and a number symbol (#) near those seen by respondents as critical for success.

Chart 13c thus sorts the *conditions* by *role* and *time period* according to how "present" they were, and lets us see which were important. It also emphasizes somewhat more the early-late dimension within role (users, administrators). But note that we have now lost the data for individuals that appeared in Chart 13b. It is also much harder to track the results for any particular condition. Matrix construction is full of this sort of tradeoff.

Chart 13d deemphasizes the differentiation among administrators and users, stresses the early-late difference, and above all takes a decisive turn toward the *dynamics* of conditions—how and why they are important. It also brings in the researcher's view of the situation. We retain the idea of specific examples, but we have lost identifiable individuals, and we have lost the capacity to make easy comparisons between users and administrators at either time period.

Any data set can be displayed in many different ways. Each way gains you some things and loses you others. The moral: Don't close up too rapidly on display format. Try several iterations; get colleague ideas and reactions.

Components in a checklist may sometimes have a meaningful structure. For example, they may fall into several clusters (see Huberman & Miles, 1984, for a clustered checklist of factors in "institutionalization" of innovations), or be ordered from peripheral to central or weak to strong.

Columns can also refer to *levels* of a site (for example, classroom, school, district).

Especially for exploratory work, it pays to have a column headed simply "Remarks," where relevant commentary of any sort can be included to aid understanding.

Advice

Don't close up too quickly on a matrix format. Consider several possibilities; ask a colleague for ideas. Look at what different formats give you and what they withhold from you.

Checklist matrices are easy to use when you know what a variable is about, and you have rather crisply specified indicators of its presence. Under these circumstances, it makes sense to collect early data on the indicators, and to use those data to refine and improve the matrix format.

In fact, a checklist format itself does a good deal to make data collection more systematic, enable verification, encourage comparability, and permit simple quantification where that is appropriate.

You must be explicit about the decision rules you follow in (a) selecting quotes and (b) making judgments or ratings. Otherwise colleagues or readers will be dubious about your conclusions—and you will probably come to doubt them yourself.

Keep quotes and ratings together in the matrix so their mutual pertinence can be assessed.

Time Required

If the written-up field notes have been coded to permit easy retrieval of segments related to each component of a check-list matrix, and fewer than a dozen or so informants are involved, the display can be assembled in one to three hours and analyzed rapidly. Most of the hard work—defining the components of the matrix—will have been done back during data collection.

We should reemphasize that the time estimates given are in our experience a reasonable range. Where

Chart 13d
Checklist Matrix on Preparedness (alternate format 3)

Conditions	Early			Later		
	Examples[a]	How important?[b]	Why important?[c]	Examples	How important?	Why Important?
Commitment						
Understanding						
Materials						
Training						
Etc.						

a. Specific illustrations, marked with A or U for administrator or user, respectively.
b. Rating—very, quite, somewhat, or not important.
c. Explanations of reasons for importance of condition, given by respondent (A or U) or researcher (R).

a particular use of the method falls in that range will depend on the researcher's skill, the theory underlying the study, the particular research question at hand, the completeness of the data, the number of informants, the number of sites, and so on.

IV.C TIME-ORDERED MATRIX

Analysis Problem

Life is chronology. One major strength of qualitative data is that they can be collected over time, following the course of events rather than being restricted to snapshots. Sequences, processes, flows can be tracked. But how to display data about time-linked events in such a way that we can readily grasp and understand (and perhaps explain) what was happening?

Brief Description

A time-ordered matrix has its columns arranged by time period, in sequence, so that one can see *when* particular phenomena occurred. The basic principle is chronology.

Illustration

In our school improvement study, we were concerned with how an innovation was changed and transformed over time during an implementation period that lasted for several years. We predicted that most innovations would show such changes as they were adapted to the needs of users and the pressures of the local situation.

Building the display. An easy way to proceed is to break the innovation down into specific components or aspects, using these as rows of the matrix. The columns of the matrix are time periods, from early through later use. If a change in a component had occurred during the time period, one could enter a short description of the change.

Chart 14a illustrates how this might look. The innovation is a work experience program for high school students. The components were those specified by the original developer of the program, as analyzed by the "configuration checklist" method developed by Loucks, Bauchner, Crandall, Schmidt, and Eiseman (1983). Note that these components, however, do not necessarily exhaust important aspects of the innovation; these are listed under "other aspects," such as time and credits, or student selection. Such aspects appear, typically, after initial fieldwork that yields the researcher direct experience with the use and meaning of the innovation.

The time periods, appearing as columns, include first the initial planning period, since one might expect that changes would occur as this innovation, a relatively demanding and complex one, was being readied for use. The three succeeding school years follow.

Entering the data. As we have noted, one needs to be very clear about what, exactly, goes into a matrix cell—and what the rules are for deciding on that entry. In this case, the analyst is looking for *changes* in the innovation, component by component. Those changes can be located in the coded field notes of interviews with innovation users, who were asked specifically whether they had made any changes in the innovation's standard format. Follow-up probes asked for parts that

Chart 14a

Time-Ordered Matrix: Changes in the CARED Innovation (a work-experience program)

DEVELOPER COMPONENTS	PLANNING PERIOD Jan.-June 77	FIRST YEAR 77-78	SECOND YEAR 78-79	THIRD YEAR 79-80
Individualization			Some tendency to "batch" students, encourage standard projects, etc.	
Student responsibility and time use	Added logs/time sheets	Added "accountability" scheme for discipline	Added system of passes for students to leave room.	Refusal to accept late work; students were failed.
Direct exposure to work experience				Some tendency to reduce individualization/exploration aspects; more long-term placements; convenience location of jobs.
Program requirements/ curriculum		Added direct instruction on basic skills, separate from job.	More competencies required	More competencies and projects required.
Learning strategies	Did not include employer seminars; intensified "competencies" experience	Wrote new "competencies". Discarded learning style instrument New basic skills mat'ls.	Student learning plan only 1 semester; more basic skills emphasis	Journal more routine communication; less counseling emphasis
Parental involvement		Parent advisory committee added.	Advisory committee mtgs dwindled and stopped.	Reduced level of detail in reporting to parents
OTHER ASPECTS Time and credits	Reduced to 4-hr time block; students must take 1 other course			
Student selection			Moved away from full-random selection to self-selection plus a few random.	Lower SES.
Program size		32 students	64 students	70 students, cut to 50 in 2nd semester; 25 for next year (juniors only)

had been added, dropped, revised, combined, or selected out for use. In some cases documentary evidence can be consulted (for instance, evaluation reports).

Which decision rules make sense for entering data? That depends in part on the extent and nature of the data available, and their sources. In this case, six or seven different people (users) were reporting on fairly clearly defined changes in the innovation, which required rather close teamwork; they monitored and discussed each other's work on a daily basis. It seems reasonable to use the decision rule that if a reported change is confirmed by at least one other staff member, and not disconfirmed by anyone else, it should be entered in the matrix.

Analyzing the data. Looking across the rows of Chart 14a, one can begin to see "drifts," or gradual shifts expressing an accumulated tendency underlying specific changes. For example, the row "program requirements/curriculum" shows an increasing tendency to make *stiffer achievement demands* on students. The component "student responsibility and time use" suggests that a process of exerting more and more *control* over student behavior is occurring (for example, the "accountability" scheme, the system of passes, and the like).

At this point, the analyst can deepen understanding of what is happening by referring back to other aspects of the field notes, notably what else people said about the changes, or reasons for them. In this example, a staff member said:

> Your neck is on the block . . . the success and failures of the students rebound directly on you. . . . There's a high possibility of accidents.

The field notes also showed that some parents had complained that "students can't handle the freedom," and that staff were worried about students "fouling up" on their work assignments on the job. So the increased emphasis on control may come from the staff's feeling of vulnerability and mistrust of students.

A third drift can be noted: *increased routinization* and *reduced individualization,* occurring mainly in the second year of operation (student "batching," reduction of unique projects, addition of various forms). The field notes showed that the staff was preoccupied with the program's demandingness ("You keep going all the time . . . you can't get sick . . . it's more than a job."); after a full year's experience, they were ready to routinize and streamline the demands that a strongly individualized program made. The reduction in *parent involvement* may also be a connected issue.

What else is happening? The portion of the matrix labeled "other aspects" provides some additional clues. The change in time and credits during the

planning period came about, the field notes show, as a result of negotiations with principals, who were very resistant to having students away from school for a full day. Here the analyst speculated that the underlying issue was the principals' opposition to the program, and suggested that the increasing achievement emphasis was a way to buy more endorsement.

We can also note that in the second year, there was an important structural shift: moving away from random student selection to self-selection. The field notes show that this decision was precipitated by principals and counselors, who opposed entry by college-bound students, and wanted the program to be a sort of safety valve for poorly performing, alienated students. Thus the program became a sort of dumping ground or oasis for such students, and principals' endorsement was somewhat higher. The addition of the summer program for the first two years was also an endorsement-buying strategy.

But look at the "program size" row. Though the program doubles in the second year, it cuts back substantially in the third year. Endorsement is not enough, apparently. (In this case, severe funding problems were beginning to develop.)

We can see that this particular matrix, as such, helps us understand general patterns of changes over time, and points us back to the original field notes to seek for explanations. The explanations can in turn be tested by looking at other changes in the matrix to see whether they fit the proposed pattern.

So the analysis could end here, and the report could either contain some text pulling together the strands we just wove or present the chart and a shorter, summarizing text. But there may be a need to do a bit more. For example, the "drifts" lok plausible, but we may have been too impressionistic in identifying them. And Chart 14a may be too "busy" and unfocused for the reader—it's more an interim analysis exhibit than a report of findings.

One way of resolving these problems is to boil down the matrix, to (a) verify the tendencies observed in the initial analysis and (b) summarize the core information for the researcher and the reader. Chart 14a could be condensed in myriad ways. One tactic is to "standardize" the several drifts by naming them, that is, finding a gerund that indicated what was going on when a change was made in the innovation, then tying that drift to its local context, inferring what the changes *mean* for the site. The result appears in Chart 14b.

Reading the "tendency" column and simply counting the number of mentions for each theme confirms the accuracy of the initial analysis. The core themes are, indeed, stiffer achievement demands ("going academic"), more control, increased routinization ("simplifying"), and reduced individualization ("standardization"). One might even try for an overarching

Chart 14b
Time-Ordered Matrix: Boiled-Down Version for Verifying
and Interpreting Changes in the CARED Innovation

Component	Tendency	Significance, meaning for site
Individualization	Standardizing	Undergoes individualization, shows streamlining as response to demandingness.
Student responsibility	Controlling, tightening up	Reflects staff feelings of vulnerability, mistrust towards students.
Exposure to work	Simplifying, standardizing	Response to demandingness; cutting back on innovativeness of project.
Program require-ments	Going academic	Shows vulnerability, marginality of project in the two high schools -- again cutting back on innovativeness of CARED.
Learning strategies	Going academic, de-individualizing, simplifying, standardizing	More "routinization" overall.
Parental involvement	Cutting back, simplifying	Response to demandingness.
Time and credits	Cutting back, going academic	Done early; reflects principals' opposition to project, etc.
Student selection	Self-selecting	Project becomes "dumping ground" but also gets stronger endorsement from counselors, principals.
Program size	Growing, then dwindling	Reflection of funding problems and possibly of under-endorsement.

label to typify the set—something like "progressive erosion" or "routinization"—and this can kick off the final text in which the researcher reports the findings. Similarly, a scan of the "significance" column helps in summarizing the underlying issues: exhaustion, lack of local endorsement, and the discrepancy between the demands of the innovation and the organizational procedures and norms in the immediate environment.

Variations

Chart 14a is a useful working matrix, in conjunction with the field notes, but it might be helpful, especially for presentation purposes, to add a column after each time period to enter the researcher's speculations about the underlying issues in, or causes of, the changes noted (endorsement seeking, routinization, and so on).

Here the time periods were relatively long (a full school year), but depending on the phenomena under study they could be shorter (semesters, months, weeks, days, hours).

The cell entries here were specific *changes*. But it is also possible to enter specific *events*, such as decisions, actions, key meetings, or crises (see also section IV.H, on "event listing").

The rows of this matrix were aspects or components of an innovation. Many other types of rows can be used in a time-ordered matrix. They might be *roles* (principal, teacher, student, parent); *event types* (planned/unplanned, decisions, critical actions); *settings* (classroom 1, classroom 2, playground, principal's office, central office); or *activity* types (teaching, counseling, formal meetings). (See also Chapter VI, on construction of displays.)

Advice

If the matrix is only descriptive of events over time, use it to develop possible explanations that can be tested by moving back to the coded field notes.

Be sure the time periods chosen are a good fit for the phenomena under study. They should be fine enough to separate events that you want to keep in sequence, rather than blurring them into one big pot.

During analysis, remain alert to what this sort of matrix can uniquely give you: timing and sequence. What occurs early, afterward, later? Look for sequences. Look for stability (in the type of matrix illustrated here, blank spaces).

After some preliminary analysis, consider whether the rows are organized in a sensible way. You may need to regroup them into "streams" or domains.

Consider whether a boiled-down, next-step matrix is needed to advance your understanding—or that of the reader.

Time Required

If field notes have been coded to permit easy retrieval of the phenomena under consideration, a matrix of the general size and sort illustrated here can usually be assembled in two or three hours; analysis and writing may take another hour or two. But a vacuum-cleanerlike matrix trying to display a very large number of events, with a less clear conceptual focus, can be expected to take longer.

IV.D ROLE-ORDERED MATRIX

Analysis Problem

People who live in organizations, like most of us, and people who study organizations, like sociologists, social psychologists and anthropologists, know that how you see life depends in part on your "role"—the complex of expectation-driven behaviors that go to make up what one does and should do as a certain type of inhabitant of an organized system. Bosses tend not to see the frustrations faced by workers, partly because they are distant from them, but partly because subordinates censor the bad news when reporting upward. The teacher's high-speed interactions with several dozen to several hundred children over the course of a day have a very different cast to them than the principal's diverse transactions with parents, vendors, secretaries, central office administrators, and teachers.

How can you display data systematically to permit cross-role comparison on issues of interest to a research study? Or to test whether people in the same role to in fact see life in similar ways? One answer is the role-ordered matrix.

Brief Description

A role-ordered matrix sorts data in its rows that have been gathered from or about a certain set of role occupants, reflecting their views.

Illustration

Once again we draw on our school improvement study. The question of interest is, "How do people react to an innovation when they first encounter it?" This general question can be unbundled into several subquestions, such as:

- Which aspects of the innovation are salient, stand out in people's minds?
- How do people size up the innovation in relation to its eventual implementation?
- What changes—at the classroom or organizational level—do people think the innovation will require?
- How good a fit is the innovation to people's previous classroom styles, or to previous organizational structures and procedures?

Building the display. Keeping in mind that we want to see answers to these questions broken out by different *roles*, we can consider *which* roles—for example, teachers, principals, central office personnel, department chairpersons, students, parents—could be expected to have some dealings with the innovation and could provide meaningful reactions to it. The matrix rows could be roles, but if we want to make within-role comparisons, the rows should probably be *persons*, but clustered into role domains. The columns can be devoted to the research subquestions.

Chart 15a shows how this approach looks. The innovation involved is an intensive remedial program in a high school emphasizing reading, and implemented in the curricular domains of English, science, and math.

Entering the data. The researcher goes through coded write-ups looking for respondent answers to questions posed formally or informally by the researcher to the various people involved. This, of course, involves some choices. Which particular people should be included? Only those who were directly involved with the innovation, or others with a stake, but less direct experience? In Chart 15a the researcher focuses on all available direct users of the innovation, plus key administrators, even if they didn't have close contact, plus department chairpersons who were not actually using the innovation but had a real stake in its use.

Here the data being entered in each cell are a brief summary of what the analyst found for each respondent in the field notes. The main decision rule appears to be this: If it's in the notes, summarize it and enter a phrase reflecting the summary. Note that there

Chart 15a
Role-Ordered Matrix: First Reactions to the Innovation

	SALIENT CHARACTERISTICS	SIZUP	ANTICIPATED CLASSROOM OR ORGANIZATIONAL CHANGES @	FIT WITH PREVIOUS STYLE OR ORGANIZATIONAL SETTING@@
TEACHERS				
+ REILLY 4th year	Highly structured	Little latitude	DK-1	DK-3
+ KENNEDY 4th year	Frightening format Overload of objectives Reams of handouts	Difficult, complicated No latitude	Teaming (loss of independence) No Scope Magazine use	Poor; user felt she would be locked into structure and others' schedules
+ FARR 1st year	Skill-oriented, organized Activities well planned Pre- & post-testing good	Simple, clear Easy to use & understand	Less freedom to change direction	Fairly good; user views self as structured, organized
+ ROGERS 2nd year	Prescriptive Rigid	Confusing Simplistic content	Working with basic students for 1st time	Composition assignments fit well; grammar, etc. simpleminded
+ FLEMING 4th year	Prescriptive Use of media Teaming Heavy monitoring	Many materials Very complex, not quite clear	Working w/ other T's Mastering all materials	DK-2
* BENNING 1st year	Objectives too broad Good content	Similar to prev. school's program, easy to use	Break down objectives Add games, activities Give objectives to kids	Close fit, when anticipated changes made
* THATCHER 2nd year	(wrote science curriculum) Skill-oriented Reading emphasis	Too detailed	DK-1	Fair; reading was new; fewer labs
# WOJICK 1st year	Variety of modes (workbooks, worksheets, computer terminals)	Easy to use; level & format right	DK-1	DK-2
# MUSKIE 2nd year	Computer terminals Short worksheets	1st 1/2 flawed; 2nd 1/2 on target Good variety	DK-1	DK-1
CENTRAL OFFICE				
MANN Superintendent	DK-2	DK-2	DK-1	Good fit: Program is a successful curriculum revision effort in district
CROWDEN Dir of Curriculum	3 strands of Level I Sequential, comprehensive Reinforcement	Works if followed Any teacher can use successfully	None -- program designed to fit structure	Close fit: same staff, teachers wrote curriculum, same auth. structure
PRINCIPAL				
MCCARTHY Tindale East	DK-2	DK-2	DK-2	Good fit: Order is maintained; no special requirements
NON-USERS				
VAN RUNKEL Science Chrmn	Science content revision Reading reinforcement Flexibility in activities	Questioned content reorg'n--would it fit tog'r?	None -- same teachers, using new curriculum	Good fit: Program replaced old curriculum
MANNHOELLER English Chrmn	Orderly curriculum w/ horizontal, vertical org'n Reinforcement of 3 strands	Concept is right Depends on its being used as set up	DK-1	Good fit: Program designed in part to fill basic English course slot

DK = don't know:

+ = English teacher DK-1 = question not asked of informant
* = science teacher DK-2 = asked, but not answered (strayed from question, didn't know answer)
# = math teacher DK-3 = ambiguous answer

@ Classroom changes question asked of teachers; organizational one asked of others.

@@ Personal style fit question asked of teachers; organizational fit question asked of others.

are also entries when data are *missing,* because the relevant question was never asked of that person, was asked but not answered, or was answered ambiguously. We can also see that the questions being asked of teachers and others (administrators, department chairs) are not precisely parallel in the last two columns.

Analyzing the data. Now we can begin looking down columns of the matrix, both within and across roles, to see what's happening. For example, attention to the entries in the first two columns shows us that many teachers—notably in English—see the new remedial program as rather *prescriptive,* with little latitude given for bending or adaptation. And the teachers who are *most* likely to have a first reaction to the innovation as prescriptive are also those who have used it the longest, suggesting that prescriptiveness was highest when the program was first introduced. A number of teachers also mention *complexity* (though, here again, first-year users are more likely to see the program as simple and easy to use, suggesting program stabilization).

When we drop down to administrators and department chairs, however, the picture is somewhat different. They are more likely to take the "big picture" view, emphasizing the "curriculum," "strands," and the like, and—though they too emphasize prescriptiveness ("works if followed . . . depends on being used as set up")—either do not give clear answers on the issue of complexity or (as in the case of the curriculum director, a major advocate of the program) say that "any teacher can use it successfully." But teachers, faced with an initially demanding, rigid program, are not so sure, it seems.

Moving to the third column of Chart 15a, we can also see role-perspective differences. Two teachers mention teaming as an anticipated change, one that curtailed their freedom and made them accountable to peers' schedules and working styles. Administrators, the field notes show, considered the teaming necessary to implement the program's several strands, and as a way of helping weaker teachers do better through learning from stronger ones, but they do not even consider it a salient change, saying either that there *are* no organizational changes required ("the program is designed to fit the structure") or that they do not know whether organizational changes were anticipated.

Finally, the fourth column shows a range of "personal fit" for different teachers, depending on their views of the content, their own styles, and the organizational issues involved. The administrators, however, uniformly emphasize good fit at the organizational level, stressing the appropriateness of the curriculum and its fit into the existing structure; the director also invokes the fact that teachers wrote it.

In short, a matrix of this sort lets us see how perspectives differ according to role, as well as within role. In this case, users from the English department who came in at the onset of the program had an initially tougher time than later users, or than math and science users. It also hints at problems that arise from these differing perspectives (for example, users' worries about teaming seem to be ignored by administrators—though they regard the teaming as critical to success).

A within-role analysis, moving across rows, shows that the superintendent, as might be expected, knows very little about the innovation and, more surprisingly, that the principal does not either. (A recheck told the fieldworker that the formal role description for high school principals in this district actually *forbids* them to make curriculum decisions, which are the province of the curriculum director and department chairs.)

Variations

This matrix emphasizes different roles as *sources* of data and perceptions. It is also possible to develop a role-ordered matrix that treats roles as targets or *objects* of others' actions or perceptions. For example, how are principals treated by teachers, students, parents, and central office personnel? What expectations or wishes do counselors, students, and parents have for the way teachers should behave?

One may want to have another, closer look at these data after identifying the main trends in the initial analysis. For example, it looks as if the findings are a function of *time of first implementation* (differences between first- and fourth-year users) and of *between-role differences* (users versus administrators). So it may be useful to boil down Chart 15a and array the information according to these two contrasts (see Chart 15b).

Chart 15b presents essentially the same information conveyed in the text on the two previous pages, which means (a) that the follow-on analysis confirms the initial observations, and that (b) with a next-step chart such as the one above, we can write less analytic text. Also, the contrasts appear more sharply, both between earlier and later users (reflecting debugging and loosening of the innovation over time) and between users and administrators (reflecting their differences of perspective and priority).

The technique used to generate Chart 15b was a simple content analysis, with the following decision rules: (a) "Standardize" the cell entries to a more generic descriptor and (b) take the modal response. As the legend to the chart shows, this wasn't always so easy to do. There are also some nagging problems: small and unequal respondent Ns, collapsing different species of administrator into one family, and missing data. All these caveats should be acknowledged, as many as possible directly on the chart. In retrospect, it's admirable that any useful conclusions could have been wrung out of data as diverse and spotty as those

Chart 15b
Role-Ordered Matrix: Example of a Next-Step Matrix to
Analyze Initial Findings (first reactions to the innovation)

Roles	Salient characteristics	Sizup	Anticipated changes	Fit
Early users now in 4th year (N=3)	Structure, prescriptiveness	Complex, low latitude	Teaming	Poor*
Later users now in 1st-2nd year (N=5)	Content focus, variety of modes	Easy to use	----#	Good
Administrators (N=5) (all combined)	Reinforcement order, integration	Fidelity of use is key	Few	Good

*Given "don't know" responses, this is inferred from analysis of other responses of 4th-year users to this set of questions
#User-unique responses.

displayed on Chart 15a. If data are thin or of doubtful quality (questionable validity, ambiguous, ungroupable), we have no business generating next-step matrices that give the misleading appearance of analytic order and adequacy. We see here the risk noted by J. A. Dawson (personal communication, 1983): that systematic methods like the ones we propose can cause researchers to present findings more strongly than they would have otherwise. All the more reason for qualitative researchers to document their procedures, leaving a clear "audit trail" for others. See section VII.C.

Advice

Clarify the list of roles you believe are most relevant to the issue at hand; avoid overloading the matrix with roles that are clearly peripheral. Differentiate the matrix by subroles (such as teachers of math or science) if relevant. Show person-level data within role domains if you wish to show the degree of within-role consensus or diversity.

Keep the questions in columns as parallel as possible for different roles.

Indicate clearly when data are missing, unclear, or not asked for in the first place.

Return to field notes to test emerging conclusions, particularly if the decision rule for data entry involves (as in this case) a good deal of reduction.

Ask for an audit of your analysis and conclusions from a colleague. Role-ordered matrices, because of our prior experience with role differences, lend themselves to too-quick conclusion drawing. For example, in Chart 15a the analyst originally emphasized teachers' reluctance to team-teach as a main conclusion, thinking of past work on teacher isolation (Lortie, 1975), and the vivid comments of several teachers. A colleague pointed out that the teaming issue appeared only for two early English users, and that the "freedom" issue for another English user seemed more related to general prescriptiveness of the innovation than to peer constraint. Preliminary analyses, like cognac, need to be distilled twice.

Time Required

If, as in this case, there is a fairly clear semi-structured interview with questions directly relevant to the columns of the matrix, and the coded data are available for relevant roles, the matrix can be constructed and data entered relatively rapidly—under two hours for a matrix of this size. Analysis and writing are also fairly rapid—an hour or so.

IV.D.a Role-by-Time Matrix

As we noticed in the preceding illustration, role-ordered matrices often turn out to involve time as well. *When* something was done by, or done to, people in a certain role is often an important issue. Box IV.D.a shows how assistance to users of an innovation was provided by different roles, over time. The analyst developed a list of types of assistance and wanted to know *when* which types were supplied by certain *roles* (superintendent or whatever).

Box IV.D.a
Role-by-Time Matrix: Illustration
Role Assistance, by Phase

	TRAINING	FIRST YEAR	SECOND YEAR	THIRD-FOURTH YEARS
SUPERINTENDENT	None	None	None	None
BUILDING ADMINISTRATION	Heavy ADV Moderate SUPP	Heavy ADV Heavy SUPP	Moderate ADV Moderate SUPP	None
DEVELOPERS	Moderate TTR, RES, SOL, SUPP	Light SOL, SUPP	Light SUPP	None
PEER USERS	Moderate FAC, SUPP	Moderate FAC Heavy SUPP	Light FAC Moderate SUPP	Light FAC, SUPP
	Spring 1976	1976-77	1977-78	1978-80

CON = Controlling
TTR = Teaching/training
SOL = Solution-giving
RES = Resource-adding
ADV = Advocacy, representing client interest
FAC = Facilitating
INQ = Inquiring, feeding back data
SUP = Supporting

We can see immediately that the superintendent is out of the picture as far as assistance giving is concerned, while initial assistance is moderate to heavy early in the game from the principal ("building administration") and from peers. Both offer support (SUP), but the principal also emphasizes advocacy (ADV), while peers provide direct facilitation (FAC). The innovation's developers provide much training (TTR), solution giving (SOL), resource adding (RES), and support (SUP) during the training, and some follow-up, but nothing in the third and fourth years. By then the innovation is running with only light facilitation and support from peers.

The chart also shows us what is *not* being done in the way of assistance: No one is directly controlling (CON) or inquiring/feeding back data (INQ).

The eight assistance types, drawn from prior work on assistance functions (Nash & Culbertson, 1977), are arranged in order of directiveness; we can conclude that the assistance provided is largely client-centered and less directive.

Using cell entries of such a general, "boiled-down" sort means that (a) a good conceptual scheme should underlie the entries, and (b) you must be very clear on decision rules for data entry. The text summarizing the analysis of the table should refer back to written-up field notes for illustration and clarification.

IV.D.b Role-by-Group Matrix

People in the various roles in an organization get work done in two major ways: by working one on one with people in other roles (principal and teacher; teacher and parent; student and counselor), and by joining together in multi-role groups (committees, faculties, task forces, and the like).

So most people in an organization are members of several different working groups. How can we display and understand this, so we can see how the "interlocking directorate" functions?

A role-by-group matrix can be organized so that we can explore which people in what roles participate in which group settings and see some initial trends. Box IV.D.b provides an illustration.

This matrix came from a small school system with 47 teachers working in one elementary and one high school. Note the following: (1) the strong administrative presence in most groups; (2) the repeat membership of several teachers, many of whom hold elective (legitimated) positions; (3) the overlapping memberships, particularly between the Administrative Team and the IPA Management Team, and the curriculum and in-service committees (field notes also show ambiguity and vagueness about the missions of these groups); and (4) the fact that only 11 of 47 teachers are involved.

Box IV.D.b
Role-by-Group Matrix: Illustration
Roles and Key Operating Groups, 1979-1980 (Carson site)

ROLES	Administrative Team	IPA Management Team	In-Service Committee+	Curriculum Committee	Salary Negotiations	Self-study Committees*
Supt	Gardner#	Gardner	Gardner		Gardner%	
HS Principal	Lantzer	Lantzer	Lantzer	Lantzer@		
Asst HS Principal	Vogelsang	Vogelsang				Vogelsang
Elem. Principal	Koehler	Koehler	Koehler	Koehler		
Counselor		Wilson				
IPA Project Director	Lowrie*	Lowrie#	Lowrie			
Librarian			MacNally#	MacNally		
Teachers, HS		W. Miller Marx	Walker	DK DK	Walker Colley	
Teachers, elem.		Steuerman Reutter	Hoffman Tabarde	DK DK	Green# Tabarde	Green# Steuerman#

* Not a member, but attends once a month.

\# Chair

+ Started by Hoffman, Lowrie & Wilson this year.

@ meets with HS dept heads

DK=Unknown

Reutter is CEA head) (Marx is 80-81 CEA head) Reutter and Green are elected "principal designees" (stand-ins during Koehler's absence)

% Serves as advisor to Board, which sends president & 2 members.

* All teachers were involved. Other chairs included 2 parents & a Board member. The over-all chair, a parent, was Hoffman's husband.

Even in this small system, many groups (classrooms, advisory committees, and so) had to be omitted. The issue is deciding which groups (and roles) are "key" for purposes of the study, or which *emerge* empirically as more prominent than others.

IV.E CONCEPTUALLY CLUSTERED MATRIX

Analysis Problem

Many studies are designed to answer a string of research questions. Sometimes that string gets to be as long as a laundry list. As a result, doing a separate analysis and section in a site report for each research question is likely to tire out both analyst and reader. The obvious solution is to cluster a few or even several research questions, so that meaning can be generated more easily.

Brief Description

A conceptually clustered matrix has its columns arranged to bring together items that "belong together." This can happen in two ways: conceptual—the analyst may have some a priori ideas about items or questions that derive from the same theory or relate to the same overarching theme; or empirical—during data collection or early analysis, one may find that informants answering different questions are tying them together, or are giving similar responses. The basic principle, however, is conceptual coherence.

Illustration

For example, in our school improvement study, we had a general question about users' and administrators' *motives* for adopting a new educational practice, and a more specific question about whether these motives were *career centered,* for example, whether informants thought they could possibly get a promotion or a transfer out of the project. We postulated here a possible a priori relationship. Then, during data collection, we began to see some inkling of a relationship between the "motives" questions and two others: a *centrality* question (whether the innovation loomed large in the daily life of a user or was one of several, equally important tasks) and an *attitude* question (whether the informant liked the new practice when first introduced to it). We wondered whether there was a relationship between people's motives and their initial attitudes toward the practice.

The best way to find out would be to cluster the responses to these questions. Not only is there a relationship to probe, but there is also a general theme (initial attitudes) and a possibility of handling three research questions at the same time.

Building the display. Assume then that one has the data from several conceptually and/or empirically clustered research questions to analyze. The next step

is to choose an appropriate *format* for analysis. Ideally, one wants a format that does several things:

- allows the analyst to have on one sheet all the responses of all key informants;
- allows an initial comparison between responses and between informants;
- enables the analyst to see how the data can be further analyzed, e.g., repartitioned or clustered;
- lends itself easily to cross-case analysis, and will not have to be redone; and
- provides some preliminary and agreed-upon standardization, common scaling, a set of content-analytic themes that all case analysts will be using.

When you are handling several conceptually/empirically related research questions together, a likely start-up format is a simple informant-by-variable matrix, as shown in Chart 16a. Thus we have on one sheet a format that includes all respondents and all responses to the four research questions. Note that we have set up comparisons between different kinds of informants (users and administrators) by clustering their responses. Finally, the format calls for some preliminary scaling or typing of the responses: types of motive, career-relevant or not, degree of centrality, valence of initial attitudes.

Entering the data. The next step is to go back to the coded segments keyed to the research questions. The analyst notes down the *motives* given by or attributed to an informant, then tries to put a label on the motive. One informant, for example, gave several motives: She heard how good the new practice was (social influence); her principal was "really sold on it" and "wanted it in" (pressure); most other teachers were using it or planned to—"It's what's coming" (conformity); using the new practice was an occasion to "keep growing" (self-improvement). At this stage, it is best to leave the start-up labels as they are, without trying to regroup them into a smaller number of headings that cover all informants; this gives the cross-case analyst more degrees of freedom while still providing a preliminary shaping of the data.

The analyst determines for each informant the *career relevance* of adopting the practice, summarizes it in a phrase or sentence, and looks for evidence on how *central* the new practice is for people, and what their *initial attitudes* seemed to be. For these two questions, the analyst makes a general rating, backing it with specific quotes. When these data are entered on the worksheet matrix, we might get something like Chart 16b.

The nature of the cell entries is worth noting. The analyst has reduced the coded segments to four kinds of entries: *ratings* (high, low), *labels* (such as self-improvement), *quotations,* and short *explanatory phrases.* The ratings and labels set up comparisons between informants and, later, between cases in the

Chart 16a
Conceptually Clustered Matrix: Motives and
Attitudes (format)

Research Questions / Informants	Motives (types)	Career relevance (none/some)	Centrality (low/mod/high)	Initial attitude (fav., neutr., unfav.)
Users U$_1$				
U$_2$, etc.				
Administrators A$_1$				
A$_2$, etc.				

cross-site analysis. The quotations supply some grounding and punch to the material; they put some flesh on the rating or label and are easily extracted for insertion in the text of a single-site or cross-site analysis. Finally, the short phrases explicate or qualify a rating, usually where there are no quotations (the "career relevance" column on the excerpt). In general, it is a good idea to add a short quote or explanatory phrase beside a label or scale; otherwise, the analyst is tempted to work with more general categories that might well lump together, for example, high centrality responses that mean different things. In face, if this *does* happen, and the single-site or cross-site analyst is puzzled about something, the qualifying words are easily at hand for quick reference.

Analyzing the data. A full-fledged worksheet usually contains more informants; this excerpt is used here for simplicity. *Reading across the rows* gives the analyst a thumbnail profile of each informant and provides an initial test of the relationship between responses to the different questions. For example, L. Bayeis *does* have career-relevant motives, sees the practice as very important, and is initially favorable. But R. Quint's entries do not follow that pattern or a contrasting one. *Reading down the columns* enables comparisons between the motives of different users and administrators as well as comparisons between these groups. It also enables similar comparisons between responses to the career-relevance, centrality, and initial-attitude questions. Not too much jumps out of the excerpted

matrix (with only five respondents), but a full matrix of ten to twelve respondents or more (see Chart 16c) will begin to show patterning.

Chart 16c assembles about as many data as a qualitative analyst can handle and a reader can follow. Notice that the analyst has decided to array informants according to their time of implementation (early users, second generation, recent users) and their roles (users and administrators) and, within the group of users, has included a *nonuser* to set up an illustrative contrast between motives for adopting and motives for refusing the new practice. As an exercise, the reader may wish to see what conclusions might be drawn from Chart 16c. Then we will suggest some that occur to us.

A simple scan down the columns of Chart 16c provides both information and leads for follow-up analyses. In the first column, "social influence" *motives* are prominent; also, there is a noticeable amount of pressure being exerted on users. The tactic of making contrasts/comparisons (section VII.B.5) is useful here. For example, there is some *career relevance* in adoption for users, but practically none for administrators. *Centrality* is high—almost overwhelming—for users, but less so for administrators. Users are less *favorable* initially than administrators. Looking across rows, we can use the tactic of noting relations between variables (section VII.A.9), and see that for two of three career-motivated users there is a relationship among the variables; high centrality and favorable attitudes are also present. But the opposite pattern (low career

Chart 16b
Conceptually Clustered Matrix: Motives and Attitudes
of Users, Nonusers, and Administrators at Masepa (excerpt)

Early Users: 1977-78	Motives	Career Relevance	Centrality	Initial Attitude toward Program
R. Quint	Self-improvement: "To get better, I had to change"..."Maybe I wasn't teaching the best ways." Pressure: "They wanted us to do it." Social influence: "Everybody was saying what Gail's doing is great."	None - improvement of practice	High: "Biggest thing I've ever done that somebody else told me to do.	Neutral: "There wasn't any appeal. They said it worked so I was going to try it."
L. Bayeis	Observation: Saw G. Norrist do it and "was impressed." Fit to personal style: "I like structure." Practice improvement: "looking around for a different way to teach reading" Novelty: "you get tired of always doing the same old thing."	Vehicle to turnkey trainer role: also became Title I Coordinator	High: "most important thing I've been involved with."	Favorable
Administrators				
K. Weelling Principal	Met need: "I was looking for a highly structured, skill-oriented reading program." Novelty, promise of practical improvement: intrigued by reading about mastery learning; wanted to see it in operation	None at first; later, appreciates the visibility	High: "Largest investment I've ever made."	Neutral, then favorable
J. Dahloff Curriculum Coordinator	Relative advantage, face validity of program: "well organized;" could be used for other subject matters. Social influence: "impressed" that outstanding teachers favored the program Practice improvement; beginning teachers ill-prepared in reading. "We didn't know what to do with them... They just had to learn on the job."	Another in a series of implementations	Moderate: "It was one thing among a lot of things I was working on.	Favorable
W. Paisly Asst. Superintendent	Social influence: "talked into it" by J. Dahloff	None	Low: "It was no big deal.."	Neutral

relevance, low centrality, and neutral/unfavorable attitudes) does not apply.

In fact, it looks as if some people who are neutral would have been favorable were they not so apprehensive about doing well. This is a good example of the merits of including a quotation or explanatory phrase in the cell so as not to pool what may be different responses behind the same label ("neutral" in this case).

Variations

In using conceptually clustered matrices for multisite studies, there is often a tension between the desire to run with the site and the obligation to set up the site report to facilitate later cross-site analyses. For instance, the data for the Masepa site in Chart 16c seem to cohere in ways that don't follow the four-column structure religiously. Note that for users, irrespective of their date of initial use, the modal pattern is social pressure, high centrality, and neutral, often mixed initial attitudes; people are backing into

what most call "the most important thing" or "biggest step" they have undertaken. Clearly, the conceptual core of the chart lies here, and the single-site analyst should fasten onto it, looking, perhaps, for an appropriate conceptual framework (such as "approach-avoidance conflict") or a descriptive gerund (such as "ambivalent innovating") to pull the material together.

The next step would be to reconfigure the chart around this theme, dropping the "career relevance" column, looking more carefully at the mix of motives, and counting up the number of informants who correspond to this profile. In other words, Chart 16c is just a way station in the site-specific analysis, where the prime objective is—and should be—to follow the data where they beckon.

On the other hand, the cross-site analytic logic requires that individual cases be set up to permit a cross-site perspective. The chief concern is that, looking across all sites, the motives-career relevance-centrality-attitude relationship can be systematically examined and tested. The relationships may not hold

Chart 16c
Conceptually Clustered Matrix: Motives and Attitudes
of Users, Nonusers, and Administrators at Masepa (full data)

Early Users: 1977-78	Motives	Career Relevance	Centrality	Initial Attitude toward Program
R. Quint	Self-improvement: "To get better, I had to change"..."Maybe I wasn't teaching the best ways." Pressure: "They wanted us to do it." Social influence: "Everybody was saying what Gail's doing is great."	None – improvement of practice	High: "Biggest thing I've ever done that somebody else told me to do.	Neutral: "There wasn't any appeal. They said it worked so I was going to try it."
L. Bayeis	Observation: Saw G. Norrist do it and "was impressed." Fit to personal style: "I like structure." Practice improvement: "looking around for a different way to teach reading" Novelty: "you get tired of always doing the same old thing."	Vehicle to turnkey trainer role: also became Title I Coordinator	High: "most important thing I've been in-volved with."	Favorable
Second Generation: 1978-79				
F. Morelly	Social influence: heard from several friends about program Opportunity, effort justification: "I took the training for recerti-fication credit. After all that, I had to follow through." Pressure: "He (Weelling) is the reason we do it here. He's so enthusiastic about it."	None – possibly stabilizing her job at the school	High: "This is the only new thing I've done since I've been out of school...I had to invest so much."	Neutral, apprehen-sive
L. Brent	Social opinion, influence: "I heard how good it was." Pressure: "(Weelling) was really sold on it. They really want it in." Conformity: Most doing it or plan-ning to in the school; "it's what's coming." Self-improvement: occasion to "keep growing"	None, possibly fear	High: "It's been a nightmare."	Unfavorable, once training began
Recent Users: 1979-80				
V. Sharpert	Obligation: requirement to obtain teaching post: "I didn't have a choice." Practice-improvement; complementing pre-service training	Ticket to teaching job in the district	High: "My first job"	Neutral, apprehensive
A. Olkin	Social influence: "heard it was good;"..."a good friend liked it" Pressure: "strongly encouraged" by Weelling and Dahloff Observation, modeling: saw G. Norrist "She really impressed me."	None: felt obli-gated by admin-istration	High: "This was really the big one for me."	Neutral, mixed feelings
S. Sorels	Observation: "It was so good for my own kids...tremendous change in reading, spelling, work habits"	Ticket to full-time teaching position	High: "This was really a big step for me--a big move..[nothing else] as high as this in my career."	Favorable: "I was excited about it."
Non User				
C. Shinder	Relative disadvantage: "My program was better." Poor fit with personal style: "too scholastic...too programmed"	None	N/A	Unfavorable
Administrators				
K. Weelling Principal	Met need: "I was looking for a highly structured, skill-oriented reading program." Novelty, promise of practical im-provement: intrigued by reading about mastery learning; wanted to see it in operation	None at first; later, appre-ciates the visibility	High: "Largest invest-ment I've ever made."	Neutral, then favorable
J. Dahloff Curriculum Coordinator	Relative advantage, face validity of program: "well organized;" could be used for other subject matters. Social influence: "impressed" that outstanding teachers favored the program Practice improvement; beginning tea-chers ill-prepared in reading. "We didn't know what to do with them... They just had to learn on the job."	Another in a series of implementations	Moderate: "It was one thing among a lot of things I was working on.	Favorable
W. Paisly Asst. Superinten-dent	Social influence: "talked into it" by J. Dahloff	None	Low: "It was no big deal.."	Neutral

for this site—but this may be a rogue site. It is important to hold onto the common set of categories, scales, and ratings for each site—even if the empirical fit is poor in one or another of these columns—until the full set of sites can be studied.

We are dwelling here on a difference in emphasis, rather than a necessary parting of the ways between site-level and cross-site analysis. Still, depending on your focus, you may well be drawn in one direction rather than the other.

Advice

Try not to use more than three or four questions when doing a conceptually clustered matrix. Otherwise, the mind will boggle. There will be too many data to *see* inclusively at one time, and too much time spent manipulating blocks of data to find clusters and covariations.

If possible, work with all the data on a single page, even if that page covers a wall or a big table. You can progressively reduce a giant chart to a more economical one by using summarizing phrases, short quotes, category headings, ratings, and so on, as in Chart 16a. Having all the data in one readily surveyable place allows one to move quickly and legitimately to a boiled-down matrix by making sure that *all* the data fit into a content-analysis scheme, and/or form ordinal or dichotomous scales.

Time Required

Assuming that one begins with all the coded segments in the appropriate piles—all the "motives" chunks together, all the "career relevance" chunks together, and so on—a chart like Chart 16c can be generated in four to six hours. As we said above, this may not be the *first* chart the analyst generates from the coded segments, but it is probably the second. A good deal depends, of course, on the number of informants; more informants will fatten the piles of coded segments, enlarge the initial chart, and make for a longer scrutiny until the patterns begin to come clear.

IV.F EFFECTS MATRIX

Analysis Problem

In most studies, the researcher is interested in *outcomes*. That interest may be cast in differing forms. An evaluator may want to know what a particular program or treatment did—what changes it brought about in its target population. A more descriptive researcher may simply want to know where things stood at the end of some process (for example, how well stabilized a newly created school is after two years). A researcher aiming at explanations will usually want to have a good look at some main dependent variables of interest (for example,

disciplinary difficulties of students, achievement, or school social climate).

These are examples of "ultimate" outcomes. That label may seem pretentious, but it only reflects the idea that the variable is the last one being looked at in a temporal or causal chain. A researcher will of course be interested too in preceding outcomes, which are usually labeled "intervening" or "intermediate."

The problem for the qualitative researcher is how to select and display data that will represent faithfully the changed state of persons, relationships, groups or organizations, seen as one or more outcomes of interest. Words are much harder to manage in this respect than numbers, where the primitive decision rules often turn out to be something like "Subtract 'pre' from 'post' scores, and proceed to the statistic of your choice." For qualitative data, clarifying just which outcomes have occurred is not always an easy process.

Brief Description

An effects matrix displays data on one or more outcomes, in as differentiated a form as the study requires. The label "effect" is used to remind the reader that outcomes are always outcomes of *something*: a global program, an independent variable, an intervening variable. There is always at least an implicit predecessor. (We will shortly turn to the question of assessing causality; see sections IV.G, Box IV. H.c., and IV.J following.) In effect, the basic principle is one of focus on *dependent* variables.

Illustrations

When an organization, such as a school, implements an innovation, there is in principle the possibility that the organization may change in some way as a consequence. Though some innovations can be "dropped in" to an existing structure, serving as a replaceable part, most innovations turn out to make demands on the system, and to have ripple effects. The organizational response often shows up in the form of something new—new attitudes, new rules, new procedures, new structures.

In the school improvement study, we wanted to study this issue. What changes in local school organizations could we see that were traceable to their having implemented an innovation?

Building the display. One first needs to get clear what the bundle called an "outcome" (in this case, organizational change) is made up of. Does it have parts or aspects? The task is one of differentiation.

Chart 17 shows how this worked out. The analyst has decided that the outcome "organizational change" has three basic parts: structural changes, procedural or operating changes, and more general relational or social climate changes. The sequence is from "hard" to "soft" aspects of change.

Chart 17
Effects Matrix: Organizational Changes After
Implementation of the ECRI Program

	Early Use 1st and 2nd yrs.		Later Use 3rd yr.	
	Primary Changes	Spin-Offs	Primary Changes	Spin-Offs
Structural	Scheduling: ECRI all morning, Rescheduling music, phys. ed. Helping teacher named: has dual status (teach/admin)	Cutting back on math, optional activities Two separate regimens in school Ambiguity of status and role	integrated scheduling, cross-age grouping in grades 2-6	less individual latitude; classroom problems become organizational problems
Procedural	No letter grades, no norms	parents uneasy 2 regimens in class teachers insecure loosens age-grading system	ECRI evaluation sheets, tightening supervision	Teachers more visible, inspectable
	institutionalizing assistance via helping teacher	in-house assistance mechanism implanted	more uniformity in work in all classes	problems, solutions more common, public
Relations/ Climate	Users are minority, band together	Cliques, friction between users, non-users	Tighter academic press Perception by teachers of collective venture	Reduction in "fun activities," projects (e.g. Xmas) More lateral help More 'public' distress

Second, the analyst, reflecting on the particular site at hand, believes that such aspects of organizational change should be displayed separately for the "early use" period (first and second years), and for "later use," when nine of the school's eleven teachers were users of the innovation.

Third, the analyst wants to distinguish between "primary changes"—those directly following from the requirements of the innovation's implementation— and those termed "spinoffs"—secondary effects, some of which may not have been fully anticipated. Since the usual convention (at least in a culture where the printed word is read from left to right) is that later events should be displayed to the right of earlier events, the analyst put the time dimension in columns and the outcome types in rows.

Note, by the way, that the primary change-spinoff division could just as easily have appeared as a subdivision of the three change types. That would permit easier comparison of, say, structural spinoffs at times 1 and 2. This illustrates a general point we want to emphasize: Any given set of data can usually be configured in a dozen or more different ways. Each way has its advantages and limitations. You usually need to try a number of format iterations before settling on one.

Entering the data. The cell entries in Chart 17 are brief phrases characterizing specific organizational changes appearing in the coded write-ups of field notes. The original question to teachers, their principal, and several central office personnel was, "Did any changes occur in the organization of the school or the district during this period?" The probes asked

specifically for structural or "set-up" changes (such as roles, connections, groups, budget, policy, space, facilities, in-service, or evaluation); for procedural changes (ways of doing things, such as scheduling, decision making, rules, help, planning time); and climate or feeling shifts (such as attitudes, dos and don'ts, relationships).

The decision rule was that any change reported and verified by a document or at least one other respondent would be reduced to a summary phrase for entry into the matrix.

Analyzing the data. (Here again we encourage the reader to take a first cut at analysis of Chart 17 before reading this.) The ECRI innovation is a relatively demanding, rather structured language arts program, taking a behaviorist approach to word recognition, phonetics, composition, and vocabulary. A look at the left side of the chart shows us that the major structural change was rescheduling previously separate language arts activities into one integrated morning period; this required rescheduling of the subjects taught by circulating teachers (music, physical education). This change in turn (see spinoff column) created two separate regimens, since the scheduling was done for two ECRI users in the first year, and five in the second year. Other teachers were on the old schedule.

Other early changes included use of mastery levels rather than letter grades, and the creation of a new helping teacher role to give assistance to new users of ECRI. We can see by moving vertically down the columns that (as has been found in much social psychological research) structural changes tend to lend to procedural changes, and in turn to climate/

attitudinal changes. In this case the pressure, insecurity, and special attention led to a "we unhappy few" climate change, where users banded together. Moving across the climate row, we can se the spinoff effect: cliques and friction.

Moving to the right half of the matrix, we can note that, since nine of eleven teachers were now involved, scheduling has become more integrated, and close supervision and uniformity are more typical. And it is clear that the fuller-scale, more regulated implementation is now seen by teachers as a collective venture. Looking across from primary changes to spinoffs, we see that teachers are both more likely and more able to express need for help, and to give and receive it.

Note what this differentiated effects matrix permits us to do: We can see how structural changes induce procedural and attitude changes; we can see how first-level changes lead to later consequences ("spinoffs"); and we can see how organizational changes flowed and developed over the three-year period. If we had simply bundled all the organizational changes reported into one content-analytic summary, all of this information would be lost.

Let's turn to one more example, presented briefly. Suppose that one were interested in sorting out, rather inductively, *all* of the "ultimate" outcomes reported as the result of some substantial intervention. In the school improvement study, that intervention was the implementation of an innovation.

Building the display. Outcomes can be sorted in one way according to their directness. Some outcomes are "direct" effects, like the "primary changes" just noted. Others are more general, of wider scope; they might be termed "meta-effects," outcomes that go considerably beyond the immediate direct effects the innovation is supposed to have. Finally, we can think of "side effects," outcomes that are quite far away from the original intention. Each of these types of effects, one suddenly realizes, can be either positive or negative. An innovation's proponents usually want one to accentuate the positive. But bad outcomes are typical in any area of human endeavor, and they should be included here.

Now, *where* can we look for outcomes? They can be *reported* by different roles (teachers or administrators), and they can be *attached* to different roles (outcomes for students, outcomes for teachers, and so on).

Finally, it is useful to consider that outcomes ought to be looked at in relation to the *intended* program outcomes—those the innovation's developer believes it will ordinarily accomplish.

Chart 18 shows how the matrix worked out. The innovation involved is a high school environment studies program. The people interviewed included three users of the innovation and two administrators.

Entering the data. The researcher has entered summarizing phrases, including *all* outcomes mentioned. Those that receive strong emphasis by the respondent, or that are confirmed by another respondent, get underlined. Where the entry represents an *inference* made by the researcher, rather than a direct paraphrase of respondent comments, it is marked with an asterisk.

Analyzing the data. Using simple *counting* (section VII.A.1), we can see immediately in Chart 18 that positive effects at all three levels outnumber negative ones. And we can also see, by comparing intended objectives with actually noted outcomes, that there is a good deal of congruence. But there are also some negative meta- and side effects that are closely intertwined with sought-for outcomes. For example, a side effect of the program is that it keeps dropouts in, but its off-campus, practical aspect also means that the program becomes a "dumping ground" for low-achieving students with discipline problems. These are the kinds of real-life contradictions that qualitative data analysis is good at surfacing *and* keeping visible throughout analysis and interpretation.

Moreover, such a differentiated-effects matrix permits analysis that would not be possible with narrative text alone, or with a content-analytic summary.

Variations

Effects displays can also be organized by specific *persons;* one can show, for example, the changes in concepts, attitudes, and behavior experienced by several different teachers as a result of their use of an innovation. Under these circumstances, the cell entries will typically be much finer and "thicker," including such items as the following:

- I'm more sensitive to kids, more aware of them individually and how I affect them.
- I learned not to fight too hard when other teachers weren't doing it right.
- You should be looking at what's good, not worry so much about where the kids are failing.
- No real change in the classroom, no.

Effects data need not only come from interviews; they can be retrieved from observation studies—or, indeed, from available quantitative information. In addition, the typical "program"—a treatment aimed at achieving outcomes—has some type of evaluation component attached to it, and has already-collected data, which can be invoked as well.

The matrices shown here concentrated on describing effects clearly, leaving implicit the issue of what caused the outcomes. It is possible to organize an effects matrix that displays the *antecedents* of various outcomes and/or adds the researcher's *explanations*

Chart 18
Effects Matrix: Direct, Meta, and Side Effects of Program

	DIRECT EFFECTS +	DIRECT EFFECTS -	META EFFECTS +	META EFFECTS -	SIDE EFFECTS +	SIDE EFFECTS -
PROGRAM OBJECTIVES Effects on Pupils	Plan & conduct env'l tasks Awareness of env'l problems					
Effects on Staff	Hands-on tasks Work w/ commun After-class work		Interdisc. skills			
Effects on Community	Inv't in env'l ed activities					
SEEN BY USERS Effects on Pupils	Env'l awareness Hands-on work		As adults, will make good env'l dec'ns in commun		Improved values Kept dropouts in + self images	
Effects on Staff	Hands-on approach Looser style		Completes env'l program here Outside workshops	Off-campus progm is dumping ground	Acquired more off-campus sites "Expert" in com. Kept user in ed.	Crystallizedhard work/low pay bec of its demands*
Effects on Community	Env'l awareness Knowledge of school programs					
SEEN BY ADMIN'RS Effects on Pupils	Hands-on work off-campus				Success experiences	
Effects on Staff			Utilizes their creativity			
Effects on Org'n			No more discipline problems Rounds out progm	Not cost-effective to transport 14 kids to site	Orientation to community	
Effects on Community						

_____ = claim made strongly by one person, or by more than one respondent

* = inference made by researcher

---

for the noted outcome (see Box IV.F.a and Section IV.G).

Advice

Unbundle outcomes carefully, then work to substruct them into a differentiated matrix. Consider two or three alternative formats before firming up.

As always, be explicit and crisp about the decision rules for data entry. Outcomes carry more intellectual and practical weight in studies than other types of variables, and, as we shall see, much rests on the clarity and validity of outcome assessments.

If your effects matrix does not include negative (undesired) outcomes, be prepared to give a good justification for the reader.

Time Required

Naturally, much depends on the degree of differentiation in the matrix, the size of the data base, and the accessibility of coded data. A matrix such as the one in our first illustration (fifteen informants, answering a specific interview question) can usually be assembled in a couple of hours, with rapid analysis following. The second illustration, which involved scanning coded interviews from four people, took slightly less time.

IV.F.a Explanatory Effects Matrix

Any effects matrix inevitably stimulates conjecture: *Why* were these outcomes achieved? What caused them—either generally or specifically? An explanatory effects matrix is a first step in the direction of answering such questions.

Here is an example of a simple explanatory effects matrix. The researcher talked to users of an innovation (the same environmental studies program that appears in Chart 18), asking them from whom they had received day-to-day, ongoing assistance, what the assistance actually consisted of, and what the effects (both short and long run) seemed to be. The results are displayed in Box IV.F.a. The researcher has entered quotes and paraphrases, aiming to get at the essence

Box IV.F.a

Explanatory Effects Matrix: Ongoing Assistance

LOCATION	USERS' ASSESSMENT	TYPES PROVIDED	SHORT-RUN EFFECTS ("STATE" OF USERS)	LONGER-RUN CONSEQUENCES (ABLE/UNABLE TO DO)	RESEARCHER EXPLANATION
Superintendent	0	None	"He's going along just for the money"	Building/expansion of program on their own	Supt was a money manager not inv'd w/ programs
Bldg Admin'n Years 1-2	+	Met w/ community Gave encouragement Buffered supt.	"We have some help here" "We're not alone" "He'll fight our battles"	Left users more time to address program issues, students, site, buses	Admin'r supported innov. programs by providing needed help to teachers
Years 3-4	0	None	"We lost our friend"	Had to fight own battles and thus learned how	Admin'r's relative in-difference probably solidified users
Developers	++	Gave ideas, help Provided framework Activity planning Positive outlook Resources	"They know their stuff" "It all makes sense" How it could work "Hey, I can do this!" "We can get equipment"	Expansion of science program to off-campus sites w/ community involvement	Dept needed money to do the program; one user needed direction and support; they got both and off they went
Peer Users	+	Helped w/ planning Gave ideas, sugg'ns Gave encouragement	How it could work Filled in gaps Not alone; there's help	Strong users of the off-campus program; they know how to do it	One user was experienced in this approach and brought others up to speed
Materials (Guides)	+	Overview, approach, and suggested activities in detail	This is really good stuff, well worked out, tried, useful	Good basis for development of own program	Mat'ls fulfilled their role: to stimulate & aid in development of local program

of the interview material appropriate for each cell. In a last column, the researcher adds a general explanation.

Such a matrix helps clarify a domain in *conceptual* terms; it's a useful first exploration tracing back—and forward—the emerging threads of causality. In this case, that involves the issue of which types of assistance cause which types of effect in users, and why.

More detailed and thorough causal analysis usually requires other methods, such as site dynamics matrices (section IV.G) or causal networks (section IV.J).

IV.G SITE DYNAMICS MATRIX

Analysis Problem

The question of *why* things happen is at the forefront of the research experience, once you are past the basic problem of understanding just *what* is happening. That question, too, is almost always a salient one for people in their day-to-day lives; questions of "why," "how come," and answers beginning with "because" appear constantly in the flow of day-to-day interaction. If you doubt this, ask the next person you meet *any* "why" question ("Why did the meeting end so abruptly?" "Why did the president veto the bill?" "Why does it get cooler when it rains?" "Why is the checking account overdrawn?" "Why did you say that?") and you will usually be presented with instant explanations. There is even a group problem-solving

technique, called "why questions," in which a chain of questions, answers, and following questions gradually clarifies a problem—or at least the *assumptions* that people are making about the problem:

Why do we have graffiti on subway cars?
    Because kids want to express their identity.
Why do they want to express their identity?
    Because they are alienated.
Why are they alienated?
    Because they have no jobs.
Why do they have no jobs?
    Because they are unskilled.

Note that quite another chain could start like this:

Why do we have graffiti on subway cars?
    Because the cars are not protected in their yards at night.
Why are they not protected?
    Because the transit budget doesn't permit it.
Why . . .

These illustrations show us several things. First, assumptions have a driving, controlling quality. The first chain assumes that explanations are to be found at the individual level; the second assumes that causes are economic and probably political. Second, there is a terrifying multitude of possible answers to any "why" question:

Why do they have no jobs?
    Because they are unskilled.
    Because they are lazy.

Because there is structural unemployment.
Because employers are prejudiced.

Third, these are only explanatory *claims*. If, as researchers, we are interested in *predicting* graffiti occurrence, or in helping someone *control it,* or in offering alternative *choices* for action, we have to go far beyond assertion, showing that there is indeed some empirical basis for the claim that Y is explained or caused by X.[4]

The qualitative data analyst, during and after data collection, is constantly trying to link data to explanations, trying to understand why specific things happen as they do—and how people in the sites explain why things happen as they do. Further, the problem is one of surfacing and making explicit the assumptions underlying these explanations. How can one display, in a preliminary way, the explanations that seem relevant to a particular question?

Brief Description

A site dynamics matrix displays a set of forces for change and traces the consequential processes and outcomes. The basic principle is one of preliminary explanation.

Illustration

Suppose that one were interested, as we were in the school improvement study, in the question of how and why an innovation induces change in the organization implementing it. That's a nontrivial "why" question, because the history of many innovations is that they are either shrugged off or absorbed into routine operating procedure, disappearing without a trace. What are the conditions under which this does *not* happen?

Building the display. If we are looking for causes, one way to begin is to look for "dynamic" issues, things that have a pushing or demanding quality. In this case, that might be "demands," or "requirements," or "strains" that the innovation carries with it. They can be in rows of the matrix. For columns we could include underlying issues or assumptions about the meaning of these demands, the organizational coping responses, and how things finally settled down, in terms of resulting organizational changes. Chart 19a shows how this works out. In this case, the innovation is a program for doing individualized educational planning for *all* students in a school district, not just those involved in special education. As such, it had been deliberately designed locally to be an organizational, districtwide change, with its procedures to be used routinely by all staff.

Entering the data. Looking through coded field notes, the analyst can pick out chunks of material marked by relevant codes. In this case, these codes were as follows:

TR-PROBS:	implementation problems
TR-ORG/PRAC:	effects on organizational practice
TR-ORG/CLIM:	effects on organizational climate
TR-SIZUP:	explanations for effects on the organization

Tha analyst has also decided to sort organizational effects into three exhaustive general classes: structural, procedural, and climate. This requires "unbundling" the TR-ORG/PRAC chunks into pieces that are really procedural and those that have a structural aspect.

The decision rule for data entry in Chart 19a is as follows: locate discriminably different "demands," and summarize in a phrase or two the essence of the demand, the coping method, and the resolution. Use only data that are not contradicted by other informants. For "underlying issue," move a level of abstraction up, drawing on one's ideas about organizational theory and the explanations site people offer, and enter concepts that seem most relevant. The question is, What is the demand a specific example of?

Note, by the way, the choices that this particular matrix closes out. (We should emphasize that *any* display forecloses some issues.) The analyst is looking only at those demand-caused effects that actually constituted an organizational change, and is tacitly excluding demands that cause *no* organizational effects, are absorbed without a trace.

Analyzing the data. In this sort of matrix, much analysis occurs during the actual data entry, which is done as noted above by moving across each row. By the time the row is filled in, the analyst knows what the dynamics have been. Then summarizing text can be written, cycling back to the written-up field notes for amplification and clarification. Here is an example of such text for the first row of Chart 19a:

> The enthusiasm of the "early settlers" in IPA was strong; teachers would often spend a weekend with one of their five children, doing special activities. But as the program expanded, there was tension: Parents somehow expected teachers to carry out all the activities. Official explanations that parents and students would have to "take responsibility" were only partially effective; the most favorable estimate was that only 25-30 percent of parents actually helped out, and a few were actually resistant to "nonschool" activities. The gap had to be filled organizationally through activities of the coordinator, who was increasingly expected to set things up and carry them out (a program on dinosaurs, visits from football heroes, trips to stables). Batching was also seen as an acceptable response at the classroom level: Units on trucking, or oceanography, could be used for subsets of interested children.

Similar analysis can proceed row by row. It is also possible to look at the types of resulting change in the last column, noting that genuine structural changes are fewer than procedural or climate changes. And

Chart 19a

Site Dynamics Matrix: The IPA Innovation as a Force for
Organizational Change in the District and Its Schools

Strains, Difficulties Created	Underlying Issues (as seen by researcher)	How Coped With	How Resolved: Type of Resulting Change
Conflicting expectations: should parents or teachers do activities?	Work load. Parent-teacher role conflict.	"Explaining" that teachers could not take primary responsibility for out-of-school activities.	Increased use of "batched" activities, many set up by coordinator (P).
View that forms and procedures were "extra", overloading.	Work load. Autonomy, resistance to control.	In-service assistance.	Repeated revision and simplification of forms and procedures; production of an operating manual. Reduction of expectations (no home visits, fewer conferences) (P).
User uncertainty and resistance to use.	Autonomy.	In-service assistance. Management Team interviews of all staff.	See above. Also, creation of in-service committee (S), with coordination through Management Team (P).
Extra time requirements.	Work load.	Initially, via volunteerism, high commitment.	Use of substitutes (P). Dismissal of school during conference days (P). Reduction of expectations (above).
Program is complex, demanding, externally funded.	Authority, coordination, accountability.	Early creation of Management Team, addition of elementary teachers.	Institutionalization of Management Team (S). Heightened expectations for teacher upward influence (C). Lowered morale when expectations violated (C).
Enthusiasm of "advocate" teachers led to peer criticism.	Autonomy.	Quieting conflicts through informal discussion. Informal coordination and referral.	Norms supporting flexibility and colleague influence within schools, and cross-school interaction (C). Increased linkage and closer interaction between schools (C). Hobby Day (P).

(S) Structural change.
(P) Procedural change
(C) Climate change.

one can look down the "issues" column to see that issues of work load and autonomy are occurring repeatedly. Cycling back over to the right column, we can see that work-load issues were in general resolved through routinization and reduction of effort. But autonomy issues were resolved in an interesting, surprising way: increased interdependence and colleague influence, *closer* linkage. When the analyst runs into such a conclusion, it poses a puzzle: How to shed light on an unpredicted finding?

One strategy is to go to other rows to find possible explanations. For example, in the row second from the bottom, we note that the Management Team was created to solve problems of coordination, and also heightened expectations for upward teacher influence. Perhaps the team is a way of trading increased influence for decreased autonomy? If we go back to the field notes, there is only partial support for that idea: The team is seen by different parties as increasing ownership, even cooptation ("Teachers are less quick to criticize if there's a colleague on the Team") and par-

ticipation. That fits, roughly. But others mention power mobilization and institutionalization as the main *raisons d'être* for the team. So we must look elsewhere.

Reviewing field notes further, the analyst comments:

It also appeared that the program induced more elementary-secondary contact and collaboration—partly because many teachers were themselves parents, and experienced the IPA program in that role (and could notice poor or partial implementation as well as benefits).

Dorry Hoffman was even able to get the revered Coach Covington to work with some of her third grade students by telling him she had some promising runnng backs.

Others also felt that the two schools were better linked, "became a team." High school people concluded that elementary school people were weird, but OK. And vice versa.

I noted that several high school teachers came to the elementary school to help with Hobby Day, an IPA offshoot (substitutes were provided). And there was a well-worked-out program for sixth graders to orient them to what life in the high school would be like the following year.

So people's willingness to be more interdependent and less autonomous seems to have been driven by direct experience in working with others, with benefits accruing. This sort of explanatory matrix, because its data are at several removes from the actual field notes, must ordinarily be used as a summarizing, clarifying, puzzle-posing (but not usually puzzle-solving) device.

Variations

Site dynamics charts, rather than starting with "strains," as this one did, can use "dilemmas"; rows can also be clustered conceptually. Chart 19b is an example, on the same topic as Chart 19a. Here the analyst has sorted the dilemmas into the familiar "structure," "procedure," "climate" triad; he also has tightened the "coping" category to specify who actually did what. This matrix, too, is limited to changes that caused friction and disequilibria. A check back to Chart 17, section IV.F, shows the full range of changes, some of which were well accepted.

As we have noted, these illustrations exclude cases of nonchange. A column could easily be added that emphasizes stability and nonchange data—particularly on outcomes that a priori might have been expected to change as a result of the initial push or strain. That in turn suggests the need for an explanations column.

Columns can also be added that directly invoke explanations offered by site personnel.

Advice

Review (or have a colleague review) the first versions of your matrix to see what you are excluding, and what analyses you will and will not be able to make.

Ask someone to look at the completed matrix and tell you what your analytic assumptions seem to be. Can alternate assumptions be made that are more fruitful?

Move back and forth regularly between the matrix and the coded field notes to (a) confirm and deepen conclusions and (b) unravel puzzles as they appear.

In writing text outlining your conclusions, *document* them with the data excerpts that led you to them. A point of emphasis: This direct documentation is very different from what has been called the "sprinkling" function of anecdotes in text, where the researcher hunts for items that will entertain or convince the reader, then "sprinkles" them here and there as needed.

Time Required

Site dynamics matrices of the size and complexity illustrated here can usually be assembled in two or three hours, if the coding scheme (as was the case here) is closely coordinated with the column headings.

If not, the task of assembling what is essentially a second-level set of generalizations/explanations becomes very much more time-consuming. And one has to rely more heavily on informal syntheses, intuitions, impressions—which in turn need to be checked back against the write-ups, making at least one complete pass through them. Expect this to take a day, maybe two.

IV.G.a Process-Outcome Matrix

A researcher, especially one carrying out an evaluative mission, often wants to trace the impact of a number of different components or processes of a "program"—often in terms of several different outcomes.

A process-outcome matrix has processes for rows and outcomes for columns. Box IV.G.a provides an illustration from Patton (1980). Cell entries, as noted, may range from direct quotations or specific activities to more abstract formulations (patterns, themes). Patton illustrates with a juvenile justice program case, where a recurring process was "letting kids learn to make their own decisions," and a recurring outcome was "keeping kids straight." That process × outcome cell in the matrix leads the analyst to look for data on actual decisions made by kids that led to their "staying straight," and conclusions can be drawn about how strong the actual linkage is between that process and that outcome.

One potential difficulty with this format is that most processes have multiple outcomes, and most outcomes have multiple antecedents. Either you have to make simplifying assumptions, as done here, *or* you have to supplement the matrix with more multiform displays, such as causal networks (see section IV.J).

IV.H EVENT LISTING

Analysis Problem

Life, as we've noted, is chronology. We live in a flow of events. Some of these events occur before other events, some after. We usually feel that there are some connections between events (for example, deciding to renovate a bathroom leads to taking out a loan, the arrival of workers, the knocking down of a ceiling, the intrusion of plaster dust in other rooms, and the purchase of new lighting fixtures).

But though we can think of ourselves as being in the midst of a sort of river of events, that metaphor breaks down, because the river's flow is not one-dimensional. Some events occur in one domain of life, others elsewhere (the plaster dust intrusion occurs while one is revising the last chapters of a new book). Some events are close to us, some distant (while the loan is being taken out, the proposed federal budget deficit is

Chart 19b
Site Dynamics Matrix: Organizational Dilemmas
Posed by ECRI Program

	Dilemma	Issue	Who Did What	How Resolved Organizationally
Structure	-Voluntary use vs scheduling, curricular complications	2 regimens in same school	Principal seeks continuity	Non-users pressured to do ECRI or leave New slots filled with ECRI users
Procedure	-voluntary, flexible use vs perceived orthodoxy	classrooms 'policed, teachers unable to make adaptations	principal enforces evaluation sheet; users take liberties on the sly	principal: no evaluation for 1 year, then tightening prescriptive use; some latitude allowed
	-complexity, pace, redundancy of program	exhaustion, calls for aid, latitude, time off task	principal creates planning period, bends rules on Title I aides, brings helping teacher office into building	
	-"losing one's pupils" in morning scheduling	½-2/3 scheduled in non-homeroom classes	principal attempts to keep number down	satisfying 1-on-1 with own pupils; contact with new children
	-assistance vs. control	'helping' teacher also controls fidelity of implementation	shifting aid to helping teacher, control to building administrator	
Climate	-users vs non-users	users form cult, resented by others	coffee room conversation dominated by ECRI	most teachers become users non-users 'vindicated' (ECRI unsuited for lower grades)

plaster dust), and others are adventitious (a loved old cat dies).

Qualitative researchers are always interested in events: what they are, when they happened, and what their connections to other events are (or were), so as to preserve chronology and illuminate the *processes* occurring (a process, after all, is essentially a string of coherently related events). Typically, these interests lead to the production of a *chronology,* a narrative, a story arranged in proper time sequence (usually without flashbacks or flashforwards). But narrative text, as we have noted, has severe disadvantages (here, mainly its size, its dispersion, and its lack of structure). Narrative text resolves only feebly the problems of multidimensionality, inter-event influence, and differential salience of events.

However, narratives are in some sense indispensable if we are to understand a complex chronology in its full richness. The problem is that going straight to a narrative from written-up field notes runs an acute risk: One can tell a story that is partial, biased, or dead wrong—even though it may look novelistic, coherent, compelling, and plausible to a reader. The event listing is a way of guarding against false chronologies.

So the problems we face in understanding event flows are those of sorting out the different domains of events, preserving the sequence, showing the salience or significance of preceding events for following events—and doing all this in an easily visible display that enables us to construct a valid chronology.

Brief Description

An event listing arranges a series of concrete events by chronological time periods, sorting them into several categories.

Illustration

In the school improvement study, we wanted to display events relevant to the adoption and implementation of an innovation at the school level, showing them by different phases or time periods of the process. How might this be done?

Building the display. Keeping the classic left-to-right convention for the passage of time, we might make columns of the matrix for successive time periods. These might be defined arbitrarily (for example, year 1, year 2, and so on), or more organically by empirically derived phases or stages of the adoption-implementation process.

Which categories might we define for different types of events? The simplest set is perhaps one dealing with the *locale* of events: school level, school district level, state, regional, or federal level. They can be rows of the matrix.

Perhaps some events are more critical than others, serving to cause new events, or move the process forward into a new phase. They could be noted or marked in some way.

Chart 20 shows how this worked out for an innovation called SCORE-ON, a pull-out laboratory for teaching remedial math and reading skills. The time

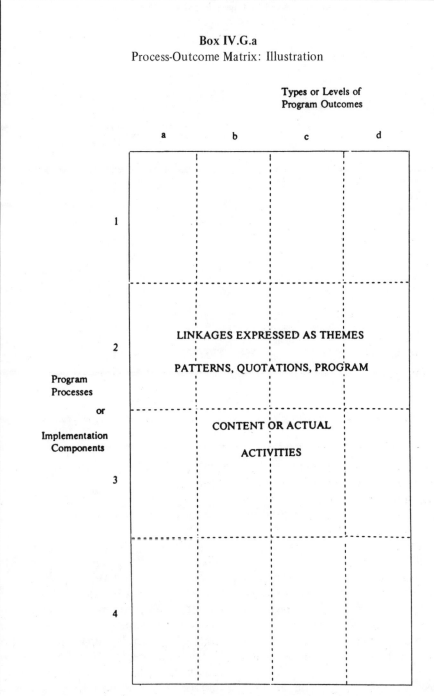

Box IV.G.a
Process-Outcome Matrix: Illustration

Types or Levels of
Program Outcomes

a   b   c   d

LINKAGES EXPRESSED AS THEMES

PATTERNS, QUOTATIONS, PROGRAM

CONTENT OR ACTUAL

ACTIVITIES

Program
Processes

or

Implementation
Components

SOURCE: Reprinted from Michael Quinn Patton, *Qualitative Evaluation Methods,* p. 319. Copyright 1980 by Sage Publications, Inc. Used by permission of the author.

Chart 20
Event Listing, Banestown Site

T I M E   P E R I O D S

LEVEL	Contextual press 1976-78	Emergence of the problem Oct. 1978	Awareness and proposal of solution Nov. 1978	Approval and preparations Jan.-Feb. 1979	Training and beginning operations March-April 1979	Expansion, new openings Sept. 1979	Budget reduction, disruption May 1980
State/Macro	minimal competency levels, testing introduced in state schools			proposal discussed, approval at state level	Smithson. middle school teachers, 2 admins. trained at D/D site (4 days, early March)		Reduction in Title I allocations
District	supplemental skills program introduced in reading and math	-alarm at failure rate -internal solutions proposed, found unacceptable	*officials see SCORE-ON at 'awareness fair' -IV-C proposal rapidly drawn up, submitted	* Smithson pupil folders screened -appointments made of Smithson lab teacher and aide	-30 4th grade pupils selected for Smithson lab -materials, technical assistance intensified for Smithson lab	-staff active in extending Smithson, launching new labs *Funding for all lab staff at Smithson taken over by Title I	*reduction in county, Title I budgets -proposed staff cuts, transfers in elementary schools
Local Schools	pressures begin to raise minimal levels			*continuation for following year planned for 5th grade in 2 middle schools; teachers named	-rooms, staffing completed for middle schools -2 other elementary schools authorized to implement in the fall	lab opens at Carington, Banestown Middle modified version opens at Smith Camp, South End	-middle schools unaffected by cuts -threat of discontinuation at Banestown Middle (conflicts)
Smithson School	large numbers of low achievers placed in FACILE classes	*4th grade teachers report 40 pupils 1-3 grade levels behind -teachers unfavorable to central office proposals	-teachers approve pull-out lab. formula	-lab teacher and aide replaced; some disgruntlement -lab room created, minimally equipped	- Smithson lab opens (late March) -preparations inadequate, materials not arrived, scheduling difficulties	Smithson expands to 45 pupils in 3rd, 4th grades -new teacher added for morning sessions	*major shifts in lab staffing announced to teachers -program to be cut back, focussed on grades 1-3, limited to 1½ posts

* barometric event

periods ("contextual press," "emergence of the problem," and so on) were initially defined conceptually, according to a general adoption-implementation model, but labels for each period were generated by the analyst based on what the core activities seemed to be during that time. A new time period was defined when a significant shift in activities occurred.

The analyst was focusing mainly on Smithson School, and wanted to have that as the most "local" of the locales (bottom row). However, the innovation was also being implemented in other schools (next row up). And events could also be sorted into "district" and "state/macro" levels, which in turn influenced the lower levels.

Finally, the analyst marked "barometric events" (those that moved the process on into the next time period or phase) with an asterisk.

Entering the data. An exploratory interview question had asked site personnel to describe the history of the innovation ("Can you tell me how SCORE-ON got started in this school?"). The follow-up probes fleshed out the sequence from innovation awareness to adoption, how and by whom key decisions were made, and the reasons involved. Other questions yielded data on outside agencies and events, and "anything else going on at the time that was important." Similar questions were asked about events during the implementation process.

The analyst looks at coded field notes (the codes in this case are any including the subcode CHRON, for chronology) and extracts accounts of specific events or occurrences, such as "Fourth grade teachers report 40 pupils are 1-3 grade levels behind," or "Officials see SCORE-ON at 'awareness fair.'"

Decision rules for data entry must be clear. In this case, the analyst defines an event as a specific action or occurrence mentioned by any respondent, and not denied or disconfirmed by anyone else. A brief phrase describing the event goes in the appropriate cell. If at least two people said that the event was important, crucial, or "made a big difference" for what happened subsequently, an asterisk is assigned.

Analyzing the data. A quick scan across the display shows us that the process of change is strikingly rapid: A problem seen in one elementary school in the fall of 1978 by the fourth-grade teachers apparently leads to the discovery and introduction of an innovation (SCORE-ON) that was in place in five district schools by the following fall.

A look at the asterisks helps explain some of the speed: the active involvement of central office officials after they saw the innovation at an awareness fair, leading to justificatory events such as the pupil file screening, and to specific school-level planning and the appointment of specific teachers to manage the remedial laboratory. We can also see that state-level competency requirements were the backdrop, and that the teachers' report of problems was probably an alarm or trigger that set off actions already fueled by concern at the district level to meet state requirements. When we note the repercussions of an externally driven budget crisis during the following school year, we can draw the inference that the original availability of Title I funds might have played a strong part in the original changes.

Given this compressed display, the analyst can now begin to piece together a coherent narrative that ties together the different streams into a meaningful account, a narrative that could only with difficulty have been assembled—or understood—from the diverse accounts in the field notes.

Here are some excerpts from the narrative the analyst produced. They should be read in conjunction with Chart 20.

> This chart calls for a more deliberate reading. Beginning in 1971 and intensifying in the years 1976-78, the State issued a series of increasingly precise and constraining documents. These texts called at first for adequate "standards of quality" in education. These standards were then outlined in the major subject matter areas. Competency testing was announced, first for grades K-3, then for 4-6. . . . After some delays, the first statewide tests keyed to these objectives for reading and math were scheduled for grade 4 in 1979 and for grades 5-6 in 1980-81.
>
> The response at the district level was to create a "supplemental skills program" in order to intensify remedial work in reading and mathematics so that minimal competency levels could be attained. . . .
>
> Schools throughout the country became more sensitized to the minimal competency obligation. . . . The implication was in the air that teachers might be held accountable for excessive rates of failure on statewide competency tests, but the pressures were still diffuse within individual schools. Teachers routinely attributed low performance to subnormal aptitude or to conditions at home over which they had no control.
>
> A special impetus was given in the fall of 1978, when the six fourth-grade teachers at Smithson noticed that they had an unusually large cohort of incoming pupils who were one or more grade levels behind in reading achievement. The number amounted to 40, about a fifth of the total. Thirty-eight of these forty had come out of the FACILE program in the first to third grades. It is not clear how so many of these pupils got to the fourth grade, but no one was surprised. The Vice-Principal says, "They got too tall, they got too bad."
>
> The teachers were worried that either promoting or retaining so many pupils would cause problems; they were leaning toward retention, but feared a massive protest by parents. Essentially, they were covering themselves, by announcing early in the year that they

> had inherited, not created, the problem. . . .
>
> The teachers contacted Mrs. Robeson, through the reading committee which she chaired. She met with them, then brought in Mrs. Bauers, the elementary supervisor. . . .
>
> During this phase, a circular announcing Federal funding in connection with the NDN came to the central office from the State superintendent. An awareness conference, presenting a series of projects, many of them keyed to remedial skill development, was to take place nearby. At Mrs. Bauers' initiative—and with an eye to a solution for the problem at Smithson school—a contingent from the central office (Mrs. Bauers, Mrs. Robeson, Mr. Rivers) attended the presentations and was attracted to SCORE-ON. It seemed a relatively flexible program, easy to integrate into the school in pull-out form. It was directed specifically to the bottom quartile in reading and math. . . .
>
> A proposal was written by Mr. Walt under title IV-C, with a request of $5,600 for training and materials. The request was cleared through the State Department, following a visit to the capital by Mrs. Bauers and Mrs. Robeson, accompanied by Alan Simens, principal of Smithson School. . . .

Note several things here: (1) The narrative helps knit together and flesh out events at different levels of the chart; (2) the analyst can add explanatory conditions or states that show how one event leads to another; (3) the return to the field notes often turns up other critical events or supporting information not originally in the display; and (4) the narrative is more understandable when read in conjunction with the display.

In short, the event listing helps ground the analyst's understanding of a complex flow of events, and increases confidence in the associated chronological account. It also lays the basis, as we shall see, for the beginnings of a causal analysis: what events led to what further events, and what mechanisms underlay those associations. For a good next step toward causal analysis, see Box IV.H.c, showing how event-listing data can be used to produce an "event-state network." Full-fledged causal networks are discussed in Section IV.J.

Variations

Event listings can be limited much more sharply to "critical incidents" (see Box IV.H.a), defined as important or crucial, and/or limited to an immediate setting.

Even more selectively the event listing can be limited to major events, each with a shorthand explanation of the connections or causal pushes that moved the process from one event to another. Figure 9 shows an example adapted from work by M. Pillet (personal communication, 1983), who was interviewing students who had interrupted their university studies and wanted to track them through subsequent experiences. The N here is one student. The succeeding

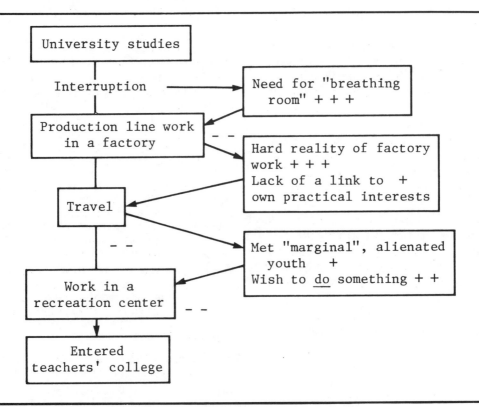

Figure 9   Event Listing: A Student's Learning and Work Experience

"experiences" are indicated in the left column; at the right we see the researcher's summary of the major forces moving the student to the next experience. The plus marks are an assessment of the strength of the various forces; the minus signs show the student's strength of dissatisfaction with the succeeding experiences.

For a careful reconstruction, the events in a listing can be dated within cells. Or the time periods can be specified much more narrowly (see Box IV.H.a). Or an event listing can cover a very brief time span (such as one hour in a classroom).

There are some recent, relatively simple statistical techniques for estimating trends and significance levels of event histories like those we have just described. See, for example, Tuma (1982).

Advice

Event listing can be done at many different levels of detail. Think first of how "micro" you want to be. Sorting out a series of candidate events on file cards can be of help in stabilizing the fineness of the approach.

Keep the rows to a maximum of four or five levels, and be sure they represent a meaningfully differentiated set of categories. Don't go finer than the study questions dictate. (In our illustration, it was not necessary to use events in the classroom locale.)

If you know in advance that you want to construct a chronology of events, then a CHRON code is essential to keep you from being overloaded with specific events. Doing an event listing for *ongoing* (not retrospectively recalled) events can be even more time-consuming unless clear codes (such as CRIT) for various types of critical events are assigned along the way.

As always, keep decision rules for data entry explicit and clean. When you enter a phrase or piece of data, it helps to have some sort of temporary tag attached so you can get back to its location in the written-up field notes (for instance, you might use 2-31 for interview 2, page 31) to clarify if needed, and to work on the production of the narrative. Be sure you have exhausted the coded data chunks before you start taking a summary look.

When the first version of the display is filled in, start a draft of a narrative summarizing it. That will require you to return to the field notes as you go. Stay open to the idea of adding new events to the listing or subtracting events that seem trivial or irrelevant.

Time Required

As always, much depends on how well coded the data are, the scope of time covered by the event listing, the fineness of detail, and the scale and complexity of the setting. An event listing like the one in our first illus-

Box IV.H.a1
Critical Incident Chart and Time Line
(excerpt from Hawthorn School)

Aug 1980		CBAM workshop for principals		District workshop for resource teachers re: composition
Sept. 1980		9/4; 9/24-29 Prindpal meets with teachers about teachers' goals for year	9/9;9/16 Principal meets with resource teacher to plan for year	9/3 District workshop for teachers on composition/ sourcebook
Oct. 1980	10/12-15 CBAM * interviews teachers	10/14 Principal has staff meeting re composition / Teachers confused about program plan committee to review*	10/23 Principal meets with resource teacher re composition	10/22 Sixth grade teacher tells principal of other teachers' concerns about innovation
Nov. 1980		11/10* Principal & resource teacher meet to plan composition & committee / Resource teacher tells principal of district ideas to clarify innovation	11/10 Principal & resource teacher meet with committee (includes 6th grade teacher) / 11/25 Resource teacher meets with committee in 2 sections-- upper and lower grades	Principal meets with various teachers to encourage work on composition-related activities / 11/25 on Committee teachers meet with others at grade level
Dec. 1980		12/1; 12/15 Principal & resource teacher meet to plan composition committee meetings / 12/1 Composition discussed at staff meeting	12/10 Resource teacher meets with committee sections to review scope and sequence / 12/18 Resource teacher meets with committee sections to plan *	12/16 Resource teacher distributes scope and sequence to all teachers

LEGEND   * refers to events that were critical in initiating writing composition as a program separate from the language arts curriculum as a whole. These events led to the development of a HAWTHORN writing program, based on teachers needs and Sourcebook guidelines.

Events boxed ☐ had a strong catalytic effect on focusing the program or on developing the principal's game plan for implementation.

SOURCE: Stiegelbauer, Goldstein, and Huling (1982). Reprinted by permission.

Box IV.H.a2
Intervention Map: Scheme for Locating Critical Incidents

Game Plan Component 3:   Consultation and Reinforcement
   Principal emphasizes need to improve in areas of language arts and composition
   by reviewing weaknesses as shown in school testing. He provides new information
   on teaching composition to help resolve weak areas and uses Resource Teacher,
   Amy Bauman and individual teachers to work with other teachers in encouraging
   use of new material.

Strategy 3.1 (135). Principal uses CAP/CAT scores to reinforce need to
   improve in areas of language arts, including composition.

   Tactic 3.1.2 (23). Principal includes language arts and composition in
      some teachers' objectives on the basis of CAP/CAT scores.

   Incidents: 27, 26, 25, 24

   Tactic 3.1.3.(145). Principal meets with upper grade teachers to discuss
      methods and goals for composition and language arts on the 1981 CAP tests.

   Incidents: 85, 86, 28, 131, 180, 75.

Strategy 3.2. (155). Principal uses key teachers to disseminate information and
   to develop staff support for composition program.

   Tactic 3.2.1.(157). Principal appoints teacher 4397 to be in charge of
      School contribution to District Magazine REFLECTIONS.

   Incidents: 44, 62, 76, 100.

SOURCE: Stiegelbauer, Goldstein, and Huling (1982).   Reprinted by permission.

---

tration can be assembled in half a day (one site, perhaps eight key informants, well-coded notes). The Pillet variant, on the other hand, was done in fifteen minutes by a researcher closely familiar with the data in a single interview.

Writing the narrative usually takes about as much time as the event listing itself. The illustration in Chart 20 led to a ten-page narrative, which required about five hours of work. Our experience has been that this is time well invested; an event listing and associated chronology represent one's first basic grasp of what happened, and suggest the subsequent lines of deeper description, analysis, and interpretation that will follow.

IV.H.a Critical Incident Chart

Sometimes a researcher wants to limit an event listing to those events seen as critical, influential, or decisive in the course of some process. A useful

approach is that developed by Stiegelbauer et al (1982), who extracted "critical incidents" occurring during implementation of a new language arts program at a school site. The process was aided by specialists in the CBAM (Concerns-Based Adoption Model) approach to the study and practice of school improvement.

In Box IV.H.a1, time goes vertically. That makes it a bit easier to examine and compare events that occurred during a given time period. The columns are not ordered, but easily could be. The dates for events make temporal ordering easy.

The chart selects only two to four critical events per month, and marks (with boxes) those seen as having a "strong catalytic effect" on determining the need for the program, or on the principal's "game plan" (strategy) for implementation. Certain events are also marked that affected a subprogram for writing skills. The authors' analytic comment is:

Relationships between events can be seen as both temporal and due to an exchange of information. In

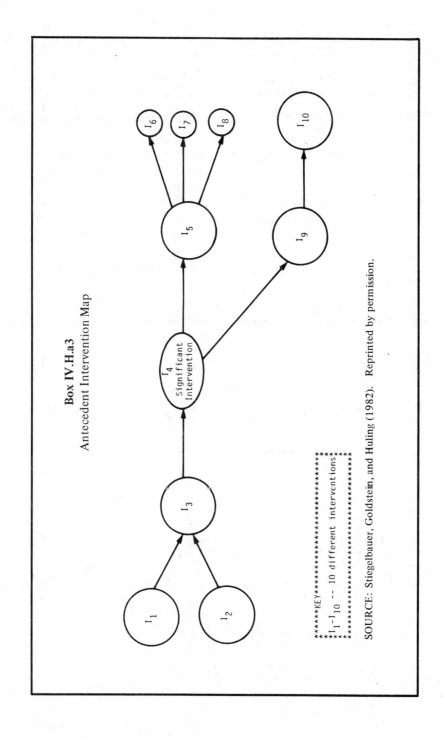

Box IV.H.a3

Antecedent Intervention Map

I_6

I_7

I_8

I_{10}

I_5

I_9

I_4
Significant
Intervention

I_3

I_1

I_2

```
*****KEY******************************
*****I₁-I₁₀ -- 10 different interventions*****
*************************************
```

SOURCE: Stiegelbauer, Goldstein, and Huling (1982). Reprinted by permission.

this school, teacher confusion about the program, discussion of teacher concerns, and new information about the program from the resource teacher all had a significant effect on program development.

Stiegelbauer et al. (1982) also employed two other mapping devices. The first was an "intervention map," which employed a hierarchical scheme (intervention "incidents" within "tactics," nested with "strategies," in turn nested within "game plans"). Box IV.H.a2 presents an excerpt, showing how the "critical incidents" can be distinguished by their scope and level within the scheme. Stiegelbauer et al. also employed an "antecedent intervention map," showing graphically how various interventions led to each other over time, as shown in Box IV.H.a3. Using all three display modes in combination enabled Stiegelbauer et al. to form a clear idea of the influence of the context and of significant actors within it as the change process went forward.

IV.H.b Growth Gradient

Events can sometimes be conceptualized as associated with some underlying variable that changes over time. That's a rather abstract characterization, which will come immediately clear with a look at Figure 5 (p. 87).

Here the analyst is interested in the main variable of *internal diffusion* of an innovation, defined as growth in the number of teachers using it. That is represented as a conventional line graph. But the analyst has attached various critical events to the line—appointments of key personnel, training, and the like—that help to expand our understanding of the movements of the main variable (for example, the sudden jump following the August 1977 workshops).

IV.H.c Event-State Network

The alert reader will have noticed that some entries in Chart 20 are not really specific events, but more general "states," such as "alarm at failure rate." Such states or conditions are not as time-limited as events, and often serve as the mediators or links between specific events.

One way to display this is to show events as boxes (the sharp edges imply specificity) and states as bubbles (round edges imply more diffuseness) and then to connect the boxes and bubbles by lines to show what led to what. Box IV.H.c shows an excerpt from an event-state network drawn from the data in the event listing in Chart 20.

Event-state networks are a simple, easy way to make sense out of an event listing. Once an event listing is done, a network can be generated rather quickly. Write one event per small card, generate "state" cards as you go, and arrange the emerging network on a big sheet of paper, drawing arrows as you go. As we will note in section IV.J, this method is an especially helpful step toward assessing causal dynamics in a particular site. Requiring the "state" cards means (a) reassessing the field notes for evidence of the consequences and/or the antecedents of specific events, and (b) surfacing your generalized understandings of what was moving events along in the process you are studying. By the time an event listing is generated, you usually have a set of implicit generalizations about why things happened as they did: Event-state networks are a way of making those ideas explicit and verifiable. They're also enjoyable and rapid—an hour or so for the size shown, *after* the event listing is complete.

It doesn't usually help to add narrative text (the display itself is much more economical and illuminating), but a summary set of comments may be helpful. However, event-state networks have their main importance as precursors to more generic causal analysis, to which we now turn.

IV.J CAUSAL NETWORK

Analysis Problem

Background. Field research, as we have said several times, is a process of progressive focusing and funneling. As data are collected, we can see more and more clearly the factors that bring the flotsam and jetsam of local events into a meaningful pattern.

These local factors are not little lizards hiding under stones turned over by the researcher in the course of investigating the local terrain. Rather, they are mental *constructions* that the analyst gradually elaborates in the course of piecing together discrete bits of data. These constructions have no physical reality "out there." They are *mental* maps, abstracted webs of meaning that the analyst lays over bits of data to give them shape without doing violence to them. In other words, piecing together local data is an *achievement*, not a given.

It is also an achievement for local informants; they too walk around with a generalized organization of experience in their heads that provides them with a frame for action and perception and explains what causes what in their world. This mental schema or map *works* for them; they can compare it with others' maps and use it to get what they are after (see Axelrod, 1976).

So, much of field research has to do with schema absorption; the analyst goes around recording individuals' mental cause maps, putting them together and making connections with his or her own, evolving map. The rub here is that the analyst has to get up to speed, with a map that is initially far more primitive than informants'. So the first attempt to take in and piece together local cause maps is usually jumbled and vague, and sometimes plain wrong. By the fourth or

Box IV.H.c

Event-State Network, Banestown Site (excerpt)

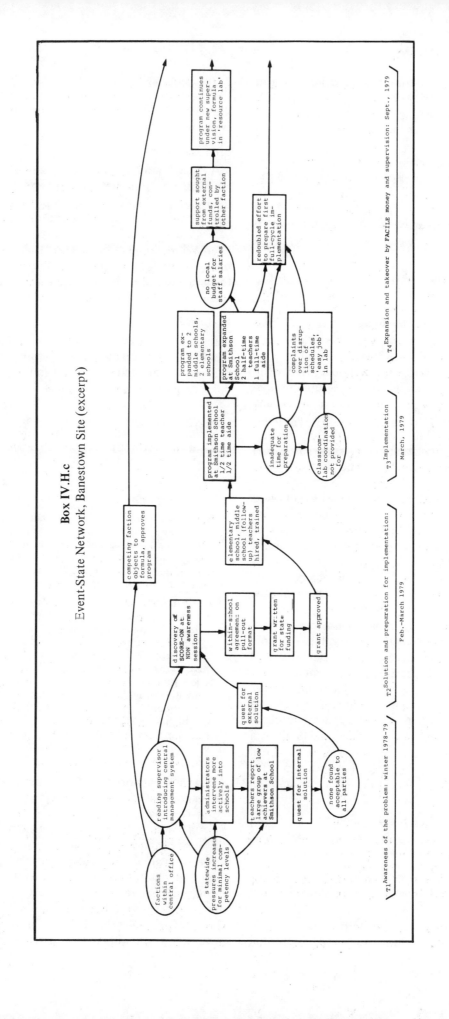

fifth attempt, however, things look brighter—and clearer. Trying to shortcut those iterations is a perilous, often self-defeating exercise, like jumping off a 40-meter ski jump after having practiced only on moguls.

Developing good causal maps that are connected with those of respondents also helps the analyst avoid getting overloaded by piles of discrete data, and produces results in a systematic, verifiable way.[5] As we shall see, causal maps can be checked out thoroughly with site personnel, long before the final report is written.

Analysis task. Field research typically has both a *descriptive* and an *explanatory* function. The researcher wants to depict the local context and what happens within it *and* to disclose the rules and reasons that determine why things happen the way they do. Until recently, the dominant view was that field studies should busy themselves with description and leave the explanations to other people with large quantitative data bases. Or perhaps field researchers, as is now widely believed, can provide "exploratory" explanations—which still need to be quantitatively verified.

Much recent experience supports a claim we wish to make here: that field research is far *better* than solely quantified approaches at developing explanations of what we call *local causality*—the actual events and processes that led to specific outcomes. And we believe that, given multiple-site data, it is possible to develop rather powerful *general* explanations. In this sense, field data can provide serious *confirmation* of plausible causal models drawn from aggregated survey data, and produce genuinely powerful explanations. We must emphasize that even the most elegant quantitative procedures (let's say cross-lagged correlations, LISREL, or path analysis) can only develop plausible possibilities, averaged across many persons and situations. To say, for example, that parental aspirations, student self-concept, and socioeconomic status "cause" college attendance is only the grossest of explanations. How the path of causality actually works in the case of a specific adolescent in a real family is a very different matter. That is what we mean by "local causality," which must be carefully understood in order to build a causal map that has more general applicability.[6]

So our basic questions are as follows:

(1) How can single-case researchers build a progressively integrated map of field site phenomena that has *local* causal significance?

(2) How can data from multiple sites be aligned to make inferential maps containing more *general* causal explanations?

In both cases, the answer lies in the creation of a "causal network" that is an abstracted, inferential picture organizing field study data in a coherent way. This section will review how to do this for a single site; sections V.G and V.H outline the multiple-site approach.

Brief Description

A causal network is a visual rendering of the most important independent and dependent variables in a field study and of the relationships between them. The plot of these relationships is *deterministic* rather than solely correlational. It is assumed that some factors exert a directional influence on others: X brings Y into being, or makes Y larger or smaller. A causal network, to be useful, also has associated text describing the meaning of the connections among factors.

Illustration

Figure 10 shows a causal network for one site. At first it may look too complex and forbidding for words. But look at one section of it (starting at the upper left) in conjunction with some text, like this:

> The first three antecedent variables (1, 2, and 4) worked out this way. The state mandate (2) for well-planned career education programs, together with assessment of local performance as less than adequate (1), led to a search for new programs (3), which proved to be a good fit (7) with district characteristics, and hence to district endorsement (8), and to adoption of the program (9).

> But these were not sufficient causes of adoption. Inadequate local funds (4) to cover existing programs led to a ceaseless search for add-on funds (6) as almost a "way of life" for the district. That search led to getting temporary external funds (14) for a three-year period; they were the other basic cause of adoption (9).

> The program, when adopted, proved to have substantial implementation requirements (10), which dictated the need for assistance (18), and also exerted a good deal of pressure for careful selection of high-quality staff (21), and for careful preparation (19) of them to carry out the program. The heavy implementation requirements (10), and to some degree the assistance provided (18) induced a good deal of user commitment (20), and in turn user skill (26) which was also high because of staff quality (21). High user skill, in conjunction with the fact that the program was quite well stabilized (27) by late 1980 brought about a reasonable degree of student impact (30).

Text and network together communicate more than either could alone. We are moving toward an explanation—not just a description—of what happened at Perry-Parkdale. The network has gotten 300-400 pages of field notes down to a few dozen boxed words and arrows on one page; it and the text tell economically how and why things turned out as they did. Furthermore, such a network can be easily corrected/verified not only by researcher colleagues, but, as we shall show, by people at the site. Finally, we can testify that developing and refining causal networks is fascinating

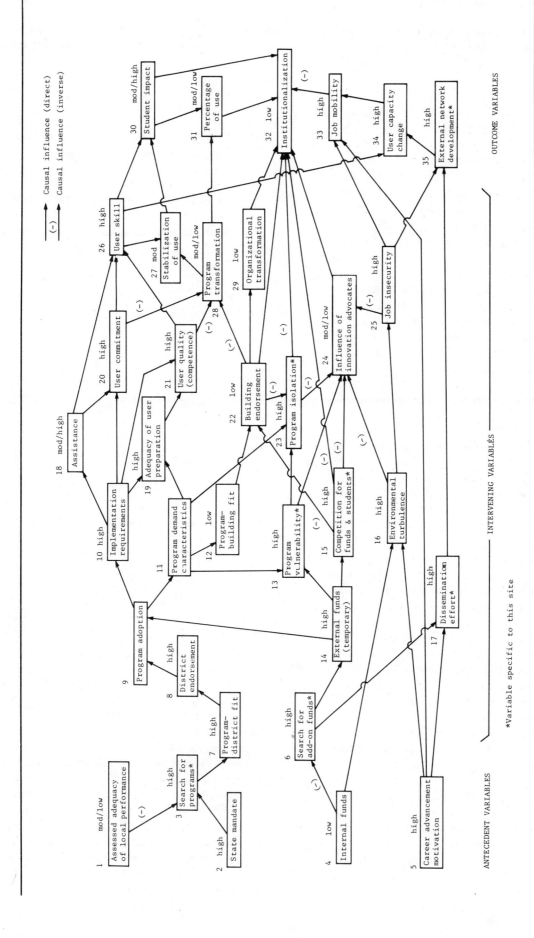

Figure 10 Causal Network for Perry-Parkdale CARED Program

and enjoyable, with plenty of "aha" experiences.

How do such networks get developed in a reliable way? Let's walk through the process.

Two general approaches to building causal networks. Basically, you have to intend from the beginning of data collection to produce a causal map, so that successive rounds of data collection, interim analysis of *all* the data, and iterations of the map itself all build toward that end. But there are two different ways of approaching the task, which can be loosely labeled "inductive" and "deductive."

In the *inductive* approach, also called constructive or generative (Goetz & LeCompte, 1981; Becker, 1958; Zelditch, 1962), the researcher discovers recurrent phenomena in the stream of local experience and finds recurrent relations among them.

These constants become working typologies and hypotheses that get progressively modified and refined as they are used in the next pass at the site. The local cause map emerges piecemeal and inductively. It is observed to have both regularity and pattern; some things only happen when others do or don't. These things and the links between them then acquire their own names or labels, cluster into probable causes and the effects they appear to engender—and the analyst has a causal network.

In the *deductive* strategy, also called "enumerative" or "conceptual" (Kaplan, 1964; Popper, 1968), the researcher has some orienting constructs and propositions to test or observe in the field. These analytic units get operationalized, then matched to a body of field data.

The deductive researcher *starts with* a preliminary causal network, and the inductive researcher *ends up* with one. In both cases, however, the initial versions are amended and refined as they are trained on empirical events and characteristics. By the end of data gathering, both species of researchers are about at the same place. Both are *substantiating* a cause-and-effect map, but the "conceptualist" has a shaken-down model and the "constructivist" has a built-up one.

The two strategies imply different start-up tactics. The deductive researcher would generate an initial conceptual framework from the best accumulated science and lore of the domain under study. The next step is operationalizing that framework with research questions, start-up codes, and some initial data-gathering devices. This implies a fair amount of front-end work. Later, the codes get enriched and reconfigured, and the research questions get answered or reframed. Most important, the conceptual framework is gradually rehashed, refined into the ultimate causal network.

By contrast, the inductive researcher would go for a more data-derived causal network—one that is dredged up progressively from the field. The ultimate model would *then* be confronted with the regnant science and lore in that domain.

As we have suggested throughout, the two strategies are more similar than conceptual purists have claimed, when one comes to grips with real data in real time. The fact that a sociologist can dredge up "grounded" institutional or cultural phenomena from the same empirical swamp the psychologist used to get intra-individual phenomena should tell us something: People need to impose conceptual frameworks on life in order to make it intelligible. But they also need the experience of *living,* in order to have meaningful ways of organizing its properties. Many epistemologists (for example, Campbell, 1975) have shown that purely conceptual models are riddled with taken-for-granted empirical assumptions—without most of which, in fact, they are incomprehensible. The reader simply fills in the blanks unconsciously while decoding the model, just as the author did in drafting it. So induction and deduction are dialectical, rather than mutually exclusive research procedures. The constructivist's inductions are informed by a personal conceptual universe, and the conceptualist's a priori frameworks contain more empirical data than at first meets the eye.

In earlier sections, we have tilted toward more front-end conceptualization. This is not only an intellectual preference, but the bitter fruit of several empirical experiences (Miles, 1979; Huberman, 1981a). In brief, without clear initial conceptualizing, we were drowned in tidal waves of shapeless data that would have taken years to analyze well. We learned—inductively—that a more deductive approach would have reduced and focused our data set without losing juice or meaning, and helped us find causal relationships faster. In what follows, we approach causal network-building from the more a priori side—while highlighting the values of doing it more inductively along the way. Most of the techniques we suggest can be used by analysts of either predilection, at points when they seem most useful.

We shall also show how several methods for within-site analysis we have covered earlier can be building blocks for the causal network.

Getting started. What you find in any quest is, of course, largely a function of what you set out to find and where you look for it. In one form or another the researcher will begin with a finite number of ideas, constructs, hypotheses, and research questions, together with some sample of people and treatments within which these ideas, constructs, and so on are likely to appear. The researcher may take an initial cut at how some of these things might fit together, just as we did in the conceptual framework (Figure 3) that was generated for the school improvement study. Note that such a framework already carries some causal freight. It makes guesses about which factors logically influence others, which ones are *likely to appear together* and which not, and which ones *have to happen first* for others to happen later (that is, directional influence). These are, of course, the conventional canons used by epistemologists to make causal inferences (for example, see Russell, 1948; Salmon, 1966; Swinburne, 1974). But the important thing to remember here is that the field researcher who begins with such a conceptual framework is not boldly going to ignore data that suggest otherwise. He or she *is*, however, going to generate research questions, codes, and samples of people and treatments that give the framework a chance of working out. A more inductively oriented researcher, by contrast, would focus initially on a more general domain or macroconcept. For example, a fieldworker might start with an interest in "servicing" and hang around a department store to see how it goes on—or, as Glaser (1978) has described, start with an interest in whorehouses and end up with "servicing" as the key to its generic processes.

In effect, no researcher can *really* begin with a *tabula rasa* mind. The question is: How soon and how systematically do I bring my assumptions and framing ideas to awareness? And how do I permit data to elaborate, correct, and extend them?

In the approach we generally favor, the first building blocks of causal analysis are the—deliberately general—*conceptual framework* (section II.A) and *research questions* (section II.B), along with the *start list of codes* (section III.B). Next come the *reflective remarks* and *added marginal remarks* in the transcriptions of field notes (see Boxes III.B.a and III.B.b). These are typically modest, data-shaping exercises. They alert the analyst to variables that go together and that contrast with other variables, and they invite a closer look at something that might be an underlying theme or pattern.

All this means that *discrete* variables are getting clumped into tentative families. If they can stay in those families through successive data-gathering and analyzing cycles, they are good candidates for a "box" in the causal network, with an arrow leading to or coming from another "box."

In a study of interorganizational linkages, for example, we found that a college of education had an active in-service teacher education program. Its faculty also served on local school district committees and got involved in community service projects. Furthermore, we found college staff to be shying away from state-level assignments and national conferences. We evolved the conglomerate notion of *localism* as a theme, putting all these indices into one bundle. Localism also seemed to lead to a *technical assistance* orientation rather than to a research or *academic excellence* orientation in the college, another

bundle of initially discrete findings. So these two variable clusters got created, linked, and, later on, incorporated into the causal network when they were observed to affect the pattern of interorganizational relations that the study was addressing.

Assembling fragments: Pattern codes, interim memos, and summaries. As shown earlier, marginal and reflective remarks often translate into *pattern codes* (section III.C). They are still bigger bites of data, and often become candidates for inclusion in a causal network. In essence, they signal a theme or pattern that makes a difference locally. For example, the "TEAMS" metaphor describing a conflict between two administrative factions in a school district (section III.B) eventually got translated into a stream of variables such as "career advancement motivation" and "climate in district office" on the causal network that eventually affected key outcome variables such as "institutionalization" of the educational innovation.

Moving up another notch, one can see how pattern codes get extended into *memos* (section III.D), then into initial attempts to pull coded data and memos together in the *interim site summary* (section III.F). This is not to say that the field researcher works this hierarchically or deliberately. But on a cognitive level, this is roughly how discrete pieces of data are combining into an evidential chain that has a beginning causal logic. One thinks, roughly, "These variables are present or absent together, while others look random or unconnected." This is a sort of "abstracting induction" (Duncker, 1945). But with more knowledge, one begins to think, "Some of these variables are coming into play *before* others, varying *with* others, or having an *effect* on others, and that effect seems to change when *other* variables are taken into account." One is, actually, using the standard canons of inductive inference: temporal precedence, covariation, and directional influence. So we have the rudiments of a cause map that contains guesses about *directions* of influence among *sets* of variables.

Operationally, however, these are little more than informed hunches about covariation that the qualitative analyst needs to check out during the next site visit—or that a colleague at another site in a multiple-case study has to try out initially on that data set. Typically, the *site analysis meeting* (section III.E) or other cross-site exchange during data collection will result in a trial of one analyst's emerging causal map on another's data.

The importance of all these devices is that they support, even force, analytical activity. They are occasions for focusing and otherwise tidying up one's thinking. So this is a good time to lay out some of the fragments of one's emerging causal map in one place. Some procedures for doing this are as follows:

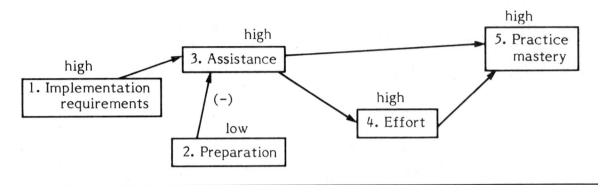

Figure 11   Causal Fragment: Mastery of a New Educational Practice

- Translate the pattern codes into variables, that is, something that can be scaled (high to low, big to little, more to less).
- Rate the variable (for instance, high, moderate, low). How much of it is there in the site?
- Draw a line between pairs of variables that covary, that is, that appear together consistently at the site, that have some kind of relationship—for example, more of one variable goes with less of another.
- Draw a directional arrow between each variable that comes first (temporally) and those later ones it appears to influence. "Influence" here means that more or less of one variable determines to some extent the rating of another. The rating of the second variable might have been different had the first one not been there.
- If two variables covary and are related but seem only to have a tepid or oblique influence on one another, there is probably another, latent variable that needs to be invented to join the two. Review the full list of codes to see if one fits here. (Section VII.A.10 has more on this tactic, called *finding intervening variables.*)

Figure 11 presents an example of a causal fragment. This one puts together themes having to do with the mastery of a new educational practice. The story can be told quickly. A demanding project with high implementation requirements (1) began with inadequate preparation (2) and was bailed out by high levels of assistance (3), which increased local efforts (4) and facilitated practice mastery (5). The minus sign indicates reverse causal influence: Low preparation leads to high assistance.

The intent here is to stimulate thinking, not to get closure. The analyst should try to assemble a few such fragments without necessarily connecting one to another. Play around; do some causal noodling. Don't try to connect variables that don't go together *empirically,* even if on logical grounds they "should." Some variables, like some blood types, don't commingle well, and the analyst can easily get led into Byzantine reasoning to decide that they do go together.[7]

A useful next step is to take these fragments out to the field during later data collection to see how, and

whether, they work. This can include some "member checks" (Guba & Lincoln, 1981), that is, submitting the diagram to an informant to get confirmation and qualifications (for instance, *some* preparation was decent, some assistance didn't have an effect on levels of effort, some users were competent and experienced enough to do without preparation or assistance and still get high practice mastery). That might suggest that the next iteration of the network should have an arrow from a new box labeled "user competence" to the "effort" variable (4) and to the "practice mastery" variable (5).

Generating a causal network variable list. About three-quarters of the way through data collection, the researcher should be ready to assemble the remaining pieces of the causal network. A useful first step is to generate the full set of network variables. This, too, is an exercise in playful brainstorming. The idea is to list all the "events," "factors," "outcomes,"· "processes," and so on that seem to be important, then to turn them into variables. For instance, the several fights between employees will become "organizational conflict." The first pass should be exhaustive, the next one more selective. That is, once a full set of variables is down, the list should be combed for redundancies and overdifferentiation (for example, three types of fighting between employees). As a rough rule of thumb, fifteen variables are probably too few and forty too many. As an illustration, Chart 21 presents a list of core variables generated in our school improvement study.

Note that such a list typically combines a "constructive" and "conceptual" approach. Some variables come directly out of the field (such as external funds, IV-C program development); others are there because the initial constructs or research questions oriented the researcher toward a search for empirical instances of them (such as program-district fit, assistance, program transformation).

In a single-site study, the variable list is a straightforward procedure. In a multiple-site study, by contrast, we are at a decisive moment. For cross-site com-

Chart 21
List of Antecedent, Mediating, and Outcome Variables

Antecedent or Start Variables	Mediating Variables	Outcomes
Internal funds	External funds	Stabilization of use
Career advancement motivation	Program adoption (NDN)	Percentage of use
Assessed adequacy of local performance	Program concept initiative (IV-C)	Student impact
Environmental turbulence	Program development (IV-C)	User capacity change
	District endorsement	Institutionalization
	Building endorsement	Job mobility
	Influence of innovation advocate	
	Implementation requirements	
	Adequacy of initial user preparation	
	Program-district fit	
	Program-building fit	
	Program-user fit	
	Assistance	
	User commitment	
	User skill	
	Program transformation	
	Teacher-administrator harmony	
	Validation effort (IV-C)	
	Stability of program leadership	
	Stability of program staff	
	Organizational transformation	

parisons, the same variables are going to be used to analyze five, ten, or twenty sites. For this to happen, theoretically *each* of the variables has to be empirically meaningful at *all* the sites. Of course, one should leave slack for the probability that there will be a handful of *site-specific* variables in addition. They are of two types: those that are influential at only one site and those that are influential at most but not all sites. In the former case, the final causal network will contain a site-specific variable, labeled as such. In the latter case, some network variables will be dropped (with an explanation) from the sites at which they contribute little to the analysis.

The process of building the list will naturally go more easily if there has been plenty of prior contact around field notes, pattern codes, memos, interim site summaries, and causal network fragments. If not, you can expect an extended period of getting people's heads together, so that variables have a common meaning.

Drawing the causal network. In principle, one could draw a full causal network for the site at this point, then go back to the field for final testing and refining. In general, we do not advise this. The risk is that network vision sets in too early. The analyst constructs a cause map and begins to use it to interpret all the phenomena of interest. A final "coherent" picture emerges *before* the individual parts of the picture have been carefully studied individually and in combination. It is as if a survey researcher began estimating a path model before looking at the distributions, cross-tabulations, and partial correlations. The answers go looking for the questions.

The better alternative is to save causal network drawing and analysis for the end—to make it the last analytic exercise. This does not rule out getting reactions to the network from the site later on, if necessary by mail, as we describe in section IV.J.a.

All the progressively multivariate, within-site analysis we have covered up to now can feed causal network analysis. Analyzing *conceptual clusters* (section IV.E), for example, allows the analyst to tease out the relationships within one of the variable families. *Effects matrices* (section IV.F) are exercises in identifying cause-effect relations. *Both* clustering and cause-effect inferencing are at work in the *site dynamics matrices* (section IV.G). In other words, causal analyses are being done incrementally; one is testing individual paths more rigorously and, at the same time, building a cognitively integrated cause map.

Finally, the *event-state network* (Box IV.H) gets us almost there. Let us illustrate how. Figure 13 shows an excerpt from the event-state network for the field site in our illustration. Figure 14 shows an excerpt from the final causal network, with the variable numbers keyed to the corresponding variables in the event-state network. There should usually be markedly *fewer* causal net variables than event-state boxes and bubbles. (This would be the case here, had we shown a fuller excerpt from the event-state network, and had we taken the three site-specific variables out of the causal network.) In most cases site-specific events and states can turn into more generic network variables spanning individual cases. For instance, everybody usually has money problems ("external funds"), school faculties support or oppose new ventures ("building endorsement"), and the innovation's champions have more or less clout ("influence of innovation advocates").

Let us now take a second look at the fully drawn causal network that appears in Figure 10, on page 133. The figure should now be easier to read. Note (a) the over-time flow denoted along the bottom and (b) the direction of all the arrows. Causal modeling assumes temporal relationships and usually assumes unidirectional ones; that is, early causes make for later effects.

Drawing the network is probably best done the same way one should analyze it: stream by stream. Some streams—unbroken chains of variables—are long: Look at the one that runs directly from box 1 through

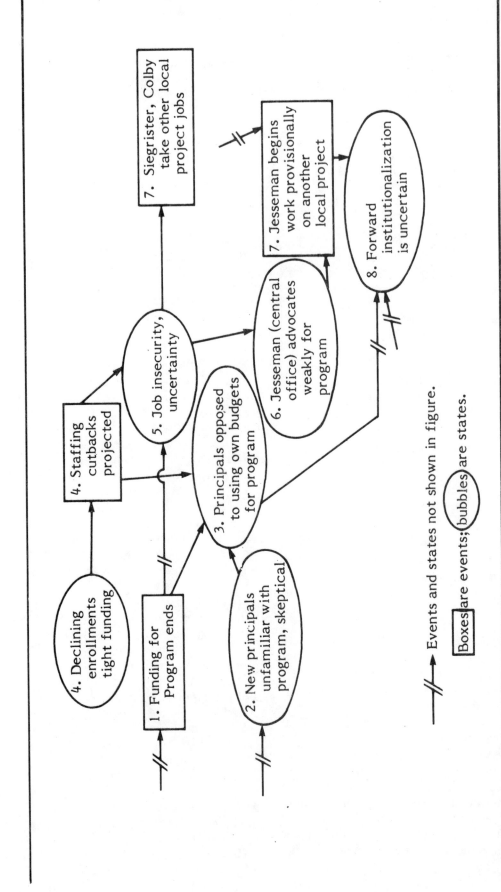

Figure 13 Excerpt from an Event-State Network

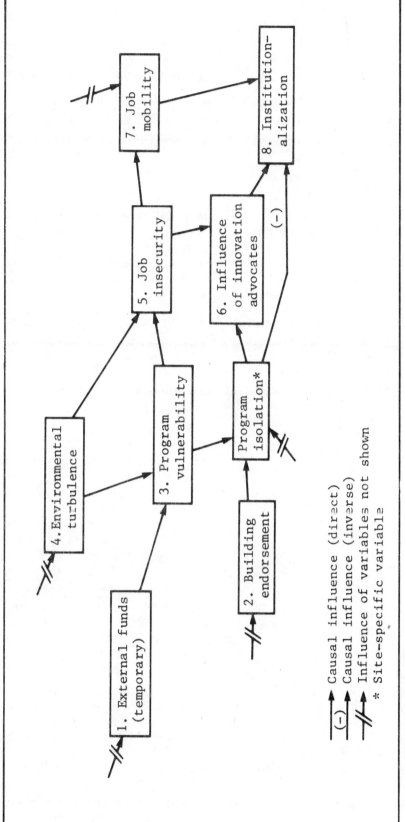

Figure 14 Excerpt from a Causal Network

The boxes in the figure, read in sequence, are:

1. External funds (temporary)
2. Building endorsement
3. Program vulnerability
4. Environmental turbulence
5. Job insecurity
6. Influence of innovation advocates
7. Job mobility
8. Institution-alization

Program isolation*

Legend:

→ Causal influence (direct)
→ Causal influence (inverse)
⫢→ Influence of variables not shown
* Site-specific variable

boxes 8, 9, 10, to 30, even to 32. Others are, conveniently, shorter; the bottom stream from 5 to 35 and 33 is a short one. Within an unbroken stream, there are usually eddies leading in different directions or ending up at the same place via a different route. They should also be drawn in.

Streams can be most easily drawn—especially if the event-state network is used as the semifinal cut—from antecedents forward in time. It is also possible to take a dependent variable and work backward, but then it is important to run it forward again to be sure the links are coherent and empirically justified. One will usually find that there are cross-stream connections, and they can be drawn in as the network evolves.

Often, these streams and eddies have a name—a scenario or theme—and this makes them easier both to analyze and to render. For example, along the bottom stream variables 5, 17, 35, and 34 have a "cosmopolitanizing" theme: People go outside their environments in connection with a new project and the experience both stretches them and sets up possible career shifts. Or again, staying along the bottom of the network, boxes 4, 16, 25, and 33 add up to a "casualty" stream: low money, high turbulence (usually in the form of budget cuts), staff instability, and ultimate staff reassignments.

Alternatively, the streams can be labeled according to the level of dependent variables, such as high student impact scenarios, low institutionalization scenarios, or high job mobility scenarios. These similarly named scenarios can be very different. For instance, as we just saw, one high job mobility scenario involves a promotion or desirable transfer, whereas another involves an unwanted reassignment or even a layoff.

These themes and scenarios should come as no surprise to the analyst. Most will have been foreshadowed in the pattern codes, memos, and interim summaries, and some will have been teased out of effects matrices and causal dynamics tables. In the causal network, the analyst traces the emergence and consequences of a particular theme and orchestrates it with others.

Finally, causal networks can have a *predictive* function. In drawing a variable stream with two or three substreams leading out to the dependent variables, one is in a position to say something like "effect Z is likely to obtain when predictors J, B, and L occur in sequence," or "to get high levels of Z, one needs high antecedent levels of J, B, and L but not necessarily of V and Q." These statements are not very meaningful in a single-case analysis, but they perk up noticeably when *several* within-case nets are showing the same or a similar pattern. More on this later (see sections V.G and V.H).

Causal network narratives. Drawing conclusions from the network should wait until the analyst has a more coherent sense of what is on it. Like all time-related representations, this one tells a story—really, several stories. One should write out a chronological narrative for each of the major streams. In this case, one starts at the beginning. Chart 22 presents the narrative for the causal network shown above.

Writing the narrative usually does several things. It forces the analyst to be less mechanistic and more coherent; turning a network into clear text requires one to be honest and explicit about what is causing what. Corrections and revisions are likely. Second, it provides an opportunity for expansion: The analyst can explain why variables are related, why they are rated differently, why some precede others, which ones matter more, and so on.

Third, both displays—the network and the text—are the basic material to be handed to a colleague for reaction and revision. In general, it is nearly impossible to map a causal network "right" the first time. Someone else who knows the data base needs to review it and suggest improvements. (Box IV.J.a shows how this can be done with site personnel as well.)

Only at this point, in our view, can a causal network be used to generate more general explanations on a multisite level. Approaches to that task are outlined in sections V.G and V.H.

Variations

It is sometimes possible to prespecify the general types of stream that a network should include (for example, in our school improvement study, the program development stream and the building/district stream) and draw it that way. However, networks have lives of their own and cannot always be precategorized without doing violence to the data.

Dobbert (1982) has described a graphic modeling approach developed by Silvern (1972) called LOGOS, which is based on systems engineering ideas. She suggests the use of cards for variables during the construction process, which aids flexibility and revision.

Advice

Causal networks are data-condensing and data-sorting exercises, not rigorous multivariate anlyses. They report themes and configurations more than "findings." Unlike the matrices shown earlier, they don't oblige the analyst to draw univocal conclusions from distributions and partitions. This is another way of saying that two analysts, working independently with the same data set, even with the same matrices and variable list, would probably not draw quite the

Chart 22
Narrative for Causal Network Shown in Figure 10

The first three antecedent variables (1, 2, and 4) worked out this way. The state mandate (2) for well-planned career education programs, together with assessment of local performance as less than adequate (1), led to a search for new programs (3) which proved to be a good fit (7) with district characteristics, and hence to district endorsement (8), and to adoption of the program (9).

But these were not sufficient causes of adoption. Inadequate local funds (4) to cover existing programs led to a ceaseless search for add-on funds (6) as almost a "way of life" for the district. That search led to getting temporary external funds (14) for a three-year period; they were the other basic cause of adoption (9).

The program, when adopted, proved to have substantial implementation requirements (10), which dictated the need for assistance (18), and also exerted a good deal of pressure for careful selection of high-quality staff (21), and for careful preparation (19) of them to carry out the program. The heavy implementation requirements (10), and to some degree the assistance provided (18) induced a good deal of user commitment (20), and in turn user skill (26), which was also high because of staff quality (21). High user skill, in conjunction with the fact that the program was quite well stabilized (27) by late 1980 brought about a reasonable degree of student impact (30).

That stream of causality refers essentially to internal program dynamics. What was happening at the *district and building* level?

Moving back to program demand characteristics (11), we note that certain aspects of the program (such as its removing students from high school control, and from high school courses and activities) caused poor fit between the program and the sending buildings (12). That poor fit led to lack of endorsement (22) from building principals, counselors, and teachers. Poor endorsement was further weakened by the presence of competition for funds and for students (15), induced by the fact that the external funds (14) were temporary in nature.

Temporary funding, together with the program's demand characteristics (11) (for example, students were visible to employers, had to be responsible, and could easily behave like "assholes") also made

for a good deal of program vulnerability (13). As a consequence, the staff tended to operate the program in a rather isolated fashion (23), to buffer it against the consequences of vulnerability when the immediate environmental endorsement (22) was weak. Certain program demand characteristics (11), such as the intensive time block, reinforced isolation (23) as well.

An added set of causal variables was also in play. The career advancement motivation (5) of key central office staff and principals operated to induce a good deal of turbulence (16) in the district. This turbulence effectively reduced the influence of those who were advocating the innovation (24); for some advocates, influence was weakened by job insecurity (25).

So although the program was transformed and altered (28) to some degree to meet the objections stemming from low building endorsement (22), achieved a modest increase in percentage of use (31) for a while, and was, as we have seen, proving reasonably effective with students (30), these factors were not enough to ensure the program's institutionalization (being built into the system) (32).

Rather, the weak building endorsement (22), the program's isolation (23), the competition for funds and students (15), and the weak exercise of influence by innovation advocates (24) resulted in weak institutionalization (32). So, it seems likely, did the departure of program staff, whose mobility (33) was driven by both career advancement motivation (5) and job insecurity (25). It also seems likely that the very user capacity development (34) induced by experience with skillful use of the program (26), enhanced by the external network of contacts (35) generated through the dissemination effort (17), also contributed to the decision of staff members (and it seems, possibly the director) to move on.

Taken as a whole, these explanations seem baroque and complex. But there is fairly clear evidence that each causal link worked as described. The chart will look less complicated if one notes that the chart contains four basic streams: the *program development* stream across the top, the *building/district* stream in the middle, the *career* stream near the bottom, and the external *dissemination/networking* stream last. In many respects the final outcomes can be seen as stemming from conflicting pressures across the streams.

---

same network. Feedback and revision will help, but essentially we are operating at a higher level of interpretive inference.

This, in fact, is the prime objective. Doing a causal network forces a more inferential level of analysis that pulls the data together in a single summarizing form. The analyst has to look at *all* the data and preceding conclusions, and map them in a coherent way. The risk, of course, is building order and purpose into events that are more loose ended, random, inconclusive, and perverse than causal networks would have them. In any event, causal analysis is an epistemological leap of faith. As Wittgenstein put it in the *Tractatus,* "Causes are superstitions." Hanson (1958, p. 64) has a slightly longer one-liner in the same vein:

Causes are certainly connected with events, but this is because our theories connect them, not because the world is held together by cosmic glue.

Procedurally, causal networking is more suggestive than definitive. The rules for drawing streams are pragmatic, and closer to heuristics than to algorithms. In part, this is because we have limited experience with the device and hesitate to be prescriptive. We should note, however, that the procedures outlined above are not primarily opportunistic and homegrown. They derive for the most part from conventional canons of inductive inference used by logicians and epistemologists: temporal precedence, constant conjunction, and directional influence. Furthermore, our empirical experience with site feedback in two separate studies was quite strongly confirmatory and supportive. Even so, we strongly advise (a) increasing the validity of any given network by subjecting it to colleague and site critique; (b) always writing accompanying text to clarify and summarize the flows; and (c) specifying carefully as you go which decision rules were employed in the construction of the network.

Finally, a causal network is only as good as the univariate and bivariate analyses whose shoulders it stands on. These in turn depend on the quality of the original codes, conceptual clusters, and matrices. This sends us back finally to the quality of the data collected and the trustworthiness of data collection methods. As in statistical analysis, good models are only as good as the measures and simpler analyses they derive from. Dross in, dross out.

Time Required

Causal network analysis is labor-intensive. Doing a network of the size illustrated takes at least a day. Writing out the narrative runs another two to three hours. Iterating and reconfiguring the network takes another half day or so. Remember, too, that this is the final work: It presumes (a) that preceding analyses have been carried out reasonably cleanly; and (b) that the results of those analyses are easily at hand.

IV.J.a Verifying Causal Networks

The causal network is the analyst's most ambitious attempt at an integrated understanding of a site. The most important factors, their interactions, and their links to the key outcomes are all plotted on the network. As careful, plausible, and exhaustive as the network may appear to be, parts or most of it could be dead wrong. One way of avoiding that outcome is to feed the network back to site informants and ask for their corrective responses.

Very often, the quality of the feedback depends on the care given to the way it is solicited. In particular, the critic has to understand what is being asked, and should work directly with the materials, rather than simply comment on them globally.

Below is a feedback form for site informants assessing the accuracy, from their perspective, of the causal network for the site. Informants should be chosen (more than one per site in different roles) who have proven reliable in the past, and who are in a position to reflect on the site's "big picture." The informant receives a one-page site overview, the network and the network narrative, and is asked to work directly with these materials in giving responses. For economy of space, we have collapsed the four-page response form into a single page (Box IV.J.a).

As a rule, people enjoy doing this kind of work. It lets them see rapidly how the researcher put the pieces together, and they can run that view against their own perspective. When that perspective is different, informants can quite easily redraw parts of the network or redraft parts of the overview. This is professional work, and we believe that people should always be offered some recompense. We provided a modest reader's fee ($25-$50).

IV.K MAKING AND TESTING PREDICTIONS

Analysis Problem

Verifying a causal network and its accompanying text by feeding them back to informants is a good way to strengthen the validity of one's findings. It is, however, vulnerable to the criticism that all actors, including the researcher, can easily succumb to a common perception that another researcher, using fewer site-immersion techniques, might not share. Social life, as the ethnomethodologists have taught us, is an issue of taken-for-granted and agreed-upon conventions that allow people to make sense of what they are doing individually and collectively. In many ways, social life is only possible through "groupthink." History, Napoleon is supposed to have said, is the version of past events that people have decided to agree upon. And field researchers, who depend heavily on local informants' perceptions in building a descriptive and explanatory map of the site, are likely to get sucked into collective perceptions that lend coherence to such a map.

There are ways, many of which we have reviewed, to avoid obvious biases in the data being collected, but few ways of getting around collective, consensual ones. Presumably, a competent field researcher is able to stay partially detached—social anthropologists call this "bracketing"—from site dynamics by virtue of outsider status and an analytical focus. But there has been virtually no hard-nosed evidence to show that this actually happens.

The opposite problem with causal network feedback is that informants may not agree—either with parts of the net or with one another. We quickly get into a Rashomon effect: People witnessing the same events give widely discrepant accounts of them. We have found, to our surprise, that there was little such discrepancy among informants, or among them and us, in the two major studies in which we fed back the causal networks. But there was *some,* and we were left sitting on it, trying to think of a satisfactory way of getting resolution.

We did find one good way of getting around these problems. It is that of testing the validity of one's findings by predicting what will happen at the site in six months or a year. Presumably, if the analysis is correct, it has implications or consequences. These can be spelled out and operationalized. The real-world results

Box IV.J.a
Response Form for Causal Network Verification

School district_____Your name_____

Your reactions to the materials you've read can be of much help in validating them. You can provide us with more confidence in our conclusions, and can show us where our explanations are partial or mistaken, and need to be revised for more accuracy.

Remember: we are asking you to think back to the way things were last June, and what led up to that state of affairs.

1. Looking at the project overview (Attachment A):

   a. What errors of fact do you see, as of last June?

   b. What differences in interpretation do you have?

      (Feel free to jot notes directly on the overview itself, if that will be easy.)

2. Now, looking at the causal network (Attachment B):

   a. Generally speaking, how accurate do you consider the network to be, as of last June? Please say a little about why you think so.

   b. Are there any important elements missing? List them here, and/or draw them in on the chart. Give each one a new number, larger than our list of numbers.

   c. Looking at the specific boxes we have used, are any of them unimportant, trivial, of little effect? Cross them off ⬛✕⬛ the network, list their numbers here, and explain briefly why they are of little value, from your point of view.

   d. Still looking at specific boxes, have we made mistakes in the ratings we have given (High, low)? If so, please write your corrections in on the network, note numbers here and give reasons for your revised ratings.

   e. Looking at the arrows between boxes, do you think they are accurate? Are they faithful to the events at your school and district? If not, please cross off arrows, or draw in new arrows. Write the numbers of the boxes involved here.
      For example:

      3 ─✕─▶ 8 shows that you crossed off the arrow between boxes 3 and 8.

      3 ─────▶ 11 shows that you wrote in a new arrow between boxes 3 and 11.

      Please explain your revisions in arrows briefly.

   f. Is our discussion of outcomes at the end of the causal network description accurate from your point of view? What revisions would you suggest to make it more accurate?

   g. If you would like to draw a revised causal network that would show your explanations of why things happened as they did, please feel free to do so here.(Or use the back of the page if you need more space.) Yours might have fewer, more, or different boxes than ours. Events in any change process are complicated, and different people see them differently. So if you would like to play the network game, enjoy!

3. Any other concluding comments or suggestions:

                    MANY THANKS FOR YOUR HELP. Please return
                    this form, and all the materials to us in
                    the stamped envelope. (Feel free to make
                    a copy for your files if you wish.)

can be checked out in a new contact with the site. The result is the qualitative researcher's version of a predictive validity coefficient that statisticians might use, for example, to see whether academic success predicts later job success.

Brief Description

Predictions are inferences that a researcher makes about the probable evolution of site events or outcomes over the following months or years. The predictions are drafted *at the time of analysis,* and submitted to site informants six or twelve months later. The informants respond to (a) the accuracy of the predictions and (b) the accuracy of the reasons given to justify the predictions.

Illustration

Generating the prediction. To show how this works, let us chain this exercise to the preceding one. Take a look back at Figure 10 in the causal network section (IV.J). Now find variable 32 on the network, "institutionalization." It has a low rating, indicating that the innovation at this site has not become a durable, built-in, routine part of ongoing operations. Note finally that the rating on this variable is a function of the several paths leading to it, both from other outcome variables (such as 30, 31) and from variables farther back on the four causal streams. Schematically, the causal network says that "institutionalization" is as low as the combined function of the variables leading up to it; they are the likely "causes" of the institutionalization "effect."

In testing the plausibility of the causal analysis, we then ask the predictive validity questions: (a) What is likely to happen to the innovation between now and next year at roughly the same time? (b) On which factors are we basing that estimate? Looking over the causal network and accompanying text, then reviewing the institutionalization checklist matrix for the site and text, the analyst decided that the program was in trouble. The checklist showed that the innovation was a peripheral one, that its benefits were less than its demands on staff, that its support was soft, that competing practices had not been eliminated, that its hard money funding was uncertain, and so on. There *were* more promising indices—the program was operating on a regular, daily basis and it was getting positive results with turned-off students—but they were buried in a pile of pessimistic indicators. The analyst predicted that the project would be phased out gradually in the course of the following year.

Making this kind of prediction is not easy. Somehow, researchers seen to escape having to make *decisions* about their data; findings "suggest," "indicate," "imply," or to take the classic, cowering pose, they "make it not unreasonable to assume" something. By contrast, generating a single, precise prediction is a bottom-line operation. The prediction is either right or wrong, usually with only a small intermediate right/wrong gray area.[8] And if the prediction is wrong, there is a good chance that some of the data supporting it are wrong too.

Justifying the prediction. How does one puzzle out the "whys" of a prediction? Back to our illustration. In part, as we just saw, the institutionalization checklist has given the site a poor report card on the ingredients for locking in the practice organizationally. The streams on the causal network (Figure 10) leading to the "institutionalization" variable are also foreboding. The project makes for a poor building-level fit (21) and is not supported by teachers or administrators (22). It hasn't worked through to a better fit by changing the organization (29). The project is vulnerable because of its demands, its isolation, and its dependence on soft money (11, 13, 14, 23). It competes for funds and students (15); its support in the central administrative office is uncertain (24) for a variety of reasons. Key project staff are about to leave (33). The number of students projected for the following year is lower than for the previous year (31). These are then the reasons for the dire prediction.

Finally, the analyst considers contextual factors and looks over trends at the site that, if continued, could have an effect on institutionalization. For example, this district had a poor track record on institutionalizing soft-money programs, and the district was currently in a "tightening-up" phase while the project was a "loosening-up" type of operation.

Taking all these indicators, the analyst then has to weight them by their degree of influence; this is also a way of getting the number down to four or five, which is all that an informant can be asked to respond to. Chart 23a shows the five that were settled on.

Looking at contrary data. If we only look for the factors supporting a prediction, we will probably make a poor one. Making a good guess is a function of weighting the odds for one outcome as against another—computing subjective probabilities on the fly. It is important, then, to consider the factors that could work *against* the prediction. To continue with the same example, there were indications that the project was well entrenched in routine operations, that it appeared to pay off for a normally hard-to-reach pupil public (in Figure 10, see the arrow from 30 to 32) and that it had *some* central office support (24). Pooling these indicators with a contextual and trend analysis of the site as a whole, the analyst came up with the four factors shown in Chart 23b that could "spoil" the pessimistic prediction.

Selecting informants. The prediction and its justification are given to key informants at the site, with a request for data on the current, actual situation about which the prediction was made. Normally one chooses

Chart 23a
Factors Supporting "Institutionalization" Prediction

A.	Poor district record of institutionalizing soft-money programs.
B.	Unlikelihood of strong support from new principals; some counselors indifferent; some elective-subjects teachers are hostile.
C.	Lukewarm support from central office.
D.	Financial squeeze in district; declining enrollments, staff cutbacks, lowered external funds. Program vulnerable because of high unit costs.
E.	"Tightening up" mandate to principals; program may be seen as a "frill," with lax control over students.

informants who (a) have proven to be reliable; (b) are in a position to know the current situation; and (c) occupy differing roles and have somewhat differing perspectives.

Analyzing feedback. How good is the prediction? How good are the supporting and spoiling factors? Chart 23a depicts a response form from one of the three site informants. Factors A through E on the top part of the chart are the "supporting factors" we listed earlier; factors A through D on the bottom part are the "spoilers" we just looked at. This informant agrees that most of the supporting factors were pertinent in determining the way things turned out one year later. The other informants made similar, but not identical judgments on all the predictors (for example, two thought central office support was stronger and that the "tightening up" was a more pertinent predictor).

As for the factors working *against* the prediction, the two high "pertinence" estimates suggest that the analyst had underrated the possibility of more external funding and the importance of the "dumping-ground" function of the project. (The two other informants agreed, but *also* felt that items C and D were influential factors that bettered the chances of institutionalization. So we are still caught in the dilemma of differing perceptions among informants—a dilemma that can sometimes be resolved by follow-up phone interviewing.)

How about the prediction itself? This had been assessed on another sheet. One can already see, however, that the prediction is probably in trouble because some of the "spoiler" factors are pertinent and important. As it turned out, our prediction was too pessimistic. The project *was* reduced in scale and its status *was* transitional—but it was still around, though barely. There was apparently stronger central office support than estimated, owing to the successful and still necessary dumping-ground function and the possibility of receiving new external funds to disseminate the project to other districts. The district office had decided to fund the project for one more year, but had cut project staff and students by half.

As the causal network in Figure 10 shows, this was a difficult prediction to make, in light of the number of streams and the fact that they did not all lead to the same conclusion. The predictions for the other outcome variables shown at the end of the net were easier to make and were on the nose. We also did better at predicting institutionalization at the other field sites.

It is also noteworthy that, although the prediction was overstated, the causal network and institutionalization checklist were still valid. Both predicted *low* institutionalization and were right; virtually all the reasons given for a phasing out were pertinent and influential. Also, the causal net *had* included countervailing evidence, such as the high student impact and the

Chart 23b
Factors Working Against "Institutionalization" Prediction

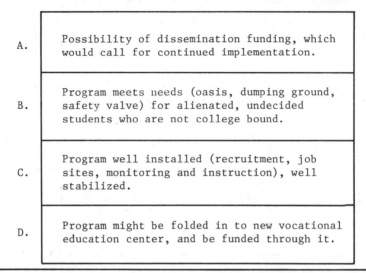

A.	Possibility of dissemination funding, which would call for continued implementation.
B.	Program meets needs (oasis, dumping ground, safety valve) for alienated, undecided students who are not college bound.
C.	Program well installed (recruitment, job sites, monitoring and instruction), well stabilized.
D.	Program might be folded in to new vocational education center, and be funded through it.

moderate to low central office support. What had happened, however, was that the *influence weightings* of these indicators were off; student impact was *more* important, support was *higher* and *counted more,* project isolation mattered *less,* and so on, than the analyst had thought.

Mechanics of feeding back predictions. Let us go somewhat more deliberately through the process of submitting the predictions to site informants.

(1) The analyst makes the predictions at the time of the analysis by taking the main outcome variables and looking at the data bearing on their causes. These data come primarily from the causal network streams, from the matrices or other summary tables in the section of the site report dealing with the outcome variable, and from contextual and historical remarks telling how the site has evolved.

(2) For each prediction, the analyst works out a set of factors supporting the estimate and another set of factors working against it. This material, with the predictors, is held by the analyst, then goes out for feedback six months or a year later to at least two site informants.

(3) An informant receives two envelopes. In the first one, the analyst defines the variable, gives the prediction, and asks the informant to judge the accuracy of the prediction by specifying the actual situation. The informant then explains his or her depiction by listing the most important contributing factors. Chart 24a shows a typical feedback form contained in the first envelope.

(4) The informant then opens a second envelope and finds the original prediction plus a pertinence table. On the table, the analyst has listed the factors that would support the prediction and factors that

might invalidate it. The informant is asked to rate the pertinence of each factor in accounting for the actual situation and to explain the reasoning behind that rating. The response form looks like Chart 24b. The logic behind the two-envelope procedure is to widen the data base (seeing whether more contributing factors are at work than the analyst had assumed) and to subject the analyst's predictors to an empirical test by being able to compare them with the informant's. Also, the informant is not "contaminated" by an externally generated framework when thinking about the prediction in the first envelope.

(5) The informant sends the two sheets, plus any additional commentary, back to the analyst.

Variations

Generating the predictions can be done in two ways—by the primary analyst or by another analyst who reviews the case report. We advise the latter procedure if possible. If a second reader cannot generate precise and well-grounded predictions from the matrices and causal network of a site report, there is something wrong with the report. Probably it is not *explicit* enough in delimiting causal streams, or in gauging the relative importance of the streams—or both.

Advice

Generating predictions is good medicine for the analyst, who has to take a tougher look at the data and address their portent explicitly. It is also a powerful validation device, even when informants' responses are equivocal. Predictions also bring in additional, well-targeted data that can be appended to a case report. Finally, as with the causal network feedback exercise, informants feel rewarded. They enjoy doing the critique and feel they have learned from it.

Chart 23c
Filled-Out Response Form from Site Informant
for "Institutionalization" Prediction

Pertinence Table:
1=not pertinent
2=pertinent, but not important
   in causing current situation
3=important factor in causing
   current situation

Our Prediction

The program will undergo a transitional year in 1980-81, during which time it will be phased out.

	Factors we thought would support our prediction	Pertinence (Write in appropriate number below)	Brief Explanation (Why you say this)
A.	Poor district record of institutionalizing soft-money programs.	2	It could have been different with a more aggressive leader sold on the idea.
B.	Unlikelihood of strong support from new principals; some counselors indifferent; some elective-subjects teachers hostile.	2	One new principal was supportive; the other not. Counselors reflected the principals' attitudes.
C.	Lukewarm support from central office.	3	This true. In four years neither the Supt nor the Deputy have ever visited the room. The new Assistant spent 30 min. there last year.
D.	Financial squeeze in district; declining enrollments, staff cutbacks, lowered external funds. Prog. vulnerable because of high unit costs.	3	
E.	"Tightening up" mandate to principals; prog. may be seen as a "frill", with lax control over students.	1	I wasn't aware of the "tightening up" toward the program. Student behavior — yes.

	Factors we thought could work against our predictions	Pertinence (as things turned out)	Brief Explanation
A.	Possibility of dissemination funding, which would call for continued implementation.	3	As long as State funds are available, a demonstration program will be available.
B.	Program meets needs (oasis, dumping ground, safety valve) for alienated, undecided students who are not college bound.	3	This year more students were less motivated than ever before.
C.	Program well installed (recruitment, job sites, monitoring and instruction), well stabilized.	1	I don't think this matters at all to the decision-makers
D.	Program might be folded in to new voc ed center, and funded through it.	1	I have not heard this said regarding the voc ed center, though I've thought it has possibilities under State guidelines which allow for student community placement under contracts with employers.

On the other hand, the exercise has some limits. Unless you go back to the field site, you are relying solely on self-report data. Also, predictions can be wrong for reasons that have little to do with their internal validity. A few unanticipated events, such as the sudden death of a key actor or a budget windfall, can wreak havoc on the best-laid projections of an analyst. It is sometimes useful to imagine the intrusion of such unanticipated events as part of the exercise—but, by definition, surprises can never be fully factored in.

Limit the number of dependent variables or outcomes for which you make predictions to a maximum of five or six, and keep the explanatory factors for each to the same number or less.

Define each of the outcome variables *specifically*, or informants will give confusing responses. For multiple variables, all can be defined in a single list.

As with causal network verification, one should not ethically expect site personnel to carry out what amounts to professional work without some form of recompense. We offered a reader's fee of $25 to $50, given five to six predictions in the two-envelope mode.

It is important to remember that for a key site figure to reflect this intensely on the current situation and its causes is likely to have *reactive effects:* He or she may take some new action as a consequence. If one has a continuing relationship with the site, such effects can be assessed through regular fieldwork. One can also

Chart 24a
Prediction Feedback Form, Part I

School District ___Dun Hollow___   Name _____

Our Predictions (Made with June 1980 data) Date _____

    I. Institutionalization: that is, the degree to which
       the Eskimo units have become a durable, built-in or
       routine part of the ongoing operations in the district.

Our Prediction

> The curriculum will not be incorporated into the district
> after the field test at Carr and Tortoise Area schools.

Your Description of the Actual Situation Since Then

Actual Situation

There are probably many factors leading to the actual situation.   The
most important ones are:

A. _____

B. _____

C. _____

(D) _____

(E) _____

(F) _____

Please rank these factors you have listed in their order of importance
by putting next to the letter A - (F) nos. 1 for the most important,
2 for the next most important, etc.

---

ask about such effects on the feedback form itself (though that in turn is likely to encourage even *more* reactivity) or through a follow-up phone call.

Time Required

Predictions take a moderate amount of time. The appropriate sections (for example, causal network) of the site report must be read closely, and there is a need to review sections containing contextual and historical material. Assuming that four to five outcomes are being predicted, and depending on the length and detail of the report, this can take between three and four hours. Then the rough-cut predictions have to be made, the supporting and spoiling factors listed and weighted, and the final predictions made. This usually adds another four to five hours. Setting up the charts, assuming the analyst does this alone, is a two-hour job. So for one site a prediction exercise will usually take one to two days, depending on the number of outcomes involved. An external analyst to whom the

Pertinence Table:
1=not pertinent
2=pertinent, but not important in causing current situation
3=important factor in causing current situation

I. **Institutionalization**; that is, the degree to which the Eskimo units have become a durable, built-in or routine part of the ongoing operations in the district.

Our Prediction

The curriculum will not be incorporated into the district after the field test at Carr and Tortoise Area schools.

Factors we thought would support our prediction	Pertinence (Write in appropriate Number below)	Brief Explanation (Why you say this)
A. Consensus at the site is that field test was unsuccessful.		
B. Eskimo units were not written into social studies K-3 curriculum.		
C. The units have little support from building principals.		
D. No innovation 'champion' at the site; the program developer is not pushing forcefully for adoption.		

Factors we thought could work against our predictions	Pertinence (as things turned out)	Brief Explanation
A. The superintendent has come out vocally in favor of adoption.		
B. Eskimo center remains within the district; the need for a program is likely to persist.		
C. Superintendent wants to strengthen working relationships with Regional Unit developing Eskimo program.		

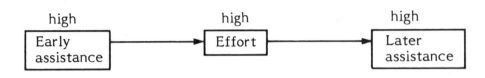

Figure 12   Nonrecursive Relationship

material is foreign will take 50-100 percent longer. Remember that time must be taken to draft a coherent cover letter explaining the exercise, and to decide which informants will receive the mailing.

Is prediction making worth the time? Yes, certainly, if you want to know how good your analysis really is, or if much is riding on it. No, if your main thrust in a study is descriptive rather than predictive or explanatory.

NOTES

1. Narrative text is of course a fine method for getting a reader to reexperience something in depth that occurred over time—as in a story, novel, or play. But reexperiencing is only one aim among many that analysts may have for themselves and their readers. See Smith and Robbins (1982) for useful suggestions for presenting results to busy audiences, including matrices, vignettes, summaries, and findings-oriented headings.

2. Such a judgment of course requires comparisons with similar figures from other sites.

3. Contexts come in still other types, of course. For useful ideas on mapping the *physical* context and the *kinship* context, see Crane and Angrosino (1974).

4. This discussion comes nowhere near covering the issues involved in explanation of social phenomena. We encourage the reader to consult Garfinkel (1981), Van Parijs (1981), and Turner (1980), and to refer to our sections IV.J, V.G, and V.H for more on the problems of ascertaining "causes."

5. This comes especially clear, for example, in the work of Smith and Keith (1971), whose case study of a new school was among the first to employ causal mapping methods.

6. This distinction is like that of Mohr's (1982), between *variance theory* (looking for explanations in terms of forces or variables acting on an individual or social unit) and *process theory* (looking for sequences of events leading to a state of affairs.)

Manicas and Secord (1982, p. 403) also stress the importance of local causality as a basis for more comprehensive explanation:

> Scientific explanation is not subsumption. Rather, it is causal explanation, and it demands that we show how in each particular case a particular causal configuration occurred that had just the achieved result. In general, explanation requires the resolution of the event into its components and a theoretical redescription of them: It requires causal analysis. As part of this process, it requires retrodiction to possible causes and the elimination of alternatives that might have figured into the particular configuration. Explanation thus requires knowledge of the causal properties of the configured structures *and* a historical grasp of the particular and changing configuration.

Finally, we concur with Geertz's (1983, p. 233) emphasis on "local knowledge" as the first order of business, and with his view that

> we need, in the end, something more than local knowledge. We need a way of turning its varieties into commentaries one upon another, the one lighting what the other darkens . . . bringing incommensurable perspectives . . . into conceptual proximity such that . . . they seem somehow less enigmatical than they do when they are looked at apart.

7. There is usually a temptation to add reciprocal or back-effect arrows. For example, in the illustration, perhaps increased effort in turn leads to more assistance, since it encourages the assister. We do *not* advise such causal flows, which are technically called "nonrecursive." They can be modeled by computer (see Gaynor, 1980 and Forrester, 1973, for good examples), but they rapidly bewilder the human brain ("after all, *everything affects everything else*"). It is usually better to stick with straight left-to-right flows that keep a temporal order. If you have a really favorite nonrecursive relationship, it can be handled as shown in Figure 12.

8. Note that the weather forecaster's ploy ("There is a 70 percent chance of rain this afternoon") doesn't let the predictor off the hook, either. Either it rains or it doesn't.

V

Cross-Site Analysis

Up to now our discussion has focused mainly on ways to describe, understand, and explain what has occurred in a single, bounded context—the "case" or site. That is the task of the traditional ethnographic researcher, where the effort is to emerge with a well-grounded sense of the local reality in a particular setting—whether it is a tribe, clan, formal organization, community—or even a culture as a whole.

More and more, as Louis (1982) and Firestone and Herriott (1983) have pointed out, qualitative researchers are using multisite, multicase designs, often with multiple methods. The aim is to increase generalizability, reassuring oneself that the events and processes in one well-described setting are not wholly idiosyncratic. Put another way, the problem is seeing processes and outcomes that occur across many cases or sites, and understanding how such processes are bent by specific local contextual variations.

The argument for studying multiple comparison groups was well put by Glaser and Strauss in *Discovery of Grounded Theory* (1967), at a time when virtually no field researchers were studying more than one setting at a time.[1] Conceptually speaking, the researcher uses multiple comparison groups to find out the kinds of social structures to which a theory or subtheory may be applicable. Having multiple sites increases the scope of the study and, thereby, the degrees of freedom. By comparing sites or cases, one can establish the range of generality of a finding or explanation, and, at the same time, pin down the conditions under which that finding will occur. So there is much potential for both greater explanatory power and greater generalizability than a single-case study can deliver. Unfortunately, Glaser and Strauss did not move on to the pragmatics of how one actually does multiple-case study work, and developing a good cross-site synthesis is not a simple matter.

Suppose, for example, that one has developed a good causal network explaining processes in a particular site. If one has a dozen such sites, just adding up separate variables as in a quantitative survey approach will destroy the local web of causality, and result only in a sort of "smoothed-down" set of generalizations that may not apply anywhere in the real world of the sites.

As Noblit and Hare (1983) put it, "A meta-ethnography must have a theory of social explanation that both preserves uniqueness and entails comparison." But how to proceed? This chapter reviews eight methods for cross-site analysis, and ten supplementary methods in our usual format.

As before, the methods are arranged from simple to complex, and from a descriptive to an explanatory emphasis. We begin with the *unordered meta-matrix*, a way of bringing together basic information from several sites or cases into one big chart. Then we consider several types of ordered matrices: the *site-ordered descriptive matrix*, where sites are sorted from high to low on some important variable; the *site-ordered predictor-outcome matrix* that leans us toward explanatory understanding; and the *time-ordered meta-matrix* that illuminates data from several sites in relation to chronology. The *scatterplot* is a graphic way to see association between variables; with the *site-ordered effects matrix* we can go even further toward explanation. Seeing recurrent relations across many sites can be accomplished through *causal modeling*. Finally, the last method aims at the seemingly intractable: drawing meaning from several *causal networks* in a cross-site network analysis.

Once again, we remind the reader that we use the term "site" by preference, to indicate a bounded context where one is studying something. But "site" is for us equivalent to "case," in the sense of "case study." So what we call "cross-site" methods can actually be used in the study of several individual people, each seen as a "case."

V.A UNORDERED META-MATRIX

Analysis Problem

Cross-site (or cross-case) analysis multiplies the data set by as many single sites as are in a study.[2] If each site produces 200-300 pages of field notes and ancillary material, we are rapidly awash in waves of data. Before this amount of data can be analyzed, it has to be *managed*. If it is managed poorly, it will be analyzed poorly.

Quantitative data analysts have similar problems—too many numbers can *also* be unmanageable—and they have applied solutions the logic of which, we think, is sound. First they make all the data compatible by *standardizing* them into the same idiom. They then reduce the amount of data by assigning the numbers to fewer distinct sets: scales, distributions, and binaries with the evocative name of "dummy variables." There are now fewer data grouped and standardized; one can then begin to see what the sets look like—how numerous, how shapely, how distinct. Looking at these "marginals" may suggest that some number sets need to be reorganized. This done, the quantitative analyst is ready *to examine the relationships between these number sets*, first pair by pair, then in combination.

These data-managing algorithms can be adapted to qualitative research in its own terms. Cross-site data also need to be standardized via common codes, outlines, and reporting formats for each case, and, within cases, common displays of commonly coded data segments. Outlines, reporting formats, and displays are all data-reductive devices for getting hundreds of pages of text down to workable units—three to four pages of text and some summarizing tables or figures.

Supposing that data from each site have been standardized in the sorts of display formats presented in the preceding chapter, the problem is how to assemble them coherently in one place. This is the first deep dive into cross-site analysis. It is also the most important one, since it will collapse the data set into clusters and partitions that will be used for subsequent analyses; this is how the analyst will *see* the data. There may be refinements in the clustering and grouping of data later on, but for now the analyst is making a commitment to a certain way of looking at what's there, making sense of it, and trying to work out the next, most likely, analytic step.

Brief Description

Meta-matrices are master charts assembling descriptive data from each of several sites in a standard format. The simplest form is a *juxtaposition* of all the single-site summarizing charts on one very large sheet or wall chart. The basic principle is *inclusion* of all relevant data. We came to call such charts, affectionately, "monster-dogs."

From there, the analyst usually moves to *partition* the data further (divide it in new ways) and *cluster* data that fall together so that contrasts between sets of sites on variables of interest can come clearer. These partitioned and clustered meta-matrices are progressively more refined, and entail some transformations of narrative text into short quotes, summarizing phrases, ratings, and symbols.

All that sounds rather abstract, so we need an illustration. The basic thing to keep in mind is that an unordered "monster-dog" that carries all the information from all the sites can be gradually refined, summarized, and reduced through partitioning and clustering, so that it becomes more *ordered*. Later, too, we'll see how meta-matrices can be ordered by *sites* (strong to weak on some variable), by *role* (administrators, users), or by *time* (early to late).

Illustration

Let us run through an example, listing each successive step.

(1) Creating the reporting format for each site. In the example shown here, the analyst is trying to answer several questions about the experience of teachers in using a new educational practice. (1) How did it look to the user? (2) What was the user doing? (3) Which feelings and concerns were paramount? (4) Which problems were looming large? And how did all this work over a long period of time?

At the simplest level, then, we have four analytic categories split into several (monthly, biannually, yearly) temporal units. The site report could then contain a section on the "experiences of use" over time; the section would comprise several pages of text and one or more summarizing displays.

(2) Building the site-level summarizing display and entering the data. The most straightforward way to start is to break the data down into the four analytic categories and show them over time in separate but commonly formatted charts. Chart 25a shows what an empty site-level display might look like (one of these for each time period). Note that, up to now, we are not dividing the data into partitions other than those suggested in the research question. We *have* decided, however, to (a) look at the four subquestions together and (b) separate them by time period. Chart 25b shows the display with data entered for one site. These are real-life data. Note that the cell entries are telegraph-style phrases boiling down what is already in the site report text. Notice too that some *selection* and grouping has probably been done. There were undoubtedly *more* feelings, problems, things done, and so on; the analyst has selected the most important ones and has clustered discrete but similar ones (for example, under problems, *several* tasks for which there was too little time = problem of too limited time). Note finally that each cell entry has several words describing the item; this is the first thing that the cross-site analyst is going to try to shrink.

Chart 25a
Site-Level Display for Unordered Meta-Matrix (format)

Teachers	Feelings/Concerns	How innovation looked	What was user doing most?	Problems
1.				
2.				
3.				
4.				
5., etc.				

Chart 25b
Site-Level Display for Unordered Meta-Matrix:
Users' Second Year of Implementation at Lido

	FEELINGS/CONCERNS	HOW INNOVATION LOOKED	WHAT WAS USER DOING MOST?	PROBLEMS
Vance	More comfortable w/ style of teaching and w/ having kids outside	Still useful, giving good direction & helpful ideas, activities	Working through materials Giving, participating in env'l educ workshops Working w/ community Off-campus site work	Time too limited for tasks to be done
Drew	Concern w/ growing number of non-achievers in forestry/ecology class	Too discovery-oriented for kids w/o biology basics; lecture style more appropriate	Adapting materials & lessons to growing non-achiever population Off-campus site work	Dealing w/ more non-achievers successfully
Carroll	Excitement with new activities, expanding science program	Same as first year	Working w/ community Giving, participating in env'l educ workshops Off-campus site work	Over-extended activity commitment

(3) Building the unordered meta-matrix and entering data. The cross-case analyst is now sitting in front of N site-level charts. If there are no more than fifteen charts with no more than five informants in each, the data can probably all go on one composite "monster-dog" sheet. If there are more, or if the site reports are formatted differently, there will have to be an intermediate step of standardization and reduction. Remember that the cross-site analyst usually *also* has four to five pages of text clarifying and deepening the entries on the chart for each site.

The unordered meta-matrix will simply be a more differentiated set-up of the site-level charts. For example, the first two columns would appear as shown in Chart 25c. Getting *all* the column entries for all the sites onto that matrix means it is going to be a big one.

Maybe they should be called "mega-matrices" rather than monster-dogs. Newsprint and a bare wall to stick it on are the best ingredients for cooking up a manageable monster-dog. But the cross-site analyst will try to distill down site-level cell entries somewhat as the work proceeds. Thus, for example, the filled-in chart for Lido in the excerpt shown in Chart 25c might appear as in Chart 25d. We are down to fewer, site-typifying words, and some symbols. Feelings/concerns have been dichotomized into positive and negative ones and each entry has a type of feeling or concern, set at about a middle range of abstraction (for example, not "comfortable" alone but with a qualification) and a short, category-grounding phrase to keep the analyst aware of what specifically was going on locally.

Chart 25c
Unordered Meta-Matrix: User Feelings/Concerns
and Other Variables (format)

Sites/Users	Feelings/Concerns	...
Lido 1.		
2.		
3.		
Masepa 1.		
2.		
3., etc.		

Chart 25d
Unordered Meta-Matrix: User Feelings/Concerns
and Other Variables (Lido data)

Sites/Users	Feelings/Concerns
Lido 1. Vance	+ Comfortable with new style, norms (lower control)
2. Drew	– Shift in target public (underachievers assigned)
3. Carroll	+ New, expanding (program, activities)

Stripping an unordered meta-matrix down to *less* information than this on the first iteration is looking for trouble. Without the qualifying and grounding task, the analyst can get quickly into comparing different species (of, say, "comfort") with no way of knowing that noncomparability was happening. When the analysis founders or when the analyst needs representative illustrations, there is no easy way to shift back down to the next lower level of analysis. One has to go all the way back to the individual charts. Doing *that* takes a lot of time and opens the door to a more sinister bias, that of looking only at *part* of the data, not at the full set (that is, all the cases).

The unordered meta-matrix, as we promised, has pruned multiple tables down to one big one that has done little violence to the original data. Such a display enables the analyst to see all the data in one (large) place. It is an early stage of analysis; the analytic categories (feelings, and so on) have been created and individual entries (such as concerns over a growing

Chart 26
Time-Ordered Meta-Matrix (format)

Type of concern	Year 1	Year 2	Year 3	Year 4
1.				
2.				
3, etc.				

number of nonachievers moving into the program) have become instances of more general analytic types (shift in target public).

From now on, the analyses and matrices will depend more on what the data have to say and on the kinds of relationships the analyst is most interested in. Let us look briefly at two such extensions, one involving within-category sorting (partitioning) and the other cross-category clustering.

(4) Within-category sorting. Let us assume the analyst wants to do some finer-grained work on the later "concerns" of users during project execution. This would involve the inspection of each meta-matrix for that period—the one for "second year," for "third year," and so on. In doing such a scan, the analyst is looking for two sets of things: (a) concerns that *change* or remain constant over time, and (b) *types* of concerns. Note that we are into the familiar clustering-and-partitioning game once again; we want fewer, distinct units of analysis. The matrix logic appears as in Chart 26.

The analyst is looking in particular to see if there are distinct types of concerns—ones that can be classified or catalogued—and if there is variation in the types of concerns over time. Under each year, there might be different signs (checks for presence/absence of a concern; ratings of "primary," "secondary" concerns, and so on). Suppose that, over time, there were more *institutional* concerns and fewer, but different *individual* concerns. This is a nontrivial finding. It suggests that mastering a new practice is not simply a matter of individual or within-classroom technical mastery, but rather that it brings institutional agendas into play as well. The analyst decides to look into this more by creating a summary tabulation of individual and institutional concerns and seeing at which of the twelve sites they were considered to be primary ones during implementation (Chart 27).

There is much useful descriptive information here for the ferreting analyst. For example, some sites have multiple troubles (such as Banestown, Perry-Parkdale), others only one kind (Masepa), and some have escaped unscathed (only ten of twelve sites have entries). Also, it looks as if individual concerns are mostly nontechnical, and institutional concerns emphasize continuation (lower priority, poor functioning, delivering on promises). Such a finding leads the analyst back to other parts of the cross-site chart to test hunches. In this case the hunch might be that projects with high technical mastery have just as many institutional concerns as those that don't. It also suggests next steps in the analysis: Let's check whether institutional concerns actually lead to cutbacks or discontinuations in the *next* time period. A simple 2×2 matrix sorting site-level data can both tell a lot and suggest to the analyst where to look next in order to get beyond a descriptive analysis to more inferential ones.

Chart 27 is the simplest way to look at the data. One can imagine fancier displays, such as one including different *levels of gravity* for each concern, one with the *sources* of the concern, one with the *consequences,* one with all these things.

(5) Across-category clustering. Now let's look at a descriptive meta-matrix that reaches across *and* takes apart analytic categories. In this example, the analyst wanted to characterize the more technical aspects of teachers' later use of the innovation. This involved working with the last two columns of Chart 25a above—what the user was doing and the problems encountered in doing it.

The procedure was straightforward. The analyst read down the last two columns of Chart 25a (the filled-in version of the meta-matrix) for each of the twelve cases, noting what users were "doing most" and the "problems encountered" in doing it. The decision

Chart 27
Summary Table: Individual and Institutional Concerns
During Later Implementation

Type of Concern/Item	Sites at Which Item Mentioned
Individual Concerns	
Relational problems-friction among project staff	Banestown, Perry-Parkdale
Motivational problems (discouragement, disenchantment, "distaste" for the practice)	Calston, Lido, Masepa, Dun Hollow, Proville, Tindale
Stamina, exhaustion, excessive demands of the project	Masepa, Carson, Plummet
Institutional concerns	
Lower institutional or district-level priority of project (with attendant lessening of rewards)	Lido, Plummet
Poor overall functioning (project as a whole, or a component)	Perry-Parkdale, Dun Hollow, Proville
Resistance, obstruction, lack of support by other staff not on project	Banestown, Perry-Parkdale, Carson
Worry whether project will "deliver" on its promises or objectives	Banestown
Continuation the following year(s)	Banestown, Calston, Lido, Perry-Parkdale, Plummet

rules were that at least two sites and optimally three would share tasks and problems and that the problems encountered in common across sites would be connected. Assembling the "doing most" responses, the analyst tried to catalogue them by looking for an inclusive gerund, something that would yield the underlying *activity* (for example, "refining"). This produced six *distinct* types of activity into which *all* instances could fit without a shoehorn. The analyst then connected the "problems encountered" to each of the activity types by (a) grouping *problems* into a

lesser number of problem types, then (b) taking the modal problem type (the one mentioned by most informants) when there was more than one. He then copied down some short quotes and summarizing phrases and set up Chart 28.

Note what the clustering has accomplished. We have gone well beyond the fragmented, site-by-site account of users' later experience as shown in Chart 25a and its following charts, and gotten closer to a focused and integrative cross-site depiction that does not read abstractly and retains a lot of the site-specific

Chart 28
Cluster Summary Table: Problems Stemming from
Major Tasks of Later Implementation at Field Sites

Task/Activity	Problem type	Illustrations
Reaching up	Difficulty in mastering more complex components	"Some parts just aren't working. They're harder than the first ones I did" (Teacher, Masepa) "I still can't monitor the children's progress...there are too many pupils to keep up with." (Teacher, Calston)
Improving, debugging	Solving specific problems, often connected to poor program design	"The bookkeeping is awful." (Teacher, Banestown). Paperwork (Perry-Parkdale, Carson). Scheduling problems (Banestown, Calston, Carson and Proville). Pupils disturbing, interrupting each other (Perry-Parkdale). "Materials [that are] not right for this age." (Dun Hollow)
Refining	Differentiating, tailoring	"needs tailoring...the time isn't there" (Teacher, Lido) Inability, despite repeated attempts, to break down groups into individual exercises. (lab teachers at Banestown)
Integrating	Combining new project with regular curriculum	"Will this destroy my own curriculum? How can I fit it in?" (Teacher, Burton) Lack of time to do both old and new (Calston, Dun Hollow, Carson)
Adapting	Accommodating the project to new inputs	"The course is all floaters now...I get the burn-outs, who sit in a daze and are hard to reach." (Teacher, Lido) Changes in released time, budget decreases (Lido); new testing requirements (Banestown)
Extending	Using components elsewhere, reorganizing practice, bringing in other segments	Trying to bring back former "stuff that worked" (Masepa); feeling "bored," looking for more stimulating materials (Tindale)

flavor. Reading across the *rows* gives a good functional sense of what, for example, "reaching up" is and what real-time problems in doing it look like. Reading down the *columns* gives a cumulative picture of what "later implementation" is technically all about. For more on' the tactic of *clustering,* see section VII.A.4.

Variations

There are many alternate paths from the basic unordered meta-matrix to variously ordered meta-matrices, which we will be looking at in succeeding sections. Sometimes, however, unordered meta-matrices are sufficient in themselves for producing summary material for a report: See the "analysis tables" described by Smith and Robbins (1982) and Lee, Kessling, and Melaragno (1981), which displayed components supporting parental involvement in various federal programs, sorted by site.

Sometimes one may wish to focus primarily on the *content* of a meta-matrix, with no reference to which site it came from. A good example appears in section V.A.a.

Advice

Don't try to move from site-level data directly to an ordered meta-matrix (as in the following sections). Look carefully first at the multiple-site, *unordered* information. Jumping to ordered meta-matrices is like going straight from marginals to regressions without any intermediate cross-tabbing or scatterplotting. A good grounding in the unordered meta-matrix helps one avoid costly blind alleys.

As we will see, it usually takes several alternative cuts before a workable and productive set of clusters and/or partitions emerges. For more on partitioning, see Chapter VI on matrix building; for more on clustering, see section VII.A.4.

Time Required

Creating an unordered meta-matrix like that described above usually takes about three to four hours; ordering exercises like those shown, about one to two hours each. Writing associated text is quicker—an hour or less. Creating the basic unordered meta-matrix and assembling the data occupy the most time. Much depends on whether the site data matrices are fully comparable and easily accessible, as well as on the number of sites, and the number of variables being looked at.

It is possible that microcomputer word-processing and data-base applications (pp. 67, 91) can speed the mechanics of basic meta-matrix assembly, and the process of clustering and partitioning it. Of course, that depends on having stored the site data in the right, retrievable form; on having some coherent, data-based ideas about clustering and partitioning; and on adequate file management and word-processing applications. There's no real way to shortcut the *thinking* time that's needed. The process of understanding a cross-site data set, even for a few variables, is one of making gradual sense. It cannot be hurried.

V.A.a Ordered Summary Tabulations

One of the first tasks in moving from a single-site to a cross-site analysis is determining how many sites share similar characteristics. In the simplest form, the analyst takes the original matrix for the single-site cases and tries to generate a cross-site matrix that gets all the data in. When the same characteristic appears in more than one site, this is noted on the matrix. But it often happens that, later on in the analysis, a new way of arranging all the sites looks promising—it will help to understand the structure of the data, across all sites. The task then is to imagine a matrix display that best captures the dimensions the researcher is interested in and that gets all the pertinent data arranged in readily analyzable form. Chart 29 shows an example of a summary tabulation from the school improvement study.

The analyst can see at a glance where there is multiple-site activity in any one of the cells by noting the numbers in parentheses. One can also tell how many different kinds of organizational changes there are within any one type by noting the number of entries in a cell. For example, "transitory changes in structure" within the innovation (upper-left cell) are not frequent and occur in no more than one site, whereas "transitory climate changes within the innovation" (two cells down) are more diverse, and show recurrence across several sites. The picture is somewhat different for durable changes. It looks as if "structural changes" (upper cell at far right) are often nonexistent, and are limited to the innovation itself or express themselves in scheduling changes alone. Even so, there are many more durable than transitory changes.

Note that this sort of tabulation deliberately *drops* the site identification of data. The aim is to be more conceptual, seeing main trends across the sites. You can, of course, attach an initial to each data bit to let you get back to the site, if you wish.

V.B SITE-ORDERED DESCRIPTIVE MATRIX

Analysis Problem

An unordered descriptive meta-matrix like the one described in V.A is a good start, but it usually leaves the analyst hungering for more understanding and more focus. What's going on? What are the real patterns of more and less X in the sites? What are some possible

Chart 29

Ordered Summary Tabulation: The Content of Organization Changes

Type of Change	Transitory Changes		Durable Changes	
	Within the innovation	In the organization	Within the innovation	In the organization
Structure	Addition of project directorships Evolving departments Creation and dropping of advisory committee	Change in locus of control, funding, and supervision	Shift in student input (5) Reorganization: more department interdependence Advisory committee Team teaching	Innovation itself (5): remedial lab, alt. school work experience program, English curriculum, accountability system None (5) Scheduling (4) Expansion of innovation to new users (3) Space for program (2) Creation of coordinator role Creation of management committee Creation of in-service committee Summer-school version of program added Increased team teaching Creation of helping teacher role
Procedures	Active, coercive student recruiting Leadership providing support (emotional, material) Leader "consultation" with teachers Non-users help users with testing Aides, parents help with instruction Increased community contact.	Innovation lapsed, is discontinued Field testing of materials Teachers exchange books Other instruction displaced	Tighter supervision, control (2) Student "batching" Routinization of forms/ procedures Charismatic leader more distant Fewer staff meetings Reduced student time in program Staff reassignment Selective use of materials.	Innovation itself (5): pupil screening, referral/intake, teaming, pullout procedures More paperwork (2) Added student transportation (2) Teacher load reduction Freeing time: substitutes, early dismissal Dropping letter grades More coordination among teachers More teacher discussion of individual students Specialist consultation for individual students Loss of teacher control over student assignment
Climate	Conflict (4): in teams between users, users-aides, departments. More cohesiveness (2), pioneer spirit, esprit User resentment (2) Less cohesiveness Tension, fear, mistrust	User-non-user conflict (2) User resentment of remedial lab Ambiguity about management committee Expectations for more upward influence violated, lower morale Resistance by principals, then support	Discouragement, burnout, loss of interest (3) Collaborative, help-giving climate (2) Cohesiveness (2) Less cohesiveness Overload Development of friendships/ enmities	Resentment re paperwork (2) Wariness about innovation More openness to innovation Norm change: flexibility, colleagueship, el-sec. interaction None: climate still good None: climate still bad More administrative awareness of the innovation

*Each item represents a change occurring at one site. Changes occurring in more than one site have numbers appended.

causes of X? Why do we see more X at one site or case and less of it in another?

Brief Description

A site-ordered descriptive matrix contains first-level descriptive data from all sites, but the sites are *ordered* according to the main variable being examined, so that one can see the differences among high, medium, and low sites. Thus it puts in one place the basic data for a major variable, across all sites.

Illustration

In our school improvement study, we were interested in the nature of a variable we called *student impact*. We had interviewed not only students themselves, but teachers, parents, administrators, counselors—and looked at formal evaluation data as well. How could one assemble this information in one place, and understand the differences between sites that showed high or medium or low student impact?

Our interviewing and data retrieval had focused not only on "direct" student outcomes (such as improved reading test scores), but on what we called "meta-level" or more general outcomes (such as increased interest in school activities) and even on "side effects" (usually unanticipated, such as "zest in program leads to alienation from regular classes"). We also wanted to be sure that we were tracking both positive (good, desirable) and negative effects of the innovation on students.

Building the display. How could the sites be ordered to begin with? The analyst can look at the relevant section of each site report and note the general level of student impact the writer of the site report had claimed. The sites are placed in rough order, then the analyst re-skims the text in each site report to see if the first impression is justified or whether the ordering should be changed.

This reading also suggests ideas for how the meta-matrix might be constructed. Chart 30a presents a first possibility. The idea here would be to read the site report selections on student outcomes, and enter a code in each cell (U for user, A for administrator, E for evaluator, S for student, P for parent, and so on). If the impact was seen as strong, the letter would be underlined; if uncertain, a question mark would be added; if the evidence was conflicting, an X would be added.

But such a display is not quite right. It abstracts and lumps the outcomes too grossly into categories such as "achievement," throwing away a lot of rich information on just *what* the outcomes were. And on reflection we can realize that outcomes might just bear some relation to desired *objectives.* Somehow they should be in the display too.

A good step at such a point is to return to the site report materials. What do they really look like, and what kind of display might accommodate them most easily? In our illustration, such a reading showed us that the data for each site were of variable robustness—ranging from detailed and thorough achievement data, interviews, and questionnaire responses to nearly unsupported opinion. Also, some programs aimed high, shooting for everything from student achievement to self-concept, while others were more focused, hoping only, say, for the improvement of reading skills. Such a range suggests the usefulness of a display more like Chart 30b. The idea here is to show what the objectives were, and to enter data in the form of phrases or sentences in the appropriate cells, marking them with code letters (U, A, E) to show the data source. This way we keep more of the raw data, and we can also see how outcomes are related to objectives.

Entering the data. One now can return to the relevant section of each site report, look for coded material on direct and meta-level outcomes, and summarize the material in a set of brief sentences or phrases, one for each distinct outcome. One can also make an effort to arrange the data in the "program objectives" and the "direct effects" columns in somewhat parallel fashion, so that comparisons can be made. Skills and achievement goals might be placed first, followed by affective/attitudinal and other outcomes. For each sentence or phrase entered, the source is marked (A for administration, U for user, and so on).

When the data are all assembled into the matrix, the analyst should review again: Are the sites correctly ordered from high to low student impact? In this case, some criteria for a "high" rating are: (1) Is the program achieving most of its aims? (2) Is it also achieving other positive meta-level and side-effects? (3) Are these judgments corroborated, either through repeated responses from one role, through cross-role agreement, or evaluation data? Weakness on criteria 1 and 2 especially should lead to lower ratings of student impact; weakness on criterion 3 may also cast doubt on a site's placement. Such a check usually suggests some reordering of sites. (Within each category, such as "high" impact, the analyst should also be trying to order the sites from "highest to "least of the high.")

Chart 31a shows how this sort of data display worked out. The rows show two sites (Perry-Parkdale, Masepa) where student impact was high, two where it was moderate (Carson, Calston), one moderate to low, and two low. (For simplicity we show an excerpted table, with only six of our twelve sites.) In order, the columns show the following: The *objectives* of the program for each site; the *direct outcomes,* both

Chart 30a
Site-Ordered Meta-Matrix: Format for Student
Impact Data (version 1)

		Direct effects		Meta-level & side effects	
		Positive	Negative	Positive	Negative
SITE 1 (highest impact)	Achievement				
	Attitudes				
	Behavior				
SITE 2 (next)	Achievement				
	Attitudes				
	Behavior				
etc					

Chart 30b
Site-Ordered Meta-Matrix: Format for Student
Impact Data (version 2)

SITES	Program objectives	Direct effects		Meta-level & side effects	
		Positive	Negative	Positive	Negative
SITE 1 (highest impact)					
SITE 2 (next)					
etc.					

positive and negative, seen by stakeholders including users, administrators, counselors, parents, evaluators, and students themselves; and *meta-level outcomes* and *side effects*. As we have noted, meta-level outcomes are congruent with the program's purposes, but affect more-general aspects of students' functioning. Note the reading program at Calston: It caused the direct outcome of improved reading skills, but by providing interesting materials and opportunities for independent student work, it caused the meta-level outcome of increased student self-direction. Side effects are more unintended: Note the alienation of Perry-Parkdale students, who liked their program's concreteness and relevance, but thereby came to dislike their regular high school's courses and activities.

Chart 31a
Site-Ordered Descriptive Meta-Matrix (excerpt): Program Objectives and Student Impact
(direct, meta-level, and side effects)

SITES	Program objectives	Direct outcomes — Positive	Direct outcomes — Negative	Meta-level outcomes and side effects — Positive	Meta-level outcomes and side effects — Negative
High impact					
Perry-Parkdale (NDN)	Basic skills (reading, math, communication, etc.). Life skills (critical thinking, citizenship). Life competencies (credit, health, etc.) Job-finding skills: career training Entry-level work skills: career training Decision-making skills Self-responsibility and initiative Matching interests/abilities to job info Understanding of others Know socioeconomic trends; career knowledge Sex role awareness Better parent-child communication	Same or better on basic skills scores U: better math (12th grade girls) E P Specific job skills S E P U Career planning and choice: aids Job readiness Job exploration attitudes positive F How interest of, ability, that to look for in job E: identify, explore career options C A Experience with world of work: headstart C U S Career, occup. knowledge E Prep. for real world of work Exper. Wkng with adults: P communication with them better U	Less exposure to academic courses C	Personal development, iden-tity. U E P Better communic w. adults Self confidence U E P S Increased attendance U Responsibility, motivation U C E P Staying in school (lower-level students) C A U Help goalless students Improved permanent job S Getting permanent job U Parent-child communication P	Some students "get lost" again after a while U Some bide time don't "deliver" U Program more effective with girls U Alienation from regular school activities C A S Irresponsibility, "can't handle freedom" P U
Masepa (NDN)	Improvement in full range of lang. arts skills (see at right) More on-task behavior Improved discipline	Increased skills: vocabulary U A F: spelling, U A: phonetics Ux, punc-tuation U, reading comprehension Ux E: written expression U, grammar Ux E: written expression U Low achievers more productive Ux	Retention levels not good U Too little diversity Student fatigue U	Concentration, study skills Fewer discipline problems A More attentive to assignments U Better academic, self-concept U More enjoyment, enthusiasm U A Work with less supervision, more responsible A U Less time loss, more time on task U A E Rapid students progress faster E	Some lagging, failing mastery tests U Boredom U
Moderate impact					
Carson (IV-C)	Increased achievement Clearer career interests Improved: self-concept as a learner More internal locus of control	Career knowledge U A C Work on new interests U		Achievement composite (use of resources) E Better classroom attitude U Attitude to school E U Self-concept as learner (HS) F Friendliness U Social studies (elem) Self-understanding U	Little effect on achievement U
Calston (NDN)	Basic reading skills, plus use of reading as tool for learning: literature appre-ciation: reading for enjoyment	Increased criterion referenced test scores A U More reading skills Ux		Learning to work independently self-managing U Self-concept, self-esteem A U Children learn independent work U Children proud to come to school A Children not competing A Reduced discipline problems A	
Moderate to low impact					
Dun Hollow (IV-C)	Eliminate stereotyping of Eskimos Knowledge of Eskimo history, customs; current life Create positive image of Eskimo culture	Some learning of culture, reduction of stereotypes U A More reading skills Ux	Information too detailed U		Some students behind in language arts U
Low impact					
Burton (NDN)	Knowledge & practical skills re political/government/ legal processes (voter education, state govt., indiv. rights)	Concept learning, by being in diff. roles U Exp. active learning approach A	No effects discernible U		

Legend for sources of data:
U = user
A = administrator
C = counselor
P = parent
E = evaluator
S = student

Underlined letters refer to mention by at least two persons.
x = presence of dissenting or conflicting opinion

162

Analysis. (Once again, try your hand at analysis before reading further.) First, looking across rows, we can see that positive effects are more frequent than negative ones—even in sites where field notes showed dissatisfaction and resentment (for example, Dun Hollow). It also seems that sites where many negative effects are noted (such as Perry-Parkdale and Masepa) are sites where much is being attempted (in terms of the program objectives column). Apparently, large efforts are more likely to spin off negative effects along with the positive ones.

Second, looking at the two right-hand columns shows us that there are significant meta-level and side effects in nearly all sites; in only the lowest-impact site (Burton) do we see none at all. Perhaps this means that the claims for meta-level changes in low-impact sites are suspect. Maybe so—they are less likely to have underlines, and have fewer instances of multiple-role confirmation (see legend).

One can also compare the projects sponsored by NDN (externally developed innovations) and IV-C (locally developed ones). In the full matrix, approximately equal proportions fall in the high, moderate, and low categories; we can conclude that program sponsorship makes no difference in student impact.

Chart 31a can also be used to answer the question of whether high-impact sites have their effect primarily on achievement, skills, attitudes, behavior, or all of these (through a detailed analysis of objectives and positive effects). We can also answer the question of who *reports* impact (administrators, users, and so on) and whether this differs in high- and low-impact sites. In making such subanalyses, it often helps to develop brief "summary tables" (see Box V.B.b).

Let's try our hand at a summary table for these data, so that the reader can see more clearly what a next-step table would look like. The analysis just made suggests two likely avenues. First, we could compare cases (sites) according to the *content of outcomes,* such as knowledge, skills, and attitudes, keeping the distinction between *direct* and *other* types of outcomes. Another possibility is to compare *degrees of achieving objectives* across cases: What proportion of the objectives for each project were actually achieved, and to what extent?

In either case, a next-step, summarizing table is going to be helpful in at least three ways: (a) providing a clearer check on how the analyst actually made the ratings of "high," "moderate," and "low" student impact; (b) allowing a finer-grained comparative analysis of the outcomes; and (c) giving the reader a more digestible visual summary than Chart 31a. In fact, the summarizing chart may be the only table the general reader will see; Chart 31a could be consigned to an appendix, or included only in reports for technical readers who want to examine the material carefully.

Chart 31b is a cut at the second option: a summarization of the extent to which each case attained its objectives. Note that the format is in the mode of a *Consumer Reports* rating,[3] to facilitate a rapid evaluation of each case and comparison between cases. This is a fairly radical condensation of Chart 31a; we are down to a set of symbols and some qualifying phrases. But it is easy enough to find one's way rapidly back to the denser matrix if something ambiguous or puzzling crops up on this one. The reader now has a readily accessible overview of impact levels within and across projects. The text accompanying such a display would need to provide contextual information, in order to compensate for the highly standardized, disembodied nature of these data; one pays a price for easy-to-read and comparable cross-case summarizing.

Notice that in the sub-entries under "overall rating" the analyst has made a differentiation that was not on Chart 31a. "Program-immediate" objectives are more concrete, attainable, and content-bound, such as "mastery of reading skills" or "knowledge of government processes." "Transfer" objectives are also tied to the program objectives, but are more general and usually harder to achieve. For example, the objectives at Carson call for "clearer career interests" (a program-immediate objective), and also for "improved self-concept as a learner" and "more internal locus of control," which are "transfer" objectives—they go beyond first-level mastery of the project content to a more generalized outcome. Note that for all cases "transfer" ratings are never higher than "program-immediate" ratings, another indication that they are harder to attain.

As is often the case in qualitative analysis, this distinction came clear only as the analyst was trying to boil down Chart 31a and noticed that there were not only different content *types* of program objectives but also different *levels,* and that any rating system would have to take that into account. This illustrates how next-step matrices can beget more inclusive, conceptually crisper findings as one works through successive iterations.

This next-step chart also surfaces something that was less clear in Chart 31a: Should the analyst place a site higher in the ordering when its project had many goals but uneven achievement (like Perry-Parkdale) than one with fewer goals and more consistent achievement (like Masepa)? The weighting can go either way, but the more focused and boiled-down display forces the analyst to decide and to make the conceptual basis of the decision explicit.

Chart 31b
Site-Ordered Descriptive Meta-Matrix, Next-Step Version
(excerpt): Program Objectives and Student Impact

SITES	Achievement of objectives no.	rating	Comments	OVER-ALL RATINGS OF OUTCOMES # Direct outcomes Program-immediate	Transfer	Other outcomes Meta	Negative
High impact							
Perry-Parkdale* (NDN)	1	partly present	math only				
	2	absent	fuzzy objective				
	3	partly present					
	4	strongly present					
	5	strongly present					
	6	strongly present					
	7	partly present	less well for girls	strongly present	partly present	strongly present	partly present
	8	strongly present					
	9	weakly present	indirect evidence for some aspects				
	10	strongly present					
	11	absent					
	12	weakly present	only 1 respondent				
Masepa * (NDN)	1	strongly present	low retention for a few	strongly present	strongly present	strongly present	partly present
	2	strongly present	boredom for a few				
	3	strongly present					
Moderate impact							
Carson * (IV-C)	1	weakly present	1 respondent, some counter-indices	partly present	partly present	strongly present	absent
	2	strongly present					
	3	strongly present					
	4	partly present	high school only				
	5	absent					
Calston * (NDN)	1	strongly present		strongly present	absent	strongly present	absent
	2	weakly present	conflicting assessments				
	3	absent					
Moderate/low impact							
Dun Hollow (IV-C)	1	partly present	reduction, not elimination	partly present / weakly present	absent	absent	partly present
	2	weakly present	1 respondent, global claim				
	3	absent					
Low impact							
Burton (NDN)	1	absent	conflicting assessments on both objectives	absent	NA	absent	absent
	2	absent					

*robust evidence (external evaluator and/or standardized test scores)

● strongly present
◓ partly present
⊖ weakly present
○ absent

#uses <u>modal</u> rating of achievement within site's objectives of this type.

NA not applicable

And as we have repeatedly insisted, the decision rules for data transformation and entry must also be explicit. How did we get from Chart 31a to 31b? The decision rules were as follows: Include as "strongly present" only those assessments of outcome made by at least two respondents or by a formal evaluator and containing no strong qualifications or countervailing indices. Ratings of "absent" mean simply that there is nothing in the "outcome" cells of Chart 31a corresponding to the program objective, or that there were no "other" outcomes (meta, negative). Intermediate ratings are justified in the "comments" column of Chart 31b. The analyst might have added a key in the second column ("achievement of objectives") to distinguish between program-immediate and transfer objectives, but this might have overloaded the chart with detail.

Variations

Variations naturally depend on the basic data structure. A first-cut site-ordered descriptive matrix can have a very large range of data in its columns. We have used up to twenty columns on occasion. We did this when we were trying to sort out a large number of site-contextual variables that might have a bearing on the degree of organizational change experienced by our twelve sites.

A large site-ordered meta-matrix is not usually fully comprehensible in the first cut, though it is a perfectly fine "reference book" for storing relevant data in one easily accessible place. Usually there will need to be next-step matrices—streamlined, boiled down, sometimes regrouped versions—before coherent analysis can take place. Similarly, one should not assume that the readers of the final report should automatically see the first "monster-dog."

The matrix in our example could probably be improved by sorting detailed types of outcome into sub-rows for each column (such as achievement, general knowledge, skills, attitudes, and behavior). That would enable cleaner conclusion drawing about types of outcome (and would give more information than the originally proposed Chart 30a).

For less complex data bases, it often helps to enter actual direct quotes from site reports, rather than constructed sentences or phrases. They give an even more direct grounding in the data for the analyst.

Advice

A site-ordered descriptive matrix is usually a fundamental first step in understanding what's going on across sites. Assuming that one has a good basis for ordering the sites, it is more powerful than an unordered matrix: Patterns can be seen for high, medium, and low sites, and the beginnings of explanations can emerge. The matrix forces the analyst to be grounded in the data from the sites, and does not allow escape into vagueness or premature abstraction. Once the matrix is formed, it also provides a good check on whether the site ordering is in fact correct.

Expect to make several cuts at the format of the matrix—and to feel somewhat anxious and overwhelmed—before you settle on the one best for your purposes. The columns have to follow directly, of course, from the form site-level data are in, but there

will ordinarily be many alternative ways of displaying the data.

Do not move too quickly to a matrix that simply has cell entries such as "adequate," "weak," "confusing," "widespread," or similar judgments. Keep as much raw data visible as you can without running into excessive size or complexity.

Recheck the ordering of sites at several points as you proceed. Ask another analyst to confirm or argue with your ordering. A valid ordering is crucial to the use of this method (see also Box V.B.a).

During analysis, first do a general "squint." What does the matrix look like—where is it dense, where empty? Draw conclusions. Then look down particular columns, *comparing/contrasting* (section VII.B.5) what things look like for high, medium, and low sites. It may also be useful to look at more than one column at a time to *note relations between variables* (section VII.A.9). (In our example, compare the "program objectives" column and the "negative direct outcomes" column, to see whether programs with ambitious objectives had more negative outcomes along with their positive ones.)

Keep in mind that more boiled-down summary tables (see Box V.B.b and Chart 30b) may be required to help you interpret a complex chart.

Time Required

For twelve sites, a descriptive site-ordered matrix of this sort can be expected to take from seven to nine hours. That will include about two hours to read the relevant sections of the site reports, and another four to five hours to create and fill in (and, if necessary, re-order) the matrix. Drawing conclusions and writing text is usually rapid—perhaps one or two hours. If the data are messy and diverse (as they were in this example), the most difficult portion of the work will be deciding on a reasonable display format; if they are cleaner and simpler, formatting will be easy. Generally speaking, time spent on an adequate site-ordered descriptive matrix is well worth the investment, since so much later analysis rests on it.

V.B.a Ordering Sites Through Summed Indices

How can one be more sure that the sites in a matrix are ordered in a valid way? Here we show a systematic method for deciding on the ordering of sites. The analyst wanted to order the twelve sites according to how much change had occurred in users. To do this, he identified a series of types of user change, and put them in a rough conceptual order (see Box V.B.a) from minimal/trivial/short-term in nature (daily routines, repertoire) to substantial (transfer to other tasks, basic constructs and attitudes). The key at the bottom shows the meaning of the cell entries.

Box V.B.a
Summed Indices: Reported Changes in User
Practice and Perception

Dimensions of change arising from implementation

Sites	Daily Routines	Repertoire	Relation-ships	Under-standings	Self-Efficacy	Transfer	Basic Con-structs, Attitudes
Masepa (NDN)	X	X	X	X	X	X	X
Plummet (IV-C)	X	X	X	X	(X)	N/A	X
Banestown (NDN)	X	X	X	X	X	(X)	
Tindale (IV-C)	X	X		X	X	X	
Carson (IV-C)	X	(X)	X	X	X	N/A	
Perry-Parkdale (NDN)	X	(X)	X	(X)	(X)	N/A	(X)
Calston (NDN)	X	X	(X)	(X)	(X)		(X)
Lido (NDN)	X	X		(X)			(X)
Astoria (NDN)	X	X	(X)	X			
Burton (NDN)		X					
Dun Hollow (IV-C)	X-0	X-0					(X)
Proville (IV-C)	X-0				N/A	N/A	

X = change claimed unambiguously by several informants
(X)= change claimed unambiguously by only one informant
X-0 = initial change, then reversion to initial practice
N/A = not appropriate/applicable
Blank = no unambiguous changes cited

To order the sites, the analyst began with a rough estimated ordering, entered the data for each site, then rearranged the rows (and sometimes columns) until the systematic order shown appeared, with Masepa at the top (all indices present and verified by several informants) to Proville (one weak change present, then reversion). The reader who is familiar with Guttman scaling will note the similarity. The final ratings given each site are shown at the right. Note the "cut points" (for example, between "mod" and "mod/low") the analyst chose to define the various ratings.

This method is time-consuming, but very thorough and explicit in ordering sites; it is good for use when much depends on the validity of the site ordering.

V.B.b Summary Tables

A matrix may often be so large and complex that it is difficult to grasp the main theme in it (see, for example, Chart 38d, section V.F). In trying to make sense of that chart, the analyst created this summary table, which shows counts of the effects of assistance that are sprinkled through Chart 38d. It collapses and summarizes the Chart 38d data.

The analyst also wanted to find out where negative effects of assistance were occurring, and added the minus marks shown, one for each instance of a negative effect. Using the summary table, he concluded, for example, that negative outcomes of assistance were more frequent in low-assistance sites, and had their effects mostly on individuals.

Summary tables, though they are restricted to counting, are often extremely helpful in understanding a complex display or in verifying a general impression. They can be produced quickly with paper and pencil. Any given matrix can usually generate several different summary tables. Another one produced from Chart 38d appears below. The analyst extracted from Chart 38d the specific effects of assistance that occurred in at least four of six sites, both high-assistance and low-assistance sites. The summary table for assistance effects on individuals was as follows:

High-Assistance Sites	Low-Assistance Sites
reducing anxiety	
increasing understanding	increasing understanding
increasing ownership	increasing ownership
feeling supported	
enlarging repertoire	
solving problems	
	increasing competence, confidence

Looking at these data, the analyst concluded:

> The recurring emphasis across sites on understanding and ownership is consistent with Fullan's (1982) view that problems *of meaning* are the central issues as users approach an innovation. For high-assistance sites, the effects noted also involve anxiety reduction/reassurance, strong support, and repertoire enlargment accompanied by problem solving. The latter two are consistent with our earlier finding that sustained assistance is more typical in high-assistance sites.

We might note in conclusion that just as summary tables aid the analyst in making sense of a larger complex chart, they are very helpful to the reader during presentation of results.

V.B.c Two-Variable Site-Ordered Matrix

The site-ordered matrices we have been looking at focus on one variable, essentially. When one is interested in the ramifications of *two* variables, the form can be easily adapted. If one is able to order the sites carefully on a well-known variable, then the columns of the matrix can include several different aspects of a less well-known variable. In Box V.B.c, the

well-known variable is users' *practice stabilization*. The analyst, ordering the twelve sites by that variable, wants to know how it is related to several aspects of *local continuation* of the practice, such as "users' attitudes," "likelihood of continued use," and so on.

This display proved very rich; the analyst wrote five pages of text from it. Looking at column 3, for example, he concluded that at the extremes, highly stabilized sites were more likely to continue, and low-stabilized ones not. He also noted that positive user attitudes (column 2) enhance the possibility of continuation, but do not guarantee it, and that project longevity (column 1) does not ensure continuation either. Column 4 proved most helpful, by the way. It was clear, for example, that lack of sustained administrative support was a prime factor in causing continuation uncertainty, and that positive administrative support, especially if accompanied by administrative fiat and codification, made continuation more likely.

This analysis also suggested some next steps: a need to "unpack" the various causes of stabilization more clearly, and to carry out additional analysis of the dynamics of the institutionalization process—the next issue beyond simple "continuation."

This method is very useful in studying the relationships between two variables thought to be associated, but where the direction of causality is unknown or ambiguous.

V.C SITE-ORDERED PREDICTOR-OUTCOME MATRIX

Analysis Problem

As we have seen in the previous two sections, metamatrices are the basic building blocks for cross-site analysis. Essentially, they get the site-level data into an increasingly economical display that allows the analyst to work with the full set of sites on one or several variables at a time. *Unordered* cross-site matrices are the basis for the important data-formatting, data-standardizing, and data-reducing functions that set up descriptive analysis. Those analyses are often made with similar but more boiled-down matrices that serve the same purpose as "marginals" (displays and computations of rows and columns) do for the survey researcher. *Site-ordered, descriptive matrices* take us a further step toward understanding patterns.

But how can we get from the descriptive to a somewhat more *inferential* level of analysis? For example, the chart in Box V.B.b answers a descriptive question: Do high assistance-giving sites have more and different effects than low assistance-giving sites? It looks as if they do. But there is another, implicit ques-

Box V.B.b
Summary Table, Showing Short- and Long-Term
Effects of Assistance, by Assistance Domain

EFFECTS ON...	For high-assistance sites (N=6)				For low-assistance sites (N=6)			
	Ongoing		Event-linked		Ongoing		Event-linked	
	Short run	Long run	Short run	Long run	Short run	Long run	Short run	Long run
The innovation and its use	25 -	24 = =	12 =	20 =	11 -	16 =	3 -	5 -
Individuals	39 =	28 = =	17 =	22 = =	19 == ==	10 -	10 = =	12 = =
The organization	12	11 =	9	13	4	0	0	0

- = negative or undesired effect (included in
numerical totals)

tion: Is more assistance likely to lead to or *produce more effects* (on the innovation, individuals, and the organization) than less assistance? In other words, are levels of assistance *good predictors* of these outcomes?

The two-variable site-ordered matrix shown in Box V.B.c begins to ask the predictor-outcome question more explicitly. The primary function of the matrix is to determine whether the levels of stabilization of a new practice contribute to the likelihood of its continued use. And the matrix also brings in *other* likely predictors: longevity of the project, users' attitudes to continuation, and other prime factors. So the analyst has on one sheet some, or possibly most, of the factors contributing to variations in a dependent variable.

The next step is to get into a multivariate prediction mode, taking those predictor or antecedent variables that we have good reason to believe are contributing to the outcomes, and assessing their separate and combined effects. How to do this?

Brief Description

Predictor-outcome matrices array sites on a main *outcome* or criterion variable, and provide data for each site on the main *antecedent* variables that the analyst thinks are the most important contributors to the outcome. The basic principle behind the matrix is *explanatory,* rather than purely descriptive; the analyst

wants to see whether these antecedents predict or account for the criterion variables.

Illustration

Let us work our way through a cross-site adventure that includes two types of site-ordered, predictor-outcome matrices, logging the successive analytic steps.

(1) Asking the prediction question. In the school improvement study, we found that some sites had an easy time during early use, and others a rougher time. What accounted for this difference? In other words, which prime factors, coming before or simultaneously with early use, were associated with more or less smoothness?

(2) Selecting the predictors. In this study, we were especially interested in a set of predictors we called "preparedness factors." For example, *prior training* in the use of the innovation was an important preparedness factor. Presumably, sites that were better prepared through prior training would have an easier time of it.

The individual site reports were equivocal; some facets of preparedness seemed to have made a difference at *some* sites, and a lot of things were happening during early use that could have added to or swamped the effects of higher or lower levels of preparedness.

Box V.B.c
Two-Variable Site-Ordered Matrix: Relationships
Between User Practice Stabilization and
Local Continuation

Extent of practice stabilization/Sites	1. End of project year	2. Users' attitudes to continuation*	3. Likelihood of continued use* (Same level or better)	4. Prime factors contributing to high/low likelihood of continuation
High stabilization				
ASTORIA (NDN)	1	Positive	High	Project mandated Heavy local transformation for good fit
TINDALE (IV-C)	3	Mostly positive	High	Local mandate well enforced Procedures codified User satisfaction
Moderate-high stabilization				
CALSTON (NDN)	2	Mixed +	Low	Budget crisis-staff cuts, reassignments
PERRY-PARKDALE (NDN)	3	Mostly positive	Uncertain	Staff turnover Uncertain funding
LIDO (NDN)	4	Mixed +	Uncertain	Lower administrative support Lower priority (new facility now available) Users' discouragement
Moderate Stabilization				
BURTON (NDN)	1	Positve	High	Parts of project written into curriculum Heavy local transformation, good user fit
BANESTOWN (NDN)	2	Positive	Uncertain	Budget crisis Staff reduced, reassigned
MASEPA (NDN)	3	Mixed	High	Project mandated Strong logistical support Improved pupil performance
CARSON (IV-C)	3	Mostly positive	High	Procedures codified, routinized Project mandated Widespread local support
PLUMMET (IV-C)	4	Positive	Uncertain	Likely staff turnover Lower district support
Low Stabilization				
DUN HOLLOW (IV-C)	3	Negative	Low	User + principal dissatisfaction No strong local advocate
PROVILLE (IV-C)	4	Negative	Nil	Other central office priorities; no advocate. Project discontinued User and principal dissatisfaction

*Researcher assessment, usually pooled from interview data and site report tables

MD=missing data

+Some wanting to continue, others not.

We needed to see in one place what was going on at all the sites. The choice was made to begin with only the "preparedness" factors as predictors, because there were already seven of them, some broken down by role type (user, principal, central office administrator). Having a manageable *number* of predictors is an important start-up criterion. So is the *logic* of the relationship; few things seemed more important for smooth early use than strong preparedness. And so are *conceptual* and *empirical* considerations. Our way of construing the innovation process included a preparedness function; numerous studies had shown it to be a strong determinant of successful early use, and many informants in this particular study were saying the same thing.

(3) Scaling the outcome and the predictors. Scaling the outcome variable (relative smoothness of early use) is a relatively straightforward operation. An analyst can simply *begin* with a scaled dependent variable—by asking informants to estimate it or by having the field researcher make an estimate in the site report. Had we been more foresightful, we probably would have done one of these things. But, like most qualitative researchers, we preferred not to foreclose too early on the choice and definition of criterion variables. We took relevant data from the individual site reports and scaled them. Respondents had been asked to list the problems encountered in the course of initial use of the innovation, and the field researcher commented routinely on the gravity of these problems. By counting the *number* of problems and the *gravity* ascribed to each, the analyst estimated the relative smoothness and ordered the sites from "smooth" to "rough." The actual procedure used is very close to the "summed indices" technique shown in Box V.B.a.

We draw attention to that chart here for two reasons. First, cross-site analysts are often in the situation of scaling—or otherwise standardizing—single-case data. Doing that means *transforming* the single-case data from a nominal or categorical variable to a dichotomous or continuous one. This is not an operation to be taken lightly. Rather—and this is our second point—it should be a self-conscious procedure with clear decision rules.

In this case, the analyst specified *how* the magnitude of "practice change" would be defined and *how* an assignment of "high" or "low" for each site would be made. He then entered the data for *all* the sites before determining cutoff points and making the assignment. Whereas survey research has most of these procedures built right into its computing algorithms, the qualitative researcher has to *define* his or her own decision rules and somewhat laboriously march the

data through them to be certain that the ordering is not getting skewed in the direction of a favored insight or arresting empirical cluster.

Scaling the "preparedness" predictors was easier. Each site report contained a "preparedness" checklist matrix (see Chart 13a, section IV.B), which could be directly converted into an ordinal scale running from "factor not in place" to "factor fully in place" (the checklist matrix was *already* scaled ordinally). Now we are ready for the site-ordered predictor-outcome matrix.

(4) Building the matrix and entering data. In this case, the predictor list is clear and the construction of the matrix (Chart 32) straightforward. The analyst works site by site, reviewing the site matrices, and forming a judgment of the degree to which each of the predictors was in place. There may well be a need to look at the associated text as well, especially in forming the judgment as to whether the predictor was decisive in affecting early implementation (see *underline* explanation in legend.) The text is also often helpful in aiding a further judgment called for: whether the factor was a facilitator or barrier (note that the analyst *does not take this for granted,* but looks for specific evidence of such near-causal attribution). It is useful to have a second analyst verify or disconfirm such judgments.

(5) Starting analysis. A first look can center on the first nine columns, ending with the ratings on "training"; these are the main "preparedness" indices. Arraying them against the twelve cases, ordered by ease of early use, yields a lot of useful information. For example, most sites are only partly prepared; NDN sites are better prepared than IV-C sites; almost everyone is well prepared on the "commitment" factor, but almost no one on the "skills" factor. Here is another example of how site-ordered matrices can furnish precious descriptive details.

(6) Testing the prediction. How does the overall prediction look? First we can try a "squint analysis." If "preparedness" were related linearly to "ease of early use," the check marks should turn progressively to broken check marks, then to zeros as we read down the columns. Perversely enough, this doesn't seem to be happening for all columns, although there is some overall thinning out of check marks as we go from smooth starters to rough starters. Notice that part of the reason the prediction is not working out is that there is too little variance; for some of the predictors (for instance, central office administrators' commitment), all or most sites have the *same* rating, or the scale is truncated (no zero ratings). This brings home the point that scaled matrices such as these live and die

Chart 32

Site-Ordered Predictor-Outcome Matrix: Degree of Preparedness as Related to Ease of
Early Implementation at Field Sites (first generation of users)

Ease of early use,[a] by sites	Commitment			Understanding			Central Resources/ Materials	Skills	Training	Prepared-ness Score[#]	Group Median	Ongoing aid/ in-service	Building-level support
	Users	Building Principal	Central Office Admin.	Users	Building Principal	Central Office Admin.							
Smooth early use													
Astoria (NDN)										19	18		
Burton (NDN)										17			
Mostly smooth[b]													
Lido (NDN)					?					17	17	0	
Mixed[b]													
Calston (NDN)										16	15.5		
Perry-Parkdale (NDN)		0		0						15			
Rough													
Banestown (NDN)					0					12	13		
Masepa (NDN)					0					8			
Carson (IV-C)										16			
Dun Hollow (IV-C)										14			
Plummet (IV-C)									0	14			
Proville (IV-C)	0									10			
Tindale (IV-C)	0						F/B			13		F/B	

[a] field researcher judgment from users' responses and/or from observation of practice in use

[b] smooth for some users, rough for others

  underline signifies field researcher estimate that factor was decisive in affecting ease of early use

F= factor facilitated early use
B= factor was barrier to successful early use

√ fully in place
√ partly in place
0 mostly absent, missing
? missing data

[#] Computed in the following way:

√ = 2 pts.
√ = 1 pt.
0 = 0 pts.
F = +1 pt.
B = -1 pt.

by the variance of their scales. If relative "ease of early use" does not *covary* systematically with levels of preparedness, the matrix is out of business for other than descriptive purposes.

Another test of the prediction can be made by converting the checks and zeros to numbers: As we have noted, the tactic of *counting* (section VII.A.1) is not irrelevant in qualitative research. This is done in columns 10 and 11. The legend at the bottom right of the chart also shows that some *weighting* has been done when facilitators or barriers were clearly present.

The "preparedness" score and group medians do show a relatively linear relationship, but the range is restricted and there are mavericks in the rough-starting sites (for example, Carson). The next thing, naturally, is to find out *why* they are mavericks. For example, Carson's high score may be a function of the fact that the "commitment" items are more numerous and may be overweighting the total "preparedness" score for a site where commitment was so strong and facilitative (columns 1-3). The analyst also checked back with the report text and broke out scores for "rough starters" and "*very* rough starters" (Banestown, Masepa, Plummet, Proville), and found the first group median to be thirteen and the second one eleven. This strengthened the linearity of the relationship between preparedness and smoothness of early use. And he looked at two more variables (see the last two columns of the chart) to determine whether these two conditions were actually present during early use.

So the numbers help. They make it far easier to manipulate the data on a site-ordered matrix when testing a hypothesis. They also make it easier for the analyst to see what is there. Finally, they keep the analyst honest; one has to look at *all* the data on the chart and use the same computing rules for *each* cell. This puts insights, hunches, strong desires, and conceptual preferences to a more stringent test.

But notice that the numbers aren't *alone* on Chart 32. The judgments that led to the numbers are still present on the chart (fully in place or not, facilitative or not, factor seen as decisive, and so on) and the researcher can easily get back to the original site charts and text—or even the coded field notes—when puzzling results turn up. Also, the numbers and weights are primitive ones, which keeps the analyst from veering off into fancier data manipulations, which would almost surely be tepid or misleading.

Still, the matrix allows for some closure. It tells us, for instance, that some requisite conditions *matter* more than others. For example, looking at the underlined cell entries along with the Bs and Fs shows that user "commitment" matters more than user "under-standing." Also, a scan of the Bs and Fs shows that being well prepared doesn't help smoothness of initial use as much as being poorly geared up hurts it. For some sites, few or none of the factors are underlined. Astoria, for instance, has the highest preparedness score, but no underlines. Something *else* must also be influencing smoothness of early use and, for the smooth sites, influencing it more than levels of preparedness. So a lot can be wrung out of a site-ordered, predictor-outcome matrix.

(7) Strengthening the prediction. What does the analyst do now? Go fishing for more predictors, look for the "something else." Once again, the choice is made on logical, conceptual and/or empirical grounds. In qualitative research, fishing is mostly an empirical recreation. What did the informants say was helping or hurting early use? How did the site-level analyst make sense of the "problems encountered" information? To derive the new predictors, the cross-case analyst goes back to individual site reports. If the site reports have been formatted in the same way, that search can be done in a few hours of reviewing the subsections and the summarizing charts.

In this particular case, the analyst derived five more variables at a low level of inference. He then did a new predictor-outcome matrix (Chart 33). Notice that all the predictors are scaled as before, either dichotomously or continuously. The analysis is also similar: looking for covariation both in the scales and in the underlines, Fs and Bs. The columns that pay off most are "actual degree of practice change" (minor change helps and major change hurts), "latitude for making changes" (higher latitude helps), and "actual size/scope of the innovation" (smaller ones have an easier time). So it looks as if smaller-scale ventures with a lesser leap from past practice to this innovation and some latitude to make changes (probably downsizing ones) is a combination accounting in part for relative ease of use. Aha! The "smooth" sites didn't *need* much preparation because they weren't taking on very much, whereas the "rough" sites were making ambitious changes that inadequate readiness could bedevil.

The analyst begins to piece together this mosaic by assembling possible patterned explanations, and cycling back to the site-level reports to see if the emerging picture makes sense. For example, here the analyst saw one cluster of sites and variables (small practice change, high latitude, and small-sized innovation) with its countervailing cluster (large practice change, lower latitude, and large innovation size). He could then look back at the site reports to see whether such animals actually existed, and whether the

Chart 33

Site-Ordered Predictor-Outcome Matrix: Additional Factors Related to Early Implementation

Ease of early use, by sites	Users (1st generation) volunteered or pressured	Actual classroom/ organizational fit	Actual degree of practice change	Latitude for making changes	Actual size/scope of innovation +
Smooth early use[a]					
Astoria (NDN)	constrainec	$good_F$	$minor_F$	$high_F$	small
Burton (NDN)	$\underline{pressured}_F$	$good_F$	$minor_F$	$high_F$	$\underline{small}_F$
Mostly smooth[b]					
Lido (NDN)	$pressured_F$	$moderate_B$	$\underline{moderate}_B$	$high_F$	small/moderate
Mixed[b]					
Calston (NDN)	pressured	$\underline{poor}_B$	$moderate_B$	$mod./high_B$	small
Perry-Parkdale (NDN)	volunteered	moderate	$\underline{moderate}_B$	$high_F$	moderate
Rough					
Banestown (NDN)	pressured	moderate	$major_B$	$high_F$	small/moderate
Masepa (NDN)	$\underline{volunteered}$	good	$major_B$	low_B	large
Carson (IV-C)	$volunteered_F$	moderate	$major_B$	$high/mod_F$	$\underline{large}_B$
Dun Hollow (IV-C)	$volunteered_F$	$poor_B$	$minor_F$	moderate	$\underline{small}_F$
Plummet (IV-C)	$\underline{volunteered}_F$	moderate	$moderate\text{-}major_B$	$high_F$	$\underline{large}_B$
Proville (IV-C)	$\underline{pressured}$ 3	moderate	minor	high	$\underline{moderate}*$
Tindale (IV-C)	$\underline{pressured}$ 2	$\underline{moderate}_B$	$major_B$	low_B	moderate/large

[a] field researcher judgment from users' responses and/or from observation of practice in use

[b] smooth for some users, rough for others

underline signifies researcher estimate that factor was decisive in affecting ease of early use

F= factor facilitated early use

B= factor was a barrier to successful early use

* substantial role changes, but for limited populations

+ as contrasted with pre-implementation size/scope. For comparison, see Chart 4, "implementation requirements".

hypothesis about size of attempted changes affecting early smoothness was plausible at each site or not (tactic: *replicating a finding*, section VII.B.9).

Variations

Predictor-outcome matrices are close, perhaps *too* close, analogues to statistical prediction procedures. They are something of a statistical albatross: no zero-order or regression coefficients, no partialing, no algorithms for entering or deleting predictors, no error terms. They can, however, be subjected to simple non-parametric analyses that test the trends and deviations thrown up by the matrix.[4] One can also look at the empirical validity of a prediction by confronting a supposedly "elegant" pattern of matrix covariation with the more mundane, local patterns actually observed in the site reports. If *no* site has a configuration corresponding to the prediction cluster that emerges from scanning the matrix, that cluster is hollow and the prediction is, literally, baseless.

Another way to go is to abandon a statistical logic altogether and switch to an analytic induction logic such as we used in section IV.J on causal networks, and will take up again in section V.G on causal models. Here we are less in the domain of probabilities (looking for good post hoc predictions) than in the arena of likely causes or determinants (providing explanations for a given outcome). Such induction is sometimes easier—both to do and to explain to others—when the predictor-outcome matrix has cell entries in symbolic, stripped-down form, like the "consumer reports" entries in Chart 34, drawn from Lee et al. (1981, p. B48). The sites are ordered by degrees of parental involvement; we can see at a glance that the key "contributing factors" are *DAC has specified authority, parent coordinator role, DAC training,* and *powerful person.*

One can also generate matrices that go from antecedents to outcomes to later consequences of those outcomes—three rather than two steps. Box V.C.c shows an example.

Advice

Let's review some of the rules of thumb sprinkled throughout this section.

(1) Use a site-ordered, predictor-outcome matrix when you want to see how several contributing factors function *together* in relation to different levels of a criterion measure.

(2) Begin work with a manageable number of candidate predictors chosen on the basis of good sense, conceptual plausibility and empirical groundedness. More than a dozen at a time is a formula for overload, *unless* you have little initial sense of what the likeliest predictors are, in which case 15-20 is a maximum

number. But this should never be a pure fishing expedition; the conceptual framework or the data from the sites should be providing strong clues from the outset.

(3) Be *very* careful when transforming site-level text into cross-site scales. Guttman-type scaling is a good, bias-deflating device here. Record and report the decision rules you used to do the scaling.

(4) Work with the matrix *descriptively* before you work with the relationships between the variables, that is, work down each column first, then start comparing columns.

(5) If there is too little variance in the matrix, be content with what you can extract descriptively, or focus solely on the variables that have some range.

(6) Test out promising patterns with simple computations. Think about the quality of the field data and consider *weighting* some of them over others (section VII.B.4).

(7) Don't let the computations get unhinged from the raw data. Keep the words and the numbers or scales together *throughout* the analysis.

(8) Expect that one matrix will lead to another, but that the next one is likely to be smaller and better informed as a result of the first one.

(9) Test your "best and final" prediction against the individual site reports to be sure that the configuration can and does actually occur locally.

Time Required

How long it takes to do site-ordered predictor-outcome matrices like these depends mainly on how many cases one has, how many predictors one loads onto the matrix, and how scale-ready and scale-worthy each one is in the single-site reports. The greater the number of cases, predictors, and transformations needed to get each predictor standardized, the longer the process. Time is also a function of how good the matrix is, that is, how well-informed the choice of candidate variables was. Random choices can go on forever. Chart 32 is probably at the middle-high range on all these counts; for twelve sites, it took about three hours to assemble and another three hours to analyze. Chart 33 took longer (about four hours) to assemble because the choice of predictors was less obvious and the data transformations greater for all the predictors.

As usual, writing final text—itself a clarifying and focusing device—went quickly; under an hour for each matrix.

V.C.a Substructing a Variable

Often, when one is trying to clarify a general variable, especially a variable used as an outcome along which to sort sites, the data seem confusing or intract-

Chart 34
Site-Ordered Predictor-Outcome Matrix: Factors Contributing to Parent Involvement

	No DAC	No Involvement							Minor Involvement					Major Involvement		
	Mt. View	Roller	King Edward	Brisbane	Benjamin Co.	Maple	Summer Place	Meadowlands	Plains	Stadium	Bonnet Co.	Kingstown	Cleteville	Redlands	Compass	Johns Co.
State Guidelines Exist, Are Implemented	○		✓					✓			✓	✓		✓	✓	✓
DAC Has Specified Authority	✓	✓		✓	✓	✓	✓				✓	✓	✓	✓	✓	✓
Parent Coordinator Role	○	○	◐	○	○	○	○	●	●	◐	◐	●	◐	●	●	●
Staff Attitude: Parental Involvement Support		✓	✓	✓	✓			✓			✓	✓				
Parent Attitude: Satisfied with Project/Professional Make Decisions	✓	✓	✓	✓	✓	✓	✓	✓				✓	✓			
Decisions Reserved for High-level Administrators		✓	✓			✓			✓			✓	✓			
DAC Training	□	▣	▣	□	□	▣	□	□	■	■	■	□	□	■+	■	■+
Powerful Person	△	△	△	△	△	△	△		◁	◁	◀	◁	◁	▲	▲	▲

○ = no PC
□ = none
△ = professional

◐ = PC dominates DAC
▣ = Title I
◀ = shared, parent and professional

● = PC supports DAC
■ = group processes
▲ = parent

■+ = group process + Title I

SOURCE: Drawn from Lee et al. (1981, p. B48).

able. Perhaps there is more than one dimension to the variable; the sites somehow don't seem to sort themselves out simply. The technique of substruction helps here. It's a way of locating underlying dimensions systematically.

In Box V.C.a we show how an analyst substructed the issue of "organizational change." The complexities of the data included the fact that in some sites the innovation was poorly implemented to begin with and couldn't be expected to induce organizational change. Also, in some sites the innovation *itself* was an organizational change, and in others it was not (that is, it was simply a small-scale classroom change). So the analyst made a 3 × 2 table to incorporate these dimensions, then sorted out the sites. Looking at sites this way, one can see that the ordering of sites should go from categories 1 through 4.

The idea of substructing, originally developed by Lazarsfeld (see Lazarsfeld, Pasanella, & Rosenberg, 1972), is discussed further as "typology construction" by Lofland (1971, pp. 22-23).

V.C.b Contrast Tables

When one is trying to understand the meaning of a general variable, perhaps an important outcome for a study, and how it plays itself out across different sites, a useful exploratory device is the contrast table. One takes a few "exemplary" sites where the variable is present in high or low form, and contrasts several different attributes of the basic variable. Box V.C.b presents an example. Here the analyst tried to "unpack" the idea of how users changed as a result of trying out an innovation, choosing three representative sites, and pulling out six relevant aspects of "user change" that he had noticed in reading site reports, such as "energy investment." The exercise aids *conceptualization* of what user change is composed of and how it works. Note: One has to read through all cases, or most, before one knows which sites are "exemplars." This process also helps locate the attributes. Contrast tables often point toward useful variables for a predictor-outcome matrix (for example, in this chart, high "pervasiveness of change" might be causing high amounts of user change). Finally, contrast tables are a very useful teaching device for readers of the final report.

V.C.c Predictor-Outcome-Consequences Matrix

Many of the meta-matrices used for cross-site analysis are descriptive; they show how the various sites cluster or diverge on variables of interest. At the next analytical level up, we can use matrices to test relationships between two, then several, variables. As we have just seen, predictor-outcome meta-matrices can also do more inferential, multivariate work by setting up and testing predictions.

Finally, it is possible to do more directly explanatory work with meta-matrices, moving beyond (probabilistic) predictions to more causal (deterministic) analyses. We could hook a chain of predictors to some intermediate outcome, then show the consequences of that outcome—the outcome of the outcome. There are three steps rather than two. See Box V.C.c. Such a chart is especially good when one is looking at an intermediate or intervening variable (in this case, assistance) that is not construed as a "final" outcome.

The first objective of the material in Box V.C.c is to predict the degree of assistance provided at the twelve field sites (which are ordered in the left-hand column). To do this, the analyst assembles the most likely predictors emerging from the individual sites and from preceding cross-site analyses.

The first three columns deal with variables that are bundled together and given a numerical weight signifying "strength of implementation requirements." Then there are three more antecedents (funding scale, central office commitment, and administrative latitude). The level of assistance is simply repeated in the next column for clarity.

But the chart has another objective, that of looking beyond assistance to its *consequences* during early implementation (column 9) and during later implementation (last column). In other words, whereas the degree of assistance was the dependent variable for the earlier analysis, it is the chief *predictor* here. But the analyst is going beyond a simple double-prediction here and also looking to see whether the predictors that best accounted for the degree of assistance make *sense* when combined with assistance level, to lead to different levels of later outcome. So we have the rudiments of a causal chain appearing in the matrix.

The same general analysis strategies as those for a regular predictor-outcome matrix can be used here. Because of the three-step aspect, expect to spend more time in analysis.

V.D TIME-ORDERED META-MATRIX

Analysis Problem

In comparing a number of sites, one often wants to know about events that have occurred over a period of time, especially those events that are indicators of some underlying process or flow. How can data from several sites be displayed in a way that respects chronology?

Brief Description

A time-ordered meta-matrix has columns that are organized sequentially by time period; the rows are

Box V.C.a
Substructed Variable: Extent of Organizational Change

<u>Have organizational changes occurred
beyond the innovation itself?</u>

		Yes	Few or None
Is the innovation in place?	Yes	Carson Masepa (1)	Plummet Perry-Parkdale Tindale Banestown Astoria (2)
	Partially, or on limited basis		Calston Lido Burton (3)
	No		Dun Hollow Proville (4)

Box V.C.b
Contrast Table: Exemplary Sites Showing Different
Degrees of User Change

Aspects of User Change	Masepa High Change	Burton Low Change	Dun Hollow Negative Change
1. Start-up discrepancy from usual practice	High discrepancy	Low discrepancy	Moderate discrepancy,
2. Pervasiveness of change	High — all facets	Low — repertoire only	Low/moderate—routines and attitudes
3. Technical mastery	Slow in coming	Rapid	Slow, then rapid
4. Energy investment	Very high	Low	High, then low
5. Negative changes reported	Some	None	Many
6. Stretched--pushed beyond voluntary change	Yes — well beyond	No	Yes — at the start

Box V.C.c

Predictor-Outcome-Consequences Matrix: Antecedents and Consequences of Assistance

SITES/Scale of Assistance	ANTECEDENT CONDITIONS							ASSISTANCE	CONSEQUENCES	
	Actual size/scope of innov.	Required practice change	Actual Classroom/organizational fit	Implementation requirements #	Scale of funding	Central office commitment to change	Admin latitude	OVER-ALL PRESENCE	Smoothness/Roughness of early implementation	Practice-stabilization (later implementation)
Substantial assistance										
Masepa (NDN)	large	major	mod/good	12	$30-50K	high	low	HIGH	very rough	mod
Plummet (IV-C)	large	mod/major	good/poor*	12	$300K	high	high	HIGH	very rough	mod
Carson (IV-C)	large	major	mod/good	12	$96K	high	mod	MOD/HIGH	rough	mod
Tindale (IV-C)	large/mod	major	mod	12	$87K	high	low	MOD/HIGH	rough	high
Perry-Parkdale (NDN)	mod	mod/major	mod	10	$300K@	mod	high	MOD/HIGH	mixed	mod/high
Banestown (NDN)	small/mod	major	mod	10	$5.6K	high	high	MOD	very rough	mod
Initial assistance, then minimal										
Lido (NDN)	small	mod	mod	7	$6.1K	low	high	LOW/MOD	mostly smooth	mod/high
Astoria (NDN)	small	minor	good	3	None	high	high	LOW/MOD	smooth	high
Calston (NDN)	small	mod	poor	9	None	mod/high	mod/high	LOW/MOD	mixed	mod/high
Nearly none										
Dun Hollow (IV-C)	small	minor	poor	7	None	low	mod	LOW	rough	low
Proville (IV-C)	mod	minor	mod	7	$180K	high→low	high	LOW	very rough	low
Burton (NDN)	small	minor	good	3	$3.1K	mod/high	high	LOW	smooth	mod

*good at district level, poor for students.

weighted sum of three variables at left, scaled 1-5.

@ IV-C funds, to adopt & disseminate NDN innovation

usually not ordered, but have the sites in arbitrary (perhaps alphabetical) order. Again, the basic principle is chronology.

Illustration

In our school improvement study, we were much interested in the question of *job mobility*—how the key people who were connected with an innovation changed jobs during the implementation period. Our look at adoption processes had already shown us that many people (up to 40 percent) liked the idea of adopting the innovation because it "might" help their job prospects. The question is, what actually happens afterward? We suspected (see section III.D, example C) that people involved with an innovation might do one of several things: Strengthen their status in their *existing* job; move *into* the innovative project when they had been out of it; *stay in* the project, but move to a new job across (same status level), up, or down; move *out* of the project—across, up, or down. Or they might actually move out of education altogether. And of course we were interested in causality: Was a person's move really stimulated or induced by experience with the innovation, or would he or she have moved anyway?

Building the display. How might one format a useful display to answer these questions? Chart 35 presents a prototype set-up. In each cell, one would enter examples of job mobility that had occurred in that site at that time period, with a descriptor showing what *kind* of mobility it was (in/out; up/down/across, and so on). Looking across rows would show the total range of job mobility examples at specific sites; looking down columns would indicate mobility at particular time periods.

But the display is too simple-minded. For one thing, it does not specify *whose* mobility we are talking about—everyone at the site, or only key people? Second, it does not tell us anything about causality— whether the job changes occurred because of the innovative project, or would have occurred for that person anyway. Third, the time periods are only vaguely defined.

Thinking about these issues led us to the display shown in Chart 36. It focuses on *key people* (with the rationale that such people are more likely to show innovation-caused effects, if they exist), and defines their number specifically, so we can see how many of them moved. Second, it defines the three time periods with a key phrase ("creation/initiation of project," for instance). And it has a column for a judgment as to whether the job mobility for each person was innovation-caused or not. The last column requires an overall judgment of the amount of mobility in the site as a whole.

The sites are not ordered, but we did want to compare the possible job mobility in two different program types (NDN and IV-C), so we separated them.

Entering the data. To fill up such a matrix, one reads through the relevant sections of the site reports, first defining people in "key" positions (advocates of the innovation, supporters, project leaders, principals, active users, and so on) for whom job movement was *possible.* Then one locates all instances of job change (including, if present, clear instances of "job strengthening"). For each instance, one enters the old job title, and characterizes the nature of the change (in/out; up/down/across). In addition, one makes a judgment based on the site report data as to whether the move was *clearly* innovation related, possibly so, or not at all.

Finally, when all data are entered for all sites, one can look across each row and make a general rating of the overall amount of job mobility for that site. The easiest way is to look at the proportion of moves to the total possible (use a decision rule, such as 0-35 percent = low; 36-70 percent = moderate; 71-100 percent = high). Extra weight can be given if unusually central "key people" (such as project directors or very active principals) are the ones moving. Usually it will be necessary to make provisional ratings for all sites, then review them again to see if they still seem correct.

Analyzing the data. A simple first step is *counting* (see section VII.A.1): We can see that there are 63 moves, of which 52, or 83 percent, are innovation-related. The 63 moves occurred in an eligible population of 123; thus a rather substantial 51 percent of key people who *could* move did so.

Mobility obviously differs by time period, as we look down different columns. Job moves are highest at the outset, when the project creates new roles and teachers move into administrative/supervisory slots. We can also see that moves are more frequent during *later* implementation, when administrators move up, or out, and teachers associated with the project take their places.

By tabulating the direction of moves, we can see that twelve teachers moved up, as did ten administrators, totaling 35 percent of the innovation-related job shifts. So innovation is not an automatic ticket to advancement.

It is also possible to explore the cases where mobility was *not* innovation-related; here the analyst has to go back to the site reports to find out what happened. It developed that people were either already planning to leave or retire, or that sudden environmental turbulence (such as massive budget cuts) ejected people from their jobs.

Chart 35
Time-Ordered Meta-Matrix (preliminary format)

SITES	Time 1 (early)	Time 2 (during implementation)	Time 3 (later)
Site A			
Site B			
etc.			

Chart 36
Time-Ordered Meta-Matrix: Job Mobility at Sites

SITES	No. key actors involved+	T1-Creation/initiation of project	Innovation-related?	T2-Early implementation (1st year)	Innovation related?	T3 - Later implementation	Innovation-related?	Overall mobility rating for site*
Astoria (NDN)	5	1 cent.office(C.O) admin.strengthens new role	✓✓	1 bldg. admin. moves up / 1 C.O. admin. moves out and over	✓/ ✓/	N/A	N/A	Moderate
Banestown(NDN)	6	1 aide moves in & up to teacher status / 1 teacher moves back in / 1 teacher prepares for move up / 1 C.O. admin. positioned for move up	✓ / ✓ / ✓ / ✓			1 tchr. moved back down / 1 tchr moved over to desirable post	0 / 0	High
Burton(NDN	9	1 C.O. admin. strengthens role	✓/			N/A	N/A	Nil
Calston(NDN)	7	1 tchr prepares for move up / 1 C.O. admin. extends authority / 1 bldg. admin strengthens position	✓ / ✓/ / ✓/			1 C.O. admin. moved out and down / 1 tchr(librarian moves out and over / 1 tchr in process of moving out	0 / ✓/ / ✓/	Moderate
Lido(NDN)	5					1 bldg. admin. moves out and up	✓/	Low
Masepa(NDN)	13			1 tchr moves up to supervisory role	✓	1 tchr moves up to supervisory role / 1 C.O. admin.retires / 1 proj.admin.moves out	✓ / 0 / 0	Low/moderate
Perry-Parkdale (NDN)	10	3 tchrs move in from less desirable jobs / 1 tchr. moves in and up to admin. post	✓ / ✓	1 C.O. admin. moves out & (tries to go) up	✓/	1 tchr moves out & over / 1 tchr moves out & back down / 1 proj. admin. moves out and up / 2 bldg. admins. move out, 1 moves up	✓ / 0 / ✓ / 0	High
Carson (IV-C)	27	2-3 tchrs move out / 2-3 tchrs move in / 1 bldg. admin. strengthens role	✓/ / ✓/ / ✓	1 teacher moves out / 1 bldg. admin. moves out	0 / 0	1 tchr(prog. coord.) moves out / 1 bldg. admin. moves out and over / 1 bldg. admin. moves up / 1 tchr moves in & up to prog. coord. role then moves out & up	0 / ✓/ / 0 / ✓	Moderate
Dun Hollow(IV-C)	7	1 regional admin. extends role	✓			N/A	N/A	Nil
Plummet (IV-C)	6	1 tchr moves in and up to admin. role / 5 tchrs move in	✓ / ✓	4 tchrs move up to supervisory role	✓	1 bldg. admin. moves out / 1 tchr moves out	✓/ / ✓/	Moderate/high
Proville(IV-C)	14	1 tchr moves in and up to admin. post	✓	1 C.O. admin moves up / 1 tchr moves in and up to admin. post	✓ / ✓	1 C.O. admin. moves out and up / 1 tchr moves in and up to proj. admin. role	✓ / ✓	High
Tindale(IV-C)	14			1 tchr moves up to bldg. admin. post	✓	1 bldg. admin.retires / 1 C.O. admin. moves out and up / 3 bldg. admins. move up	0 / ✓ / ✓	High

+People in key roles connected to the project
for whom job mobility was possible

*Researcher estimate based on proportion of actual job moves to total
of key actors, with higher weighting for moves by people immediately
responsible for, or crucial to, the innovation (ex: project director).

Legend:

✓   Yes, clearly
✓/   possibly, in part
0   no

N/A = not applicable

Still other analyses can be made. We can see that, by and large, IV-C projects, except for Dun Hollow, have substantial mobility (37 moves in 5 sites), while NDN projects range more widely and average lower (29 moves in 7 sites). A step back to the site reports shows that most IV-C projects, being self-developed rather than imported, tended to require new coordinative and supervisory roles. Also, 3 of the 5 were relatively large-scale projects, while NDN projects tended to be "add-ons" or "drop-ins" with fewer demands.

Variations

This particular chart could be differentiated with subcolumns for teachers, project administrators, building and central office staff, which might make for easier analysis.

Of course, time-ordered meta-matrices can be designed for a wide range of events in addition to the one focused upon here (innovation-connected job moves). Staying with the general area of school improvement as an illustration, other events could include the following: assistance efforts (such as workshops or in-service training); modifications in the innovation; extension of the innovation to new users; changes in school structure or procedures; or specific managerial interventions aimed at aiding implementation. It is important only that (a) a reasonably clearly defined class of events is specified, related to some general variable of interest; and (b) the available data permit the identification of the period when the event occurred.

We should not be too harsh about defining "events" as the only candidates for such a display. In principle, one could also do a time-ordered meta-matrix on "states," more fuzzily defined. For example, we might want to show the states of innovation users' feelings and concerns (confusion, overload, anxiety, satisfaction, pride, commitment, and so on) when they first encountered the innovation, then during early use, and during later, more stabilized use. If the time linkages of such states can be determined validly, then good analysis is possible.

We have stressed ordering of the matrix by time, but there is no law that says such a matrix could not be site-ordered as well. If so, one can see more clearly what the patterns of movement in high-mobility sites are, and how they differ from low-mobility sites.

Advice

This sort of display works best when a reasonably clear *class* of time-related events (or states) needs to be examined. For looking at the *general* flow of events in a site, see *event listing* (section IV.H) and associated boxes.

Try to specify the events (or states) being examined rather clearly, so good comparability exists across sites. Be sure that you have identified sensible and comparable time periods across sites, and that you can unambiguously locate the particular event or state in a particular time period.

Use summary tables (Box V.B.b) to pull together and look at data from the display if it is complicated, or the totals in a row or column are not easily visible.

Time Required

The display illustrated here took about three hours for reading the site reports and making a rough-cut matrix, then another three hours for making the refined matrix and entering the data. Analysis and writing occupied another hour, though more could have been spent (in this case the analyst was eager to move on to understanding the *causes* of mobility, and could not wait to dig into them more deeply). Generally speaking, if adequate time is spent in specifying the events and developing codes (like up/down/across, in this case), the analysis can go quickly; if the events are blurrily defined, extracting meaning will be much more time-consuming.

V.E SCATTERPLOTS

Analysis Problem

Many of the cross-site analytic techniques discussed up to now involve the display of all the cases on common dimensions so the analyst can see how the cases line up. Scanning these data in matrix form can tell the analyst something about how they should be further partitioned and clustered, and perhaps something about trends over time. But the matrix logic is one of creating categories or cutoff points, then seeing into which bin the cases will fall, so that a "contingency" analysis can be made.

Matrices, in other words, throw away a lot of useful information on how close or far apart the sites are on dimensions of interest—how they cluster, and how clusters relate to each other. Something a bit more *spatial* is needed.

Sometimes, the analyst will want to plot each of the sites on two or more axes to see exactly how close to or distant from one another they are. This is closer to a scatterplot logic, as used to make sense of correlation coefficients, or to a "vector" logic as used in statistical factor analysis. How can qualitative data be displayed in similar ways?

Brief Description

Scatterplots are figures that display data from all sites on two or more dimensions of interest that are related to one another. Data from sites are carefully scaled, and laid out in the space formed by respective "axes," so that some determination of similarity and contrast between the sites can be made. The principle is bivariate (or multivariate) analysis of relationships in coordinate-defined space.

Illustration

In the school improvement study, we were struck by how much users "bent" the innovation during project execution. Few of these projects came out looking like the developer's model. Gradually, it became clear that most of these modifications were made with the explicit or implicit approval of local administrators, who granted "latitude" to users to make appropriate changes.

Since, in most cases, administrators had leaned hard on users to adopt the new practices, we wondered whether there was some kind of implicit bargain here. Perhaps users were being allowed by administrators to modify the project locally as a palliative to their feelings about being pressured to adopt. If that hypothesis were borne out, there should be a clear relationship between levels of pressure and levels of latitude.

This relationship was not probed in each of the case studies, but only began to emerge during cross-site analysis. So the analyst had to transform the original site-level data to some common metric, then find a way of arraying them that tested the relationship.

Building the display/entering data. Figure 15 shows what the analyst did. He scaled each site on a "pressure to adopt" continuum and a "latitude" continuum, then created two axes and plotted each case on them. As he went back to the site reports to do this, he noted that for some sites latitude, or pressure, *differed* as between early and later implementation. That could be accommodated on the display by showing two values for such a site, with an arrow indicating the direction of change.

Analyzing the data. It looks as if the hypothesis doesn't pan out; if it had, most of the sites would have clustered in the upper right quadrant (high pressure, high latitude), and we have only a single case there (Astoria). In fact, it looks as if the *opposite* hypothesis is being borne out.

In short, administrators who pressure people to adopt keep up the pressure in the form of low latitude; where adoption pressure is weaker, users get more latitude. However, note the interesting drift in four of the six higher-pressure sites: Latitude was slightly higher during later implementation. So maybe once the innovation has started in, administrators relent a bit, and there is something to our bargaining hypothesis after all. But the negotiation comes later than we had thought.

Going back to the site reports helped clarify things further. For example, the analyst found that only in

Astoria (tactic: *checking the meaning of outliers*, section VII.B.6) was there an explicit initial bargain with payoffs struck between administrators and users. And there turned out to be plenty of data supporting an administrative message like this one to users, notably in Dun Hollow, Calston, Masepa, and Tindale:

> You're going to do this. Start out doing it like the developer wants. Later, you can make changes.

And the moderate pressure at Proville was accompanied by a central office bargaining stance toward principals that sounded like this:

> We want to try this and we want at least token collaboration from you.

Variations

Illustrations such as Figure 15 can carry still more freight. For example, they can easily accommodate more sites. Site data can also be differentiated (for instance, by using separate symbols for measures of administrators and users in each site). With some care, it is possible to plot three dimensions, but graphic clarity is very important, else interpretations are difficult.

The scatterplot can also be simplified back down to a contingency table format. See Box V.E.a for an illustration that gained power by comparing two such tables from different time periods.

For another illustration, Chart 37 is drawn from Firestone and Corbett (1979); see also Firestone and Corbett (1981). It gives a quick scan of the relationships between two key variables. The authors hypothesized that a rational, collective planning cycle within a school would increase local "ownership" in the sense of heightened commitment to the changes undertaken. They classified their eleven cases on "ownership," and on the degree of progress through a rational planning cycle. The relationship is there, and nearly linear; there are no cases in the extreme off-diagonal cells. Still, there is a slight "belly" in the table: Low ownership goes more with fair progress through the planning cycle than with poor; medium ownership goes about equally with fair to good progress. That suggests that planning progress is *not* causing ownership by itself, but that other factors are intervening to suppress ownership. To find out more about what is actually causing what, we need to go back to site reports—which the authors did, cell by cell, looking at similarities. (Note that we should also consider the possibility that reverse causality is at work—higher ownership induces more planning progress.)

Advice

Scatterplots are very useful when the analyst is trying out a hypothesis or is in a still more exploratory mode calling for some way to "see" all the cases in two-

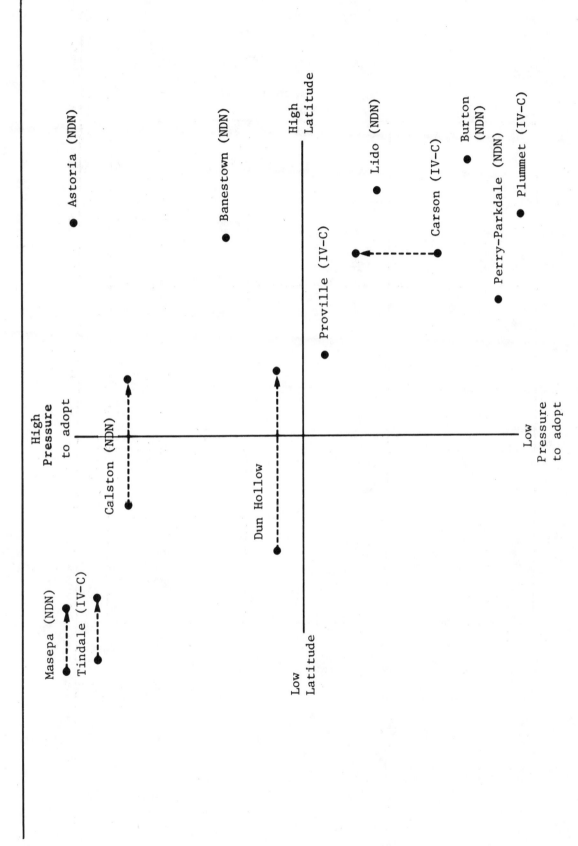

Figure 15   Scatterplot: Relationship of Pressure to Adopt and Degree of Latitude Given to Users at Twelve Sites

Chart 37

Scatterplot (contingency table format): Comparison of Interim Process Outcomes

Progress Through the Planning Steps

	Poor	Fair	Good	
High			Fa Ol Pa (3)	(3)
Medium		Su Gr (2)	Ne Ru (2)	(4)
Low	Ur (1)	Ri Bi Mi (3)		(4)
	(1)	(5)	(5)	

"Ownership"

NOTE: Pa = Patriot; Mi = Middleburg; Ru = Rural District; Fa = Farmcenter; Ur = Urban; Ri = Riverside; Su = Suburb; Ne = Neighbortown; Gr = Green Hills; Bi = Bigtown; Ol = Oldtown.

dimensional space. Plotting the cases spatially is also a good way to make more precise determinations about which sites form clusters (see Box V.E.a).

Because figures like these call for a careful "scale score" rather than an impressionistic rating, the analyst has to do finer-grained work than the site-level researcher probably did. This may call for a review of the appropriate section in the site report, in order to pick up more differentiated cues. Techniques such as summed indices (Box V.B.a) can be used. If careful scaling is not possible, then a contingency table is better.

As usual, it is important not to settle for conclusions drawn from the display alone. One must clarify and confirm (or qualify) the conclusion through reference back to site reports.

Time Required

Figures such as these are relatively easy to construct and fill in. If the cross-site analyst has data in an easily scalable form, the data can be scaled and entered for a dozen cases in an hour or so. If not, scaling can be time-consuming (as in Box V.B.a). But, often, the variables of concern have already been scaled or categorized for some other analysis—then we are talking about ten or fifteen minutes for a procedure that is usually quite illuminating.

Drawing conclusions and taking a confirmatory look at site reports and writing text may occupy another hour. More sites, more time, naturally.

V.E.a Scatterplots over Time

Scatterplots can be useful when they display similar variables in sites over two or more time periods. In this example, the analyst was trying to find out whether the amount of assistance given to people executing an innovation aided (a) early implementation "smoothness," and (b) later "stabilization" of the practice. He was looking for a display that would line up all twelve sites on these three dimensions. The best bet looked like Box V.E.a. The analyst already had sorted sites into the categories noted, so plotting was quick. One can see at a glance—one of the benefits of such a display—that the sheer amount of assistance does *not* predict early smoothness or later stabilization. But there *are* families of sites. The analyst drew lines around what looked like reasonable families, then thought about what they meant.

In the first time period, family A was sites with high assistance and rough implementation, while B was sites with low assistance and smooth implementation. Why should the relationship go that way—seemingly *backwards* from expectations? The analyst suddenly realized that a *third* factor was in play. The Family A

sites were all attempting large innovations (see chart, Box V.C.c). So, he reasoned, even large amounts of early assistance are unable to achieve smoothness if the innovation is big. The Family B sites don't need much assistance, because their innovations are small. Family C is a different kettle of fish: Their innovations are large, but enjoyed little assistance. The analyst labeled this family "assistance incompetence."

Turning to the scatterplot in the second time period, the analyst noted that Family A stayed the same: High assistance eventually paid off in moderate to high stabilization for large-scale innovations. Family B, with almost the same membership as before, achieved good stabilization for its innovations with minimal assistance. The weak assistance in family C probably hindered eventual stabilization.

Note that cycling back to the site reports is always needed. For example, why did the weakly assisted, large-scale innovation stabilize in Dun Hollow? It developed that teachers themselves helped each other, and did considerable rewriting and adaptation of the curriculum materials. We see here that anomalies and deviant cases always need careful follow-up in the site-level data; they have to be accounted for satisfactorily, and usually strengthen conclusions (see section VII.B.6 on *checking the meaning of outliers*).

V.F SITE-ORDERED EFFECTS MATRIX

Analysis Problem

So far we have been mostly pursuing data display and analysis methods that concentrate on *describing* a state of affairs, or *explaining likely causes* of a state of affairs. There is another kind of analysis problem: Understanding the *effects* of a particular variable, seen as a stimulus, an antecedent, or a probable cause. We looked at this in section IV.F for the single-site situation. Causal displays—for single or multiple cases—tend to be implicitly modeled like this:

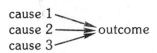

Effects displays, examining the diverse results occurring from a single variable, are structured like this:

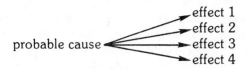

So when one has a number of sites where an important or salient "cause" is expected to have a variety of

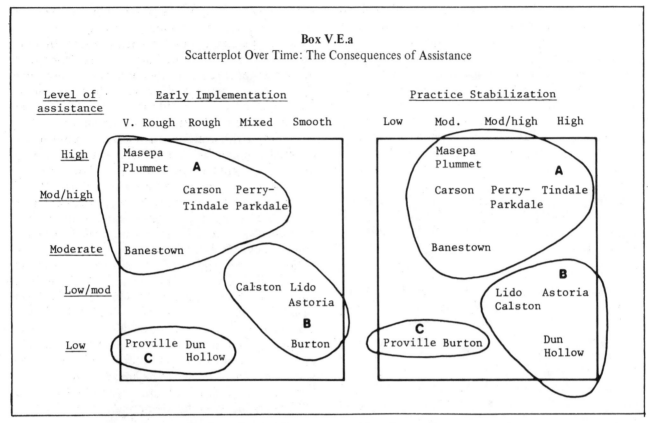

Box V.E.a
Scatterplot Over Time: The Consequences of Assistance

results, the question is how to display relevant data in order to see how the effects play out, across sites where there is a greater (or smaller) amount of the basic cause. Usually one also wants to see whether the effects are "sortable" into various categories.

Brief Description

A site-ordered effects matrix sorts the sites by degrees of the probable cause and shows the diverse effects for each site. The effects may be clustered or categorized to help understanding. Again, the focus is on *outcomes,* dependent variables.

Illustration

In our school improvement study, one of the main variables in which we were interested was *assistance* provided to users of an educational innovation. We knew that assistance might be of various *types* (for example, special training, supplying resources, or giving emotional support); we also knew that some assistance was *event-linked* (for example, a brief workshop) and other assistance was *ongoing* (for example, a principal's troubleshooting assistance given from day to day). And we expected that the assistance might have *short-run effects* (such as feeling clearer about the innovation), and *longer-run consequences* (such as improved skill in using it). The

problem here is how to sort all these features out in a manageable display.

Building the display. A first cut at a possible display could look like Chart 38a. This display could be repeated for "event-linked assistance." A natural first step is to read through the relevant sections/displays in the original site reports to see what the information there looks like, and whether it can be sorted into the proposed display. Doing this also helps to generate a list of possible categories for short-run effects (for example, "increased understanding," "more motivation," "reduced isolation") and long-run effects (such as "getting funds," "increased legitimacy of the program," "routinization of the innovation"). When the analyst has done this for many/most of the sites, he or she can subsume the list of specific effects into fewer, more general bins. In our case, both short- and long-run effects could be sorted into three general kinds: those effects on the *innovation* and its use, those on *individuals,* and those on the *organization.* So a possible refigured format could look like Chart 38b.

The idea here is to enter specific types of effects (a phrase, usually) in appropriate cells. If one returns to the site reports (and/or the lists of effects already generated), it is possible to see whether this format will work. It depends on how many different types of effects there are. If there are only a few, the matrix will

Chart 38a
Site-Ordered Effects Matrix (preliminary format)

EFFECTS OF ONGOING ASSISTANCE

Sites	Types	Short-run effects	Long-run consequences
high 1.			
assis- 2.			
tance 3.			
to 4.			
low 5.			

Chart 38b
Site-Ordered Effects Matrix (version 2 of format)

		SHORT-RUN EFFECTS					LONG-RUN EFFECTS				
		SITES high..................................low					SITES high..................................low				
EFFECTS	on the innovation										
	on users										
	on the organ- ization										

not be too unwieldy. But if there are a lot, one will have to do better—especially if there's a wish to include the differentiation between "ongoing" and "event-linked" assistance effects. We can also see that having two sub-matrices for short- and long-term effects may get confusing.

Supposing a very wide range of effects, the next iteration of the format could look like Chart 38c. This looks more workable. Remember that a preliminary list of categories had already been developed for the headings. We can show the whole range of detailed effects and enter information in each cell. For each site we can show that that specific effect did or didn't occur, and possibly even whether it was a long-term or short-term effect. Let's see.

Entering the data. Reading from a particular site report, one can locate the effects noted and can enter a check mark in the appropriate row for that column for each effect. But what about the problems of short-run and long-run effects, and event-linked and ongoing assistance? There are several options. One is to enter O for ongoing and E for event-linked assistance, plus 1 if the effect was short-run and 2 if it was long-run. That would provide maximum differentiation in the display—data would not be smoothed over or lost—without complicating it excessively.

Chart 38d shows what the complete overall display, with all data entered in, looks like. It looks complicated

Chart 38c
Site-Ordered Effects Matrix (version 3 of format)

SITES, by assistance provided.

	Substantial					Moderate		Low	
Effects on the innovation									
1.									
2.									
3.....									
Effects on individuals									
1.									
2.									
3.....									
Effects on the org.									
1.									
2.									
3.									
4....									

at first—but the *data* are rich and complex, and need a complex display.

We can note another refinement that developed as the analyst pondered over categories. The effects of assistance for the *innovation* could be roughly temporally ordered, with initial or "front-end" effects, such as "planning, developing," and "sense of goals" arrayed at the top, and later or "back-end" effects, such as "program expansion" and "program dissemination" coming toward the bottom. A similar ordering could be done for effects on *individuals.* But the analyst found that the categories for effects on the *organization* could not be sorted by temporal order. (There's little conceptual basis for assuming that "conflict resolution" or "trust" or "improved problem solving" would necessarily come early or late during implementation.)

Naturally, as the data are entered, site by site, a few new categories appear and should be put in the temporal order that *seems* appropriate. For example, on Chart 38d, "routinization" should clearly go toward the bottom of the list of individual effects, but not as far down as "continuation."

Analyzing the data. A good first step here, as is often the case, is a quick and dirty "squint analysis." One can see by scanning down columns that all sites, even those where there is nearly no assistance, show assistance effects on the *innovation* and (even more

numerously) on the *individual. Organizational* effects are least frequent, and occur in all but two sites (Calston and Burton).

It is also visible from a squint that (a) high-assistance sites have a wider *range* of effects than low-assistance ones; and (b) low-assistance sites are less likely to experience assistance effects that occur *late* during implementation (such as "program dissemination").

The next steps in analysis, given the complexity of the table, require the use of summary tables (see chart, Box V.B.b) collapsing the data from Chart 38d to confirm or correct the "squint" impressions and comparing the content of effects in high- and low-assistance sites. For example, one can see (in Box V.B.b) that low-assistance sites show more negative effects on individuals than do high-assistance sites. Or a content summary table (same section) can show that problems of increasing understanding and ownership occur in *both* high- and low-assistance sites.

Variations

Most site-ordered matrices are far simpler than this illustration, which involves not only temporally ordered effects in three major categories, but complicated cell entries (short- and long-term effects, event-linked and ongoing assistance). Effects matrices can be simplified by "unpacking" them (for example, in this case, doing separate matrices for event-linked and ongoing assistance), by making simpler cell entries (checks, for

An antecedents matrix is ordered by the outcome variable, and shows all the variables that seem to be at work in inducing changes in it. The easiest way to proceed, after the subnetworks have been identified as in step 2, is to scan through them for the variables that appear on, say, at least one-third of the subnetworks. You may want to add variables that are conceptually important as well.

Box V.H.a shows an example of an antecedents matrix for the outcome variable "student impact." Note that the variables are *clustered* conceptually under general headings to make understanding easier. An "immediate" cause is considered one not more than two steps back from the outcome. (Going further back than this tends to bring in everything but the kitchen sink, and the analysis gets blurred.) A "remote" cause is still on a stream connected to the outcome, but further back. A remote or immediate cause should also have its strength (high, moderate, or low) entered. Some variables will either not be on a direct stream or not be on the network at all—leave those cells blank.

During analysis, it helps to take each column, one by one, and summarize the finding. For example, we can see that "user commitment" is high and immediately causal in three of the five high-impact sites, and a remote cause in the other two; is a high or moderate remote cause in the moderate-impact sites; is not causal at all in moderate/low sites; and is low in low-impact sites. So user commitment, even though it is often a remote cause, has a real bearing on eventual student impact.

When all the variables have been reviewed and the text written, it helps to make a general summary. Here is one for the chart:

> It appears that high student impact is more likely when *user commitment* is high, when *program transformation* is either held to a minimum or is a corrective to an initially overambitious start, and when strong *assistance* takes place, resulting in *practice mastery* and *stabilization of use.* The presence of *administrative pressure* is a remote cause of student impact—but only, it appears, when it translates into willingness to restrict program transformation, to supply strong assistance, or do both.

What we have here is an overview statement—which could be used, in fact, to construct a preliminary cross-site causal model (see section V.G). We have gotten an idea of what variables are most powerful antecedents of the outcome.

But such a model would only be a smoothed-down, averaged version of what really happens site by site. It is now necessary to begin the process of looking for "families" of sites that share the same scenario. To do this, one can do site-by-site comparisons across the columns, looking for similar patterns.

It also helps to start with sites that have the same general level of outcome (such as the high-impact ones). When the matrix suggests a plausible pair, the original subnetworks can be examined to see if they, and their component streams, are a reasonable match. The same pattern-matching operations we have already described are in play.

We have now gotten to the same outcome—a set of coherent scenarios explaining what happened in the sites. As before, they need to be verified (step 4).

The antecedents matrix is an easy way to see the big picture without getting swept away in myriad specific streams and going under for the third time. The main thing to remember is that the matrix *takes apart* the causal flows, and genuinely powerful conclusions cannot be drawn from it. One must always go back to the actual local flow of causality, and sort networks into families—not individual variables, out of sequence.

Doing an antecedents matrix adds some to analysis time, but it often saves you from the overload and incoherence that are likely when trying to do stream-by-stream analysis, especially with more than a few sites.

Variations

We consider cross-site causal networking to be in its infancy, and expect future analysts to improve on it as they work out alternative techniques of conclusion drawing. It is not clear, for instance, whether one would get more than one or two replications of a causal stream with an N of only 5-6 cases, or whether these procedures are cost-effective with an N of more than 15-20 cases.

Researchers being ambitious creatures, the obvious next threshold is cross-site analysis of *several* outcomes at once. We have also tried our hand at this with reasonably good success, although there is often cause for relaxing one or another of the decision rules, else one get ensnarled in thickets of boxes and arrows. However, the same decision rules do apply when one is contending with a single or with multiple outcome measures. For example, using the same analytic procedures outlined earlier, we derived four multiple-outcome scenarios for the twelve cases in the school improvement study. Figure 21 is a causal network grouping four cases into one scenario (a total of five outcome variables was used).

Here the analyst, discarding site-specific variables, was able to map consistent flows across the four sites, defined as a "family" sharing a common scenario by the fact that they had high student impact and user capacity change, but only moderate percentage of use and institutionalization. (The consistent mapping is in part achieved by accepting correspondences such as "moderate/low" rather than a harsher criterion such

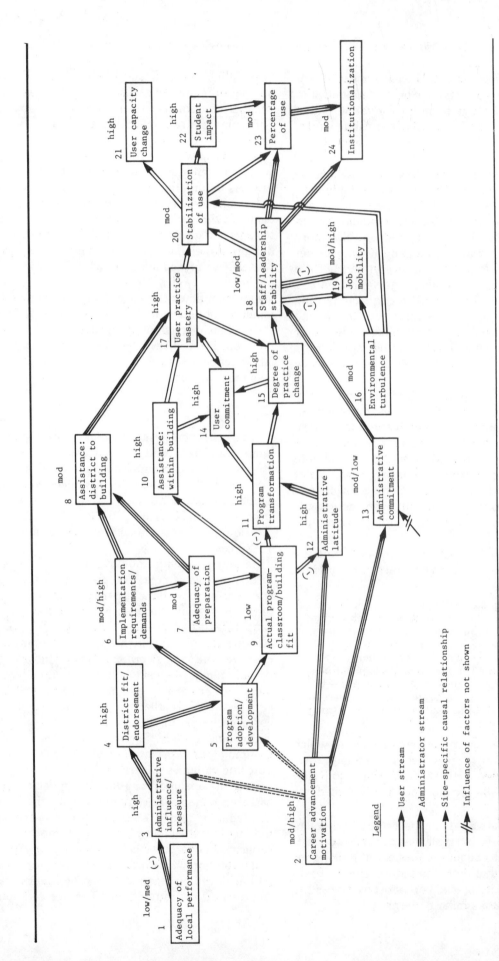

Figure 21 Scenario 2: Moderate/High Outcomes from High Mastery and Low Settledness

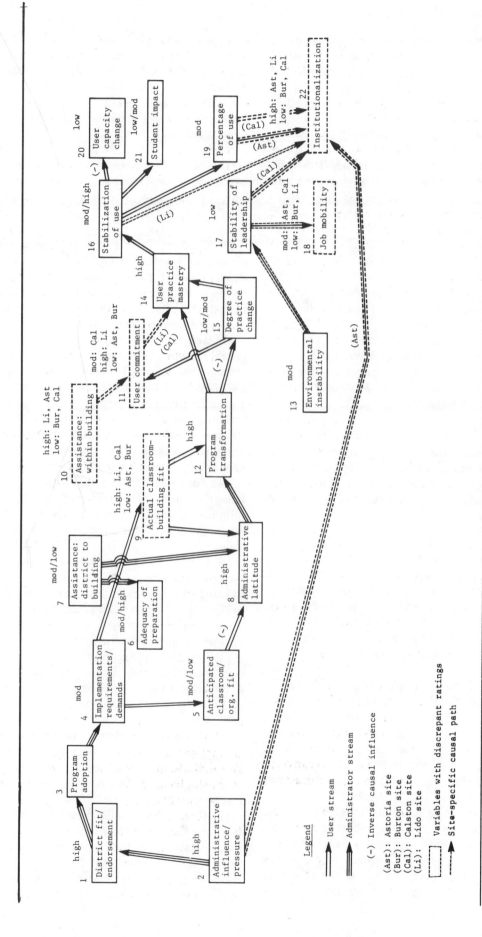

Figure 22   Scenario 3: Moderate/Low Outcomes from Program Blunting/Downsizing

207

as full agreement.) The critical factors appear to be high user mastery accompanied by only moderate stabilization of use. Note that the analyst also found that causal flows were somewhat different for users and administrators, suggesting that role-specific causal networks could be generated as well.

Not all multiple-outcome scenarios come out so nicely. In Figure 22 we have four sites grouped in one causal network with five outcome variables. As before, there are some distinct causal streams for users and administrators. But there are several instances where either the *ratings* or the *paths* are discrepant among the set of four cases. For example, the variable boxes surrounded by broken lines (for example, 9, 10, 11) have discrepant between-site ratings. Also, some of the paths are case-specific (such as those linking variables 19-22, 11-14, 17-18). Still, the overall scenario is plausible (moderate to low outcomes are likely when administrators allows users a lot of latitude [8] to transform the innovation [12] to make it "easier to use"). Even though the innovation is used stably (16), its "downsizing" results in less capacity change (20) and student impact (21), along with lower percentage of use (19) and institutionalization (22).

What about the intersite discrepancies on this multisite, multioutcome network? On balance, they are far fewer than the correspondences. Furthermore, the discrepancies can be shown directly on the network itself without overloading the display—and the reader can get back easily to the original site network to understand more.

Advice

Cross-site analysis can yield explanatory accounts that make good logical and empirical sense, using a simple set of arithmetical and inferential procedures. The exercise gets somewhat more unwieldy when more than one dependent variable is cranked into the analysis, but the use of the same decision rules can produce overarching findings that are equally compelling.

Cross-site causal network analysis is feasible mainly because the analyst includes attention to the microanalytical level, such as individual "paths" or "streams." It is important to be able to see the big picture, but the more general insights gained from an antecedents matrix, as in Box V.H.a, ultimately have to be run back through the lens of site-specific streams. One must not lose sight of the web of *local causality*.

An important corollary, however, is that this exercise should be *derived* from other, less inclusive cross-site analyses. If the causal network findings are inconsistent with, say, the site-ordered predictor-outcome analyses or the site-ordered effects matrices, something is wrong. In other words, the more "bivariate" cross-site

analyses and simpler "multivariate" ones should lead inferentially to the more encompassing pattern-matching we try for in cross-site analysis. There has to be an evidential trail, and the analyst has to be able to follow it not only *up to* the causal network analysis but also *back down* from the causal networks to the constituent analyses.

A few, more specific, bits of advice:

(1) The analyst should always keep the network narratives close at hand. It is possible that site accounts with the same set of core variables aligned along a similar sequenced stream actually mean different things.

(2) Don't try for a theme or scenario name until several sites have been looked at. There is usually a stray predictor or two in a stream, and the analyst needs to wait until these strays can be separated out from those variables appearing consistently, which will give the name to the stream.

(3) Be cautious about giving tacit *weights* to individual network variables. Presumably, the ones with more arrows leading to them are more significant, but a stream-level analysis cancels this out. In fact, a variable with too many arrows leading to it becomes a nuisance, since it multiplies the possible number of streams. Unlike path-analytic models, our networks have no regression coefficients to show how significant any substream (two or more connected variables) is. We do, however, have the *narrative*, which usually tells the reader which factors count most and which relationships are especially meaningful. So, once again, the analyst should keep the words and diagrams together.

(4) It is a good idea to have a second person *replicate* the analysis (section VII.B.9) with the same networks, narratives, and core list of variables. It is easy to slip into believing that streams from two sites are the "same"; another analyst may well note an obstinate exception ignored in the first run.

(5) If a cross-site scenario doesn't square with one or more depictions in the narrative, the scenario needs to be redone. In other words, the narrative is the prime piece of evidence, of which the causal network is a schematic depiction.

(6) If the person doing the cross-case analysis is other than the one doing the individual causal network site analysis, the cross-site account should be fed back to the single-site analyst to verify that his or her site has not been misrepresented.

(7) Remember, finally, that the objective of moving from the locally causal to the translocally causal is to derive a wide-ranging, more generalizable explanation. Not only does that explanation have to make *local* or context-informed sense, but it should also make *theoretical* sense. It should fit with an extant or

emerging account of *why* phenomena like these, seen across multiple instances, are likely to come together as they did.

Time Required

Although it may look forbidding at first, cross-site causal network analysis turns out to be pleasurable and not overly time-consuming. For example, the *single*-outcome "job mobility" analysis discussed here took about a working day from the time the analyst began work with the 12 networks and narratives. Steps 2 and 3 (isolating and matching streams across cases with similar outcome levels) took about 4 hours. Step 4 (double-checking the decision rules, looking at cases with contrasting outcomes) took about 3 hours. Writing text finished the day. Recall that in this analysis we had 12 networks, each containing 35-40 variables.

The alternate strategy using an antecedents matrix typically takes slightly more time. Marking the networks (12 here) and creating the matrix typically takes 3-4 hours, drawing conclusions and writing text another hour, then moving back to the clustering of sites into common scenarios, extracting prototypical subnetworks and writing text another 5-6 hours.

Doing cross-site network analysis is enjoyable; one is making sense of things in an integrative way, with the "aha" rate never being zero. The price of the enjoyment, though, is a certain obsessive care. You have to take the time to (a) exhaustively account for the full set of cases and (b) back out of certain dead ends. Taking the latter first, dead ends are streams that, finally, need to be broken up, that *make no sense*, although they seem common across cases, because they don't square with the narratives. It is important to tell yourself that this is a *necessary* part of an analytic process that is bound to lead *somewhere*—ultimately.

Second, the full set of cases has to be accounted for—a far more stringent criterion than in probabilistic analyses. If, let us say, the predictor ratings or sequences for networks with low levels of an outcome measure, as contrasted with the high cases, do not allow the analyst to meet decision rules 6 and 7 (consistent contrasts), the analyst must find out *why*. This can usually be resolved in the narratives, but it takes time.

Exhausting all the cases means, typically, that several scenarios are found. For example, we usually found four basic scenarios across twelve sites, emphasizing somewhat different variable sets. Here's a typical set of scenarios for the dependent variable "student impact":

Enforced, supported mastery, high impact (two sites)

Stabilized, committed mastery, high to moderate impact (six sites)

Weak commitment, low impact (two sites)

Program-blunting, low impact (two sites)

Taking on more than one outcome across cases is quite labor-intensive, to put it genteelly. Figures 21

and 22 took roughly two days each to derive. One should plan on interspersing this work with physical exercise, or one can become seriously disoriented and incoherent with friends and relatives. Also, expect to have dreams with unceasing arrays of boxes and arrows that never quite interconnect . . .

NOTES

1. For a more condensed discussion, see Glaser and Strauss (1970).

2. There are no clear rules of thumb as to the number of sites that can be managed in qualitative analysis, without simply regressing to numbers. We tend to feel that once past 15 or so sites, serious gaps in understanding of local dynamics begin appearing. But note that successful cross-site qualitative studies have been carried out with site Ns of up to 57 (see Smith & Robbins, 1982). One useful strategy involves first analyses on a representative subsample of sites, then replicating these (see section VII.B.9) on the remainder. But we need to learn much more about the possibilities and limitations of cross-site analysis with large numbers.

3. We are indebted to Rolf Lehming for suggesting this format.

4. We have experimented, for example, with Nishisato's (1979) dual scaling procedure.

5. The literature on various forms of quantitative causal modeling is large, and growing by leaps and bounds. We cannot possibly encompass it here, or do more than point to various useful treatments (such as Li's (1975) discussion of path analysis; Asher's careful overview (1976); Blalock's original classic (1964) and his more recent overview (1971); James, Mulaik, and Brett's (1982) material on confirmatory analysis, with a practical training emphasis; Gaynor's (1980) reports of nonrecursive "system" modeling; and Fornell's (1982) collection reviewing "second-generation" approaches to quantitative causal modeling, including LISREL, PLS, and others).

Developments in causal modeling have done a great deal to help researchers manage and understand multivariable data in a coherent, non-self-deluding way. We should note, however, that much of this literature deals with the technical problems of measurement and data manipulation involved, and little of it deals with the basic problem we are discussing in this section: model building, or how one moves from a list of "associated" variables to an integrated, causally coherent picture.

Excessive preoccupation with technical problems can easily lead to final models where the findings make no sense. Worse, when a finding makes no logical or theoretical sense, but is quantitatively "sound," the researcher can get seduced into making stretched, forced explanations. The great strength of qualitative causal models is that they can always be run back against the reality of events in the field site for verification.

6. This was, however, done with subsites in our study of interorganizational links between educational institutions.

7. Note that for simplicity we have omitted another associated substream (see full network): 10, 19, 21, 26, thence to 34 and 33. Early user preparation and selection, producing competent users (even without assistance) was also a factor in the level of user skill attained.

8. It is worth pointing out here that a lot of the inferential "pattern matching" that qualitative analysts do within and across cases involves the kind of simple counting and contrasting in rules 1-3 above: noting that some things always happen together, that others happen more or less often in similar sequences, that there are several instances of X and only one or two of non-X, and so on. Underneath most qualitative analyses are such necessary estimates of frequency, intensity, and covariation. In fact, one can't *get* to rule 4 above (comparing outcome themes) without the preliminary counts and comparisons of rules 1-3. So there is plenty of simple computing in qualitative work—just as there is constant inductive sense-making in quantitative work (as, for example, in factor analysis or cluster analysis procedures).

VI

Matrix Displays

Some General Suggestions

Matrices of various types are so pervasive throughout this book that it may be useful to offer some summarizing suggestions for building and using them.[1] For general suggestions on building and using displays of other types, see our Advice sections for *scatterplots* (section V.E), *context charts* (section IV.A), *causal networks* (section IV.J), and *causal models* (section V.G). In turn, we offer ideas on building matrices, on entering data, and on analysis. For each area we suggest some modest rules of thumb derived from our experience.

VI.A BUILDING MATRIX DISPLAYS

We should begin this section with some hortatory remarks. Matrix construction is interesting, easy, and satisfying. It is not arcane, forbidding, or obsessive, but an enjoyable problem-solving activity.

Most of the matrix formats described in this book were conceived, literally, in a few minutes. Developing them and working them through was naturally a longer process. But we have repeatedly had the experience, in running training workshops using this book, of formulating a research question and some data types, then asking participants to "make a matrix" that would answer the question. The average participant does the task in 15-25 minutes, with a good deal of surprise and pleasure.

Furthermore, that exercise usually produces in a group of, say, 25 people, at least 20 discriminably different matrix designs, each with different types of data entries. *Each* can be used to answer the research questions; *each* has certain advantages and certain limitations (see section IV.B, Variations). This under-

scores a basic point: There are no fixed canons for constructing a matrix. Rather, matrix construction is a creative—yet systematic—task that furthers your understanding of the substance and meaning of your data base, even before you begin entering information. Thus the issue is not whether one is building a "correct" matrix, but whether it is a *functional* one that will give you reasonable answers to the questions you are asking—or suggest promising new ways to lay out the data to get answers. At a deeper level, the message of this book is not "Use these matrices," but "Think in terms of matrices, and invent a format that will serve you best."

Matrix Elements

Here we provide a simple checklist—aspects of matrices about which to make choices during the design process. We are essentially considering how to partition the data.

(1) Descriptive versus explanatory intent. Are you essentially trying to lay out data to see "what's there," or do you want to extract some explanations as to *why* things happen as they do? The latter intent usually requires more careful attention to various forms of ordering (see below).

(2) Single-site versus multiple-site data. Are you focusing on describing/explaining phenomena attached to a single research setting (an individual "case," a family, a group, an organization, a community) or to several settings, from which reasonably comparable data have been collected? If the latter, rows or columns will have to be devoted to sites.

(3) Ordered versus nonordered. Are you essentially placing data in rows and columns that represent

descriptive categories, one by one, or are those categories ordered in some way—by strength or intensity of a variable, by time, by roles of participants, by sites that have different levels of some key variable? Once past initial description, some form of ordering is usually warranted.

(4) Time-ordered versus not. Ordering matrices by time is a special case of the above. If a matrix is time ordered, it enables the analysis of flow, sequences, perhaps cycles and chronologies, and maybe causes and effects.

(5) Categories of variables. Here there is an almost infinite set of possibilities. Which types of rows and column can there be? Here we offer two brief lists adapted from Lofland (1971) and Bogdan and Biklen (1982). One list refers to the size of the social unit being examined:

individuals

roles

relationships, pairs

groups

settings (places or locales within sites)

sites as wholes

Another list refers to what social units are doing, in effect:

specific acts, behaviors (what people do or say in detail)

events (marked-off happenings or occurrences)

activities (regularly occurring, connected sets of behavior)

strategies (activities aimed toward some goal)

meanings, perspectives (how people construe events)

states (general conditions)

processes (ongoing flows, changes over time)

Once you are clear about the *types* of rows and columns, there are usually further partitioning decisions. For example, if you are working with "roles" as columns, then *which* roles: teachers, students, administrators? And are department heads shown separately, lumped with teachers, or with administrators?

(6) Two-way, three-way, N-way... The simplest matrices, as in quantitative data display, are organized in two dimensions. You have a choice to move to more complexity if the data demand it. Subdividing each column in a parallel fashion for each column permits a "three-way" matrix, even though the data are still displayed in two dimensions; subdividing rows in the same way permits a four-way analysis. More complexity is always possible, but going further than four-way tables probably means you should be breaking out submatrices for more clarity.

(7) Cell entries. Finally, there are always choices about the level and type of data to be entered. For example, one can include

direct quotes, extracts from written-up field notes;

summaries, paraphrases, or abstracts;

researcher explanations;

ratings or summarized judgments;

combinations of the above.

Rules of Thumb for Matrix Building

Given these choices, what can we say informally about the best and easiest ways to build matrix displays? We'll state these brisky, as softly given advice rather than as harsh dicta.

(1) Keep the display on one large sheet, even if that sheet covers a wall.

(2) Don't try to include more than 15-20 variables in rows or columns; 5-6 is more like it.

(3) Expect to make a preliminary format, and to iterate it several times after entering data.

(4) Get a colleague to look at your formats, to help you detect the assumptions you are making, and to suggest alternative ways to display your data.

(5) If the matrix is an ordered one, expect to transpose rows and columns for a while until you have a satisfactory version.

(6) Consider regrouping a complex matrix containing many rows or columns into "streams" or adjacent "families."

(7) Always stay open to the idea of adding new rows or columns, even late in your analysis operations.

(8) Keep rows and columns fine-grained enough to accommodate meaningful differentiations in the data, but not so fine as to bury you in overdiscriminative detail.

(9) Keep in mind that any particular research question may require a *series* of matrices; for example, an initial unordered descriptive matrix, leading to a small summary table, then to various ordered, more boiled-down, matrices. Think ahead to this possibility, but allow new matrix forms to *emerge* as the analysis proceeds. They invariably do.

VI.B ENTERING MATRIX DATA

The choice of data for entry into matrix cells, and the operations involved in doing it, are critical issues in qualitative data analysis. *The conclusions drawn from a matrix can never be better than the quality of the data entered.* A completed matrix may look coherent and plausible, and may be fascinating—but if the data have been poorly collected in the first place, or entered in a hasty, ill-partitioned, or vague way, the conclusions must be suspect.

Rules of Thumb for Data Entry

(1) Be clear about the *level* (the "thickness") of the data you want to enter. Will you be entering "thick" descriptions, direct quotes, close-up detail? Will you be making a short summary or paraphrase? Will you be making more general summary judgments or global ratings?

(2) Remember that any matrix is displaying only a small percentage of the available data. Even for "thick" entries, there is a great deal of selection from the mass of field notes. And for more boiled-down entries, everything depends on your knowing—and others' knowing—just how you did the boiling down.

So, keep an explicit record of the "decision rules" you followed in selecting data chunks for entry (for example, the nature of agreement among respondents, researcher confidence in the data, or the basis for making ratings). This record should be generated as a *log* as you proceed—otherwise you may delude yourself retrospectively, forget how you did it, or shift your decision rules during the process (see section VII.C for specific self-documentation suggestions).

(3) Use codes to locate material for entry. Use a method of "tagging" the location of the data chunk in the written-up field notes, so that you can easily get back to it in context if need be.

(4) Be open to using numbers, either direct quantities, or judgments in the form of ratings or scales (decision rules on the latter must be clear). If you do use numbers, keep *words* together with the numbers in the matrix to clarify, support, and deepen their meaning.

(5) It pays to take unusual care when you are trying to scale any variable on which you will order sites (cases) in a multisite matrix. Unclear ordering will enfeeble all subsequent analyses. The same holds true for any major dependent variable—for example, the outcome variable in a predictor-outcome matrix. If the outcome is poorly scaled, then all the predictor analyses will be founded on sand.

(6) When data are missing, ambiguous, or were not asked for from certain respondents, show this explicitly in the matrix.

(7) Early in the game, get a colleague to review a filled-in matrix, along with your decision rules and written-up field notes, to check the procedural adequacy of your work. This will go best if you have kept a thorough log of the data entry process as noted under point 2. Such audits are time-consuming (they take about half the time an original data entry and analysis process took), but are important to use selectively to check on the "confirmability" of the procedures you used.

VI.C ANALYZING MATRIX DATA

The test of any matrix is what it helps you understand—and how valid that understanding is. As Chapter VII shows, there are many specific "tactics" for data analysis, each with its advantages and pitfalls. We won't go into them here, but content ourselves with some general advice.

Rules of Thumb for Matrix Data Analysis

(1) Start with a quick scan—a "squint analysis" down rows and across columns to see what jumps out. Then verify, revise, or disconfirm that impression through a more careful review.

(2) In site-ordered matrices, make a first sweep through the data for each site, one at at time, to be sure that your descriptive understanding is clear at the site level before you try to understand cross-site patterns.

(3) For initial descriptive matrices, which are often large and complex because of the need to "get it all in," use summary tabulations (Box V.B.b) to clarify your understanding. Then check back with the larger matrix to be sure you have not oversimplified or distorted your conclusions.

(4) As conclusions begin forming in your mind, write text explaining them. The process of writing usually leads to reformulation, added clarity, and ideas for further analysis. Writing is itself a form of analysis.

(5) Emerging conclusions almost always need to be checked against written-up field notes. If a conclusion does not ring true at the "ground level" when you try it out there, it needs revision. Systematic procedures like those we suggest can sometimes lead to unjustified feelings of certainty about conclusions. Look at the *raw* data to guard against this.

(6) In writing semifinal text explaining the conclusions drawn from the matrix, include specific illustrations from written-up field notes. In doing this, avoid the "sprinking" of vivid or interesting examples to spice up the narrative. Rather, look for genuinely representative exemplars of the conclusions you are presenting. If you cannot find them, something is wrong with the conclusions—revise.

(7) Remember that analysis has ultimately to go beyond summation and reach up to explanation (see Noblit, 1982). Checking the conclusions against the data is only half the meaning-establishment task. The

other part has to do with the conceptual import of those conclusions, how they tie into your or someone else's theory of social behavior. Matrix analyses that yield verifiable but meaning-poor conclusions are of no use to anyone.

(8) Document the analysis procedures followed (see section VII.C for methods), and ask for an occasional audit from a colleague, especially during your early work.

(9) In developing final report text, think carefully about the data the reader will need. In many cases, the complete matrix you used should also be presented to the reader, who can thereby follow and verify your conclusions. In other cases, a summary table or boiled-down version may suffice. And in still others—which ought to be the rarest, in our view—you may conclude that text with illustrations will be sufficient. Where basic matrices are *not* presented, you owe the reader a clear explanation of the display and analysis methods used to get to the text.

The tradition of presenting basic data is deeply ingrained in reports of quantitative data analysis, so much so that it would be unthinkable for a researcher to present conclusions without data tables or without reference to working documents containing them. Our advocacy is that the same norms should apply to qualitative researchers. Successive data displays should be a normal part of reporting conclusions.

NOTE

1. For added suggestions on "matrix thinking" as a way to aid conceptualization and research planning, see Hage (1972) and Patton (1981, chap. 6).

VII

Drawing and Verifying Conclusions

The many types of displays we have outlined always involve a general analysis *strategy*, a systematic approach to finding meaning in a set of data. But as we have seen, general strategies, in qualitative research as in war, are not enough. There will always be a flow of specific analysis *tactics*, ways of drawing and verifying conclusions that the analyst employs during the process.

VII.A TACTICS FOR GENERATING MEANING

In this section we discuss twelve specific tactics for drawing *meaning* from a particular configuration of data in a display. Usually, we will describe the general analysis situation being faced, explain the tactic, then give one or more examples, often referring back to previous sections. We will also refer to others' work for examples. If we can muster advice, it will be presented too. Our approach will be brisk; the test of these tactics comes in the using.

People are meaning-finders; they can make sense of the most chaotic events very quickly. Our equilibrium depends on such skills: We keep the world consistent and predictable by cognitively organizing and interpreting it. The critical question is whether the meanings found in qualitative data through the tactics outlined here are valid, repeatable, *right*. The following section (VII.B) discusses tactics for testing or *confirming* meanings, avoiding bias, and assuring the quality of conclusions.

Here is a quick overview of the tactics for generating meaning, numbered from 1 to 12. They are roughly arranged from the descriptive to the explanatory, and from the concrete to the more conceptual and abstract. *Counting* (tactic 1) is a familiar way to see "what's there." *Noting patterns, themes* (2), *seeing plausibility* (3), and *clustering* (4) help the analyst see "what goes with what." *Making metaphors* (5), like the preceding four tactics, is a way to achieve more integration among diverse pieces of data. Differentiation is sometimes needed, too, as in *splitting variables* (6).

We also need tactics for seeing things and their relationships more abstractly. These include *subsuming particulars into the general* (7); *factoring* (8),

an analogue of a familiar quantitative technique; *noting relations between variables* (9); and *finding intervening variables* (10).

Finally, how can we assemble coherent understanding of data? The tactics discussed are *building a logical chain of evidence* (11) and *making conceptual/theoretical coherence* (12).

VII.A.1 Counting

In qualitative research, numbers tend to get ignored. After all, the hallmark of qualitative research is that it goes beyond how *much* there is of something to tell us about its essential *qualities*.

However, as we noted earlier, there is a lot of counting going on when judgments of qualities are being made. When we identify a theme or pattern, we are isolating something (a) that happens a number of times and (b) that consistently happens in a specific way. The "number of times" and consistency judgments are based on counting. They are not *only* counting exercises, but they are *also* counting exercises. When we make a generalization, we amass a swarm of particulars and decide, almost unconsciously, which particulars are there *more often*, matter *more* than others, *go together*, and so on. The moment we say something is "important" or "significant" or "recurrent," we have achieved that estimate in part by making counts, comparisons, and weights.[1]

So it's important in qualitative research to know, first of all, that we *are* sometimes counting, and to know *when* it's a good idea to work self-consciously with frequencies. There are three good reasons to resort to numbers: to see rapidly what you have in a large slice of data; to verify a hunch or hypothesis; and to keep yourself analytically honest, protecting against bias. Let's review each briefly.

Seeing what you have. Numbers, we noted earlier, are more economical and manipulable than words; one "sees" the general drift of the data more easily and rapidly by looking at distributions. For instance, in the school improvement study, we asked informants why they were using the new school practices we were studying. We got a mass of answers from several informants at each of twelve field sites. It *seemed* that a lot of people were saying they had been pushed, more or less gently, into these projects rather than diving in voluntarily. To see more clearly, we did a content analysis of the responses, totaled them, and derived Chart 41.

It turns out that 62 percent of the respondents mention pressure and constraint. And, counterintuitively, very few of the practices were adopted to solve problems. There also seemed to be a general "professional development/capacity enhancement" theme (challenge, shaping projects, professional growth). *Seeing* that theme, gauging the importance of the "constraint" motive, noting the infrequent problem-solving incentive, were all helpful. We saw the overall trends, got some new leads, saw some unexpected differences. All this helped in the subsequent *non-quantitative* analysis. Even within a *single site*, that kind of exercise would have been a useful one.

Verifying a hypothesis. Section V.C, Chart 32, is probably the best example of this. We reasoned that good preparation was the key to smooth initial use, so we simply created and computed a preparation "index" and set it against an estimate of smoothness of early use. Except at the extremes, we were wrong. But, by doing the counts, we saw at *which* sites we were wrong and *why* this appeared to be the case. We then set aside the numbers and followed up those leads.[2]

Keeping analytically honest. We had expected from the start that careers would be important in these school improvement projects. The more data we got, the more it seemed that "innovating" was a vehicle for moving up, in, over, or out (seldom *down*). The finding seemed important, potentially controversial, and might have been a result of our expectation. So we actually counted up the number of job moves (75 for 12 sites) and estimated how many could be attributed to the innovation (83 percent were). Afterwards, we felt far more comfortable about the claims we were making; for example, it seemed that only 35 percent of the job-related shifts were upward ones, contrary to our early impression.[3]

The last illustration is an important one. As a qualitative researcher, one works to some extent by insight and intuition. There are moments of illumination. Things "come together." The problem is that we could be wrong. There is a near-library of research evidence to show that people habitually tend to *overweight* facts they believe in or depend on, to *forget* data not going in the direction of their reasoning, and to *"see"* confirming instances far more easily than disconfirming instances (see the review in Nisbett & Ross, 1980). We do this by differentially weighting information and by looking at *part* of the data, not all of it. Doing qualitative analysis of all the data with the aid of numbers is a good way of seeing how robust our insights are.

VII.A.2 Noting Patterns, Themes

When one is working with text, or less well-organized displays, one will often note recurring patterns, themes, or "Gestalts," which pull together a lot of separate pieces of data. Something "jumps out" at you, suddenly makes sense. We have already discussed this under "pattern coding" (section III.C); such patterns can often be found under the heading of repeated themes, causes/explanations, interpersonal relationships, and theoretical constructs.

Some examples of patterns from our school improvement study:

- The frequent citing of a "miracle case" (a failing student who was rejuvenated by the innovation) as either an explanation or a justification for the project.
- "Organic coping" as a problem-solving style in a certain staff group.
- The use of "administrative latitude"—freedom to alter an innovation in return for trying it at all.

Pattern finding can be very productive as an analysis strategy when the number of sites and/or the data overload is severe. Stearns, Greene, David, et al. (1980), for example, studied 22 sites, all implementing a new law on education for handicapped children. Fieldworkers generated unstructured "pattern" statements of findings from more than one site; these were gradually reduced to a few hundred "propositions," ordered into 21 categories. This procedure used fieldworkers' knowledge of the sites well, and did not involve close coding of all field notes. See section III.D.a for more detail.

The human mind finds patterns so quickly and easily that it needs no how-to advice. Patterns just "happen," almost too quickly. The important thing, rather, is to be able to (a) see *real* added evidence of the same pattern; (b) remain open to disconfirming evidence when it appears. As Ross and Lepper (1980) point out, beliefs (in this case in the existence of a pattern) are remarkably resistant to new evidence. Patterns need to be subjected to skepticism—one's own or that of others—and to conceptual and empirical test (Does it really make sense? Do we find it elsewhere in the data where predicted?) before they represent useful knowledge.

VII.A.3 Seeing Plausibility

The faithful fieldworker Boswell (1791) reports that Dr. Johnson said, "Patriotism is the last refuge of a scoundrel." With good reason: A noble sentiment can easily be exploited for other purposes. There's a crude parallelism to the idea of "plausibility" as a last-refuge tactic for drawing conclusions.

Chart 41
Reasons Given for Adoption by Users

Reasons/Motives	Number of Respondents Mentioning Item (N = 56)
Administrative pressure, constraint	35
Improves classroom practice (new resources, relative advantage over current practice)	16
Novelty value, challenge	10
Social (usually peer influence)	9*
Opportunity to shape projects	5
Professional growth	5
Gives better working conditions	3
Solves problems	2
Provides extra money	1
Total	86

*Seven mentions were from one site.

It often happens during analysis that a conclusion is plausible, "makes good sense," "fits." If a colleague asks you how you came to the conclusion, or what you based it on, the initial answer is something like, "I don't really know. . . . It just feels right." Many scientific discoveries initially appeared to their authors in this guise; the history of science is full of global, intuitive understandings that, after laborious verification, proved to be true. So plausibility, and intuition as the underlying basis for it, is not to be sneered at.

But, as we have noted, people are meaning-finders, even in the most genuinely chaotic data sets. Patterns can be found even in random data, as the activities of numerologically obsessed people show. So plausibility can easily become the refuge of, if not scoundrels, analysts who are too ready to jump to conclusions. As we remark later, "Plausibility is the opiate of the intellectual."

During documentation of our own analysis efforts (as in section VII.C), we often found ourselves giving the "plausibility" basis for conclusions we drew, particularly in the early stages of analysis. Nearly always, it developed, the "plausibility" was an initial impression that needed further checking through other conclusion-drawing tactics, or through verification efforts. Plausibility in this sense was a sort of pointer, drawing the analyst's attention to a conclusion that looked reasonable and sensible on the face of it—but what was the real basis involved?

Here's a brief illustration. The analyst in our school improvement study was trying to order twelve school sites on "percentage of use" of the innovation—the number of teachers in a school or district eligible to use an innovation (such as a reading program) who in fact *were* using it. On the face of it this looks simple: the ratio of two numbers. The sites could be sorted into a few categories: full, moderate, minimal percentage of use. But as the analyst proceeded, life looked more complicated. His documentation comment was:

The categories are OK, but they don't form an ordinal scale. Much depends on the size or scale of what is being attempted in the first place.

This was based, the analyst said, on "plausibility. . . . Seems clear on the face of it."

The next step was to get more systematic. The analyst went through several iterations of a chart displaying the data until Chart 42 appeared. In the course of this, the analyst also realized that percentage of use in the district and in the school were quite different things, and he clustered sites accordingly.

We can now see that the initial "plausibility" basis had to be supplemented by *clustering* (realizing that Astoria, Calston, and Lido were all dealing with a specialized population of students) and by *splitting a variable* (building-level and district-level percentage of use). The final four clusters of schools fall in an order that has a clear basis (substantial use in building and in district; full in building, less in district; moderate to full, but for a specialized, hence less demanding, population; and clearly minimal use). The analyst can also order the sites within each category.

So the moral is something like this: Trust your "plausibility" intuitions, but don't fall in love with them. Subject the preliminary conclusions to *other* tactics of conclusion drawing and verification.

Chart 42
Site-Ordered Meta-Matrix: Percentage of Use, by Sites

SITES by Percentage of Use / Substantial	In the building				In the district				Eligibility criteria	Remarks
	Years of use	# users in bldg.	Eligible users in bldg.	% of use	Yrs. of use	# users in dist.	Elig. users in dist.	% of use		
Carson (IV-C)	3	20	20	100%	3	42	42	100%	All regular teachers in dist(1 elem, 1 HS)	Mandated as of Fall '79.
Masepa (NDN)	3	9	11	82%	4	36	43	84%	All tchrs, grades 3-7, 6 schools	Mandated as of April, 1980.
Tindale (IV-C)	4	29	36?	80%?	4	48	60?	80%?	Eng. math & sci. tchrs for lower-track students, 2 HSs. 60= max. of tchrs ever using innovation.	Not clear what maximum student population is.
Full in buildings, less in district										
Plummet (IV-C)	4	25	25	100%	4	N/A	N/A	?	Innovation is complete school; all present staff eligible.	Unknown whether school deals with all of potential target population (delinquents, 11 high schools).
Perry-Parkdale (NDN)	3	6	6	100%	3	N/A	N/A	?	Innovation is self-contained program; all present staff elig.	Program accomodates 3% of total jrs. and srs. from 2 HSs; unknown what "eligible" population is.
Banestown (NDN)	1½	3	3	100%	1½	10?	DK	?	Innovation is remedial lab; all lab staff eligible.	Used in 5 schls of large county system.
Moderate to full for specialized population										
Astoria (NDN)	1	5	5	100%	2	DK	DK	100%?	All 1st-grade tchrs & aides (92 schools).	Prog. mandated as of Fall '78; actual percentage of use throughout district unknown.
Calston (NDN)	2	2	2?	100%?	4	4	4--50	100% to 8%	Narrow definition; all intermediate teachers in schools with an interested principal (N=2)	Pct. of use for all 25 schools in district is 8%
Lido (NDN)	4	3	5	60%	4	3	5	60% to 8%	High school science teachers, in the one high school.	In princ. all 36 HS tchrs are elig. since innov. is interdisciplinary. Pct. use would thus be 8%
Minimal										
Burton (NDN)	1	1	5	20%	1	3	20?	15%?	All social studies tchrs, in 4 high schools.	Use defined as "experimental" during first year.
Dun Hollow (IV-C)	2½	2	13?	15%?	2½	3	84	3%?	All primary teachers (grades 1-3 in 7 elem. schools	Use defined as "field testing."
Proville (IV-C)	3	0	11 to 36?	0	3	0	44 to 144	0%	44 voc. ed. tchrs in 4 HSs and/ or 100 classified personnel.	A discontinuation as of Spring '79.

? Missing or inconclusive data.

Incidentally, a somewhat more trustworthy tactic involves *lack* of plausibility. When a conclusion someone is advancing "just *doesn't* make sense," it's a bit safer to rule it out. But not completely safe. Counterintuitive or puzzling findings can sometimes be extraordinarily stimulating and rich, so they should be allowed their day in the sun too.

One final comment. Most conclusions drawn during analysis are *substantive*, based on the content. But the analyst is constantly drawing *procedural* conclusions along the way as well: to transpose two rows in a matrix; to add or discard a column; to collapse the data into a summary table; to change a decision rule for data entry. Our experience is that "plausibility" is often a reasonable guide for such decisions, and laboring to try other tactics, or to "verify" the procedural decision, is unnecessary. Of course, it's important, as we have said many times, to *show* the procedural decision made (the final matrix, the operative decision rules, and so on).

VII.A.4 Clustering

In daily life, we are constantly sorting things into classes, categories, bins: Something that doesn't move around but grows is called a "plant"; something that moves around and has babies is called an "animal"; something that moves around, has four wheels and an engine run by fossil fuels and carries people is called an "automobile." Most categories require *other* categories to define them: "wheel," "engine," "babies."

As we have already noted in our discussion of coding (section III.B), the qualitative analyst is looking to see, as LeCompte and Goetz (1983) put it, "What things are like each other? Which things go together and which do not?" The categories or classes used by the analyst may be preexisting (for school districts: urban, suburban, rural) or they may emerge from the data ("controlling," "directive," "facilitative," and "neglectful"), as found by Berman and Weiler in their study of districts in California school improvement projects (Degener, 1983). Typically, as Bulmer (1979) points out, they emerge from an *interaction* of theory and data.[4]

Clustering is a tactic that can be applied at many levels to qualitative data: at the level of events of acts, of individual actors, of processes, of settings/locales, of sites as wholes. In all instances, we are trying to understand a phenomenon better by *grouping*, then *conceptualizing* objects that have similar patterns or characteristics. Here are some illustrations.

Davis (1959), quoted in Lofland (1971), was studying the *acts* of cab drivers who were more interested in receiving a larger tip. They clustered this way:

fumbling in the making of change

giving the passenger a hard-luck story

making fictitious charges for services

providing a concerted show of fast, fancy driving

displaying extraordinary courtesy

At the level of *actors*, in our school improvement study we asked teachers to draw pictures of how their high school looked to them—which people and groups were involved. This led to categories of teachers such as "goners," "boy coaches," "girl coaches," and the "old new guard" (see section IV.A).

At the level of *processes*, we were able to cluster the activities involved in coping with the problems of later implementation of an innovation (Chart 28, section V.A):

reaching up

improving, debugging

refining

integrating

adapting

extending

These clusters took a good deal of summarizing and reworking before they came clear. A simpler example comes from our study of teachers' and administrators' job mobility, which fell rather easily into these categories:

moving in

moving out

moving up

moving in and up

moving out and up

moving over

It is also possible to make clusters of *settings* or locales. For example, in schools, we might sort places where people interact into these clusters:

formal instructional (classrooms, gyms)

informal instructional (library, club room)

formal adult work (meeting room, office)

informal adult association (teacher lunchroom, restroom, corridor)

mixed (cafeteria, playground)

Finally, as we have seen in the school improvement study, it's possible to sort *sites* as complex wholes into meaningful clusters. For example, in Box V.E.a, we show how twelve sites were sorted into three "families," according to the level of assistance provided and roughness/smoothness of early implementation, then the later degree of practice stabilization. Using more complex data—causal networks—as the base, section V.H shows how the twelve school sites could be clustered into four different scenarios: "casualties," "success-driven advancement," "opportunism," and "career crystallization."

We can see from these various examples that "clustering" is a general name given to the process of using and/or forming categories, and the iterative sorting of things—events, actors, processes, settings, sites—into those categories. Where lower-level, less complex things are being sorted (events, actors, and the like), the clustering tactic typically relies on aggregation and comparison ("What things are like each other/unlike each other?"), and is naturally closely interwoven with the creation and use of codes, both at the first level (section III.B) and the pattern-coding level (section III.C). As the analyst works at clustering processes, settings, and sites, the clustering operations become more and more complex and extended—just as sorting things into "animals" and "plants" is a (perhaps deceptively) simpler task than sorting various kinds of four-wheeled machines (automobiles, trucks, golf carts, airplanes, ski-lift gondolas, typewriter tables, and floor polishers) into sensible clusters.

The typical problem in making clusters at these more complex levels is that the entities being clustered have many attributes that you initially expect are relevant to the clustering task. A simple way to proceed is the "site-by-attribute matrix." Listing sites as rows and attributes as columns lets you see the whole picture. By inspection of the columns, you can find which attributes are critical in differentiating sites. Then "families" of sites can be formed by cutting up the rows of the matrix and re-sorting them. Each family shares the same set of critical attributes. See Miles, Farrar, and Neufeld (1983) for an example.

Clustering can also be seen as a process of moving to higher levels of abstraction (see section VII.B.7 on *subsuming particulars into the general*). Figure 23 presents an excerpted illustration of a content-analytic technique called a "dendrogram," drawn from Krippendorff's (1980a) excellent summary. The analyst was clustering various advertising appeals, using a treelike display.

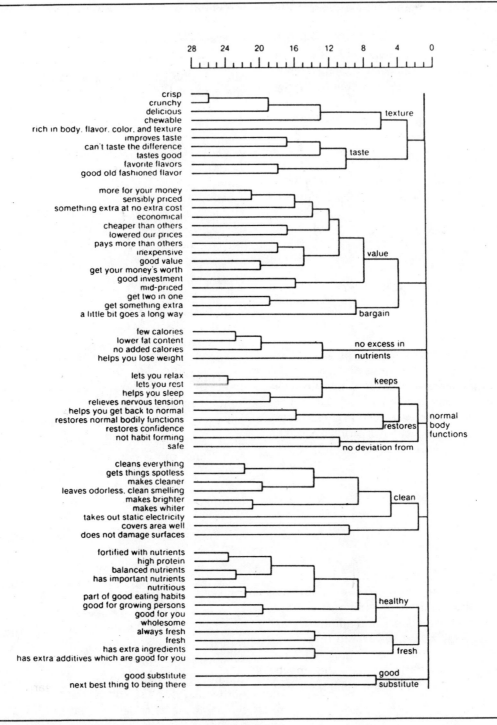

Figure 23 Illustration of Clustering, Using Dendrogram Method
SOURCE: Krippendorff (1980a). Reprinted by permission.

As this example suggests, the qualitative analyst need not assume that clustering techniques have to be completely self-invented. There is a long tradition of content-analytic techniques dealing directly with issues of coding, unitizing, and clustering qualitative data that can be very helpful (see, for example, Holsti, 1968, 1969; Berelson, 1971; Pool, 1973; Krippendorff, 1980b; Monge & Capella, 1980).

Clusters, like the results of other conclusion-drawing tactics, must be held lightly in the analyst's mind; premature closure is to be warded off. And they naturally need to be verified, as well. For example, does a cluster *"outlier"* (section VII.B.6) really belong to cluster A, or more appropriately to cluster B? Are the data being used fully *representative* (section VII.B.1) of the universe of events, actors, or settings being studied?

VII.A.5 Making Metaphors

Surprisingly, most of the case studies we have read are baldly matter-of-fact. The emphasis is put on description and, near the end, on interpretation and meaning, but both exercises tend to be taken literally, even actuarially. Most of this material is not—how shall we say?—riveting. Nor is it particularly illuminating in the way a piece of fiction can be. Though most novelists would cringe at being called "social scientists," many surpass the best qualitative researchers in communicating complex social reality. Consider Proust, Dreiser, Balzac, Austen, Nabokov, Updike, Oates, and Garcia Marquez. Their appeal is that they dramatize, amplify, and depict, rather than simply describe, social phenomena. The language itself is often figurative and connotative, rather than solely literal and denotative. Part of this has to do with the use of metaphors, analogies, symbols, and other allusive techniques of expression.

We are suggesting that qualitative researchers should not only *write* metaphorically, but also *think* metaphorically. For instance, it seems to us that "mother's separation anxiety" is a less appealing, less suggestive, *and* less theoretically powerful descriptor than is "the empty nest syndrome." Why do we say this? For one thing, the metaphor is richer, more *complete*. Instead of a clinical character trait (anxiety), we have allusions to an important environmental setting ("nest"), the idea of nurturance aching for a newly absent (but grown-up) object, and the acknowledgement that all this has taken a good deal of time up to now. Instead of focusing only on a mother's inner states, we can see new theoretical possibilities (maybe if socialization for independence was weak, the child will regress).

What else is true of metaphors? They are *data-reducing devices*, taking several particulars and making a single generality of them. For instance, the "scapegoat" metaphor pulls together facts about group norms, treatment of deviants, social rituals, and social rationalizations into one package. This is not to be sneezed at. Qualitative researchers looking at mountains of field note write-ups are grateful for *any* device that will reduce the bulk without locking out multiple avenues for analysis.

Metaphors are also *pattern-making devices*. For example, in the school improvement study, we found at one site that the remedial learning room felt like an "oasis" for the pupils sent there for part of each day. The metaphor "oasis" pulls together separate bits of information: The larger school is harsh (like a desert); not only can students rest in the remedial room, but they can get sustenance (learning); some resources are very abundant there (like water in an oasis); and so on. Such metaphors also help to place the pattern noted in the larger context (in this case, the harsh, resource-thin school).

Metaphors are also excellent *decentering devices*. You have to step back from the welter of observations and conversations at the field site and say, "What's going on here?" Since metaphors won't let you simply describe or denote a phenomenon, you have to move up a notch, to a slightly more inferential or analytical level. The remedial learning room doesn't *look* like an oasis, and perhaps no one is actually *describing* it that way, nor is anyone behaving literally like an exhausted Bedouin under a date palm.

Finally, metaphors or analogies are ways of *connecting findings to theory*. The "oasis" metaphor makes one think of how institutions develop compensating mechanisms to reduce the stress they put on role occupants, or of how they nurture as well as isolate deviants. Or one starts considering social control mechanisms more generally.

The metaphor is halfway from the empirical facts to the conceptual *significance* of those facts; it gets the analyst, as it were, up and over the particulars en route to the basic social processes that give meaning to those particulars. For instance, Glaser (1978) advises the field researcher struggling to make sense of social phenomena to attach metaphorical gerunds to them (such as servicing, bargaining, becoming). In so doing, one shifts from facts to *processes*, and those processes are likely to account for the phenomena being studied at the most inferential level.

For more on metaphor, see Ortony (1979), Lakoff and Johnson (1980), and Johnson (1981).

Now a few words of advice for metaphor-makers.

(1) Looking for metaphors too early in the study is dangerous. To begin with, it distracts one from the work at hand—collecting the information, following leads, observing closely. It also leads to making judgments on the basis of too few facts. Finally, it clamps down too quickly on the meaning of what one is studying. Psychologists call this "premature closure." You become all too quickly wedded to your metaphor; it *sounds* good, other people resonate to it (it sounds good to them, too); it makes you feel insightful. You start to look around less and to project the metaphor increasingly on things that are, at best, remotely

related to it. Better to wait until about two-thirds of the way through data collection, when you have a strong body of information to draw from, and still some time to test the validity of the image on the site during late visits.

(2) The best way to generate metaphors is to be cognitively playful, to say to oneself, "What's the gerund there?" or "If I only had two words to describe an important feature at this site, what would they be?" or "What are people doing here?" The trick is to move from the denotative to the connotative.

(3) Interaction helps. Groups stimulate their members' thinking by increasing the inputs, bringing in ideas from a new angle, making one decenter from one's cognitive ruts, and creating a contagiously playful thinking environment.

(4) Know when to stop pressing the metaphor for its juice. When the oasis starts to have camels, camel drivers, a bazaar, and a howling sandstorm, you know you're forcing things. Use it as long as it's fruitful, and don't overmetaphorize.

VII.A.6 Splitting Variables

"Westward the course of empire takes its way." So wrote George Berkeley in 1752 in *On the Prospect of Planting Arts and Learning in America*. To Berkeley, the main direction was obvious. It sometimes seems equally "obvious" that the course of qualitative data analysis is toward *integration*—ever and ever greater linkage among variables, expressed at a more and more powerful level.

But just as there was plenty of colonial push to the south and to the east, there are many times when differentiation is more important than integration. The analyst must say, "Stop!" That wonderful variable isn't really one variable, but two, or maybe even three. You must have the courage to question what might be called "premature parsimony."

Splitting variables can occur at many points during analysis. At the stage of initial conceptualization, it pays to "unbundle" variables rather than assume a monolithic simplicity. For example, the checklist matrix shown in section IV.B splits the general variable of "preparedness" to carry out an innovation into ten subvariables or components, ranging from states of the user ("commitment," "understanding," "skills") to the availability of materials and actions taken by administrators ("time allocation," "inservice").

When coding schemes are being developed and elaborated, splitting is often useful. For example (section III.B), our study originally had a code TR-ORG, used for instances of change in the school as an organization as a result of innovation use. Initial fieldwork showed clearly that this variable should be split to distinguish among organizational changes that were *practices*, such as staffing, scheduling, planning, use of resources, and an equally important, "softer" variable, organizational *climate* (norms, interpersonal relationships, power, social networks).

When matrix formats are being designed, variable-splitting is also a very useful strategy; more differentiation lets you see differences that might otherwise be blurred or buried. For example, in box IV.F.a, the analyst who wanted to study and explain the effects of various types of assistance to teachers realized very early that the variable "effects" of assistance should be separated into *short-run* effects (the user's immediate "state" after receiving assistance) and *longer-run* effects (what the user was able, or unable, to *do* as a result of the assistance).

Similarly, as conclusion drawing proceeds, the analyst will often realize that a variable needs to be split. In section V.A, where the issue was the feelings and concerns of innovation users, the analyst was struck by the fact that some concerns, as originally expected, were *individual* ones, such as discouragement, fatigue, or friction with others, and many other concerns were essentially *institutional* in nature, such as changes in district priorities, poor overall functioning of the project, or uncertainties about project continuation. This led to the summary tabulation in Chart 27.

Sometimes creating a two-variable matrix, as in Box V.B.c, helps to clarify whether splitting a variable will be illuminating or not. In this case, the analyst was struggling with the relationship between user "practice stabilization" and the "continuation" of the innovation locally. The first look at continuation emphasized users' *attitudes* to continuation as the indicator. That made sense: A stabilized innovation ought to evoke more positive attitudes on the part of its users. But the relationship was quite weak. Users from almost all sites had positive attitudes to continuation; only in very low-stabilized sites were there negative attitudes. This suggested splitting the "continuation" variable into two parts: users' *attitudes* toward continuation and their estimates of the *probability* of continuation. Adding a column to the matrix led the analyst to pay dirt. The probability variable turned out to illuminate the relationship between stabilization and continuation more clearly than the attitude one, because it took into account factors beyond individuals, such as district support, staff turnover, and funding difficulties.

In sum, when is variable-splitting a good tactic? The first answer is: Split in early stages (conceptualizing, coding) to avoid monolithism and blurring of data. The second answer is: Split a variable when it is not relating as well to another variable as your conceptual framework (or other available data) have led you to expect.

Finally, we should remark that variable-splitting is not a virtue in itself. Extreme differentiation leads to complexity and atomization, poor mapping of events and processes. When you split a variable, it should be in the service of finding coherent, integrated descriptions and explanations.

VII.A.7 Subsuming Particulars into the General

Clustering, as we have seen, involves clumping things together that "go together," using single or multiple dimensions. That process is often an intuitive, first-level process, corresponding to ordinary coding (section III.B).

A related tactic involves asking the question, "What is this specific thing an instance of? Does it belong to a more general class?" This tactic corresponds to many of the types of "pattern code" we outlined in section III.D. The analysis is taking a step up, trying to locate the immediate act, event, actor, or activity in a more abstractly defined class. That class may have been predefined, or it may have emerged as a result of memoing (section III.D). Here is an illustration.

LeCompte (1974), looking at a classroom, noted that the following events fell into a cluster:

- Teacher vacuums room twice daily.
- Students cannot leave in afternoon until they wash their desks.
- Teacher refers to personal hygiene when reprimanding students.
- Teacher says, "Children who come to school looking like that [soiled shirt] you just can't expect to do the same kind of work as the others."

At first glance, this is simply a cluster of behaviors dealing with cleanliness. But LeCompte also noticed that children's statements about the cleanliness issue tended to parallel the teacher's. Furthermore, most of the items (a) recurred and (b) had a strong regulatory emphasis. She concluded that the general class here was "cleanliness norm"—a shared set of standards about appropriate and inappropriate behavior.

Glaser (1978) uses this tactic during his "constant comparative method," looking for "basic social processes," such as negotiation or bargaining, that are a more general class into which specific behaviors (for example, bickering, arguing, refusing, offering, soothing) can be subsumed.

In our school improvement study, we noted specific statements made by teachers and administrators, such as:

- If you want to depart from the guide, ask me and also tell me why you want to do it and how it will fulfill the guide's objectives.
- The basic philosophy is there, but the use of (the innovation) is flexible, and doesn't require use of all units.

- In this program you're like a robot . . . but I learned that if I wanted to change something I would just go ahead and do it. . . . I learned to cut corners and do it just as well.

These statements can be subsumed into a more general class: The presence of high or low *administrative latitude* given to teachers to adapt or alter an innovation, a variable that turned out to be very important in explaining the amount of adaptation that occurred.

Note that the process of moving up a step on the abstraction ladder is not a mechanical or automatic process. For example, all three statements above could be seen as an instance of the more general class "adherence to objectives," if one attends to such phrases as "the guide's objectives," "basic philosophy," and "do it just as well." Here the analyst was convinced, through the presence of many other statements, that the question of administrative action restricting or permitting latitude was the more important general class.

In short, subsuming particulars into more general classes is a *conceptual* and theoretical activity (Glaser, 1978) in which the analyst shuttles back and forth between first-level data and more general categories, which evolve and develop through successive iterations until the category is "saturated" (new data do not add to the meaning of the general category).

Arbitrary movement up the abstraction ladder gets a researcher nowhere. Suppose that you observed a teacher writing his name on the blackboard on the first day of school. That specific action can be subsumed in a larger class of "written communication," then in a larger class of "information transmission," then in a still-larger class of "human action." That is a sort of taxonomic classification without useful meaning, however. Depending on the purposes of the study and the assumptions of the researchers, the action might more fruitfully be classified as an instance of "thoroughness of preparation," "reassurance/anxiety reduction," "group control through legitimacy," or "institutional perpetuation."

One cannot decide in a vacuum which of these classes is "right" or "best." There must be a clear linkage to the study's conceptual framework and research questions. *And* one must repeatedly move back down the abstraction ladder, as Korzybski (1933) always counseled, to "find the referent": the concrete instance that's being alluded to when a phrase such as "institutional perpetuation" is being used in an analysis.

VII.A.8 Factoring

"Factoring" comes from factor analysis, a statistical technique for representing a large number of measured variables in terms of a smaller number of unobserved, usually hypothetical variables. These second-order variables ("factors") may be largely uncorrelated, or have some "communality," overlapping with each other. In either case it is possible to identify general themes, giving a name to the statistically identified factor or factor cluster. What is the qualitative researcher's analogue?

Most of the tactics covered here are designed to do two things: to reduce the bulk of data *and* to find patterns in them. Clustering, making metaphors, moving up the abstraction ladder are all pattern-forcing exercises. The task is essentially that of saying to oneself, "I have a mountain of information here. Which bits go together?" When I derive a pattern code (section III.C), I am really hypothesizing that some disparate facts or words *do* something in common or *are* something in common. What they do or are is the "factor," and the process by which we generate it is "factoring." Time for an illustration.

Our study concerned interorganizational arrangements linking a university or college with a set of surrounding schools. At one successful site in a midwestern state, we collected some study-relevant characteristics of the state college. Most were coded "COLL-CHARS," so we could easily yank them out and list them. Here is the list:

- service is a central objective
- few contacts with state-level agencies
- small-scale projects
- low publishing rate by staff
- little research activity
- numerous outreach activities to surrounding schools
- concern for following up on preservice training with in-service training
- college staff active on community councils
- use of area teachers as resource people in activities
- majority of within-state college staff
- few cross-university discipline contacts

How can one "factor" the list? The reader might like to scan these items to see what factor might underlie them. Then we'll share our try.

Let's list the items again and see how the analyst, in the course of successive scans, identified the commonalities (shown between slash marks).

- service is a central objective / activist, client-centered /
- few contacts with state-level agencies / not looking beyond own region /
- small-scale projects / operating on scale of community /
- low publishing rate by staff / service over academic orientation /
- little research activity / *idem* /
- numerous outreach activities to local schools / service again; localism, too /
- concern for following up on preservice training with in-service training / keeping connected to graduates in local area /

- college staff active on community councils / service; *local* investment, again /
- use of area teachers as resource people in activities / practical focus; nonacademic orientation, again /
- majority of within-state college staff / not looking beyond region, again /
- few cross-university discipline contacts / *idem*; also nonacademic orientation /

The same themes recur: Activism, client-centeredness, localism, nonacademic orientation. We settled on a double-barreled theme we called "localism/ activism." All of the characteristics fit into this theme without a conceptual shoehorn. From these eleven particulars, which most of the people we observed or interviewed had in common, we had derived a general characteristic.

We also noted that the large state university, another site in the same state, had different characteristics. It, too, was activist, but it was *not* localist. Its principal client was the state, not the city in which the university was located. There was more cross-university contact, and publishing was higher. So perhaps we had a bipolar factor in our study, "localism versus cosmopolitanism" with the effect of activism "controlled," analogically speaking. Now we are factoring at a slightly higher level of abstraction, using multiple sites to do a sort of "second-order factoring." It gets us to still fewer overarching themes or constructs that subsume bigger chunks of the data. We get there by asking the question, "What is there a *lot* of in one place that there is *little* of in another—and are they comparable things?"

Then comes the more consequential question, "Do these contrasts make any *meaningful* difference, or are they essentially decorative?" The factors have to contribute to our understanding of the case or of its underlying dynamics. Otherwise, they are no more useful than the big, gift-wrapped boxes that unpack into a succession of smaller, but equally empty gift-wrapped boxes, leaving us at the end with a shapeless heap of ribbon and cardboard.

In this case, the localism/cosmopolitanism factor, when associated with the activism factor, was very helpful in explaining why some school-university arrangements were very successful and others limped along.

VII.A.9 Noting Relations Between Variables

The idea of relations between variables has already been prefigured in our discussion of conceptual frameworks (section II.A), which we suggest can economically be thought of as sets of boxes and arrows; boxes are variables, and the arrows show relationships between them. Once an analyst is reasonably clear about what variables are in play in a situation, the natural next query is, how do they relate to each other?

What sort of relations can we envision between two variables A and B? A variable is something that *varies*. Thus we might have:

(1) A+ , B+ (both are high, or both low at the same time)
(2) A+ , B− (A is high, B is low, or vice versa)
(3) A↑ , B↑ (A has increased, and B has increased)
(4) A↑ , B↓ (A has increased, and B has decreased)
(5) A↑ then →B↑ (A increased first, then B increased)
(6) A↑ then →B↑ then A↑ (A increased, then B increased, then A increased some more)

(These don't cover all the possible permutations, of course.) Relationship 1 is a direct association: Both variables are high (or low) at the same time. For variables that are "all or nothing," this relationship can be read as follows: When A is present, B is also present, or both may be absent. Relationship 2 is "inverse." With relationship 3, we are noting that *changes* have recently occurred in A, and in B, in the same direction; 4 is the inverse. No claims are necessarily being made that the changes are linked; they are just present. In relationship 5, we verge toward causality: A has changed, *then* B changed (and—not shown—there is a reasonable belief that A "could" have caused B). If A is an evening of heavy drinking and B is a headache the next morning, there's a presumptive connection. But there's probably little likely connection—in most cases—if B is a morning headache and A is the announcement of the new city budget. (Still, if the headache belongs to the Mayor, maybe . . .)

Finally, in relationship 6 we see a mutual ("non-recursive") relation: A change in A leads to a subsequent change in B, then to a subsequent change in A. Of course the strength of these associations can vary: We can have decisive, strong, clear relationships—or feeble, weak, ambiguous ones.

The basic analysis tactic here involves trying to discover what sort of relationship—if any—there is between two (or more) variables. The important thing to keep in mind is that we are talking about variables, concepts, not necessarily specific acts or behaviors. Even when we are focusing on specific *events*, there are usually underlying or more general variables involved. The event of an evening of heavy drinking and the event of the morning headache do not quite affect each other directly. All sorts of variables are at work: the presence of certain esters in the beverage involved and the body's ability to metabolize alcohol, the amount consumed, the time intervening, and so on. So, we concur with Glaser (1978), who says that the researcher is "making theoretical statements about the relationship between concepts, rather than writing descriptive statements about people."

How are relationships detected? We argue in this book that matrix displays are an especially economical way to see them: Data bearing on two or more variables can be arrayed for systematic inspection, and conclusions drawn.

For one illustration, consider the relationship we wanted to explore between the "centrality" of an innovation to a person's interests and the initial attitude held toward it. Are people more favorable to a "central" innovation than one that is more superficial in their life space? Perhaps, indeed, we might find that people are more negative when an innovation looms large in their scheme of things. Turning to section IV.E, Chart 16c, we can see a matrix displaying data on these two variables (and others). Scanning down the columns for "centrality" and "initial attitude toward program," we can see that there is indeed some relationship, though it is not a tight one. For users, the centrality is always high and initial attitudes are neutral or favorable; only one is unfavorable. And it looks as if early apprehension is at work with the "neutral" teachers.

We cannot know what the consequences of moderate or low centrality are for teachers, because we have no such cases. There is more of a range of centrality for administrators, but no clear pattern in terms of attitudes. So we have only modest support for the idea of a positive relationship. The analyst might want to go back to the field and hunt for some low-centrality teachers to fill out the picture—and/or turn to other associations with positive attitude—such as "career relevance," in Chart 16c. There the range is wider—and it looks as if there may be a clearer relationship: For the teachers (and administrators) where there is no career relevance, the attitudes are neutral or unfavorable; in the case where career relevance grows (Weelling), attitude becomes more positive; and for two of three teachers who have high career relevance, initial attitude is positive.

That example shows how pairs of variables were associated within one site. For an illustration that uses data from multiple sites, see section V.C, Chart 32, where the analyst was trying to relate a number of variables, such as user commitment and user understanding, to another variable, "ease of early use." He concluded, for example, that user commitment had a stronger relationship with ease of early use than did user understanding. This conclusion was based on how fully "in place" the conditions were prior to early use, and on the assessment of the conditions' "facilitating" or "barrier"-like status (note that the display includes causal judgments, marked as F and B, made by the researcher, based on the field data).

For a third example, also with multiple sites, turn to section V.E, where we see a scatterplot (Figure 15).

The researcher thought that an administrator's early pressure on teachers to adopt an innovation might lead to the negotiation of a sort of compensatory bargain, where the administrator agreed to allow for adaptation—gave "latitude"—in return for the teachers' willingness to proceed. But the scatterplot in Figure 15 shows otherwise: The initial pressure to adopt seems to be accompanied by *low* latitude. It's the sites with initial *weak* adoption pressure where the administrator allows a good deal of adaptation (Perry-Parkdale, Burton, Plummet, for example).

Note, though, that the analyst picked up on the issue of how things *evolved* during later implementation (see arrows), pointing out that in four of six high-pressure sites, latitude increased slightly during later implementation. Thus, he concluded, "Perhaps there is something to our hypothesis . . . though the negotiation comes later than we had thought."

As we have noted at a number of points, people tend to think in causal terms. The risk in trying to understand relationships between two variables is jumping too rapidly to the conclusion that A "causes" B, rather than that A happens to be high and B happens to be high. Here it helps to shift to verification tactics, such as proposing and *checking out rival explanations* (section VII.B.10), *ruling out spurious relations* (section VII.B.8), or *using extreme cases* (section VII.B.7).

Drawing in skeptical colleagues to use one or more of these tactics can be very useful. One friend of ours says that any causal statement made about a social situation should immediately be reversed, to see whether it looks truer that way:

> "The students are late to class because they hate the teacher." (resistance driven by dislike)

> "The students hate the teacher because they are late to class." (lateness, caused by other reasons, leads to dislike—perhaps mediated by the teacher's reactions to tardiness)

That example may sound a little fanciful, but the reversal exercise is useful. In our school improvement study, as we note in section VII.A.12, we considered this statement:

> "Teacher involvement and commitment lead to more effort in using the innovation."

We entertained the reverse:

> "High teacher effort leads to teacher involvement and commitment."

This made good theoretical sense, in terms of cognitive dissonance theory. And the data had already shown us several examples of sites where early strong teacher effort led to later increases in commitment.

VII.A.10 Finding Intervening Variables

It often happens during analysis that two variables that "ought" to go together according to your conceptual expectations or your preliminary understanding of events at the site have only a tepid or inconclusive relation. A puzzle encountered almost as frequently is the case of two variables that *do* go together, but without making much sense. The analyst cannot quite figure out *why* they go together.

In both of these conditions, looking for *other* variables that may be in the picture is a useful tactic. Perhaps a third variable Q is confusing, depressing, or elevating the relationship between A and B, so that if you "controlled" for Q, the relationship between A and B would become clearer:

$$A———\overset{Q}{?}——→B$$

Or perhaps the third variable actually fills out a reasonable chain, mediating or linking between A and B:

$$A → Q → B$$

Let's take the last case first. In section V.G, we found that school sites that had adopted innovations bearing large associated funding changed their organization structures and procedures more than those adopting less well-funded innovations. That leaves a great deal unexplained. As we noted, you can't change organizations just by throwing money at them. Why should it be that a well-funded innovation "induces" more organizational change?

In this case, the analyst created a site-ordered matrix of other possible correlates of organizational change, ranging from "environmental pressure" to "problem-solving orientation," "implementation requirements," and "administrative support." A careful scan showed that the original relation (Figure 24a) could be understood much more realistically when several other variables entered the picture (Figure 24b). Here we see that "size of funding" is part of a web of other variables. Larger innovations (1) carry more funds with them (2). The funds increase the support administrators give (4), but so do the heavier implementation requirements (3) of larger innovations. Organizational change (6) comes from at least three sources: the direct requirements of the implementation itself (3), administrative support (4), and the degree to which implementation is successful (5). As we can see, administrative support is a very central intervening variable.

In this case, the effort to clarify a plausible but puzzling relationship led to a much clearer—if more complex—formulation. Simpler cases of finding intervening variables also exist. For example, we found that *administrative pressure* to use an innovation was associated with its eventual *institutionalization*. That looked puzzling, until we discovered that sites where there was administrative pressure were also those

Figure 24a Two-Variable Relationship

where *organizational changes* had occurred—and these in turn supported institutionalization.

Now let's turn back briefly to the other sort of puzzle: where the relationship between A and B is tepid when it "ought" to be hot. The tactic here is also to examine a series of other candidate variables that may be "depressing" or confusing the relation between A and B. Chart 32 (section V.C) shows that *preparedness* of innovation users (commitment, understanding, resources, and so on, summed to a general variable) is not a *very* brilliant predictor of *smoothness* of early implementation (note, for example, the fairly high preparedness scores in the rough-starting sites of Carson, Dun Hollow, and Plummet). So getting people ready and prepared is not enough to guarantee early smoothness. What else might be in the picture?

The analyst went back to the written-up field notes, and located a series of five other variables that might affect smoothness: Were users pressured to adopt? Did the innovation fit their previous ways of working? How much did the innovation demand of them? Did they have latitude for making changes? How big was the innovation? These were displayed in a site-ordered predictor-outcome matrix (Chart 33). Presto! It came very clear that the main issue making for smoothness/roughness was the size of the innovation. Even if people were well prepared, if the innovation was large and demanding, early implementation was rough.

We might note that finding intervening variables is easiest when there are multiple examples of the two-variable relationship to look at, contrast, and compare. In our illustrations, these were *sites*. But the same principle can be used to examine multiple instances of *actors*, *settings*, or *events*.

VII.A.11 Building a Logical Chain of Evidence

We have been talking a good deal about patterns, metaphors, clusters, and themes. In these cases, what happens is that discrete bits of information come together to make a more economical whole that, analytically speaking, is more than the sum of its parts. How do we actually *accomplish* this? Is there some kind of heuristic or algorithm we can use?

Let's begin with an illustration. In the study of interorganizational arrangements between schools and universities, we happened upon one case that looked particularly successful. It was a "teacher center," connected to a rural state college and undertaking a variety of in-service training activities for schools within a radius of some 60 miles.

We tried to develop a logical chain of factors that could be leading to success, as seen from the state college side and from the school side. Figure 25 shows them. The logical chain of evidence goes like this. The state college might regard service and outreach activities as very central (1). Since that is in fact so, we would expect college staff to see the benefits (2) of a teacher center as high (they did). That should in turn lead to higher resource commitment (3) to the center; such commitment was found in the form of money and staff. Looking at the school side, we found few other opportunities for in-service help (5), and a shortage of good teaching materials (6); both of these should lead to high perceived benefits (7) from using the center—*if* the center did in fact give good in-service help and provide new materials. As it turned out, the high resource commitment did permit that; teacher center assets (4) and extent of use (8) were high.

This is, of course, a stripped-down version of a far more intricate case. But it does illustrate how one builds an evidential chain. To come out with such a chain some minimal conditions have to be met. For example, *several* informants with *different* roles have to *emphasize* these factors *independently*, and *indicate the causal links*, directly or indirectly (for example, "We didn't have any other facility to go to to find out about new materials, so the center looked good" = the link between 5 and 7). The researcher has to *verify the claims* (for instance, the actual funds committed, the lack of alternative resource sources, the activities actually undertaken). *Countervailing evidence* has to be accounted for.

How does building a chain of evidence differ from the "causal network" method we've already described in section IV.J? This approach is more tactically, specifically oriented. Building a chain of evidence is more painstaking at each step, more demanding of variable-to-variable logical coherence. There are more occasions of "If that were true, we should find X. We do find X. Therefore . . ."

Furthermore, *the relationships have to make sense*; the logical basis for the claim that "perceived benefits"

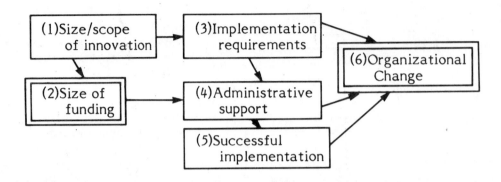

Figure 24b   Two-Variable Relationship with Intervening Variables

translate into "resource commitment" must be incontrovertible. The *chain must be complete*; the stream from antecedents to outcomes should stand alone. For instance, in the figure shown, the link between 3 and 4 is not so obvious. One might have committed resources and come up with another model or another center with different characteristics. Committing resources doesn't translate automatically into, let us say, craft-oriented resource materials. Something is missing.

The field researcher constructs this evidential trail gradually, getting an initial sense of the main factors, plotting the logical relationships tentatively, testing them against the yield from the next wave of data collection, modifying and refining them into a new explanatory map, which then gets tested against new cases and instances. This is the classic procedure of analytic induction, well codified by epistemologists. It has been used in qualitative research, such as Lindesmith's (1947, 1968) celebrated studies of opiate addiction, to make a case for the necessary and sufficient causes of social behavior. See also Smith and Manning (1982, pp. 280-295) for more on this method.

At its most powerful, the method uses two interlocking cycles. One is called "enumerative induction," in which you collect a number and variety of instances all going in the same direction. The second is called "eliminative induction," in which you test your hypothesis against alternatives and look carefully for qualifications that bound the generality of the case being made. When qualitative researchers invoke "progressive focusing," they are talking about enumerative induction, and when they get into "constant comparisons" and "structural corroborations," they are switching into a more eliminative inductive mode of work. The "modus operandi" logic used in several professions as a troubleshooting device—for forensic pathologists, garage mechanics, clinicians, detectives, classroom

teachers—is a good example of a back-and-forth cycling between enumerative and eliminative induction.

VII.A.12 Making Conceptual/Theoretical Coherence

When you are trying to determine what someone's behavior "means," the mental exercise involves connecting a discrete fact with other discrete facts, then grouping these into lawful, comprehensible, and more abstract patterns. With the preceding tactics, we are moving progressively up from the empirical trenches to a more conceptual overview of the landscape. We are no longer dealing just with observables but also with unobservables, and are connecting the two with successive layers of inferential glue.

The next, perilous step, is to move from metaphors and interrelationships to *constructs*, and from there to *theories*. That is, we need to tie the findings of our study to overarching, across-more-than-one-study propositions that can account for the "how" and "why" of the phenomena under study. Let's illustrate this abstraction-making process.

In the school improvement study, we came to notice that people at some of the field sites were literally exhausting themselves in the course of using new instructional practices. We also found that these people were making strong claims that the practice had substantially improved reading scores or children's attitudes toward school. The interesting part was that hard data to substantiate the claims were either nonexistent or gave little support to the claims.

These are the "facts" from which *we*, as analysts, made a pattern. Field site informants could—and did—agree with the facts, but they didn't put them together as we did. To some extent, we were only able to *see* the pattern because things were happening

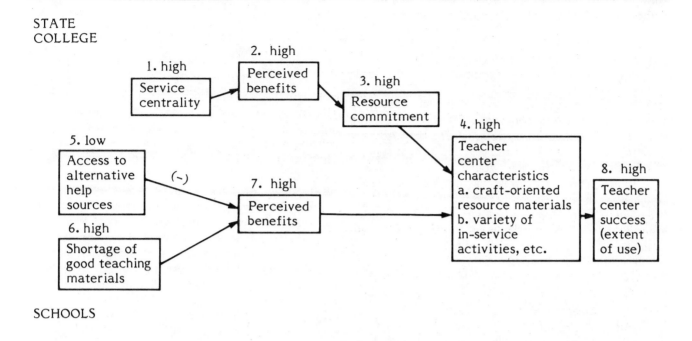

STATE
COLLEGE

1. high — Service centrality

2. high — Perceived benefits

3. high — Resource commitment

4. high — Teacher center characteristics a. craft-oriented resource materials b. variety of in-service activities, etc.

5. low — Access to alternative help sources

6. high — Shortage of good teaching materials

7. high — Perceived benefits

8. high — Teacher center success (extent of use)

(—)

SCHOOLS

Figure 25   Example of a Chain of Evidence Supporting an Observed Outcome
NOTE: (—) = inverse influence.

otherwise at *other sites*, such as less investment, fewer claims, or more accurate claims. This, of course, is where multisite field research is so useful; it provides contrast and variance.

Let's call the pattern we saw "consensual delusion"— everyone agrees that more is happening than really is. The metaphors might be "groupthinking," or "self-deluding" or "wish fulfilling." We could also sketch out a logical flowchart like the one shown in Figure 25 to get a fix on *how* this happens at the several sites. But we're still within the confines of our study; we can't converse meaningfully with other social scientists except in the sense of reporting replication of an existing finding.

The analyst now has to ask, "Are there any broader constructs that put these facts together the way I'm putting them together?" In principle, as we noted earlier, the metaphors should help. The first one points toward group behavior, the next one toward individual cognitive process, and the third one toward motivational dynamics.

In this instance, we picked up an appropriate and powerful construct from cognitive social psychology: effort justification (Lawrence & Festinger, 1962). In order to justify the effort expended, one "sees" more results than are objectively there. This led us on into

the domain of cognitive dissonance, and how people learn to love that for which they have suffered.

Where does this get us? For starters, it tells us that our finding has a conceptual analogue, which lends more plausibility to the finding *and* to the concept, which is now empirically grounded in a new context. It also helps to explain *why* such a pattern occurs. And it throws light on larger issues (such as how people, at our sites and more generally, cope with uncertainty). Finally, the construct can be trained back on our sites to explain related but puzzling phenomena. For example, we can now see *why* objective criteria (the test scores) are being systematically ignored when, in fact, they are widely available.

We have progressed here from the bottom up— from the field to the concepts. The steps are: (a) establishing the discrete findings, (b) relating the findings, (c) naming the pattern, and (d) identifying a corresponding construct. As we showed earlier in the book (Chapter II), it's perfectly legitimate, and often desirable, to work from the top down, from a conceptual framework to the collection of information testing its validity. Of course, you have to stay open to the idea that the concept is inapplicable, or has to be bent or discarded when you see the data. Concepts without corresponding facts are hollow, just as facts without concepts are, literally, meaningless.

VII.B. TACTICS FOR TESTING OR CONFIRMING FINDINGS

Having spent some time on particular ways of making and interpreting findings at different levels of inference, we now confront the issue of validity. As we have said often, qualitative analyses can be evocative, illuminating, masterful, and downright *wrong*. The data, looked at more scrupulously, don't support the conclusions drawn. Researchers double-checking the site come up with different findings. Site informants, asked to provide feedback on the findings, contest some or all of them, very plausibly. The phenomenologist chuckles, reinforced in the idea that there is no single reality out there to get "right." The psychometrician, from the polar opposite stance, concludes the nonstatistical research is an albatross.

The problem, as we have discussed in more detail elsewhere (Huberman & Miles, 1983a), is that there are no canons, decision rules, algorithms, or even any agreed-upon heuristics in qualitative research to indicate whether findings are valid and procedures robust. This is changing, but very slowly. Some recent work (Guba, 1981; Dawson, 1979, 1982) has provided general guidelines, and we are doing our best in this book to operationalize ways of testing/confirming findings.

Let's take a longer view of the problem at hand. Most qualitative researchers work alone in the field. Each is a one-person research machine: defining the problem, doing the sampling, designing the instruments, collecting the information, reducing the information, analyzing it, interpreting it, writing it up. A vertical monopoly. When we read the reports, they are most often heavy on the "what" (the findings, the descriptions) and wafer thin on the "how" (how one got to the "what"). In most cases, we don't read how, exactly, the researcher got from 500 pages of field notes to the main conclusions drawn, and we don't know how much confidence we can place in them. Researchers are not being obtuse. It's just that they have very little that is systematic to draw upon.

The other part of the problem appears when we look at research on information processing by individuals. There's a long research tradition (Meehl, 1954, 1965; Goldberg, 1970; Dawes, 1971) showing that human judgments are consistently *less* accurate than statistical/actuarial ones—and even that "expert" judges are worse than untrained ones (Taft, 1955). Oskamp (1965) found that experts felt more and more *confident* of their erroneous judgments as they got more accurate information, without modifying the initial judgments. (Think of the lone fieldworker out there, trying to collect trustworthy data, with few or no actuarial procedures to help.)

Why are such errors made? There's a long tradition of research on how people attribute causality (Heider, 1944; Kelley, 1967, 1972) and form judgments (Kahnemann & Tversky, 1972; Nisbett & Ross, 1980). The most recent findings, baldly put, are that most people are rotten scientists, relying heavily on pre-existing beliefs, and making bias-ridden judgments. They don't act like scientists: They don't keep track of frequencies, make probabilistic estimates, sample representatively, or make accurate deductions.[5]

What these works don't tell us is when and how scientists behave like laypeople. The suspicion is that they do so often. For example, Kahnemann and Tversky (1972) have studied the "availability heuristic": Data that are "vivid" rather than "pallid" tend to be noticed, registered, retrieved, and used more frequently. As a result, one overweights the importance and frequency of concrete, immediate inputs. One personally experienced or witnessed dramatic event "means more" than several one has read about. Think now of the fieldworker who witnesses a crisis or a dramatic conflict on site, then makes inferences about the significance of the event—and still other inferences about what the site is like when he or she is absent.

So we need to be especially watchful in qualitative research about the multiple sources of potential analytic bias that can weaken, or even invalidate, our findings. Some of these biases have been identified in mainstream anthropological textbooks, along with some pointers for avoiding them (for example, see Wax, 1971). The archetypical ones include the following:

(1) *the holistic fallacy:* interpreting events as more patterned and congruent than they really are, lopping off the many loose ends of which social life is made

(2) *elite bias:* overweighting data from articulate, well-informed, usually high-status informants and underrepresenting data from intractable, less articulate, lower-status ones

(3) *going native:* losing one's perspective or one's "bracketing" ability, being coopted into the perceptions and explanations of local informants

It's useful to note that each of these three biases corresponds, respectively, to one of the three major judgmental heuristics identified by researchers: "representativeness," "availability," and "weighting." We recommend Nisbett and Ross (1980) as a good guide to this literature, and a help in avoiding self-delusion.[6] We'll also draw on this literature in discussing tactics for testing/confirming findings, a task to which we now turn.

The twelve tactics for confirming conclusions are numbered as before. They begin with tactics that are aimed at assuring the basic quality of the data, then move to those that check findings by various contrasts, then conclude with tactics that take a skeptical, demanding approach to emerging explanations.

Data quality can be assessed through *checking for representativeness* (1); *checking for researcher effects* (2) on the site, and vice versa; and *triangulating* (3) across data sources and methods. These checks may also involve *weighting the evidence* (4), deciding which kinds of data are most trustable.

Looking at differences tells us a lot. *Contrasts/ comparisons* (5), *checking the meaning of outliers* (6), and *using extreme cases* (7) are all tactics that test a conclusion about a "pattern" by saying what it's *not* like.

How can we really test our explanations? *Ruling out spurious relations* (8), *replicating a finding* (9), *check-out out rival explanations* (10), and *looking for negative evidence* (11) are all ways of submitting our beautiful theories to the assault of brute facts, or to a race with someone else's beautiful theory.

Finally, a good explanation deserves attention from the very people whose behavior it is about—informants who supplied the original data. The tactic of *getting feedback from informants* (12) concludes our list.

VII.B.1 Checking for Representativeness

When we come up with a "finding" in a field study, we quickly assume it to be typical, representative, an instance of a more general phenomenon. But *is* it? And, if it is, *how* representative?

In their numerous studies of the "representativeness heuristic" used by individuals to calculate base rates and sample sizes, Tversky and Kahneman (1971) showed how biased we are in moving from particulars to generalities. From one or two concrete, vivid instances, we assume there are dozens more lurking in the bushes—but we don't verify whether or how many there are, and there are usually fewer than we think. People typically make a generalization, then illustrate it ("For example, my friend X . . . "), but would be hard put to come up with several more instances of a supposedly widespread occurrence. To compound the problem, people as information seekers—and processors—are far more likely to see *confirming* instances of original beliefs or perceptions than to see disconfirming instances, even when disconfirming instances are more frequent (for example, see Edwards, 1968). Still, more ominously, Kahneman and Tversky (1972) were able with little effort to catch mathematical psychologists in the act of making biased inferences from samples to populations. What, then, of the fieldworker who, Prometheuslike, is doing all the sampling, measuring, and inference-making *de novo*?

Operating alone, without any standardized or validated instruments, the field researcher runs several risks of generalizing inappropriately from specific instances. Here are some of the most common pitfalls, and their associated sources of error:

Pitfall	Source of Error
sampling nonrepresentative *informants*	overreliance on accessible and elite informants
generalizing from nonrepresentative *events* or activities	researcher's noncontinuous presence at the site; overweighting dramatic events
drawing inferences from nonrepresentative *processes*	nonrepresentative informants and events; heavy reliance on plausibility; good fit into emerging explanation, holistic bias

The first pitfall highlights the fact that the researcher can talk only with people who can be contacted; some people are easier to contact than others, especially when the researcher has limited time on site. This problem in itself signals something particularistic about these people. Their accessibility may be connected with work load, lack of cooperativeness, or both.

We should also emphasize that anthropologists have often warned of fieldworkers' tendency to rely too much on articulate, insightful, attractive, and intellectually responsive informants; such people often turn out to be in the local elite. For a good discussion of the atypicality of persons chosen as prime informants, see Dean, Eichorn, and Dean (1967).

The second pitfall also results from the researcher's noncontinuous presence; you have to infer what is happening when you are not there. In particular, when the researcher observes a dramatic or salient event (a crisis, an argument), there is the tendency to assume it has "built up" when one was absent, or that it "symbolizes" a more general pattern. These are plausible, but certainly not airtight, inferences.

Finally, in looking for underlying processes explaining the phenomena you have studied closely, you naturally draw heavily from the people, events, and activities you have sampled to derive the most plausible account. But if the samples are faulty, the explanation cannot be generalized beyond them.

"Plausibility" is, unfortunately, the optiate of the intellectual. If an emerging account makes good logical sense and fits well with other, independently derived analyses within the same universe, you lock onto it and begin to make a stronger case for it; this constitutes the "confirmability" bias studied by Edwards (1968) and others. Anthropologists call this the "holistic bias": The researcher sees all the main facets of the site "coming together" to form a meaningful pattern—one more meaningful and more patterned than the loose-endedness and contradictory nature of social life warrants.

Elementary safeguards: Some illustrations. The real dilemma with selective sampling and abusive generalizing is that you can sllide incrementally into these biases, with the first layer preparing the ground for the next. Gradually, you are prisoner of your emerging system of comprehending the site. There is no longer any possibility, cognitively speaking, to "stand back" or "review critically" what you have observed up to then. What you now understand has been accumulated very gradually from within, not drawn validly from without. If you want to stand back and review critically, you are going to need someone *else* to do it—or you must build in safeguards against self-delusion. We have already addressed the former approach (second readers, auditors, second field-workers), so let us illustrate some safeguards.[7]

In our study of linkage between universities and local school districts, we were on the lookout for—and felt we were drifting into—the three pitfalls listed earlier. For example, each researcher covered several institutions in a state, which meant discontinuous field visiting. We wondered whether there were informants we were systematically missing when we interviewed school and university staff, even though these people assured us that we had sampled broadly. Our first safeguard was to look for the outliers (see section VII.B.6), in order to check the representativeness of those with whom we had talked. As a second safeguard, we asked for the personnel rosters of the districts and the university, and randomly sampled eight informants from each one for interviewing. As it turned out, we *had* been in danger of sampling a biased group.

Here is a second example, from the same study. Informants often talked about one type of project, saying that this was the most frequent activity sponsored by the university. We began to wonder if informants were confusing frequency with impact; did they *remember* this activity type most because it seemed to have been the most practice-relevant? So we took the last two years' newsletters, extracted a calendar of activities, and counted and content analyzed them. Informants had, in fact, misled themselves and us by overweighting one activity type.

A final example from that study corresponds to the third pitfall. There were periodic policy board meetings between delegates from the university and school districts. We tried to be present at them since they represented the formal, more decisive meeting ground between the two parties. Gradually, it appeared that university staff were dominating them; the university delegates spoke more often and longer than the school people, and most decisions went their way. We

thus entertained the hypothesis of a university-dominated arrangement, an idea that fitted the data we had. But to check it, we reverted once again to a wider sampling procedure and observed *other* meetings between the two parties, notably ones that (a) were less formal and did not involve representatives or delegates; or (b) were also formal, but not as prominent as the policy board. This was salutary; we ended up having to qualify our initial hypothesis. In less formal, less prominent meetings, school people held their own in the decision making.

We suggest that you *assume* you are selectively sampling and drawing inferences from a weak or nonrepresentative sample of "cases," be they people, events, or processes. You are guilty, until you prove yourself innocent. You can do this by extending the universe of study, in at least one of four ways: (1) simply *increase the number of cases*; (2) look purposively for *contrasting cases* (negative, extreme, countervailing); (3) *sort the cases systematically* (perhaps using substructing, as in Box V.C.a) and filling out weakly sampled case types; and (4) *sample randomly* within the total universe of people and phenomena under study. The last two procedures are especially recommended. They correspond, not haphazardly, with the "stratification" and "randomization" conventions used by experimental researchers to enhance internal validity. But while the experimental researcher uses the conventions *early*, as anticipatory controls against sampling and measurement error, the qualitative researcher typically uses them *later*, as verification devices. That allows you to let all the candidate people and data in, so that the most influential ones will have a chance of emerging. But you *still* have to carry the burden of proof that the patterns you ultimately pinpoint are, in fact, representative.

VII.B.2 Checking for Researcher Effects

"Outsiders" to a group influence "insiders," and vice versa. So it is with the researcher who disembarks in a field setting to study the natives, whether in a familiar culture or a more exotic setting. The researcher is likely, especially at the outset, to create social behavior in others that would not have ordinarily occurred. This, in turn, can lead the researcher into making biased observations and inferences, thus "confounding" (a nice term in this instance) the "natural" characteristics of the setting with the artificial effects of the researcher-native relationship. Unconfounding them is like threading one's way through a hall of mirrors.

So we have two possible sources of bias here: (a) the effects of the researcher on the site and (b) the effects of the site on the researcher. Both topics have been treated at length in methodological textbooks, more so by experimental or laboratory-based researchers than by field-study methodologists. The latter are less worried about the first kind of bias (bias a) because the field researcher typically spends enough time on the site to become part of the local landscape.[8] This, of course, increases the danger of the second kind of bias (bias b): Being coopted, going native, swallowing the agreed-upon or taken-for-granted version of local events.

For simplicity, we discuss these biases in terms of what is happening during site visits. It is important to remember that they influence *analysis* deeply, both during and after data collection. The researcher who has "gone native" stays native during analysis. The researcher who has influenced the site in un-understood ways suffers unaware from that influence during analysis.

Bias (a) occurs when the researcher disrupts or threatens ongoing social and institutional relationships. People now have to figure out who this person is, why he or she is there, and what might be done with the information being collected. While they are figuring that out, informants will typically switch into an on-stage role or special persona, a presentation of self to the outsider. (They have *other* personae, of course, for fellow insiders, as Goffman, 1959, has so graphically described.)

Even after this preliminary dance, informants will typically craft their responses in such a way as to be amenable to the researcher and to protect their self-interests. For some analysts (for example, Douglas, 1976), local informants' interests are fundamentally in conflict with those of the researcher, who might penetrate to the core of the rivalries, compromises, weaknesses, or contradictions that make up much of the basic history of the site and that insiders don't want outsiders to know about—either because *other* outsiders aren't meant to find out or because the social equilibrium among local actors depends on those facts being kept private. So the researcher, who is usually interested in uncovering precisely this kind of information, must *assume* that people will try to be misleading and must shift into a more investigative mode.[9] (For more detail on useful tactics, see section VII.B.4, on *weighting the evidence.*)

It is probably true that, fundamentally, field research is an act of betrayal, no matter how well intentioned or well integrated the researcher. One makes public the private and leaves the locals to take the consequences.[10] But that is not the only way bias (a) can occur. In some instances bias (a) can team up with bias (b) to create artifactual effects, as a result of the complicity between researcher and local actors. This is the famous "experimenter" effect, studied intensively by Rosenthal (1976).

We have been caught napping several times on this one. For instance, we studied one field site in the school improvement project that was about to phase out the project we had come to see. For some mysterious reason, the phase-out decision was suspended during our time on site, The reasoning, which we unraveled after several more days on site, was that the practice *had* to be better than it appeared since people had come from so far away to see it. Mixed in also was the desire to avoid a public indictment; the researcher, and the public reading the research or talking with her, might convey the impression that the school had botched the project.

Bias (a) can take still other forms. For example, local site informants can implicitly or explicitly boycott the researcher, who is seen variously as a spy, a voyeur, or a pest. Or the researcher can inhibit local actors. After several days on site and multiple interviews with informants, people aren't sure any more how much the researcher has found out and assume—wrongly in most cases—that the researcher knows *too* much. This then triggers bias (b). The researcher accordingly becomes more reassuring or, alternatively, moves into the investigative-adversarial mode. Both strategies are likely to affect the data being collected.

Assuming then, that the researcher has only a few months, weeks, or even days on site, how may these two interlocking forms of bias be countered? Below is a short shopping list of suggestions, many of which are treated in far more detail in the mainstream methodological literature (for example, see Pelto & Pelto, 1978; Lofland, 1971; Adams & Preiss, 1960; Wax, 1971).

(a) Avoiding biases stemming from researcher effects on the site:

- Stay as long on site as possible; spend some of that time simply hanging around, fitting into the landscape, taking a lower profile.
- Use unobtrusive measures where you can. (Webb, Campbell, Schwartz, & Sechrest, 1965; McCall & Simmons, 1969).
- Make sure your mandate is unequivocal for informants: why you are there, what you are studying generally, how you will be collecting information, what you will do with it.
- Consider coopting an informant—asking that person to be attentive to your influence on the site and its inhabitants.
- Do some of your interviewing off site, in a congenial social environment (cafe, restaurant, informant's home), by way of reducing both your threat quotient and your exoticism quotient for informants.
- Don't inflate the potential problem; you are not *really* such an important presence in the lives of these people.

(b) Avoiding biases stemming from the effects of the site on the researcher:

- Avoid the "elite" bias by spreading out your informants; include people not directly involved in the focus of your study (peripheral actors, former actors).
- Avoid cooptation or going native by spending time *away* from the site; spread out site visits (see Whyte, 1943, on "temporary withdrawal").
- Be sure to include dissidents, cranks, isolates— people with different points of view from the mainstream, people less committed to tranquility and equilibrium in the setting.
- Keep thinking *conceptually*; translate sentimental or interpersonal thoughts into more theoretical ones.
- Consider coopting an informant who agrees to provide background and historical information for you and to collect information when you are off-site (the cooptation may be more useful, in bias-reduction terms, than the information provided).
- Triangulate with several data collection methods; don't overly depend on *talk* to make sense of the setting.
- If you sense you are being misled, try to understand, and focus on *why* an informant would find it necessary to mislead you. Follow that trace as far upstream as you can.
- Don't casually show off how much you *do* know; this is a covert plea for confirmation that deludes only the person making it.
- Show your field notes to a second outside reader. Another researcher is often much quicker to see where and how a fieldworker is being misled or coopted.
- Keep your research questions firmly in mind; don't wander too far from them to follow alluring leads, or drop them in the face of a more dramatic or momentous event.

As with all such lists, following some items gets you in trouble on others. For instance, if a researcher has only eight days on site, spending much of it in off-site interviewing may be too costly. Or, one may be coopted by the informant one is trying to coopt.

Supposedly, bias detection and removal take time. The more time you have, the more layers you can peel off the setting to get to the meatiest, explanatory factors, and the less subject you are to either of the biases described above.

However, we take that with a grain of salt. Long exposure can just push up bias (b) and make bias (a) harder to see. We reiterate that people who are discreet, savvy in the environment under study, and conceptually ecumenical are often able to get to the core of a site in a matter of days, sidestepping both types of researcher bias and coming away with higher-quality data than others could have compiled after several months' work, if at all. In that sense, it's possible that the methodologists demanding months or years on site before valid data can be obtained are confusing time with competence.

VII.B.3 Triangulating

In psychological testing, an important part of the internal validation process is checking a new item or test against other, already validated, measures of the same skill or construct. If they concur—overlap, correlate strongly—the new item or test has good "concurrent validity." Until recently, qualitative research had no comparable all-purpose term. One spoke of "corroboration" or, somewhat loosely, of "cross-validation" or of "multiple validation procedures," (see Becker, 1958) to ensure the dependability of a field-study finding. In all instances, since there was typically no *external* measure to check the new finding against, one looked to other internal indices that should provide convergent evidence. Webb et al. (1965) coined a term for this procedure that stuck: triangulation. In addition, their depiction of the process was an apt one; they spoke of validating a finding by subjecting it to "the onslaught of a series of imperfect measures."

Stripped to its basics, triangulation is supposed to support a finding by showing that independent measures of it agree with it or, at least, don't contradict it.[11] The measures are imperfect in that the researcher usually invented them on the spot, and we know little about their validity or reliability. They are also imperfect because they usually come from the same "instrument," that is, observations made or conversations recorded by the researcher alone. When the same instrument—in this case the same person—is both establishing and corroborating a finding, we have what amounts to a potential cognitive conflict of interest.

Bias, however, is not inevitable. Detectives, car mechanics, and general practitioners all engage successfully in establishing and corroborating findings with little elaborate instrumentation. They often use a *modus operandi* approach, which consists largely of triangulating independent indices. When the detective amasses fingerprints, hair samples, alibis, eyewitness accounts, and the like, a case is being made that presumably fits one suspect far better than others. Diagnosing engine failure or chest pain follows a similar pattern. All the signs presumably point to the same conclusion. Note the importance of having different *kinds* of measurements, which provide repeated verification.

How can the qualitative researcher apply a *modus operandi* approach to the testing of field study findings? Essentially, we have been saying throughout this book that this is precisely how you get to the finding in the first place—by seeing or hearing multiple instances of it from different sources, and by squaring the finding with others it needs to be squared with. Analytic induction, once again.

But it is important to make certain that the several indices chosen are indeed independent, sturdy, of different types and sources, and congruent. Let's look at an example. At one field site in the school improvement study, we found what looked like a highly successful practice. Virtually all the people we talked with made this claim, and the test scores looked good. To make certain of the finding, we assembled the most likely sources of evidence:

(1) test scores for first-year and second-year pupils whose teachers were and were not using the practice
(2) testimony of teachers using the practice
(3) testimony of teachers *not* using the practice
(4) testimony of pupils
(5) observations of the practice
(6) samples of pupils' work
(7) hands-on work with the practice in the classroom
(8) testimony of local administrators
(9) observation of classrooms *not* using the practice
(10) analysis of the program manual and materials

Notice that we have compiled different *sources* of evidence, using different *methods* and operating at different *levels* of the school. Most indices were *corroborative* or verificatory indicators of success, while some were more *contrasting* and *inferential* indicators. (We looked at comparable test scores for nonusing pupils, observed nonusing classrooms, and talked with nonusing teachers to see whether different or lesser results were obtained when other methods were used.)

Finally, putting some of the indicators together yielded some *multiple* and more *causally linked* evidence. For example, we analyzed the program manual and materials (10 on the list) to determine whether, in fact, the results could flow conceptually and logically from the features of the program itself. We then conducted observations in the classrooms to make sure that teachers were putting into practice the same program described in the manual. Looking at work samples provided another check on this, as did a check on pupils scoring high on the tests in relation to low-scoring pupils: Were they further ahead in the program? Triangulation here consisted of retracing the most plausible causal chain from program design to execution to interim outcomes (work samples) to ultimate outcomes (test scores), trying to get more than one type of measure from more than one source for each link in the chain.

The process sounds more obsessive and sophisticated than it really is. It is easy to sit down and imagine where one can find or double-check sources of corroborative, contrasting, and causally linked information. It is also relatively easy to get data from multiple *sources* (people with different roles, deviant and mainstream

informants) using multiple *methods* (such as talking with people *and* observing routine life at the site). See also the thoughtful discussion by Jick (1979).

It also helps to be on the lookout for a *new* source of data—a new informant or class of informants, another comparable event or setting. A new source forces the researcher to "replicate" the finding in a place where, if valid, it should reoccur (see also section VII.B.9).

Finally, we can triangulate with different *researchers*. They can be taking parallel mesures at the same time, or following up a finding to confirm it.

Perhaps our basic point is that triangulation is a state of mind. If you *self-consciously* set out to collect and double-check findings, using multiple sources and modes of evidence, the verification process will largely be built into the data-gathering process, and little more need be done than to report on one's procedures.

VII.B.4 Weighting the Evidence

Any given preliminary conclusion is always based on certain data. Maybe we should use the word some historians have employed: "capta." There are events in the real world, from which we "capture" only a partial record, in the form of raw field notes, from which we further extract only certain information in the form of write-ups, which we then call "data." There is in turn further reduction, selection, and transformation as these data are entered into various displays.

Some of these data are "better" than others. Fortunately, the qualitative analyst can exploit that fact beautifully in verifying conclusions. If the data on which a conclusion is based are known to be stronger, more valid than the average, then the conclusion is strengthened. Stronger data can be given more weight in the conclusion. Conversely, a conclusion based on weak or suspect data can be, at the least, held lightly, and, optimally, discarded if there is an alternate conclusion with stronger data back of it.

Basically, there is a very large range of reasons that certain data are stronger or weaker than others—essentially, the question is one of validity (Dawson, 1979, 1982). We cannot be encyclopedic here, but will suggest a number of markers the analyst can use in deciding whether to give more weight to some data than to others.

First, data from some *informants* are "better." The informant may be articulate, thoughtful, and reflective, and may enjoy talking about events and processes. Or the informant may be knowledgeable, close to the event, action, process, or setting with which you are concerned. In our study, for example, we gave more weight to school superintendents' judgments about forward budget categories than we did to those of teachers.

Second, the *circumstances* of the data collection may have strengthened (or weakened) the quality of the data. Here is a partial list (see also Sieber, 1976; Becker, 1970; Bogdan & Taylor, 1975):

Stronger Data	Weaker Data
Collected later, or after repeated contact.	Collected early, during entry.
Seen or reported firsthand.	Heard secondhand.
Observed behavior, activities.	Reports or statements.
Fieldworker is trusted.	Fieldworker is not trusted.
Collected in official or formal setting.	Collected in informal setting.
Volunteered to field-worker.	Prompted by fieldworker question.
Respondent is alone with fieldworker.	Respondent is in presence of others, or in group setting.

Finally, data quality may be stronger because of a fieldworker's *validation* efforts. These may be of several varieties:

- checking for researcher effects (section VII.B.2) and biases
- checking for representativeness (section VII.B.1)
- getting feedback from informants (section VII.B.12)
- triangulating (section VII.B.3)
- looking for deception
- looking for ulterior motives

We might comment briefly on the last two, since they haven't been attended to in other sections. Douglas (1976) emphasizes the idea that, regardless of the degree of trust a fieldworker may feel has been developed, people in field sites nearly always have some reasons for omitting, selecting, or distorting data, and may have active reasons for *deceiving* the fieldworker (not to mention deceiving themselves). If the fieldworker has actively entertained such a view of particular respondents, and of a particular set of data from them, *and* has done something to validate the data, more confidence is justified. The interested reader should consult Douglas (1976) for a wide range of specific interventions. Here are a few:

- Check against "hard facts."
- Check against alternative accounts.
- Look for "the trapdoor"—what's going on beyond the obvious.
- Share own personal material to open up the respondent.
- Assert your knowledge of "what's going on" and see if respondent buys it.
- Summarize a state of affairs and ask the respondent to deny it.
- Name possible ulterior motives, and see respondent response (denial, acknowledgment).

Fieldworkers who rely mainly on "trust" may quail at such interventions or dismiss them as too intrusive. Nevertheless, Douglas makes a good case for such validating tactics when the object of investigation has good reasons for being evasive and/or self-deceiving (some of his studies have included people who had attempted suicide, clients of massage parlors, habitues of nude beaches, and police who work in emergency rooms). And even for less dramatic settings, we have found that it pays to be suspicious, to expect to be lied to sometimes, to look for respondent self-deception, and to push respondents from time to time on such matters.[12]

Two added suggestions: First, we have found it useful to keep a running log of data quality issues (often in the form of reflective or marginal remarks on the field notes; see Boxes III.B.a and III.B.b) together with recurrent efforts to improve data quality in subsequent site visits.

Second, when approaching final write-up of a site analysis, it is useful to summarize one's views of data quality. Here is an example from a site report in our school improvement study, which appeared after the researcher summarized the number of interviews (46), informal talks (24), and observations (17) held during three site visits:

The data base is probably biased toward administrators and central program personnel (3-6 interviews apiece), and may underrepresent those of normal program users, and certainly those of peripheral (and more disenchanted) people. So the information may be fuller about the ins and outs of operation as seen by key operators, and thinner on what day-to-day life in the Carson schools is like, with the IPA program as a feature in that life.

Though some interviews were brief, I had no difficulty in re-interviewing people whose opinions seemed crucial or especially illuminating.

I have moderately good retrospective data on the first and second years of the program, except for assistance provided. Data on the current year's operations are quite full, except that I observed no actual student-parent-teacher conferences in the high school. The only key informant I missed talking to was the former IPA director, Helena Rolland. It could also be argued that I should have interviewed Mark Covington, as the archetypal coach. But with these exceptions the coverage was thorough.

Dictation from field notes was done 14-32 days after Visit #1, 28-49 days after Visit #2, and 10-30 days after Visit #3. Interim phone calls were usually written up immediately after the call, with one or two exceptions. In spite of the write-up delay, I experienced little decay from notes. Where puzzling or meaningless notes could not be reconstructed, this was marked in the field notes and noted during dictation; such indications appeared, however, for only 3-5 percent of field notes.

Editorial comment: The researcher's confidence about "little decay" is almost surely self-deluding. The probable loss of detail will need to be compensated for by triangulation and by looking for repeat examples from the same respondent. And comments from "disenchanted" people should probably be given more weight in conclusion verification.

VII.B.5 Making Contrasts/Comparisons

A time-honored, classic way to test a conclusion is to draw a contrast or make a comparison between two sets of things—persons, roles, activities, sites as a whole—that are known to differ in some *other* important respect. This is the "method of differences," which goes back to Aristotle, if not further. (The contrast between experimental and control groups was not invented by R. A. Fisher.) A few examples from our work:

- When we looked at preparedness (section IV.B, Chart 13a), the comparison showed that administrators were enthusiastic about the innovation, but users were bewildered—a picture that fit with other aspects of their roles: Administrators press for adoption, users have to do the actual implementation work.
- Comparing *sites* that had many negative effects of implementation with those that had few (section V.B, Chart 31a) showed us that such sites were also ones where demanding innovations were being tried.
- Comparing *program sponsorship* (NDN versus IV-C, section V.B, Chart 31a) showed us that there were *no* differences in final student impact, a finding that fit with prior expectation.
- Contrast tables (Box V.C.b) comparing *sites* on, for example, amounts of user change, made it clear that "change pervasiveness" might be causing user change.
- Predictor-outcome matrices (section V.C) array sites by high and low *outcomes*, and use that leverage to examine the impact of a wide range of possible predictors. In our example, the comparison was between roughness and smoothness of implementation; which predictors were present in smooth sites but not in rough ones (Charts 32, 33)?
- Comparing job mobility during the middle, early, and later portions of projects showed (section V.D, Chart 36) the effects of *timing* and project development; more people moved *in* at the beginning and *out* toward the end.

The method of comparisons is so pervasive throughout social science that we won't introduce other examples. Some notes, however:

(1) Mindless comparisons are useless. The trick is to be sure that the comparisons being made are the right ones, and that they make sense.

(2) The results of a comparison should themselves be compared with what *else* we know about the roles, persons, groups, activities, or sites being compared.

(3) Take a minute before you display a comparison, and think, "How big must a difference be before it makes a difference? And, how do I think I know that?" You don't have a significance test to fall back on.

VII.B.6 Checking the Meaning of Outliers

For any given finding, there are usually exceptions. The temptation is to smooth them over, ignore them, or explain them away. But *the outlier is your friend.* A good look at the exceptions, or the ends of a distribution, can test and strengthen the basic finding. It not only tests the generality of the finding, but protects against self-selecting biases.

For example, in the school improvement study, we happened on one site where the new practice was seen by many teachers as a *miraculous cure* for local ills. Although teachers found it hard to get on top of, the project eventually led to dramatic increases in reading and composition scores. Enthusiasm was high.

To test the generality of the finding, we asked about people who either hadn't adopted the practice or had used it and found it wanting. After some thought, our key informants came up with one each.

Our interviews with these two people were instructive. First, we found that the reasons given for *not* adopting were opposite to—and thereby coherent with—the reasons given by the other informants *for* adopting. And we found that the dissident user had *not* really mastered the innovation in the way the contended users had. We already had good evidence linking technical mastery to positive results. So our findings were strengthened, and we understood far better *why* deviant cases were deviant.

So, was the innovation a "miracle cure"? Perhaps—but only if it were technically well carried out. Furthermore, these dissidents told us there were more people like them around than advocates had admitted.

We realized then that we had oversampled contented users and, in a sense, had been "sucked in" to the taken-for-granted version of events among local actors. In widening the sampling of discontented users thereafter, we got a somewhat different, and more intricate, picture of the site.

The second part of the illustration suggests that, very often, there are *more* exceptions or deviant cases than one realizes at first, and that one has to go looking for them. They don't come calling, nor do we think spontaneously of sampling for them. After all, they are inconvenient—not only hard to reach or observe, but, more fundamentally, spoilers of the artfully built, coherent version of site dynamics at which the researcher has arrived.

Remember, too, that outliers are not only people; they can also be discrepant *sites,* atypical *settings,* unique *treatments,* or unusual *events.* You need to find the outliers, then verify whether what is present in them is absent or different in other, more mainstream examples (see also the discussion of *using extreme cases*, section VII.B.7).

A good illustration appears in Section V.E, Figure 15, where the Astoria site proved to be an outlier. Most other sites had *high* pressure to adopt the innovation, and gave *little* latitude to users, or vice versa—little pressure and lots of latitude. Only in Astoria was there high pressure *and* high latitude. Why should this be? A look back at the site report showed that some careful administrator-teacher bargaining had been going on: The administrator said the innovation was mandated, but agreed that it could be flexibly adapted. Astoria was also the only parochial school in our sample, suggesting that authority was less questioned. This exploration gave us more confidence that the basic finding was right.

Finding outliers is easier when you have good displays. Sites, settings, events, people can be shown along a distribution. If you are still collecting data, display what you have and go for the outliers. If things are closely clumped (no apparent outliers), consider where you might go to find some outlying persons, events, settings. And, on following up, be cognitively open to the eventuality that the exceptional cases are, it turns out, the modal ones.

VII.B.7 Using Extreme Cases

We have just described the use of *outliers* (section VII.B.6) in deepening preliminary conclusions. Outliers of a certain type, which we'll call extreme cases, can be very useful in verifying and confirming conclusions.

Here we can use two illustrations from Sieber (1976). The first involves extreme *situations*. Sieber asks us to imagine a situation in which an educational innovation failed, then to look at the possible antecedents of that failure. If we found that in a particular site there were many *positive* factors—such as high motivation to innovate, access to resources, and implementation skills—but that *administrative support* was lacking, we could argue persuasively that in this site we have found the key factor responsible for the failure. In effect, Sieber suggests, this is a tactic of "holding *everything else* constant"—looking for the most extreme case, where there *should* have been success, but there wasn't. Note that this tactic requires conceptual and/or empirical knowledge of the variables involved; it cannot be done in a vacuum.

The second sort of extreme case Sieber mentions is *persons* known to have a strong bias. For example, suppose that you are talking to a very conservative administrator, whom you know from past contact is inclined to be rather defensive. You ask him why the teachers he works with are reluctant to try innovations. He answers that it's due to a lack of cooperation and

support on his part. That answer is very persuasive because you wouldn't expect this particular administrator to make such a statement at all. So its truth value is probably high.

To put this another way: Look for the person in a site who would have most to gain (or lose) by affirming or denying something, and pop the question. If you get a surprising answer (for example, the person who has much to gain by denying the statement/question in fact affirms it), then you can be more confident. Of course this requires that you have a good prior understanding of the person's typical stance and biases, not a superficial impression or stereotype.

In a way, this is another style of differentially *weighting evidence* (section VII.B.4). For example, if you are interviewing people you know to be enthusiastic proponents of an innovation, their comments on the innovation's warts and trouble spots should be taken quite seriously.

VII.B.8 Ruling Out Spurious Relations

Suppose that you have been able through assorted ingenious tactics to establish that variable A is indeed related to B, perhaps causally. Before breathing a sigh of relief and proceeding to the next conclusion, it pays to consider that the picture you are drawing:

$$A \rightarrow B$$

may in fact be more accurately portrayed as

where some third factor is in play, causing both A and B to occur.

This is an old problem, which statisticians have dealt with well. We can draw a nice example from Wallis and Roberts (1956), describing a study from the *Journal of the American Medical Association*. Researchers noted that polio patients who traveled longer distances (average, 85 miles) to a hospital were more likely to die than patients who traveled little (average, 7 miles) and were more likely to die sooner (50 percent died within 24 hours, versus 20 percent). They concluded:

> The greater mortality in the transported group, occurring shortly after admission to the hospital, is a manifestation of the effect of long transportation during the acute stage of illness.

Wallis and Roberts suggest that another, third variable may be influencing both A (transportation) and B (mortality). It is *seriousness of the initial attack*. All the patients were seen in a certain hospital, Willard Parker, a noted center for treatment of contagious diseases. Polio patients who lived farther away were probably only brought to Willard Parker if their conditions were

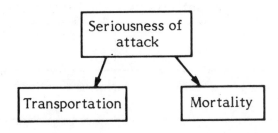

Figure 26a Possible Explanation of Spurious Relationship

serious; milder cases would be treated nearer their own homes. Thus the picture develops as shown in Figure 26a. This interpretation can be checked out through the sort of display found in Figure 26b, with Ns and mortality rates entered in the cells.

And, as Wallis and Roberts faithfully point out, even if the reanalysis could be done, and it supported "seriousness of attack" as the real issue, one would have to do additional ruling out. Perhaps those coming from a distance had poorer basic health to begin with. Perhaps they came from an area where a particularly virulent strain of polio was widespread. And so on.

Finding a candidate third variable is not always easy, particularly if the original explanation "makes sense," as the transportation-mortality link seemed to at first glance. The Willard Parker researchers did think of one third variable—length of prior illness—which showed no real difference. Then they stopped, not realizing that the "Willard Parkerness" of Willard Parker was probably in the picture. Had they been able to recruit Wallis and Roberts as "friendly strangers" part way through their analysis, the story might have been different.

The moral for qualitative researchers is the same. When two variables look correlated, especially when you think they are causally associated, wait a beat, and consider whether some third variable might be underlying/influencing/causing them both. Use a knowledgeable but detached colleague to help in the search. Then consider new displays that will give you a clean look at such third variables and their effects.

Doing this in a more than cursory way takes time, so it is worth it mainly when you have a major (but perhaps surprising) conclusion, or one on which a lot is riding, in practical terms.

VII.B.9 Replicating a Finding

As we showed in section VII.B.3, findings are more dependable when they can be buttressed from several independent sources. Their validity is enhanced for having been confirmed by more than one "instrument" measuring the same trait or outcome.

Still, the fact that in most cases one person is doing all this measuring with homemade instruments is grounds for precaution. Once a researcher has latched onto a hypothesis that makes powerful sense of the site, it's the dickens to get rid of it. Confirmation seems, almost magically, to come from all quarters. New interviews, observations, and documents all appear to bring verification, and to fit together coherently. Disconfirming evidence is absent or feeble. This is a heady and extremely dangerous moment, and it usually means that the researcher is knee-deep in the "holistic fallacy": putting more logic, coherence, and meaning into events than the inherent sloppiness of social life warrants. How to protect against this?

One line of attack is to think in terms of *replication*, which is the bedrock of science. If I can reproduce the finding in a new context or in another part of my data base, it's a dependable one. If someone else can reproduce it, better still.

There are several ways of doing this. At the most elementary level, the fieldworker is replicating in the simple act of collecting new information from new informants, from new settings and events. New data bolster or qualify old data; in fact, one begins to collect new data *in order to* test the validity and generality of the old.

At a notch higher in the confidence scale, one can test an emerging hypothesis in another part of the site or data set. This amounts to "if/then" reasoning: If I find this *here*, then I should find it—or something coherent with it—*there*, too. For instance, in one study we gradually got the picture that school administrators in the district office were aggressively promoting changes in three local schools, bypassing the school principals. This looked important, because it could realign the entire power-influence network within the district. Teachers, for example, could short-circuit

	Local patients	Distant patients
Mild attack		
Severe attack		

Figure 26b Display for Testing Explanation in Figure 26a

their principals and go directly to the central administrative office. We reasoned that, if this were true, the principals would have relatively little detailed understanding of the practices being so implemented, even though they were happening in that principal's own building. So we conducted open-ended interviews with the principals, simply asking them to tell us about the practice. As hypothesized, there was a good deal of hemming and hawing, even in the very small schools that principals could cover easily.

Such a test is more rigorous; it's harder to bootleg researcher bias into it. Even stiffer tests can be made. For example, in another study, we came up with the hypothesis that a "localist" orientation at a college or university was more promising than a more "cosmopolitan" orientation when the college undertook collaborative work with surrounding school districts. To test this, we had "saved" one college in the sample for study later on. We operationalized what we meant by localism and cosmopolitanism (see section VII.A.8), described for the other sites just how the two variables were associated with successful collaborative projects, then went to the new (most localist) site and tried to determine whether our hypothesis was viable. (It was, but needed some qualifying.) Others (see Stake and Easley, 1978) have used this kind of staggered replication device even more methodically.

Some brief words of advice:

(1) In cross-site studies, replication is an important part of the basic data-collection effort. Emerging patterns from one site need to be tested in others. They usually surface in some of the methods we described earlier: pattern codes, memos, site analysis meetings, interim site summaries. One should therefore be prepared, in the course of fieldwork, to do the kind of corroborative and replicative testing described here and in section VII.B.3.

(2) If provisions aren't made in advance for replications later in the study, they won't happen; there is inevitably too little time and too much information still to compile.

(3) Doing replication at the end of fieldwork, during final analysis and write-ups, is very difficult and less credible. To test a hypothesis in another part of the data set assumes that all the requisite data are there for the test to be made. They usually aren't, unless the researcher has made sure to collect them beforehand in anticipation of just such an exercise.

VII.B.10 Checking Out Rival Explanations

Thinking that there may be rival explanations to account for the phenomenon one has carefully studied and masterfully unraveled is a healthy exercise in self-discipline and hubris avoidance. But that thought often gets lost in the shuffle. During data collection, you are often too busy making minimal sense of the welter of stimuli. Later on, you tend to get married to your emerging account, and usually opt for investing the scant time left to buttress, rather than to unhorse, your explanation. Then, during data analysis, it is often too late to "test" any other explanation than the one arrived at; the data necessary for doing that in any but a cosmetic way just aren't there.

So, in qualitative research, there appears at first blush to be little of the kind of rival hypothesis-testing that Platt (1964) praises so much when he speaks of "strong inference." Platt, drawing on fields such as molecular biology, emphasizes (a) developing alternative hypotheses; (b) specifying critical experiments, the outcomes of which will exclude one or more hypotheses; (c) carrying out the experiments; and (d) recycling until a satisfactory conclusion is reached. But in most social settings, we cannot easily conduct the series of carefully controlled, elegantly scaffolded critical experiments that theoretically—but seldom practically—do away with equivocal findings from competing studies. Maybe we shouldn't worry too much about trying rival hypotheses on our data, since our rivals will cheerfully do it for us afterwards. (Somehow, though, *their* conclusions don't match the ones *we* would have reached had we done the same exercise.)

We claim that the search for rival explanations is usually more thorough in qualitative research than in survey research or in most laboratory studies, and that it is relatively easy to do. The competent field researcher is looking for the most plausible, empirically grounded explanation of local events from among the *several* competing for attention in the course of fieldwork. You are not looking for *one* account, forsaking all others, but for the best of several alternative accounts. This is rendered beautifully, we think in Umberto Eco's novel, *The Name of the Rose* (1982, pp. 311-312), in the following exchange between the protagonist and his foil:

Guillaume: I have a number of good hypotheses [for explaining a series of events], but no overriding fact to tell me which is the best . . .

Adso: So then you must be far from finding the solution?

Guillaume: I'm very close, but I don't know to which one.

Adso: So you don't only have one solution?

Guillaume: Adso, if that were the case, I'd be teaching theology at the Sorbonne.

Adso: So in Paris they always have the right solution?

Guillaume: Never, but they're very confident of their errors.

Adso: What about you? Don't you make errors too?

Guillaume: Often. But instead of imagining one, I try to imagine several. That way I don't become a slave of any one error in particular. (translated from the French)

The trick, then, is that of holding on to several possible (rival) explanations until one of them gets increasingly more compelling as the result of more, stronger, and varied sources of evidence. Looking at it from the other end, you give each rival explanation a good chance. Is it maybe *better* than your main love? Do you have some biases you weren't aware of? Do you need to collect any new data?

Foreclosing too *early* on alternative explanations is a harbinger of bias, of what psychometricians call "systematic measurement error." One locks into a particular way of construing the site and selectively scans the environment for supporting evidence. Discounting evidence is ignored, underregistered or handled as "exceptional"—and, as such, *further* increases one's confidence in one's thesis.[13]

On the other hand, we should note that closing *too late* on alternative explanations builds too weak a case for the best one. It also adds enormous bulk to the corpus of data. So, rival explanations should be looked at fairly promptly in fieldwork, and sustained until they prove genuinely inviable—or prove to be better. This should happen if possible before the bulk of fieldwork is done. The same principle applies to analysis done

after fieldwork. Check out alternative explanations early, but don't iterate forever.

It is usually difficult for the analyst who has spent weeks or months coming up with one explanation to get seriously involved with another one. The idea may have to come from someone else who is not on the site and has the cognitive distance to imagine alternatives, to be a devil's advocate. You can ask a colleague (preferably from another discipline), "Here's how I see it and here's *why* I see it this way. Can you think of another way to look at it?" We also heartily commend the use of what Platt (1964) calls "The Question": "What could disprove your hypothesis?" Or, "What hypothesis does your analysis *disprove?*"

It also helps to fasten on to discrepant information—things that "don't fit" or are still puzzling. The trick is *not* to explain them away in light of one's favorite explanation—that's a piece of cake—but rather to run *with* them, to ask yourself what kind of alternative case *these* bits of information could build, then check them out further.

See section V.E, Figure 15, for an illustration of checking rival explanations. Explanation 1 was that high pressure to adopt an innovation will be accompanied by plenty of latitude to change it, which administrators grant in a bargain with users. Explanation 2a turned up when the analyst cross-tabulated the data: Pressure and latitude are *inversely* related. Explanation 2b noted that *some* bargaining was going on, but much later during the relationship; the inverse finding was essentially upheld. Note that in this case the rival hypothesis wasn't dredged up from the depths of the analyst's mind or presented by a "stranger" colleague, but was forced on him by the data.

A useful rule of thumb is this: During final analysis, first check out the merits of the "next best" explanation you or others can think of as an alternative to the one you preferred at the end of fieldwork. "Next bests" have more pulling power than fanciful alternatives. For more on rival explanations, including many fascinating problem exercises for practice, see Huck and Sandler's (1979) text.

VII.B.11 Looking for Negative Evidence

This tactic is easy to describe, but given people's pattern-making proclivities, not naturally come by. Essentially, when a preliminary conclusion is in hand, the tactic is to say, "Are there any data that would oppose this conclusion, or are inconsistent with this conclusion?" This is a more extreme version of looking for *outliers* (section VII.B.6) and for *rival explanations* (section VII.B.10); you are actively seeking disconfirmation of what you think is true.

Einstein is supposed to have said, "No amount of evidence can prove me right, and *any* amount of evidence can prove me wrong." That is right, in the abstract, but most of us act as if the converse were true. Our beautiful theories need little data to convince us of their solidity, and we are not eager to encounter the many brutal facts that could doom our frameworks.

As Glaser and Strauss (1967) have remarked, "There are no guidelines specifying how and how long to search for negative cases," so it's never quite clear what "enough" effort is. For a good case study of such an effort, see Kidder's (1981) account of Cressey's (1953) classic study of embezzlers.

The easiest way to proceed is to commission a skeptic to take a good cut at the conclusion at hand, avoiding *your* data display, and seeking data back in the written-up field notes that would effectively disconfirm your conclusion. If such evidence is found, do your best to rejoice, and proceed to the formulation of an alternative conclusion that deals with the evidence. If such evidence cannot be marshaled in, say, half the time it took you to do the analysis, more confidence is justified.

But note what might be called the "delusional error." Absence of negative evidence can *never* be decisive as a confirmatory tactic. As in this exchange:

> *Therapist:* Why do you have that blue ribbon on your little finger every day?
>
> *Patient:* It's to keep elephants from following me.
>
> *Therapist:* But there are no elephants here.
>
> *Patient:* See? It's working.

VII.B.12 Getting Feedback from Informants

One of the most logical sources of corroboration is the people with whom one has talked and whom one has observed. After all, an alert and observant actor in the setting is bound to know more than the researcher ever will about the realities under investigation (see Blumer, 1969). In that sense, local informants can act as a panel of judges, evaluating singly and collectively the major findings of a study (Denzin, 1978).

Feeding findings back to informants is a venerated but not always executed practice in qualitative research. It dates back at least to Malinowski's fieldwork in the 1920s, and has been used in numerous field studies since then. More recently, Bronfenbrenner (1976) classified feedback to informants as a source of "phenomenological validity," and Guba (1981) built it into his repertoire of devices for assuring the "confirmability" of findings, using the sociologists' term "member checks." Other researchers (such as Stake,

1976) have made the case for feedback a quasi-ethical one—informants have the right to know what the researcher has found—and still others, more and more numerous, are feeding back findings because people at the site are making this a precondition for access.

Earlier (in sections IV.J and IV.K) we showed two techniques for feedback to site informants. The first one required the reader to comment on a short summary of findings, then to evaluate the accuracy of a causal network encapsulating the higher-inference findings. In the second, the researcher generates predictions that should play out if the findings are valid, then submits them to site informants for verification a year later.

There is an important distinction to be made about the *timing* of such feedback. In a more or less deliberate way, researchers are *continuously* getting feedback in the course of data collection. When a finding begins to take shape, the researcher checks it out with *new* informants and/or with *key* informants, often called "confidants." The check-out process may be more indirect with the former than with the latter, who are often built into the study as sources of verification (for example, Becker, Geer, Hughes, & Strauss, 1961; Lofland, 1971; Whyte, 1943). The delicate issue here, of course, is that of introducing bias (see section VII.B.2). Feeding things back in the course of a study may change informants' behaviors or perspectives.

There are good reasons for conducting feedback after final analysis instead of during data collection. For one thing, the researcher knows more. You also know better what you know—are less tentative, have more supporting evidence, can illustrate it. In addition, you can get feedback at a higher level of inference: on main factors, on causal relationships, on interpretive conclusions. Finally, the feedback process can be done at this point in a less haphazard way. You can lay out the findings clearly and systematically, and present them to the reader for careful scrutiny and comment. As we showed in sections IV.J and IV.K, it is crucial that the reader be able to connect to the feedback—understand it, relate it to local experience and perceptions, *do* something with it (draw on it, cross out parts and add others, and so on). So *formatting* the feedback is crucial. Sending back an abstract, an executive summary, or the concluding chapter, without transforming it into the language of the site—which the researcher has come to learn in the course of field research—is of little value if one is seriously after verification.

Some advice:

(1) If you don't plan deliberately for this exercise—setting aside the time, doing the transforming of

write-ups into site-comprehensible language and formats, leaving time and space to incorporate the results of the exercise into one's final write-up—it probably won't happen. Once again, there will be too many competing claims on your time.

(2) Think carefully about displays. As with analysis, matrices and figures work much better than text alone to help local site informants access the information. Better still, people will find it easier to get an overview, to see how the pieces fit together.

(3) Providing information at more macroanalytical levels of inference (such as main factors and relationships, plus causal determinants) has to be done very carefully, by working up from particulars. If this isn't done, informants may discount the whole exercise because the overarching findings look wrongheaded or incomprehensible. Or they may swallow these macro findings whole, because they read so "scientifically." As the symbolic interactionists have shown convincingly (see Blumer, 1962), people don't act toward social structures or institutions or roles; they act toward *situations*, and are likely to understand meta-situational language only to the extent that it is directly connected to these situations.

Still, as we have remarked, people in sites *do* make maps of their reality.[14] Those maps may not coincide with the researcher's, but if we can cast our pictures, and feed them back, in an informant-friendly way, they can at the minimum be acknowledged. Beyond this, there is the possibility of mutual enlightenment.

(4) Counterpoint: Think very carefully before feeding back *any* specific incident. Will anyone's self-esteem, job chances, or standing in the organization be damaged by the report? (One of us once fed back first-draft site reports to people in five sites and was threatened with lawsuits in four of the five, because of specific incidents in the reports—even though the incidents were accurately reported.)

(5) Don't expect that informants will always agree with you or with one another. If they always did, life at the site would be more conflict-free than you probably found it to be. People have wildly varying perceptions of the same phenomenon—popularized in the so-called Rashomon effect. One should be aware that there are several reasons informants might reject the conclusions or interpretations a field researcher submits to them. Guba and Lincoln (1981, pp. 110-111) have reviewed them succinctly and well. To recapitulate:

- The informant is not familiar with the information.
- The informant doesn't understand it (jargon, lack of sophistication or awareness).
- The informant thinks the report is biased.
- The information conflicts with the informant's basic values, beliefs or self-image.
- The information is in conflict with the informant's self-interest.
- This is not the way the informant construes or puts together the same information.

General implication: The occasion of data feedback is an occasion to learn more about the *site*, not only about your feedback.

VII.C DOCUMENTATION AND AUDITING

The Problem

Most journals require authors of empirical studies to report on their procedures as an integral part of the article. The formats are often so familiar that the author can almost fill in the blanks when writing sections on sample, methods, and data analysis.

These conventions serve two purposes. First, they are a *verification* device the reader can use to track the procedures used to arrive at the findings. Second, the reporting procedures furnish details that *secondary analysts* can use to double-check the findings using other analytic techniques, to integrate these findings into another study, or to synthesize several studies on the same topic. Such secondary analyses depend upon the author's reporting such basic details as means, standard deviations, error terms, derived scores and scales, marginals, and various validity and reliability coefficients.

There is, in other words, a *technology* for reporting on empirical research and a corresponding technology for verifying the report. But these tools seem confined to statistical studies. Most qualitative researchers are uncomfortable in the reporting straitjacket we have described, but they don't have an alternative to fall back on. There is no corresponding technology for qualitative studies. Lofland (1974, p. 101) says it well:

> Qualitative field research seems distinct in the degree to which its practitioners lack a public, shared and codified conception of how what they do is done and how what they report should be formulated.

On the face of it, this is a curious state of affairs. One of the strengths of qualitative research is precisely its capacity to *describe* in detail the empirical phenomena under study. Qualitative studies are rich in descriptions of settings, people, events, and processes, but they usually say little about *how* the researcher got the information, and almost nothing about *how* conclusions were drawn.

The problem, of course, is that we can't verify or do secondary analysis of a study in which procedures are so opaque. We are left with vague criteria: the "plausibility," the "coherence," or the "compelling-ness" of the study—all evocative but ultimately hollow terms. The researcher can *always* provide a plausible account and, with a careful editing, may assure its coherence. If the writing is good, we will be won over by the undeniability and vividness of the report. But, as we saw earlier, plausible and coherent accounts can be terribly biased, and vividness lands us in the "avail-ability" heuristic, whereby we overweight concrete or dramatic data.[15]

So we have the unappealing double bind whereby qualitative studies can't be verified because researchers don't report on their methodology, and they don't report on their methodology because there are no established canons or conventions for doing so. (There may be other reasons as well—for instance, the implicit assumption that a qualitative study is such a person-specific, artistic, or phenomenal act that no one else can viably verify or replicate it—but that takes us too far afield, out of science altogether.) How then to break out of this dilemma?

If an area of study has no clear boundaries or parameters, one customarily begins by *describing* that universe. This, in fact, is precisely why qualitative research is heavily descriptive. As Brandt (1974) has noted, we don't know which variables are particularly significant in natural settings until we have detailed descriptions of their characteristics and influences. Without such descriptive information, the wrong prob-lems are selected for study, inappropriate hypotheses are tested, and erroneous inferences are made.

The same logic can be applied to qualitative *methodology*. We can't—and shouldn't—get too far into methodological canons until we know what quali-tative researchers are *doing* when they do qualitative research. As Mills (1959) noted many years ago:

> Only by conversations in which experienced thinkers exchange information about their actual ways of working can a useful sense of method and theory be imparted.

We need to know many things in these conversa-tions. Which kinds of qualitative designs do researchers actually use? How are sampling decisions actually made? What does the instrumentation look like, and how does the researcher know whether it is measuring accurately what it was meant to measure? More funda-mentally, how does the researcher get from hundreds of pages of field notes to a final report? How are the data aggregated, reduced, partitioned, analyzed, interpreted? Until we can share clear descriptions of qualitative research procedures,[16] we can't even talk about them intelligibly with one another—let alone set up conventions for verification.

Outline of a Solution

One has to begin, then, by describing one's pro-cedures clearly enough so that others can reconstruct them and, further down the line, corroborate them and do secondary analysis. Guba (1981) and Guba and Lincoln (1981) have provided a good orienting map for doing this. They take the metaphor of the fiscal auditor who examines the books of a company to determine whether accounts have been kept satisfac-torily and whether the "bottom line" is correct. Making such an audit depends on the auditee's having documented income, outlays, and transfers. As Guba puts it, there has to be an "audit trail." Without the trail, one cannot determine the dependability or the confir-mability of the bookkeeping.

Another researcher should be able to follow the audit trail and verify the accuracy and legitimacy of the procedures used to establish the researcher's finding. Guba and Lincoln are not very specific on what an audit trail looks like or on how the auditor actually proceeds. They suggest generally that researchers document procedures with samples of interview notes or observations, and that researchers keep a sort of ongoing diary or log. Fortunately, Halpern (1983) has succeeded very well in operationalizing these ideas into specific and auditing procedures, and shows a case study.

Illustration

Over the past three years, we have developed seven successive versions of a documentation form for use by qualitative researchers. We used it, in fact, to get a better fix on the methods outlined in this book. It was only by scrupulously recording how we went about working with nonnumeric data that we could gauge the dependability of our procedures and, at the same time, pass them on to others (Huberman & Miles, 1983a). The challenge here, of course, is to come up with a documentation form that meets several criteria: facility and rapidity of use, easy transfer into a methodological report, easy access and comprehen-sion by a second reader, and believability/validity. There are some clear trade-offs—for example, com-prehension and believability usually mean the form cannot be tossed off rapidly, but requires some time and care.

We show here (Chart 43) version VII of our form, a streamlined version of some earlier elaborate efforts. Naturally, we encourage others to experiment with this form, revising it as they go. The nature of good documentation—and good auditing—is something we will have to discover inductively.

First of all, note that the form covers only procedures used to *analyze* data; another form is needed to cover

Chart 43
Qualitative Analysis Documentation Form

QUALITATIVE ANALYSIS DOCUMENTATION FORM

M.B.Miles, A.M.Huberman   Version VII
NIE G-81-0018   3/83

Analyst _____   Date _____   FORM NO. _____

1. Research issue being explored: _____

2. In this analysis task, what, specifically, were you aiming to do? (Give context and a short rationale; say whether focus is exploratory or confirmatory; make the connection with earlier analyses.)

3. Description of procedures. Work sequentially, keeping a log or diary of steps as you go through the analysis. Use a second sheet if needed. If the analysis task changes substantially, use a new form, redoing items 1 and 2 above.

SPECIFIC DATA SETS IN USE*	PROCEDURAL STEPS (number each one, explain what was done, and exactly how it was done) @	DECISION RULES# followed during analysis operations	ANALYSIS OPERATIONS (enter codes) Readying data Drawing Confirming for analysis conclusions conclusions		CONCLUSIONS DRAWN from these specific analysis operations; give substance in brief.	RESEARCHER COMMENTS, reflections, remarks on any of the preceding.

*Indicate whether single or multi-site. May include: field notes; write-ups; summaries;documents; figures; matrices; tables;tape recordings; photos; film/videotapes; others (specify).

Explicit list of actual rules used for "readying" data (clustering, sorting, scaling, etc.); may also apply to drawing/confirming conclusions.

@ PROVIDE ALL RELEVANT EXHIBITS; give each a letter, describe briefly, and also give numbers of procedural steps where used.
    Work notes/work sheets: _____
    Interim data displays: _____
    Final data displays: _____
    Final text written(excerpts): _____

sampling, instrumentation, and data collection. The form is focused on a single research question or issue (item 1). Item 2 asks the researcher to explain, generally, what the analysis was designed to do, and to situate it in the context of other analyses. Item 3 then calls for a fairly complete description (written as a log or diary during analysis), including the *data sets* in which the analysis was conducted, the *procedural steps*, the *decision rules* used to manage data, the *analysis operations* involved, the preliminary *conclusions* to which the analysis led, and any concluding *comments*. All this information goes on a single sheet, so that the analyst can log in the successive analytical steps and a reviewer can quickly grasp what was done.

The researcher appends all relevant *exhibits* (materials used or developed in the course of analysis), so the reviewer can look at them and determine whether the procedures, decision rules, and conclusions are congruent with the data in use.

Let's walk through the form, explaining and commenting on its use. Items 1 and 2 help orient an auditor to the analysis enterprise. It is important to take *one* analysis task per form. Of course a string of procedures will be involved, but if the general task changes (for example, from summarizing the general nature of the data to defining a precise set of predictors), a new form should be used.

The *data sets* should be clearly enough described so that an auditor can find them in your files. Some, of course may appear as *exhibits* (see below).

It is essential to fill out the section on *procedural steps* as you go; much gets lost in recollection. Use practical, nonformalistic terms. Here are some examples:

- Reviewed preliminary matrix format, entered data from 2 sites.
- Tried a cross-tabulation of program type by ease of implementation; abandoned after several entries.
- Reviewed meta-matrix, decided to lump Lido site with Astoria and Carson.
- Went through causal network, reviewing links, adding and subtracting links to make final version.
- Scanned Chart 38d and Box V.B.b, comparing high- and low-assistance sites.
- Wrote text based on preceding step.

Noting the exact *decision rules* used is important, especially for any operations involved in "readying" data for entry into diplays or the like. Making them explicit as you go is very useful; it reduces error and can aid self-correction. Here are some examples:

- Theme was coded as present for an informant if mentioned repeatedly or with strong affect during the interview.
- Item entered in display if mentioned by more than 1 informant at sites with more than 3 informants; at sites with fewer users, entered if mentioned by 1 informant with no contradiction from others.
- "Smoothness of use" was a fieldworker judgment drawn from the interview responses and/or from observation of the practice in use; more weight given to observation data.
- If judgments of value of assistance sources varied in strength, the final rating gave more weight to the source closer to the user (for example, assistance from principal, materials, peers had more weight than assistance from external consultants).
- Rating of ± given when implementation smooth for some users, rough for others. Otherwise, ratings followed *modal* response.
- "Immediate causes" of the outcome were defined as two steps or less back along the causal network. "Distal causes" were on the causal stream leading to the outcome, but further back. "Other" variables were off the stream, or not on the network.
- A "strong" predictor had to be present in the majority of high-assistance sites, and absent in at least 40% of low-assistance sites.
- Cutting point between "high" and "moderate" sites made when half or less of the indicators were absent.
- When contradictory data given on adoption date, gave more weight to those informants on site from the beginning, and who were actively involved.

Making decision rules explicit is most critical for data-readying operations, but may also be important for conclusion drawing and confirmation as well. A reader will usually want to know *how* and *why* you concluded that variable A was a stronger predictor than variable B of the outcome, and how you verified or confirmed that conclusion.

For tracking *analysis operations*, we have provided a code list (Chart 44). Scanning the list will serve as a kind of prompt for the analyst, both helping to label the operations followed, and suggesting other avenues that might be followed. Note that though we have clustered the codes for convenience into three general categories, many of them may fall into any of the three categories. For example, COH (conceptual and theoretical coherence), though it appears under "drawing conclusions," can also be used to confirm or test conclusions. Or SUB (subsuming data under a higher-level variable) can be seen as readying data for analysis or as a way of drawing conclusions.

Note that many of the items, along with the logic underlying their use, come from chapters in this book. We have the problem here of deciding just how we will talk about qualitative analysis procedures when documenting them. Since there is no common language, and there are a variety of partial dialects from different disciplines, we tried to find items that will have meaning to most researchers. Note that there is some borrowing from statistical terminology, and some adaptation from the terminology of analytic induction.[17]

Chart 44
Code List for Analysis Operations

Readying data for analysis

TAB	tabulating coded segments
MAT	filling in matrices
CLAS	classifying, categorizing
RANK	ranking/weighting data
SUMM	summarizing phrases, generating key words
SUB	subsuming data under higher-level variable
SCAL	scaling, summing indices
COMP	computing, tabulating
SPLT	splitting one variable into two
PAR	partitioning
AGG	aggregating

Drawing conclusions

PLAUS	seeing "plausibility" only
MET	generating metaphors
GES	seeing a Gestalt
COUNT	counting/frequencies
CEN	establishing central tendencies
VAR	establishing variance, differences (contrasts, comparisons)
CLUS	clustering
FAC	establishing factors
REL	establishing relationships between variables/sets of variables
LOG	logical chain of evidence
INTV	establishing intervening/linking conditions
COH	conceptual/theoretical coherence
CAUSE	determining directional influence
TEMP	determining temporal order/temporal relationships

INF	making inferences
INF-COMP	by computations
INF-DED	by deduction
INF-IND	by induction (e.g., determining antecedents, covariates, consequences)

Confirming conclusions

REPR	checking for representativeness
RES-EFF	checking for researcher effects
BIAS-CONTR	control for bias (specify)
TRI	triangulation
TRI-DATA	from different data sources
TRI-METH	from different methods
TRI-CONC	conceptually (different theories)
TRI-RES	from different researchers
CONT	systematic contrasts/comparisons
OUT	use of outliers, exceptions
EXTR-SIT	extreme situation verification
EXTR-BIAS	extreme bias verification
WT	weighting of evidence
EMP	empirical evidence from elsewhere
FALSE-REL	checking false relation due to third variable
RIV	test of rival explanation
NONEG	absence of negative evidence
REPL	replication
FB	corroboration from informant feedback

It probably doesn't matter much *which* terminology we use to generate a common, agreed-upon language for describing qualitative research procedures; we need one badly enough that we should begin with an imperfect one and clean it up collectively.

Note, finally, that certain terms are *missing*. There are no items for noting "insights," "bracketing," "structural corroboration," "disciplined subjectivity," or even "constant comparisons." This is because it isn't clear what, operationally, these terms mean—how they are procedurally *done*. We suspect that the labels we have given to items on the list contain the building blocks of these approaches and of many others.

The next to last column of the form asks for the researcher's substantive *conclusions* in capsule form; they do not need to be detailed, and reference can be made to the final text in which they appear (see below).

In the last column, the researcher is free to reflect, make remarks, comment on confidence in the conclusion, or vent any feelings that are relevant. Such asides help clarify the meaning of the analysis episodes being reported.

We repeatedly found that supplying all available *exhibits* was crucial for an auditor. It is simply impossible to understand analysis procedures followed without direct recourse to such exhibits. The final *text* is especially important—it's the end of the audit trail.

Advice

(a) It's hard to know how detailed documentation should be until you try it. Our usual experience was that any given major research question usually involved a flow of seven or eight analysis *episodes*, each lasting from one to four hours: *one sheet per episode.*

(2) Work usually goes faster with a two-step procedure. First, while actually conducting the analysis, the researcher logs in the procedural steps, decision rules, and conclusions, giving enough detail to be clear, and assembles the exhibits (tables, work sheets, text, and so on).

Then, when the analysis is complete, the researcher reviews the raw material, cleaning it up where needed and adding analysis codes, and then fills out the more reflective part. It's *not* a good idea to do a thorough *reflection* on your analysis while *doing* the analysis. You need all the energy you can spare for the analysis itself.

The log is crucial. The dictum is this: If it isn't on the documentation form or your original worksheets, you didn't do it. Avoid "laundering" or retrospective "enlightenment." Do not let incomplete documentation forms pile up. Complete them as you go.

(3) Use the lists as cues for procedures or techniques you *aren't* using but could use. This will turn up automatically as you notice yourself using the same codes frequently; it probably means that you are relying too heavily on too few devices.

Time Required

Documenting your steps methodically adds time to analysis itself. Sometimes it's fun and very helpful; sometimes it isn't. Still, we think it is an indispensable operation that will become, sooner or later, a requirement for published qualitative research.

Our experience with later versions of our form varied widely depending on complexity of the analyses being carried out. Generally speaking, for an analysis that occupies two hours, using Form VII, you can expect to spend 10 minutes or so doing concurrent logging, and another 15-20 minutes in refining, coding, and reflecting on the experience. For a longer analysis task (say, 4-5 hours) logging will take 20 minutes or so, and coding/reflection 30-40 minutes. Thus documentation at the level we have been trying can be expected to require something like 20 percent of total analysis time, given the current state of the art. Notice that documentation is not a separate, onerous task carried out for "someone else," but a method of improving the immediate analysis task as it's carried out, advancing the sophistication of later analyses, *and* deepening the confidence one has in final conclusions. So, though it may be possible to reduce documentation time incrementally with further experience, that 20 percent is a good investment in research quality.

Computerized methods, as Conrad and Reinharz (1984) note, show special promise, since the analytic steps and procedures used can be easily recorded, displayed, and shared with other researchers.

Doing a careful audit of an analysis using the form and exhibits can be expected to occupy 40-50 percent as much time as the original analysis. Corollary: Auditing should happen *selectively*, early in a study's analysis work, and on items about which there is reason to be especially careful.

NOTES

1. For some epistemologists, there is no antithesis between qualities and quantities. Kaplan (1964) argues that quantities are *of* qualities, and that a measured quality *has* just the magnitude expressed in its measure. Hook (1953) claims that qualitative *changes* are the cumulative result of variations in quantities. Beyond a certain limit of quantitative change, there is a transformation from differences of *degree* to differences in *kind*—as in changes of weather, emotions, structures, relationships, and the like. This is the so-called third law of dialectics and it is worth considering before we dismiss the arithmetic of qualitative analysis.

2. It is worth recalling that "mainstream" qualitative researchers resort routinely to frequency counts for verifying hypotheses. In symbolic interactionism, this is known as "behavioral validity" (Denzin, 1978, pp. 22-24). The researcher observes whether a social phenomenon appears in an actor's behavioral repertoire and, if so, at which frequency, in which situations, at which times. The greater the frequency of appearance across times and situations, the greater the behavioral validity.

3. See McCall's (1969) "data quality control index," a counting procedure used by anthropologists to control biases stemming from premature conclusion-drawing.

4. The traditional philosophical position here notes the supposedly insoluble "paradox of categorization" (Scheffler, 1967): "Observation contaminated by thought yields circular tests; observation uncontaminated by thought yields no tests at all." In spite of this, categories *do* happen, practically speaking, in the interaction between someone thinking and a set of data. Each influences the other.

5. See Sadler (1981) for a thoughtful, empirically based discussion of thirteen "information-processing limitations"; they include problems such as data overload, persistence of first impressions, inattention to unreliability in data, and overweighting of novel information. A practical checklist could easily be constructed from the article to guide analysis activities.

6. See also the "inventory of biases" assembled by Martinko and Gardner (1983); the fifteen types range from "evaluation of behavior" to "enhancement of contrast" and "mind-reading."

7. For a more detailed and comprehensive treatment of safeguards against self-delusion, see Becker et al. (1961).

8. For a good discussion of researcher effects on the site, see Schwartz and Schwartz (1955).

9. Douglas (1976) has something of an obsession with this issue, but he has astutely catalogued and dissected the various evasions, lies, and fronts visited on researchers by informants (see especially pp. 55-82). He has, in this connection, a marvelous quote from John Leonard: "It took me a long time to discover that the key thing in acting is honesty. Once you know how to fake that, you've got it made" (p. 55).

10. Writer Joan Didion once noted: "I am so small, so neurotic, and so inoffensive that people invariably forget an important point: The writer will *do you in*."

11. If they *do* contradict it, and you have only two measures, you are stuck with a deeper question: Which do you believe? On this topic, one of us wrote:

> The rhetoric of triangulation, a term drawn from the field of surveying, implies that three elements of a triangle are known. . . . Where there are two data points, all we have is a

measure of agreement or disagreement. . . . Real triangulation requires additional information, which may be data from an actual third source (one whose position relative to the two other sources is known); a more general theoretical explanation that subsumes the apparent disagreement; or information about the trustworthiness of the two sources drawn from other data (the assistant superintendent is known to be a liar; the survey item is unreliable, and so on). (Miles, 1982)

12. See also Van Maanen's (1979) discussion of the differences between "operational" (observed) data, and "presentational" data, which involve respondents' efforts to maintain or enhance *appearances*. He also notes two other sources of data invalidity: Respondent *ignorance* and taken-for-granted *assumptions*.

13. We should remember that explanations are not loose bundles of particular facts, but interrelated mental *constructions* that hold the particulars together. When people register or comprehend a bit of information, they automatically include its *causes*, not just its particulars (Sherman & Titus, 1982). We think in terms of connected explanations. Undoing a thought (or a fact) means unbundling the whole causal stream of reasoning to which it belongs. So a few contrary facts can threaten the whole system, which is why we are loath to notice them—as laypeople *or* as social scientists—and why we are usually unaware that we *are* blocking them out.

14. Precisely *how* map making happens, and what it implies when we try to determine how people make sense of their social environments are two of the key constructs in ethnomethodology. See Garfinkel's (1967) discussion of "reflexivity."

15. It is sometimes argued that certain consumers of research—such as policymakers, managers, and the general public—are uninterested in "verifying" the methods used in qualitative research. It is more nearly accurate to say that they are *less* interested. But even such audiences raise such questions as "Who did you talk to anyway?" "How do you *know*?" "Where'd you get *that* recommendation?" Methodological reporting is still needed to assure nonresearcher audiences of the strength of the conclusions reached.

16. Such descriptions need not be highly codified to be useful. See the well-done case accounts in Hammond's *Sociologists at Work* (1964), the methodological report by Lee et al. (1981), the five-case comparison by Firestone and Herriott (1983), and the reports of analysis episodes in Huberman and Miles (1983a).

17. To suggest that there are qualitative analogues to statistical procedures (such as covariation, clustering, partitioning) does *not* mean that we use precisely the same *procedures*. But the goal is the same. (Some qualitative researchers have, though, recommended explicitly that the logical structure of quantitative procedures be used to orient qualitative analysis. See Becker, 1958.) In the same vein, analytic induction is a good analogue for the kind of sifting and interpretive work one does in the field, but we needn't replicate precisely the same procedures or the same theorems.

VIII
Concluding Remarks

REFLECTIONS

Writing this book has naturally confirmed the old saw that teaching something deepens your understanding of it. The process of clarifying and formulating the ideas in this book has extended our grasp of qualitative data analysis methods a good deal. We have tried to share our learnings along the way in the form of specific advice; later in this section we will add some general suggestions.

Throughout the book, we have tried to stay practical, close to the reader's elbow, talking aloud as we went, offering both variations and advice. Many methodological texts are heavy on theory, with bland examples that always seem to work out clearly, even effortlessly. Yet when one actually comes to grips with collecting and analyzing real-life data, things seldom work out that way. Research-in-use is almost always more intractable, disjointed, and perverse than research-in-theory, and we have tried to take careful account of that fact.

One clear implication is that methodological quagmires, mazes, and dead ends are not necessarily a product of researcher incapacity, but of social science data themselves. Like the phenomena they mirror, they are usually complex, ambiguous, sometimes downright contradictory. Doing qualitative analysis means living for as long as possible with that complexity and ambiguity, coming to terms with it, and ultimately passing it on to the reader in a form that clarifies and deepens. Small wonder, then, that the mechanics of analysis seem formidable or elusive, and that most qualitative researchers have shied away from making them explicit.

We have found, paradoxically, that making the steps of analysis explicit makes them *less* formidable—makes them manageable. One doesn't need prolonged socialization or arcane technologies. The core requisites for qualitative analysis seem to be a little creativity, systematic doggedness, some good conceptual sensibilities, and cognitive flexibility—the capacity to undo rapidly one's way of construing or transforming the data, and to try another, more promising tack. None of these qualities is contingent on a

battery of advanced "methods courses." In doing this book, we have had the recurrent impression of creating a self-help book for researchers, rather than that of coining a new, only remotely accessible set of methods. That is, we think, a hopeful sign.

We are aware that our approach will enrage some people and delight others. We have advocated measures that amount to goring the oxen of some traditionalists and of some latecomers to the scene. To those who feel that analysis is an intuitive, nearly incommunicable act, we have insisted that analyses can be workably replicated, and that to be taken seriously one should be fully explicit about what is being done each step of the way. To those who feel that serious explanation must involve converting words into numbers and manipulating the numbers according to conventional statistical canons, we have said that there are better, more powerful methods of data analysis that illuminate the web of local causality. To those enamored of long narrative accounts full of "thick description," we have counterposed the idea of compressed, focused displays that permit systematic analysis. To those of all stripes who believe that qualitative data analysis requires years of training and apprenticeship, we have offered a sampling of commonsensical but rigorous techniques that can be quickly mastered—and developed further in the service of a stronger methodology.

To those colleagues who feel pleased with what we have done, for whatever reason, we express our cautious pleasure—along with a strong plea for skeptical testing and revision of the methods we have outlined here. In no other way can the field advance.

ADVICE

Throughout the book, we have provided detailed advice on a method-by-method basis. Here we offer some generalized last words of encouragement to our colleagues, of whatever persuasion.

"Think display." Given a research question or a puzzling issue in a qualitative data base, consider what forms of display are most likely to bring relevant data

together in a way that will permit good conclusion drawing.

Be open to invention. The range of useful displays we were able to create in a short time was quite wide; the displays others have created reinforce our belief that the universe of useful displays is very large and, like other universes, is constantly expanding.

Expect iteration. The mode of analysis we have advocated throughout the book involves shuttling between data reduction, display, and preliminary and verified conclusions. New data enter the picture, new display forms evolve, conclusions get bent and revised. All of these will have back effects on each other, effects that are crucial to the evolving analysis.

Seek formalization, and distrust it. We have steadily emphasized a structured approach to understanding meaning in qualitative data. Becoming more systematic—*not* more positivistic, we should emphasize—strikes us as a priority for those who wish to advance analysis methodology. At the same time, however, increased formalization carries its own risks: narrowness, overconfidence, obsessiveness, blindness to the emergent—and the risk of orthodoxy. The field does *not* need a narrow set of canons that will strike fear into the hearts of graduate students and inspire endless casuistry and disputation.

Stay self-aware. Our own experience showed us vividly how useful it is to maintain a part of one's attention on the *processes* involved in analysis—from the selection of research questions through the creation of displays, data entry, conclusion drawing, and verification. Only through such sustained awareness can regular self-correction occur—not just during specific analysis episodes, but over time, as the methods themselves iterate and develop. We have suggested supports for self-awareness in the form of documentation logs and "friendly stranger" colleagues who can counter one's taken-for-granted approaches and suggest alternatives.

Share methodological learnings. The methodological sections of most reports of qualitative studies are thin. Methodological articles on analysis issues and approaches are all too rare. We believe that anyone who wants to advance the craft of qualitative analysis owes it to colleagues to communicate what has been learned to others. We advise stronger methodological emphasis in articles and books drawn from qualitative data, and encourage reports of training methods in courses and workshops that have successfully expanded analysis skills. We urge much parallel and divergent effort, in order to develop gradually a stronger, clearer consensus on how to draw valid conclusions from qualitative data.

In sum, we hope that more and more qualitative researchers will tell each other, concretely and specifically, just how they went about it, and what they learned. Perhaps we can all be as vivid and rich in describing our own work as we are in describing the inner and outer lives of the people we are studying. We owe them, and ourselves, at least that much.

References

Adams, R., & Preiss, J. (Eds.). (1960). *Human organization research.* Homewood, IL: Dorsey.

Asher, H. B. (1976). *Causal modeling* (2nd ed.). Beverly Hills, CA: Sage.

Axelrod, R. (Ed.). (1976). *Structure of decision: The cognitive maps of political elites.* Princeton, NJ: Princeton University Press.

Bailey, K. D. (1982). *Methods of social research* (2nd ed.). New York: Free Press.

Becker, H. S. (1958). Problems of inference and proof in participant observation. *American Sociological Review, 23,* 652-660.

Becker, H. S. (1970). *Sociological work.* Chicago: Aldine.

Becker, H. S. (1978). Do photographs tell the truth? *After Image, 5,* 9-13.

Becker, H. S., Geer, B., Hughes, E. C., & Strauss, A. L. (1961). *Boys in white.* Chicago: University of Chicago Press.

Becker, H. S., Gordon, A. C., & LeBailly, R. K. (1984). Field work with the computer: Criteria for assessing systems. *Qualitative Sociology, 7*(1-2).

Berelson, B. (1971) *Content analysis in communication research.* New York: Hafner.

Blalock, H. M. (1964). *Causal inferences in nonexperimental research.* Chapel Hill: University of North Carolina Press.

Blalock, H. M. (1971). *Causal models in the social sciences.* Chicago: Aldine.

Blumer, H. (1962). Society as symbolic interaction. In A. Rose (Ed.), *Human behavior and social processes* (chap. 9). Boston: Houghton Mifflin.

Blumer, H. (1969). *Symbolic interactionism: Perspective and method.* Englewood Cliffs, NJ: Prentice-Hall.

Bogdan, R. C., & Biklen, S. K. (1982). *Qualitative research in education.* Boston: Allyn & Bacon.

Bogdan, R., & Taylor, S. J. (1975). *Introduction to qualitative research methods.* New York: John Wiley.

Bolton, R. (1982). *We all do it but how? A survey of contemporary field note procedure.* Claremont, CA: Pomona College.

Brandt, R. (1974). *Studying behavior in natural settings.* New York: Holt, Rinehart & Winston.

Bronfenbrenner, U. (1976). The experimental ecology of education. *Teachers' College Record, 78*(2), 157-178.

Bruyn, S. (1966). *Human perspective in sociology.* Englewood Cliffs, NJ: Prentice-Hall.

Bulmer, M. (1979). Concepts in the analysis of qualitative data. *Sociological Review, 27*(4), 651-677.

Campbell, D. T. (1975). Degrees of freedom and the case study. *Comparative Political Studies, 8,* 178-193.

Conrad, P., & Reinharz, S. (1984). Computers and qualitative data. *Qualitative Sociology, 7*(1-2).

Cook, T. D., & Campbell, D. T. (1979). *Quasi-experimentation: Design and analysis issues for field settings.* Chicago: Rand McNally.

Cook, T. D., & Reichardt, C. S. (1979). *Qualitative and quantitative methods in evaluation research.* Beverly Hills, CA: Sage.

Crandall, D. P., & Associates. (1983). *People, policies and practices: Examining the chain of school improvement* (Vols. I-X). Andover, MA: The Network, Inc.

Crane, J. G., & Angrosino, M. V. (1974). *Field projects in anthropology: A student handbook.* Morristown, NJ: General Learning.

Cressey, D. R. (1953). *Other people's money: A study in the social psychology of embezzlement.* New York: Free Press.

Cronbach, L. (1975). Beyond the two disciplines of scientific psychology. *American Psychologist, 30,* 116-127.

Davis, F. (1959). the cabdriver and his fare: Facets of a fleeting relationship. *American Journal of Sociology, 65,* 158-165.

Dawes, R. (1971). A case study of graduate admissions: Applications of three principles of human decision-making. *American Psychologist, 26,* 180-188.

Dawson, J. A. (1979). *Validity in qualitative inquiry.* Paper presented at the meeting of the American Educational Research Association.

Dawson, J. A. (1982). *Qualitative research findings: What do we do to improve and estimate their validity?* Paper presented at the meeting of the American Educational Research Association.

Dean, J., Eichorn, R., & Dean, L. (1967). Fruitful informants for intensive interviewing. In J. T. Doby (Ed.), *An introduction to social research.* New York: Meredith.

Degener, D. (Ed.). (1983). Improving school improvement: New study shows that most school improve under SIP. *Research and Educational Practice in the Far West,* February.

Denzin, N. K. (1978). *Sociological methods.* New York: McGraw-Hill.

Dobbert, M. L. (1982). *Ethnographic research: Theory and application for modern schools and societies.* New York: Praeger.

Douglas, J. (1976). *Investigative social research.* Beverly Hills, CA: Sage.

Dow, J. (1982, December). *The combined use of computers and audio tape recorders in storing, managing and using qualitative verbal ethnographic data.* Paper presented at the meeting of the American Anthropological Association.

Dreitzel, H. P. (1970). Introduction. In H. Dreitzel (Ed.), *Recent sociology* (Vol. 2). London: Macmillan.

Duncker, K. (1945). On problem-solving. *Psychological Monographs, 58*(5).

Eco, U. (1982). *Le nom de la rose.* Paris: Ed. Grasset.

Edwards, W. (1968). Conservatism in human information processing. In K. B. Kleinmuntz (Ed)., *Formal representation of human judgment.* New York: John Wiley.

Erickson, F., & Wilson, J. (1982). *Sights and sounds of life in schools: A resource guide to film and videotape for research and education.* East Lansing: Institute for Research on Teaching, College of Education, Michigan State University.

Faust, D. (1982). A needed component in prescriptions for science: Empirical knowledge of human cognitive limitations. *Knowledge, 3,* 555-570.

Filstead, J. (1970). *Qualitative methodology.* Chicago: Rand McNally.

Firestone, W. A., & Corbettt, H. D. (1979). *Rationality and cooperation in external assistance for school improvement: A preliminary report of the RBS experience.* Philadelphia: Research for Better Schools.

Firestone, W. A., & Corbett, H. D. (1981). Schools vs. linking agents as contributors to the change process. *Educational Evaluation and Policy Analysis, 3*(2), 5-18.

Firestone, W. A., & Herriott, R. E. (1983). The formalization of qualitative research: An adaptation of "soft" science to the policy world. *Evaluation Review, 7,* 437-466.

Fornell, C. (Ed.). (1982). *A second generation of multivariate analysis.* New York: Praeger.

Forrester, J. (1973). *Principles of systems.* Cambridge, MA: Wright-Allen.

Freeman, D. (1983). *Margaret Mead and Samoa: The making and unmaking of an anthropological myth.* Cambridge, MA: Harvard University Press.

Fullan, M. (1982). *The meaning of educational change.* Toronto: OISE Press, and New York: Teachers College Press.

Garfinkel, A. (1981). *Forms of explanation: Rethinking the questions in social theory.* New Haven, CT: Yale University Press.

Garfinkel, H. (1967). *Studies in ethnomethodology.* Englewood Cliffs, NJ: Prentice-Hall.

Gaynor, A. K. (1980). *A dynamic model of mathematics curriculum change in an urban elementary school.* Paper presented at the meeting of the American Education Research Association.

Geertz, C. (1973). Thick description: Toward an interpretive theory of culture. In C. Geertz, *The interpretation of cultures.* New York: Basic Books.

Geertz, C. (1983). *Local knowledge: Further essays in interpretive anthropology.* New York: Basic Books.

Glaser, B. (1978). *Theoretical sensitivity.* Mill Valley, CA: Sociology Press.

Glaser, B., & Strauss, A. L. (1967). *The discovery of grounded theory: Strategies for qualitative research.* Chicago: Aldine.

Glaser, B., & Strauss, A. L. (1970). Discovery of substantive theory: A basic strategy underlying qualitative research. In W. Filstead (Ed.), *Qualitative methodology* (pp. 288-297). Chicago: Rand McNally.

Goetz, J. P., & LeCompte, M. D. (1981). Ethnographic research and the problem of data reduction. *Anthropology and Education Quarterly, 12,* 51-70.

Goffman, E. (1959). *The presentation of self in everyday life.* Garden City, NY: Doubleday.

Goldberg, L. (1970). Man versus model of man: A rationale, plus some evidence, for a method of improving on clinical inferences. *Psychological Bulletin, 73*(4), 422-432.

Guba, E. G. (1981). Criteria for assessing the trustworthiness of naturalistic inquiries. *Educational Communication and Technology Journal, 29,* 75-92.

Guba, E. G., & Lincoln, Y. S. (1981). *Effective evaluation.* San Francisco: Jossey-Bass.

Hage, J. (1972). *Techniques and problems of theory construction in sociology.* New York: John Wiley.

Halpern, E. S. (1983). *Auditing naturalistic inquiries: Some preliminary applications. Part 1: Development of the process. Part 2: Case study application.* Paper presented at the meeting of the American Educational Research Association.

Hammond, P. E. (Ed.). (1964). *Sociologists at work.* New York: Basic Books.

Hanson, N. (1958). *Patterns of discovery.* Cambridge: Cambridge University Press.

Havelock, R. G., Cox, P., Huberman, A. M., & Levinson, N. (1983). *School-university collaboration supporting school improvement* (Vol. 4). Washington, DC: American University, Knowledge Transfer Institute.

Heck, S., Stiegelbauer, S. M., Hall, G. E., & Loucks, S. F. (1981). *Measuring innovation configurations: Procedures and application.* Austin: University of Texas, R&D Center for Teacher Education.

Heider, F. (1944). Social perception and phenomenal causality. *Psychological Review, 51,* 358-373.

Herriott, R. E., & Firestone, W. A. (1983). Multisite qualitative policy research: Optimizing description and generalizability. *Educational Researcher, 12*(2), 14-19.

Holsti, O. R. (1968). Content analysis. In G. Lindzey & E. Aronson (Eds.) *Handbook of social psychology: Vol. 2. Research Methods* (2nd ed; pp. 596-692). Reading, MA: Addison-Wesley.

Holsti, O. R. (1969). *Content analysis for the social sciences and the humanities.* Reading, MA: Addison-Wesley.

Hook, S. (1953) Dialectics in science in history. In H. Feigl & M. Brodbeck (Eds.), *Readings in the philosophy of science.* New York: Appleton.

Huberman, A. M. (1978). *Evaluation of three objectives of an experimental primary school: Summary of outcomes.* Bern: Swiss Scientific Research Council.

Huberman, A. M. (1980). *A further replication study of autonomous and dependent behavior in unstructured learning environments.* Geneva: Faculty of Psychology and Education, University of Geneva.

Huberman, A. M. (1981a). Splendeurs, misères et promesses de la recherche qualitative. *Education et Recherche, 3*(3), 233-249.

Huberman, A. M. (1981b). *School-university collaboration supporting school improvement: Vol. 1. The midwestern state case.* Washington, DC: American University, Knowledge Transfer Institute.

Huberman, A. M., & Miles, M. B. (1983a). Drawing valid meaning from qualitative data: Some techniques of data reduction and display. *Quality and Quantity, 17,* 281-339.

Huberman, A. M., & Miles, M. B. (1983b). *Innovation up close: A field study in 12 school settings.* Andover, MA: The Network, Inc.

Huberman, A. M., & Miles, M. B. (1984). *Innovation up close: How school improvement works.* New York: Plenum.

Huck, S. W., & Sandler, H. M. (1979). *Rival hypotheses: "Minute mysteries" for the critical thinker.* London: Harper & Row.

James, L. R., Mulaik, S. A., & Brett, J. M. (1982). *Causal analysis: Assumptions, models, and data.* Beverly Hills, CA: Sage.

Jick, T. D. (1979). Mixing qualitative and quantative methods: Triangulation in action. *Administrative Science Quarterly, 24,* 602-611.

Johnson, M. (Ed.). (1981). *Philosophical perspectives on metaphor.* Minneapolis: University of Minnesota Press.

Kahneman, D., & Tversky, A. (1972). Subjective probability: A judgment of representativeness. *Cognitive Psychology, 3,* 430-454.

Kaplan, A. (1964). *The conduct of inquiry.* Scranton, PA: Chandler.

Kelley, H. (1967). Attribution theory in social psychology. In D. Levine (Ed.), *Nebraska Symposium on Motivation* (Vol. 15). Lincoln: University of Nebraska Press.

Kelley, H. (1972). Causal schemata and the attribution process. In E. E. Jones et al. (Eds.), *Attribution: Perceiving the causes of behavior.* Morristown, NJ: General Learning Press.

Kelley, H. (1973). The process of causal attribution. *American Psychologist, 28,* 107-128.

Kidder, L. H. (1981). *Selltiz, Wrightsman & Cook's research methods in social relations* (4th ed.). New York: Holt, Rinehart & Winston.

Korzybski, A. H. (1933). *Science and sanity.* Clinton, CT: Colonial.

Krippendorff, K. (1980a). Clustering. In P. R. Monge & J. N. Capella (Eds.) *Multivariate techniques in human communication research* (pp. 259-308). New York: Academic.

Krippendorff, K. (1980b). *Content analysis: An introduction to its methodology.* Beverly Hills, CA: Sage.

Lakoff, G., & Johnson, M. (1980). *Metaphors we live by.* Chicago: University of Chicago Press.

Lazarsfeld, P. F., & Barton, A. H. (1972). Some principles of classification in social research. In P. F. Lazarsfeld (Ed.), *Qualitative analysis: Historical and critical essays.* Boston: Allyn & Bacon.

Lazarsfeld, P. F., Pasanella, A. K., & Rosenberg, M. (1972). *Continuities in the language of social research.* New York: Free Press.

LeCompte, M. D., & Goetz, J. P. (1982). Problems of reliability and validity in ethnographic research. *Review of Educational Research, 52:* 31-60.

LeCompte, M. D., & Goetz, J. P. (1983). *Playing with ideas: Analysis of qualitative data.* Paper presented at the meeting of the American Educational Research Association.

Lee, D., Kessling, W., & Melaragno, R. (Eds.). (1981). *Parents and federal education programs: Vol. 7. Methdologies employed in the study of parental involvement.* Santa Monica, CA: System Development Corporation.

Levine, H. G. (1982). *Data storage and retrieval systems for use in participant-observation research.* Paper presented at the meeting of the American Anthropological Association.

Lewis, O. (1963). *Life in a Mexican village: Tepoztlan revisited.* Urbana: University of Illinois Press.

Li, C. C. (1975). *Path analysis: A primer.* Pacific Grove, CA: Boxwood.

Lindesmith, A. (1947). *Opiate addiction.* Bloomington, IN: Principia.

Lindesmith, A. (1968). *Addiction and opiates.* Chicago: Aldine.

Lofland, J., (1971). *Analyzing social settings: A guide to qualitative observation and analysis.* Belmont, Ca: Wadsworth.

Lofland, J. (1974). Styles of reporting qualitative field research. *American Sociologist, 9,* 101-111.

Lortie, D. C. (1975). *School teacher: A sociological study.* Chicago: University of Chicago Press.

Loucks, S. F., Bauchner, J. E., Crandall, D. P., Schmidt, W. B., & Eiseman, J. W. (1983). *Setting the stage for a study of school improvement.* Andover, MA: The Network.

Louis, K. S. (1982). Multisite/multimethod studies. *American Behavioral Scientist, 26*(1), 6-22.

Mailer, N. (1959). *Advertisements for myself.* New York: Signet.

Manicas, P. T., & Secord, P. F. (1982). Implications for psychology of the new philosophy of science. *American Psychologist, 38,* 390-413.

Manning, P. (1977). *Police work: The social organization of policing.* Cambridge: MIT Press.

Markus, H. (1977). Self-schemata and processing information about the self. *Journal of Personality and Social Psychology, 35*(2), 63-78.

Martinko, M., & Gardner, W. (1983). Training manual for researchers, Florida Study of High-Performing Principals. Tallahassee: Florida State University.

McCall, G. (1969). Data quality control in participant observation. In G. McCall & J. Simmons (Eds.), *Issues in participant observation* (pp. 128-141). Reading, MA: Addison-Wesley.

McCall, G., & Simmons, J. (1969). *Issues in participant observation.* Reading, MA: Addison-Wesley.

Mead, M. (1928). *Coming of age in Samoa.* Magnolia, MA: Peter Smith.

Meehl, P. (1954). *Clinical versus statistical prediction.* Minneapolis: University of Minnesota Press.

Meehl, P. (1965). Clinical versus statistical prediction. *Journal of Experimental Research in Personality, 63*(1), 81-97.

Miles, M. B. (1979). Qualitative data as an attractive nuisance: The problem of analysis. *Administrative Science Quarterly, 24,* 590-601.

Miles, M. B. (1980). Innovation from the ground up: Dilemmas of planning and implementing new schools. *New York University Education Quarterly, 11*(2), 2-9.

Miles, M. B. (1982). A mini-cross site analysis. *American Behavioral Scientist, 26*(1), 121-132.

Miles, M. B., Farrar, E., & Neufeld, B. (1983). *Review of effective schools programs: Vol. 2. The extent of adoption of effective schools programs.* Cambridge, MA: Huron Institute.

Miles, M. B., Sullivan, E. W., Gold, B. A., Taylor, B. L., Sieber, S. D., and Wilder, D. E. (1978). *Designing and starting innovative schools: A field study of social architecture in education* (Final report, NIE Grant G-74-0051. ED 170 828-834). New York: Center for Policy Research.

Mills, C. W. (1959). On intellectual craftsmanship. In C. W. Mills, *The sociological imagination.* New York: Oxford University Press.

Mishler, E. (1979). Meaning in context: Is there any other kind? *Harvard Educational Review, 49*(1), 1-19.

Mohr, L. B. (1982). *Explaining organizational behavior.* San Francisco: Jossey-Bass.

Monge, P. R., & Capella, J. N. (1980). *Multivariate techniques in human communication research.* New York: Academic.

Mulhauser, F. (1975). Ethnography and policy-making: The case of education. *Human Organization, 34,* 311-315.

Nash, N., & Culbertson, J. (Eds.). (1977). *Linking processes in educational improvement: Concepts and applications.* Columbus, OH: University Council for Educational Administration.

The Network, Inc. (1979). *Conceptual framework: A study of dissemination efforts supporting school improvement.* Andover, MA: Author.

Nisbett, R. E., & Ross, L. (1980). *Human inference: Strategies and shortcomings of social judgment.* Englewood Cliffs, NJ: Prentice-Hall.

Nishisato, S. (1979). Dual scaling and its variants. *New Directions for Testing and Measurement, 4,* 1-12.

Noblit, G. W. (1982). *Not seeing the forest for the trees: The failure of synthesis for the desegregation ethnographies.* Paper presented at the meeting of the American Education Research Association.

Noblit, G. W., & Hare, R. D. (1983, April). *Meta-ethnography: Issues in the synthesis and replication of qualitative research.* Paper presented at the meeting of the American Educational Research Association.

Ortony, A. (Ed.). (1979). *Metaphor and thought.* Cambridge: Cambridge University Press.

Oskamp, S. (1965). Overconfidence in case-study judgments. *Journal of Counseling Psychology, 29*(3), 261-265.

Patton, M. Q. (1980). *Qualitative evaluation methods.* Beverly Hills, CA: Sage.

Patton, M. Q. (1981). *Creative evaluation.* Beverly Hills, CA: Sage.

Pelto, P. J., & Pelto, G. H. (1978). *Anthropological research: The structure of inquiry* (2nd ed.). Cambridge: Cambridge University Press.

Platt, J. R. (1964). Strong inference. *Science, 146,* 347-353.

Pool, I. de S. (1973). *Handbook of communication.* Chicago: Rand McNally.

Popper, K. (1968). *The logic of scientific discovery.* New York: Harper & Row.

Redfield, R. (1930). *Tepoztlan: A Mexican village.* Chicago: University of Chicago Press.

Rist, R. C. (1980). Blitzkrieg ethnography: On the transformation of a method into a movement. *Educational Researcher, 9*(2), 8-10.

Rosenthal, R. (1976). *Experimenter effects in behavioral research.* New York: Irvington.

Ross, L., & Lepper, M. R. (1980). The perseverance of beliefs: Empirical and normative considerations. In R. A. Shweder (Ed.), *Fallible judgment in behavioral research* (pp. 17-36). San Francisco: Jossey-Bass.

Runkel, P. J., & McGrath, J. E. (1972). *Research on human behavior.* New York: Holt, Rinehart & Winston.

Russell, B. (1948). *Human knowledge: Its scope and limits.* New York: Simon & Schuster.

Sadler, D. R. (1981). Intuitive data processing as a potential source of bias in naturalistic evaluations. *Educational Evaluation and Policy Making, 3,* 25-31.

Salmon, W. (1966). *The foundations of scientific inference.* Pittsburgh: University of Pittsburgh Press.

Scheffler, I. (1967). *Science and subjectivity.* New York: Bobbs-Merrill.

Schwartz, N., & Schwartz, C. (1955). Problems in participant observation. *American Journal of Sociology, 60,* 343-354.

Sherman, R., & Titus, W. (1982). Covariation information and cognitive processing: Effects of causal implications on memory. *Journal of Personality and Social Psychology, 42,* 989-1000.

Sieber, S. D. (1976). *A synopsis and critique of guidelines for qualitative analysis contained in selected textbooks.* New York: Project on Social Architecture in Education, Center for Policy Research.

Silvern, L. (1972). *Systems engineering applied to education and training.* Dallas: Gulf.

Smith, A. G., & Louis, K. S. (Eds.), (1982). Multimethod policy research: Issues and applications. *American Behavioral Scientist, 26*(1).

Smith, A. G. & Robbins, A. E. (1982). Structured ethnography. *American Behavioral Scientist, 26,* 45-61.

Smith, H. W. (1975). *Strategies of social research.* Englewood Cliffs, NJ: Prentice-Hall.

Smith, L. M. (1978). An evolving logic of participant observation, educational ethnography and other case studies. In L. Shulman (Ed.), *Review of research in education* (Vol. 6). Itasca, IL: Peacock.

Smith, L. M., & Keith, P. (1971). *The anatomy of educational innovation.* New York: John Wiley.

Smith, R. B., & Manning, P. K. (Eds.). (1982). *Qualitative methods.* Vol. II of *Handbook of social science methods.* Cambridge, MA: Ballinger.

Snow, R. (1974). Representative and quasi-representative designs for research in teaching. *Review of Educational Research, 44,* 265-292.

Spiro, M. E. (1982). *Oedipus and the Trobriands.* Chicago: University of Chicago Press.

Spradley, J. (1979). *The ethnographic interview.* New York: Holt, Rinehart & Winston.

Sproull, L. (1981). *Microethnography: A research strategy for understanding behavior in organizations.* Pittsburgh: Carnegie-Mellon University.

Sproull, L. S., & Sproull, R. F. (1982). Managing and analyzing behavioral records: Explorations in non-numeric data analysis. *Human Organization, 41*(4), 283-290.

Stake, R. (1976). *Evaluating educational programs: The need and the response.* Washington, DC: OECD Publications Center.

Stake, R., & Easley, J. (Eds.). (1978). *Case studies in science education.* Urbana, IL: Center for Instructional Research and Curriculum Evaluation.

Stearns, M. S., Greene, D., David, J. L., & Associates. (1980). *Local implementation of PL 94-142: First year report of a longitudinal study* (SRI Project 7124). Menlo Park, CA: SRI International.

Stephenson, W. (1953). *The study of behavior.* Chicago: University of Chicago Press.

Stern, R. P. (1977). *DTA's computer-based data management system.* Chicago: Center for New Schools.

Stiegelbauer, S., Goldstein, M., & Huling, L. L. (1982). Through the eye of the beholder: On the use of qualitative methods in data analysis. In R&D Center for Teacher Education, *Qualitative and quantitative procedures for studying interventions influencing the outcomes of school improvement* (R&D Report 3140). Austin: R&D Center for Teacher Education, University of Texas.

Swinburne, R. (Ed.). (1974). *The justification of induction.* London: Oxford University Press.

Taft, R. (1955). The ability to judge people. *Psychological Bulletin, 52*(1), 1-23.

Templin, P. A. (1982). Still photography in evaluation. In N. L. Smith (Ed.), *Communication strategies in evaluation.* Beverly Hills, CA: Sage.

Tuma, N. (1982). Nonparametric and partially parametric approaches to event history analysis. In S. Leinhardt (Ed.), *Sociological methodology, 1982* (pp. 1-60). San Francisco: Jossey-Bass.

Turner, B. A. (1981). Some practical aspects of qualitative data analysis: One way of organizing the cognitive processes associated with the generation of grounded theory. *Quality and Quantity, 15*(3), 225-247.

Turner, S. P. (1980). *Sociological explanation as translation.* New York: Cambridge University Press.

Tversky, A., & Kahneman, D. (1971). The belief in the law of small numbers. *Psychological Bulletin, 76*(2), 105-110.

Van Maanen, J. (1979). The fact of fiction in organizational ethnography. *Administrative Science Quarterly, 24,* 539-611.

Van Maanen, J. V. (Ed.). (1983). *Qualitative methodology.* Beverly Hills, CA: Sage.

Van Parijs, P. (1981). *Evolutionary explanation in the social sciences: An emerging pradigm.* Totowa, NJ: Rowman & Littlefield.

Wagner, J. (Ed.). (1979). *Images of information.* Beverly Hills, CA: Sage.

Wallis, W. A., & Roberts, H. V. (1956). *Statistics: A new approach.* New York: Free Press.

Wax, R. (1971). *Doing fieldwork: Warnings and advice.* Chicago: University of Chicago Press.

Webb, E. J., Campbell, D. T., Schwartz, R. D., & Sechrest, L. (1965). *Unobtrusive measures.* Chicago: Rand McNally.

Werner, O. (1982). Microcomputers in cultural anthropology: APL programs for qualitative analysis. *BYTE, 7,* 250-280.

Whyte, W. F. (1943). *Street corner society.* Chicago: University of Chicago Press.

Wilson, S. (1977). The use of ethnographic techniques in educational research. *Review of Educational Research, 47,* 245-266.

Wolcott, H. (1980). How to look like an anthropologist without really being one. *Practicing Anthropology, 3*(2), 56-59.

Yates, G. R., Jr. (1977). *The DTA computer system.* Chicago: Center for New Schools.

Yin, R. K. (1981). The case study as a serious research strategy. *Knowledge, 3,* 97-114.

Yin, R. K., with Quick, S. K., Bateman, P. M., & Marks, E. L. (1978). *Changing urban bureaucracies: How new practices become routinized* (R-2277/NSF). Santa Monica, CA: Rand Corporation.

Zelditch, M. (1962). Some methodological problems of field studies. *American Journal of Sociology, 67,* 566-576.

Index

About the Authors

Matthew B. Miles is Senior Research Associate, Center for Policy Research, New York. A social psychologist, his primary interests have been in the assessment of planned change efforts in groups and organizations. His research and development work since 1955 has focused on educational innovation, intensive group training, R&D management, organization development, and knowledge dissemination and utilization. His books include *Learning to Work in Groups, Innovation in Education, Organization Development in Schools, Measuring Human Behavior, Learning in Social Settings,* and *Whose School Is It Anyway?* He has conducted qualitative research since 1974 in studies of the creation of new schools and the implementation of educational innovations; the latter work led to *Innovation Up Close* (Plenum, 1984), coauthored with Michael Huberman. His current research focuses on "effective schools" improvement programs and the role of change agents.

A. Michael Huberman is an educational psychologist. He is currently Professor of Education at the Faculty of Psychology and Education, University of Geneva, Switzerland, and has also conducted research at the American University and at Stanford University. His areas of specialization are adult learning, knowledge dissemination and utilization, and educational innovation. His books include *Understanding Change in Education, Models of Adult Learning and Adult Change, School-University Collaboration Supporting School Improvement,* and *Solving Educational Problems.* His work in qualitative methods began in 1975 with a study of "informal" teaching and learning environments. At present, he is engaged in research on teachers' professional life cycles and on pupils' self-regulation processes.

Chart 38d
Site-Ordered Effects Matrix: Effects of Ongoing and Event-Linked Assistance, by Sites

EFFECTS OF ASSISTANCE / On the innovation and its use	Substantial assistance provided						Initial assistance, then minimal			Nearly no assistance		
	Masepa	Plummet	Carson	Tindale	Perry-Parkdale	Banestown	Lido	Astoria	Calston	Dun Hollow	Proville	Burton
Planning, developing		02 E2	012	012 E2	01	E1	012	01		01	02	
Validating, confirming			012	01 E1	E12			E2				
Sense of goals, direction, priority		012-E1 2-	02	01 E2		02					01	
Increasing legitimacy of innov		E12				E2			E1			
Obtaining funds			01		01 E2						02 E12	
Aiding start-up, launching	01	012	02		E1	01 E1			02		02	
Preparing/adding materials		02	02	E1		012	02	01	012-	01-2		
Providing general frame/model				01		E12	01					
Aiding good-quality implementation		02	02-E1				02	01-E2	02	01-2	02-	
Maintaining program	012		02	02		E2						
Program regulating, managing	012		012			012						
Protecting, saving program		012			01-	E12	02					
Program adaptation, alteration	012	E2	02-E2-	E2-	E2	E1	02	012		E1-2-		01
Program strengthening	01	E2				02						
Program expansion	01					E2	02					
Program continuation (district)		02		E2				E2			012	
Program evaluation			01	02	012 E2							
Program dissemination		E2				012						
USER ASSESSMENT	++/ *	++/ +	+ to/ + +	+ / +	+ to/ + +	+ /+ to ++	+ to/ ++	+ to/0 to ++/ +	0 to/ + -	+/+	+ to/+ to +/-	+ / *

On individuals

	Masepa	Plummet	Carson	Tindale	Perry-Parkdale	Banestown	Lido	Astoria	Calston	Dun Hollow	Proville	Burton
Reducing anxiety, reassuring	02		012E12	01 E2	01 E12	E1			02 E2			01
Reducing ambiguity, uncertainty			01-E1						E2	01-		
Increasing understanding, coherence, concepts			012E2	012 E1	012 E12	E1	01	01		E1-	E1 2	
Reducing resistance			02-E2-	E2-		01			E2		01- E1-2- 01	
Reducing frustration, resentment		01- E2-		E1-	01			E2-		E1-2-	E1-2-	
Increasing optimism, hopefulness		E1										
Stimulating, motivating	01		E1							01		
Catharsis, blowing off steam				01								
Increasing interest, ownership	012	E2	012E2	E2	01 E2	012E2		012 E12	E2	01- E1	01-	012
Feeling supported, encouraged, backed	012	01,2-	01		012	012	01	01	01	E1	01-	
Feeling pressured, policed	01			012 E1						02		
Increasing autonomy		02	02	012-	02							
Mobilizing energy			02 E1			01				E2		
Saving energy, reduction of tasks	01			012				012	02	01		
Enlarging repertoire	01	E2	01 E1-		E2	01				01		01
Solving short-run problems	012		01	01 E12		012E12			E12	01-		
Increasing satisfaction, enjoyment			01 E2							01- E1-		
Teaching/refining skills	01		02			01				02		
Routinization			01	02 E2	E2							
Increasing competence, mastery, confidence			012 E1	02 E2	02 E12		01		02	02		02
Continuation (indiv. level)						02						
USER ASSESSMENT	++ / *	+/ + +	+ to/+ to -	+ to+/+ to -	+ to/ + to ++	+ to /+ ++	+ to/ * ++	+ to/+ to ++/ -	+ to/ + -	+ to/+ to -	+/+ to -/-	0 to/ * +

On the organization

	Masepa	Plummet	Carson	Tindale	Perry-Parkdale	Banestown	Lido	Astoria	Calston	Dun Hollow	Proville	Burton
Conflict resolution		01	02								01	
Reducing isolation, aiding linkage			E2	01 E2		01	01			01-		
Increasing cohesiveness, trust	02	01 E2	E12	02+ E12	01			E2				
Increasing collaboration		02		E2	02							
More innovative climate		02										
Improved problem solving		E1			E2							
Increasing morale			01									
Establishing implementation "team"			012-E2	E2		E12	01					
Building assistance infrastructure			012 E12		E2	E12						
Coordination, improved organization		01		E1		02						
Lower dependency on assisters			012-									
Built links to external environment		012 E1,2	01									
USER ASSESSMENT	++/*	++/+	+ to/ + +	+/+ to +	+ to/ * +	+ to/++ / ++	+ / *	+ / +	NA/NA	+ to/ NA 0	+/NA -	NA/*

0 = ongoing assistance
E = event-linked assistance effect

- = effect was negative, or opposite

1= short-run assistance effect
2= long-run assistance consequences

* effects of event-linked assistance not assessed
NA = not applicable

User Assessment
++ very effective
+ effective
0 neutral
± mixed
- ineffective

example), or by having fewer effect categories (though the risk is getting them too abstract and general).

Advice

Effects matrices are especially useful when one anticipates a wide diversity of effects from a general cause. Complicatedness is a natural result of effects diversity. The use of summary tables helps to verify or disconfirm impressions from the larger display. But the summary table's conclusions usually need to be rechecked against the original display. For example, low-assistance sites (chart, Box V.B.b) seem to have more negative effects on individuals. But a recheck with Chart 38d shows that most of these effects occurred in only two sites (Proville and Dun Hollow), not in sites where there was minimal later assistance (Lido, Astoria, Calston).

As with other site-ordered displays, everything depends on the accuracy with which the sites are ordered. For example, in Chart 38d, one must be fairly sure that Masepa has very substantial assistance, and Tindale less, though still of the "substantial" variety, and that Proville has "nearly no" assistance. Otherwise no conclusions about the effects of varying amounts of assistance can be drawn with any validity.

As the display is being built and even as data are entered in the supposedly "final" format, stay alert to simple ways of adding other data. For example, the analyst here added a minus sign to cells where the effect was clearly negative or opposite to that intended by the assister. That was easy to do, nonconfusing, and did not involve extensive recoding or alteration of the basic matrix.

It is usually easier to show effects by rows rather than columns, simply because there is more space to write headings there. If the aim is to show the full, detailed range of effects, resist the temptation to collapse categories.

Time Required

This illustration took about 4 hours for creating the basic display (alternating with reading and categorizing site report materials), 5½ hours to enter data from all 12 sites, and only 2½ hours for analysis and write-up (6 pages). Once the data are in one place, analysis can go quite quickly. The summary tables typically require only a few minutes each to produce.

V.G CAUSAL MODELS

Analysis Problem

Carefully ordered meta-matrices, like predictor-outcome matrices, time-ordered matrices, or effects matrices, can begin to tell us a lot about *what* goes with *what*. Variable by variable, we can understand that X comes before Y, and more of X goes with more of Y, that *less* of Q goes with more of Y, and perhaps that J looks unrelated to Y—unless, maybe, if you take varying levels of K into account. This is all rather atomistic, though. There remain two problems.

The first is beginning to transcend mere "association" (the weasel word of quantitative researchers) and to arrive at something like a judgment that variable X not only precedes Y in time, but looks connected to it in such a way that should X go up for some reason, we would expect Y to go up or down, as well. The second problem is how to go beyond mere list-making (X, Q, and J with K controlled are all predictors of Y) to something like an integrated set of relationships among the variables: In short, a *model*. In practice, these problems usually need to be solved together.[5]

We have already discussed (section IV.J) the multifold problems of assessing local causality and of forming a sensible, data-grounded causal network. The question at hand is this: Given multiple-site data in ordered matrix form, and a set of variable-by-variable conclusions, how can a researcher integrate those findings into a general model of the variables involved that specifies causal connections clearly?

Brief Description

A causal model is a network of variables with causal connections between them, drawn from multiple-site analyses. Although empirically grounded, it is essentially a higher-order effort to derive a testable set of propositions about the complete network of variables and interrelationships. The principle is one of theory building.

Illustration

Here we can use another example from the school improvement study. The question was, in what way do users of an innovation change their "practice" after using the innovation—and what determines greater or lesser amounts of practice change?

Since causal modeling is a second-order activity drawing on other displays, we depart here from our usual format.

Preliminary display: Outcomes. An analyst thinking about causal modeling usually has to clarify the basic dependent variable. Is it monolithic, or does it have several parts? Can some display of data from all sites help to clarify this?

One line of analysis goes like this. Divide the dependent or outcome variable into aspects or components; make a rough ordering of the sites by degree of presence of the overall variable; and see if the components have variance—that is, are differentially present. For example, a component present only in

Chart 39
Summed Indices: Reported Changes in User Practice and Perception

	Dimensions of change arising from implementation						
Sites	Daily Routines	Repertoire	Relation-ships	Under-standings	Self-Efficacy	Transfer	Basic Con-structs, Attitudes
Masepa (NDN)	X	X	X	X	X	X	X
Plummet (IV-C)	X	X	X	X	(X)	N/A	X
Banestown (NDN)	X	X	X	X	X	(X)	
Tindale (IV-C)	X	X		X	X	X	
Carson (IV-C)	X	(X)	X	X	X	N/A	
Perry-Parkdale (NDN)	X	(X)	X	(X)	(X)	N/A	(X)
Calston (NDN)	X	X	(X)	(X)	(X)		(X)
Lido (NDN)	X	X		(X)			(X)
Astoria (NDN)	X	X	(X)	X			
Burton (NDN)		X					
Dun Hollow (IV-C)	X-0	X-0					(X)
Proville (IV-C)	X-0				N/A	N/A	

X = change claimed unambiguously by several informants
(X) = change claimed unambiguously by only one informant
X-0 = initial change, then reversion to initial practice
N/A = not appropriate/applicable
Blank = no unambiguous changes cited

"high" sites is presumably "deeper," harder to achieve than a component that appears in nearly all sites.

We have already shown how this worked out for the issue of user practice change in Box V.B.a; we repeat that chart here for clarity (Chart 39). Here we can see that the "user practice change" outcome is not monolithic. Components of it such as "basic constructs, attitudes" and "transfer" (of learnings to new situations) appear only in high-change sites, while others (such as "daily routines" and "repertoire") appear in nearly all sites, regardless of how much user practice change occurred. Thus we have "unbundled" the outcome, finding that some aspects of it change more easily than others. Note that this process is an interactive one. The various dimensions came from inductive examination of teachers' reports of their changes after using the innovation; the analyst tried to sort them out in a rough order of "depth," meanwhile sorting out the sites in a rough order of "overall impact." Both orderings shifted; rows and columns were transposed several times until the analyst came out with the result.

Preliminary display: Predictors and outcomes. Next, we need to look at the question of which predictor variables might be associated with the outcome.

Chart 40
Predictor-Outcome Matrix: Predictors of Magnitude of User Practice Change

EARLY IMPLEMENTATION REQUIREMENTS

Magnitude of change, by sites / Predictors	Required practice change*	Project Size/scope	Classroom/organizational fit	Index of early impl. requirements	General attitude during implementation	Administrative Pressure Direct: Strong-arming	Indirect: exhorting, reinforcing
High Change							
Masepa (NDN)	major	large	mod/good	14	+	high	high
Plummet (IV-C)	mod-major	large	good/poor #	12	+	low	high
Moderate Change							
Banestown (NDN)	major	small/mod	moderate	10	+	mod	high
Tindale (IV-C)	major	large/mod	moderate	12	+	high	high
Carson (IV-C)	major	large	moderate	13	+	low	high
Perry-Parkdale (NDN)	mod-major	mod	moderate	10	+	low	low/mod
Moderate-low change							
Calston (NDN)	moderate	small	poor	9	+	mod.	mod.
Lido (NDN)	moderate	small	moderate	7	+	low	mod.
Small – no change							
Burton (NDN)	minor	small	good	3	+	low	mod
Dun Hollow (IV-C)	minor	small	poor	7	–	mod.	low
Proville (IV-C)	minor	moderate	moderate	7	–	mod.	mod.
Astoria (NDN)	minor	small	good	3	+	low	low

*Discrepancy between users' customary instructional practices and those required to implement the innovation at the time of initial use.

#Good in the district, poor for needs of incoming students

Recall that we have already shown in section V.C how to make a site-ordered predictor-outcome meta-matrix.

The analyst in this case chose to order the sites in terms of overall intensity of the outcome (holding in abeyance for the moment the idea that sub-outcomes seemed to be differentially achievable), and picked a number of predictors that seemed to have been important on a site-by-site basis in inducing larger degrees of user practice change. The final display appears in Chart 40. For exercise, the reader may want to scan the chart and draw some preliminary conclusions about the weight of the different predictors.

In this case, the analyst concluded that "required practice change," "project size/scope," and "classroom/organizational fit" were all associated with degree of user practice change. (This conclusion involved a careful look at deviant cases. For example, the analyst noted that the moderate-sized program at Proville was simply sabotaged by dissatisfied users, so there was no opportunity for user practice change to occur. The small [institutionally speaking] project at Calston nevertheless was an ambitious one for the individual teachers involved.)

The analyst also noted that "attitude toward the innovation" was a poor predictor, since it was largely positive, except in sites where discontinuations took place (Dun Hollow, Proville).

Finally, the analyst saw that "administrative pressure" of a direct sort was by itself not a *very* good predictor. But if it was combined with *indirect* pressure (exhortation, reinforcing), the consequences were clear: A carrot-and-stick approach was associated with greater user practice change.

Building the causal model. Now the analyst must begin reflecting: How can the results of these two displays be integrated into a meaningful explanatory model? One rule of thumb is to order the model temporally. So the question is, which variables of those found relevant occur *first* in time, which occur along the way during implementation, and which might be seen as early and later outcomes?

The second rule of thumb is this: Consider which variables might reasonably be expected to have a direct *impact* on other variables, both preceding them in time, and having a plausible direct connection.

The third rule is, note what people at the site say when asked for explanations. What causal linkages do they claim are present? Consult the field notes.

The fourth rule is, consider what available research and theory have to say about causal connections. In this case, past studies of implementation and individual learning theory might suggest relationships among variables.

Using these rules, the analyst has to "noodle" for a while. As with other network-type displays, it helps to put variables on cards, move them around into various configurations, and look at the connections that seem sensible. And since the process is a creative, synthesizing one with a good dose of serendipity thrown in, it helps to have a colleague look at the first few versions.

Figure 16 shows the model that finally emerged from this process. Let's look at some of its aspects. First, the analyst concludes that the innovation's "implementation requirements" are logically prior to what happens when it is implemented. So he places *innovation size/scope, classroom/organizational fit,* and *required practice change* as antecedents of some aspects of user practice change. But *which* aspects? Chart 39 suggests that the easiest (hence possible earliest) things to change are *classroom routines.* The analyst, reflecting a minute and reviewing site data, also realizes that such routines are being changed, not by magic, but by the form of organization of the project and the way it is carried out in classrooms. So he poses those as the immediate "user practice" changes during early implementation.

Where should *administrative pressure* fit in the model? It occurs mainly during early implementation, the field notes show, and the analyst reasons that it probably has a direct effect on classroom and project organization and users' routines: The pressure and exhortation serve to keep the immediate short-run practice changes in place. Prior implementation research tends to support this linkage (see Fullan, 1982). Note that the analyst, still using the four rules of thumb presented above, also postulates that the pressure has weaker, later effects as well (dotted lines): It encourages positive *attitudes to the innovation* itself (through the exhortation and reinforcement), and it makes it more likely that users will *transfer* their learnings to other subjects and teaching tasks.

The assumption being made here is that administrative pressure, in its blend of direct and indirect aspects, will not alienate teachers from administrators, as a direct-only approach might. Such pressure should have the consequence of keeping user learnings salient and visible, so that the possibility of transfer to new situations is higher. Naturally, assumptions like these must (a) be made explicit as the work proceeds; (b) be checked with the data and one's colleagues.

Now once the initial user changes in practice have taken place, what is a reasonable model that would get us to the other, "deeper," outcomes noted on Chart 39? It almost surely is not a simple chain $W \rightarrow X \rightarrow Y \rightarrow Z$. We have to consider how succeeding types of change in teachers might influence and feed each other. Here

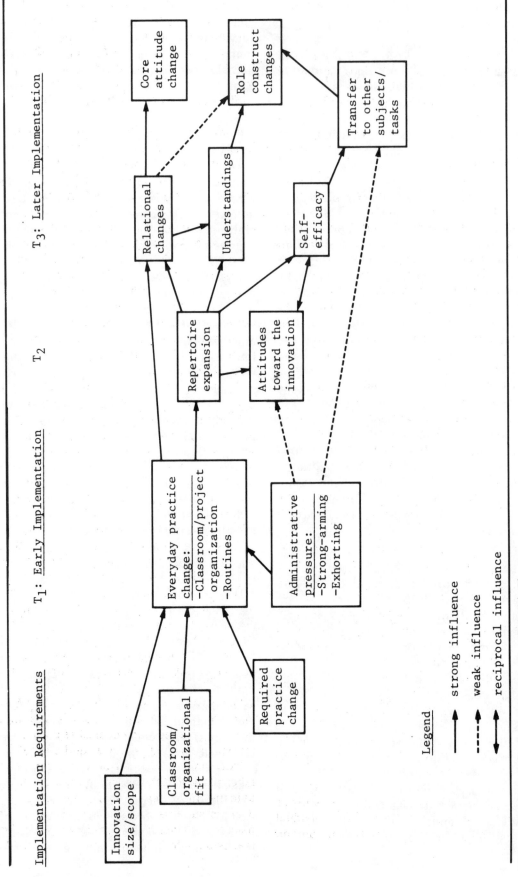

Figure 16 Causal Flowchart Tracing User Practice Changes

again the four rules of thumb apply. The analyst also has the outcome orderings from Chart 39 as an empirical start.

The analyst says that the project's *routines,* given some teacher experience with them, lead to *repertoire expansion* (teachers have new things they now know how to do). That expansion of repertoire, he reasons, is probably satisfying (increased skills usually feel good), thus by inference we might expect increased positive *attitudes to the innovation.* Checking back with the original site report and the field notes gives (a) clear examples supporting those causal links; and (b) no examples of disconfirmation.

These two practice changes have further consequences. An expanded repertoire leads to *relational changes* (for example, more willingness to share one's new knowledge with other teachers); in some cases, the analyst notes, the innovation's routines themselves bring people into new working relationships (as in the case of team teaching, the collaboration between a teacher and an aide, or a work experience program for students). But the repertoire expansion also deepens teachers' *understandings*—of classroom dynamics, of their own and pupils' roles, and, in some cases, of school and district dynamics. Finally, both repertoire expansion and positive attitudes to the innovation lead to increased *self-efficacy* (put schematically: I am more skilled in doing this good new thing, therefore I feel good about myself professionally). These formulations, once again, need to be checked through cycling back to Charts 39 and 40—and to the analyst's knowledge of other research.

And how do we get to the final, "deepest" set of outcomes? The analyst postulates here that later on, after a good deal of implementation time has elapsed, *core attitude changes* (such as, "I learned to let go of the child," "I was learning to be flexible," "how to trust students when you have no control over them") come essentially from the teacher's working relations with peers as well as with students themselves. Second, he proposes that *role construct* changes (for example, reconceptualizing "structured" teaching as productive rather than authoritarian) come essentially from basic understandings, *and* from the successful experience of transfer to other subjects and tasks. (Here the assumption is that such transfer has a "cosmopolitanizing," "generalizing," and possibly "reinforcing" aspect.) *Transfer,* itself, comes mainly from self-efficacy, in this model: The better I feel about my competence, the more likely I am to try my new ideas and practices in other aspects of my work.

Thus endeth the explication. Note that another analyst could well have come out with a somewhat different model. The rules of thumb may be weighted differently, or they may turn up alternative, equally compelling accounts. For example, one might postulate that *core attitude* changes are unlikely if there has been no change in *self-efficacy;* they cannot flow solely from *relational changes.* But this is not a major change in the model; independent analysts using the rules of thumb, the same data base, and assumptions that are not wildly different will be likely to come up with a similar causal picture.

It is important to subject the "final" version to verification. You might subject your model to the depredations of colleagues (including earlier analysts, if any), who can help you clarify the assumptions you are making and suggest alternative views. (The tactic is *checking out rival explanations,* section VII.B.10.) And, given a causal model with which you are reasonably satisfied intellectually, return once again to the written-up field notes for evidence of disconfirmation or needed revision.

Variations

It sometimes helps to make submodels that are wholly linear (W→X→Y→Z) as a simplifying strategy (see section V.G.a). It is also useful to consider a backward mapping approach, in which one begins with final outcomes and reasons back along the causal byways ("Which variable, in principle, would have to be changed in order to induce this change?").

This particular outcome variable (user practice change) turned out to be nonmonolithic, and, conceptually speaking, its parts could plausibly be seen as influencing each other. If you are primarily interested in *processes* and the outcome variable is a straightforward, simple one (for example, percentage of teachers using an innovation in a school), then the modeling will naturally ramify on process issues.

Advice

To reiterate: Expect to do several versions of the model. Use a simple technology (cards or the like) that permits flexibility in rearrangement. Get advice and argument from colleagues. Do not close up too fast.

Return repeatedly to field notes to check, test, and extend the model. It will usually help to cut back to the preceding matrices, with a good look at deviant cases and outliers. When a specific site does not fit the model, CHANGE THE MODEL to accommodate that information, rather than try to explain away the "inconvenient" information.

It often happens that you feel blocked, unable to understand how variable A could lead to variable C in any plausible way. For example, in the school improvement study, we started a causal model that led from "size of project funding" to "organizational change." (More expensive projects were also those that transformed the local school and district.) But, as

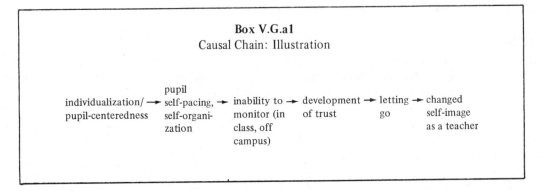

Box V.G.a1
Causal Chain: Illustration

individualization/ pupil-centeredness → pupil self-pacing, self-organization → inability to monitor (in class, off campus) → development of trust → letting go → changed self-image as a teacher

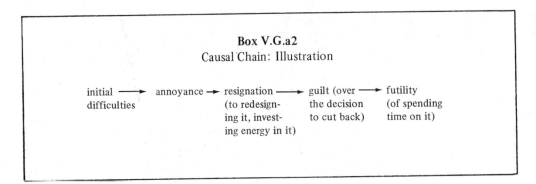

Box V.G.a2
Causal Chain: Illustration

initial difficulties → annoyance → resignation (to redesigning it, investing energy in it) → guilt (over the decision to cut back) → futility (of spending time on it)

the saying goes, you can't change organizations by throwing money at them. There had to be one or more intervening variables in the picture. These turned out to be features of the implementation process, such as administrative support (which was greater for more expensive projects). Use the tactic of *finding intervening variables* (see section VII.A.10).

The classical way of testing a model is to apply it to fresh data, a new site. If you have such data easily at hand, wonderful. You might also make a braver and riskier choice that involves basic research design decisions from the very beginning of the project: holding out one or more sites from the initial analysis, without analyzing them. The causal model can now be tested cleanly. This approach is usually difficult or infeasible if one's sites are few in number and complex, as was the case in our school improvement study.[6] You cannot avoid partial analysis during data collection itself, even if you resolutely decide otherwise. But if your sites or cases are large in number and less complex (for example, interviews with individual students about their choice of careers), it's much more feasible to have a "holdout" sample for model-verifying.

Time Required

Assuming that the preliminary display work has all been completed and a list of strong candidate variables for the model assembled, a causal model of the size shown here can be put together in its first version

relatively rapidly: an hour or less. But the dictum here comes from Norman Mailer (1959): "Do not understand me too quickly." Discussing the model with colleagues, cycling back to the displays and the field notes, and revising may take another three to four hours.

V.G.a Causal Chains

During the early stages of causal modeling, it helps to make simplifying assumptions about what leads to what, placing causes and effects in a linear chain. Box V.G.a1 presents an example, drawn from an analyst's effort to understand how it might be that teachers using an innovation that stressed individualization and pupil-centeredness came to experience a change in themselves they called "letting go."

Such a chain helps the analyst lay out explicitly what may be causing certain phenomena. Though the chain does represent a simplification, that very simplification carries with it the seeds of a fuller explanation. As the analyst remarks:

> We have left out some steps. For example, pupil-centeredness also leads to relational closeness and to a better grasp of individual ability levels and emotional states. Trust then develops as a result of the bond between staff and pupils—"trust violation" was a common leit-motif at many sites. There is something like an implicit contract between parties that pupils going off campus will not "betray" their teachers in return for pastoral care...[or that] in classroom-

bound projects pupils will complete their work and do the requisite exercises or mastery tests in return for individual help with difficult concepts or operations.

Such chains can of course be used to study less constructive processes. Box V.G.a2 presents one explaining why an initially ambitious innovation was eventually discontinued, with energy expenditures dwindling steadily.

The useful thing about such causal chains is that they require little elaboration or textual explanation. They are a rapid, simple way to communicate with colleagues (and final readers) about the meaning of a process. They must ordinarily be elaborated and linked with other chains to form causal models, as in this section, or within-site causal networks (section IV.J). See also the remarks in section IV.G on site dynamics matrices.

V.H CAUSAL NETWORKS— CROSS-SITE ANALYSIS

Analysis Problem

In section IV.J, we went into some detail on how to make an inclusive, explanatory analysis of single-site data using causal network analysis. We believe that causal networks have much utility and power in accounting for the principal outcomes in which the site-level researcher is interested. Such analysis is the last, most inferential step, building hierarchically from pattern coding, tests of bivariate relationships, conceptual clustering, and predictor-outcome analysis.

The question naturally arises as to whether these site-level analyses can be loaded into a *cross-site procedure* that produces inferences for a larger population of sites. Can it be managed? Is such an analysis meaningful? At first glance, the operational question appears to be the more pertinent. How does the analyst juggle a dozen such networks, each containing up to 30-35 variables that are presumably put together in site-specific ways? But the question of meaning is crucial too.

The answer to both questions is yes. Doing a cross-site analysis with a core list of variables determined to have significance across several sites is the most powerful way to move from a partial to an interpretive explanatory account. And it, as with single-site analysis, is the ultimate analytic step after the analyst has built from unordered to site-ordered meta-matrices and scatterplots, then to multiple-site effects matrices. As for the manageability of such an analysis, we have found that the basic operations are very similar to those used in single-site causal networking. In brief, it can be done.

Brief Description

Cross-site causal networking is a comparative analysis of all sites in a sample on variables estimated to be the most influential in accounting for the outcome or criterion measures. The analyst looks at each outcome measure and examines for each site the stream of variables leading to or "determining" that outcome. Streams that are similar or identical across sites, and that differ in some consistent way from other streams, are then extracted and interpreted. The basic principle is that of developing one or more meta-networks that respect the individual site networks.

Illustration

Since cross-site causal networking involves manipulating several sets of boxes and arrows at the same time, it can be confusing to explain. So let us try to break down the successive analytic steps into smaller chunks. We shall also make the reader's task easier by working from an example already discussed and by taking an outcome variable that lends itself easily to cross-case analysis.

Step 1: Assembling the causal networks. We shall assume here that the analyst has the basic building blocks discussed in section IV.J, that is, the *list of core variables* (see Chart 21) and the *causal network* (see Figure 10), along with the *narrative* (see Chart 22), for each of the sites. In our school improvement study, for example, we had 12 such networks and narratives, incorporating a core list of some 35 variables, together with a half-dozen site-specific variables. It helps to have the networks up on a wall or other display surface.

Step 2: Isolating the causal "streams" for each case that lead to the dependent variable being analyzed. This is the major task. Let us assume, for purposes of illustration, that the analyst wants to see how an outcome called "job mobility" is determined in a study looking at people's role and career shifts.

Let's begin by looking at the predictors of that outcome for one site. Let's start with an exhibit we have already seen (section IV.J), the causal network for the Perry-Parkdale site (Figure 10). Figure 17a presents the network once again, marked up to help our analysis. The job mobility box is at the far right, midway in the list of outcome variables (box 33). It is rated "high"; there was a lot of shifting of staff out of the project, to different roles within the district, to similar roles in another district, or out of education altogether. (To see how this rating was made, take a look at Chart 36, section V.D.)

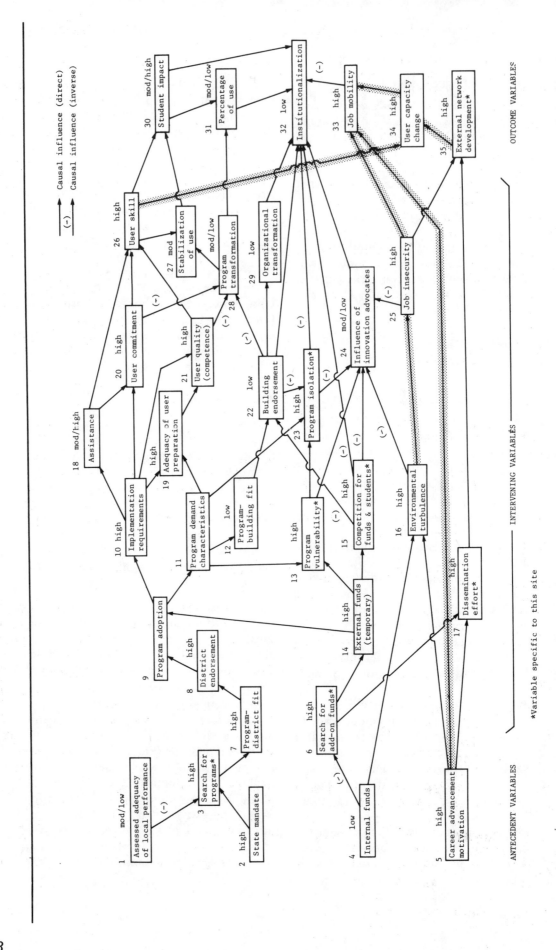

Figure 17a Causal Network for Perry-Parkdale CARED Program (immediate causes of job mobility marked)

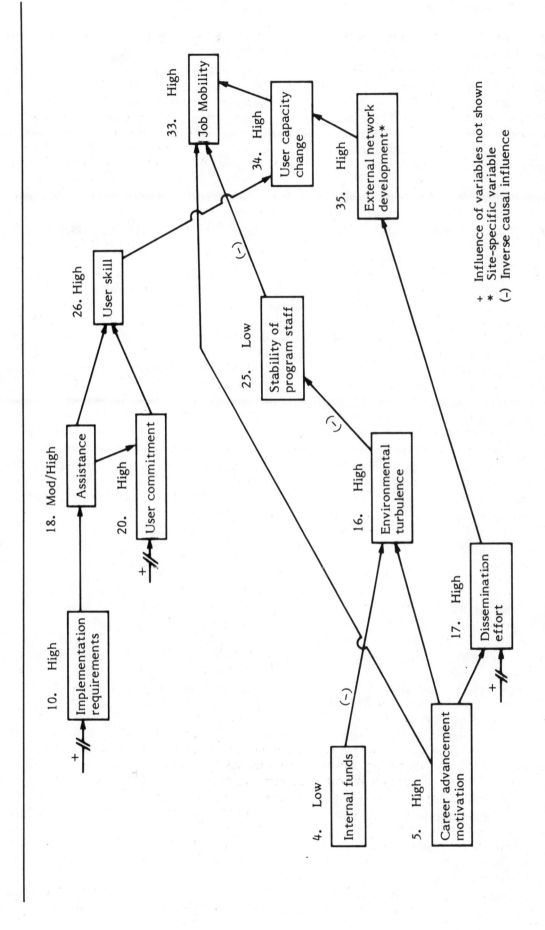

Figure 17b Subnetwork: Variable Streams Leading to High Job Mobility at Perry-Parkdale Site

The box has three arrows leading to it from boxes 25, 34, and 5. Two of those boxes, in turn, have others leading to them along what we have called a "stream." The streams leading to job mobility are easy to see if one draws backwards from box 33 to preceding boxes, using a felt-tip marker. It helps to go only two steps back from the outcome measure. The boxes reached that way can be thought of as "immediate" causes of the outcome; earlier boxes on the causal stream are "remote" causes.

Working from the bottom of the display, let's look at the streams. One goes from 5 and 17 (remote causes) on through 35 and 34 to 33 (job mobility). The next is 5 directly to 33. The third stream is 5, 16, 25, 33. The fourth stream is closely connected to the third: 4 (remote), 16, 25, 33. And the fifth stream, taking a reasonable starting point just after program adoption, runs from the remote causes 10 through 18 to 20, then to the immediate causes 26 and 34 to 33.

To make the analysis easier to follow, let us extract the streams from the causal network, as shown in Figure 17b. What we have done here is to extract the *subnetwork* of variables leading to the outcome of job mobility. To understand the five streams within that subnetwork, we have two tools. First, we can read across the stream to see what is happening, that is, what the theme or logical succession is. To do that, we have the variable labels and their ratings. For instance, take the substream 5-17-35. The message here is that key actors at the field site were interested in getting promoted (5), which led to a more energetic effort to disseminate (17) the innovation they had developed to others outside their home district (35), where, presumably, some interesting jobs might be found.

To be sure that such an interpretation is plausible, we have the second tool: the causal network narrative (see section IV.J, Chart 22, the narrative for the site discussed here). The narrative nails down the context, shows the temporal and causal relationships mapped on the network, and explains *why* the variables are chained as they are.

Let's take up each stream. The stream 4-16-25-33 looks ominous: Low funds, high turbulence, high job insecurity, low stability of program staff, high job mobility. Reading the narrative confirms our impression that this is a "casualty" scenario: Low funding led to local uncertainties about continuing the project, which caused project staff to be shifted to other jobs. We can lump another stream into the same scenario: 5-16-25-33. It adds the "career advancement motivation" variable and thereby strengthens the "casualty" notion; people did not get promoted or reassigned to desired job slots, even though they had hoped to. But the stream 5-33 qualifies that; some people *did* get where they wanted via the project. For now, let us call this an "opportunism" stream.

Others also made desirable job shifts, but in what looks like a more socially redeeming way. This is shown on the fourth stream: 5-17-35-34-33. The dissemination effort may be fed by career advancement motives, but the process of spreading the project to other districts develops training and consulting skills (capacity changes) that are then used on the next job. Reading the narrative to get a clearer sense of what is happening here yields a "career crystallization" theme: People doing the disseminating realize that they want to go on doing this kind of work, rather than return to their old jobs.

Now for the last stream: 10-18&20-26-34-33. First, how did we know to *begin* that stream at variable 10 rather than, say, at variable 1 or variable 2, where the stream "really" began? Here, again, we can use our two tools. The logical theme in this stream has to do with project mastery, so one begins with the setting for that mastery process, that is, just after "program adoption" (variable 9 on the full network). And the narrative confirms that hypothesis. The stream itself is upbeat: Local staff take on a stiff project (high implementation requirements), receive decent assistance, develop strong commitment, master the project (high user skill), develop thereby new capacities, and move to desirable new jobs. Let us call this scenario "success-driven advancement."[7]

Step 3: Matching the variable streams to other cases with the same outcome. This step can be carried out in two different ways, depending on the analyst's preferences. The first way involves "pattern matching" (Campbell, 1975), on a site-by-site basis; we outline that approach here. The second way, an initially more macro approach for those who would like to see how specific *variables* perform across all sites, involves the creation of an *antecedents matrix* (Box V.H.a) showing immediate and remote causal variables in all the subnetworks for the complete set of sites.

The issue in the "pattern matching" approach is discovering whether a pattern found in one site plays out in other ones as well, suggesting a common scenario. Are the same core variables involved? Are the ratings (high, moderate, low) the same?

Let us take more or less at random another high job mobility site, extracting the streams leading to that criterion variable. Figure 18 presents the result. This one is far easier to contend with. There are only two streams leading to the "job mobility" variable, and both turn around the same scenario. If one looks back at the "casualty" stream for the first (Perry-Parkdale) case, three of the same variables (internal funds, environmental turbulence, stability of program staff) are here, are in the same sequence, and have identical ratings.

Let's try another case. Figure 19 shows the extracted portion. This is clearly another "casualty" case. If we

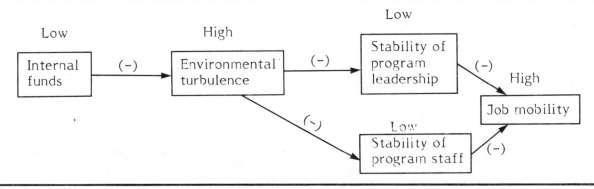

Figure 18   Subnetwork for Job Mobility, Calston Site

extract the site-specific variable ("climate in district office") and the "external funds" variable, we have the same variables, identically rated, as in the first network we examined, although not in the same order; here, the "internal funds" variable comes after, not before, the "environmental turbulence" variable. But reading the narrative produces the same, sad scenario of dashed career hopes; the shift in sequence means little.

Let us look at one last example, a somewhat more complex one. Figure 20 shows the extracted streams leading to high job mobility. By now the reader can probably dissect the network more rapidly. There are three arrows leading to high "job mobility," but five possible streams: The first one—variables 20-18-26-36-37—should be familiar; it is the "success-driven advancement" stream we saw at Perry-Parkdale, at least in the *immediate causal variables,* those closest to the criterion measure: skill, capacity change. The sequence is the same and the ratings are identical. Let's try another stream, say, 27-31 & 38-37. This looks like the "opportunist" scenario at Perry-Parkdale, with some more fleshing out (the "stability variables" are the intervening processes at work). Finally, let's take a third stream: 39-38-37. This is the same sequence as the final three predictors in the Calston "casualty" scenario, which itself is virtually identical to the Perry-Parkdale "casualty" scenario. To confirm this, the analyst rereads the causal network narratives for the three cases.

At the end of this analysis, the forty-odd streams for the twelve cases fell into the four families we have identified: Casualty scenarios, opportunism scenarios, success-driven advancement scenarios, and career crystallization scenarios. Slightly more hybrid streams—as, for example, the remaining substreams on Figure 17 above—usually entailed an additional variable or an additional path to the same two or three immediate predictors closest to the "job mobility" variable.

Moreover, the analyst can move up an analytical notch and cluster *sites* rather than individual streams.

For example, both Perry-Parkdale and Plummet have successful *and* unsuccessful job mobility scenarios; some people get what they are after and others don't. This also obtained at other sites; we could group them at the *site* level as "win-lose" scenarios.

Step 4: Verifying the scenarios for similar and contrasting outcomes. Whichever strategy (stream-by-stream or antecedents matrix) the analyst has followed, it is time to confirm the emerging scenarios. Here are the decision rules that the analyst uses to decide whether two streams belong in the same scenario, or, to take Campbell's term, have "matched" patterns. In all, there are seven such rules, of which we have used five in the illustrations shown above. First, these five:

(1) All (or all but one or two) of the core predictor variables on the stream are the same.
(2) The most immediate predictor variables—the two or three closest to the outcome measure—are the same and are in the same sequence.
(3) The common predictors have the same ratings (high, moderate, low).
(4) The outcome theme is the same (e.g., "casualty," "success-driven advancement").
(5) The narrative confirms the similarity or identity of the outcome theme derived from the stream of variables in the network.

Let us note in passing that the analyst is doing three different things to determine similarity of pattern. First, there is simple *counting,* which can be done rapidly with the aid of antecedents matrices (Box V.H.a): number of identical predictors, number of similar sequences, identity of ratings (rules 1-3). Next, there is *matching of outcome themes* from a stream of predictors—in short, getting a plausibly similar theme from two sets of four or five variable flows (rules 1-4). Finally, there is *comparison of the outcome themes with the narratives*—again, matching semantic units of two different sorts (rule 5). So we have both a somewhat "arithmetic" and a more structural or "qualitative" form of analysis operating together.[8]

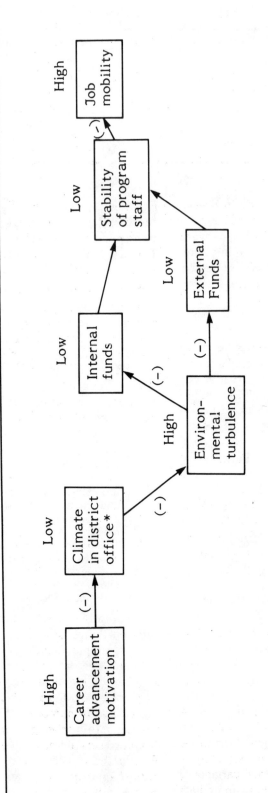

Figure 19 Subnetwork for Job Mobility, Banestown Site

*Site-specific variable.

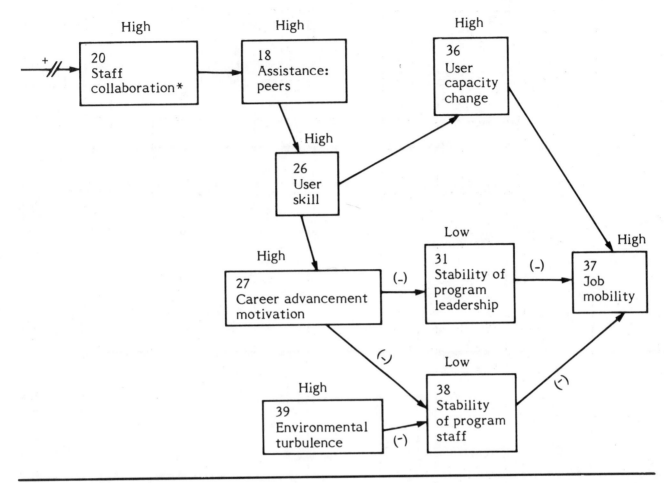

Figure 20 Subnetwork for Job Mobility, Plummet Site

*Site-specific variable.

+Influence of variables not shown on network.

We now need the two last decision rules to round out the picture:

(6) The outcome themes are different (or absent) in cases with a differently rated outcome variable (e.g., low job mobility).

(7) In these differently rated cases, the predictor variables closest to the outcome variable are different or, if the same, are rated differently.

These rules were used by the researcher to complete or test the analysis (not shown here). They bring home the point that in a sample of cases we have not only comparability but also *variability*. There are moderate and low job mobility cases, and we have to be sure that their causal flows are either different or contrary to the ones obtaining in the high job mobility sites.

Ideally, the low sites would have some of the *same* variables in the *same or similar sequences* as for the high cases, but the *ratings* would be different. For example, *high* internal funds, combined with *low*

environmental turbulence and *high* staff stability, would lead to *low* job mobility—the opposite of the casualty scenario, but with the same variables in the same order. This, of course, *strengthens* the analysis and increases its explanatory power. It is the qualitative analyst's version of testing or estimating the significance of a causal path with structural equations. We can now say with more confidence that job mobility is caused by a combination of funding, turbulence, and staff stability, since both high and low mobility result from the same interaction of these variables.

V.H.a Antecedents Matrix

Sometimes it is easy to get lost in the welter of stream-by-stream matching across sites. The need is to get a general fix on the variables that seem to be leading to the outcome in question.

Box V.H.a
Antecedents Matrix: Antecedents of Student Impact

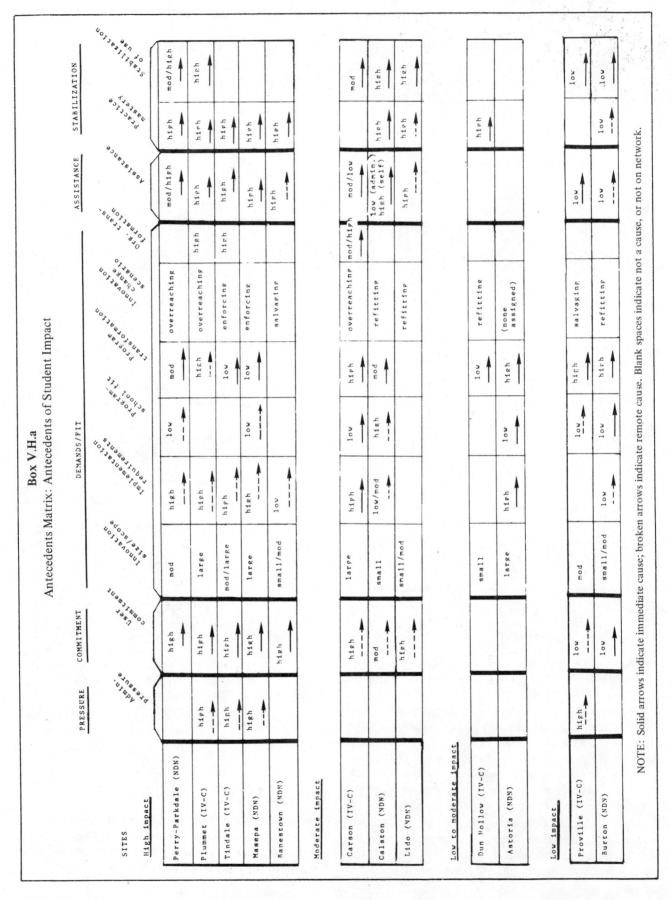

NOTE: Solid arrows indicate immediate cause; broken arrows indicate remote cause. Blank spaces indicate not a cause, or not on network.